Crisis On The Frontier

The Third Afghan War And
The Campaign In Waziristan
1919–1920

CRISIS ON THE FRONTIER

THE THIRD AFGHAN WAR AND THE CAMPAIGN IN WAZIRISTAN 1919–1920

by

Brian Robson

SPELLMOUNT

*Or what king, going to encounter another king in war,
will not sit down first and take counsel whether he is
able with ten thousand to meet him who comes against
him with twenty thousand?*
Luke 14.31

To Jessica, Ellen, Max, Theo and Guy

British Library Cataloguing in Publication Data:
A catalogue record for this book is available from the British Library
Copyright © Brian Robson 2004, 2007

ISBN 978-1-86227-403-7

First published in the UK in 2004 by
Spellmount Limited
The Mill, Brimscombe Port,
Stroud, Gloucestershire GL5 2QG
This paperback edition 2007

Tel: 01453 883300 Fax: 01453 883233
Website: www.spellmount.com

1 3 5 7 9 8 6 4 2

The right of Brian Robson to be identified
as the author of this work has been asserted by him
in accordance with the Copyright, Designs
and Patents Act 1988

Printed in Great Britain by Oakland Book Services.

Contents

PART TWO: WAZIRISTAN

List of Maps

Preface

Inevitably, I owe a debt of gratitude to many people and institutions for help generously given. In particular, I am grateful to the Director and Council of the National Army Museum for permission to quote from original material and for photographs in their ownership; to the Trustees of the British Library for the same courtesy; to Mr Glenn Mitchell, of Maggs Bros, for providing me with copies of scarce documents temporarily in his care; to Major Michael Barthorpe for sharing his extensive knowledge of uniforms and operations on the Frontier; to Major M C R Devlin for the generous loan of family papers on the Baldwin affair; to Mr S C R Burton for similarly sending me copies of the Adjutant's diary of the 2nd Battalion, North Staffordshire Regiment; to Mr Andrew Cormack and his colleagues at the Royal Air Force Museum, Hendon; to the Director and staff of the Imperial War Museum; to Major Harrap and Mr Bill Norman, of the Duke of Wellington's Regiment, for the loan of papers on the regiment's part in the Third Afghan War, and to Mr Clive Morris, Curator of the Queen's Dragoon Guards' Museum. Finally, I am indebted to the Comptroller of Her Majesty's Stationery Office for permission to quote from material within the Crown copyright. Above all, I am grateful to my publisher, Jamie Wilson, for his patience, and to my copy editor, David Grant, than whom there can be no better or kinder.

I have used the term 'Pathan' throughout rather than the philologically correct 'Pashtun'. 'Pathan' has been in common English usage for at least 150 years and to use the unfamiliar 'Pashtun' now seems to me pedantic and confusing; Sir Olaf Caroe, the standard authority, clearly took the same view. I have however used the terms 'Pashtu' and 'Pakhtu' for the 'soft' and 'hard' forms of the language.

Generally, I have omitted all diacriticals from spellings – they are a needless complication for the general reader while the specialist can put them in for himself. Similarly, I have used those spellings of proper names, e.g. Ghilzai or Simla, which are likely to be most familiar to the non-specialist. All transliterations are approximations and arguments about whether it should be Ghilzai or Ghalji, for example, are significant only for philologists. In older works, the term 'Wazirs' was often used to cover both Wazirs and Mahsuds; indeed, one sometimes comes across the term 'Waziri Mahsuds'. Caroe has shown clearly that they come from different branches of the tribal family tree and I have therefore made the same clear distinction.

British operations on the North-West Frontier of India are very rapidly passing into history – anyone who fought, for example, in the Third Afghan War would now have to be well into his second century and there can be very few, if any, still living. Even for the last major campaign on the Frontier, in 1937, participants would have now to be over 85. Yet the Frontier played a major part in the history of British India, and of the Indian and British armies, and it lives on in the British folk memory through the writings of Rudyard Kipling. Generations of soldiers, both British and Indian, learnt their soldiering ABC there; it was a training ground for high command for Montgomery, Alexander, Auchinleck and Slim, to name but a few more recent commanders. It may have been, in many ways, an old-fashioned type of warfare, but it taught in a very stark way the basics of tactics and command. No one who had had to place a picquet on the hills of Waziristan or the Khyber was likely to forget the basic principles of speed and movement, and the sound of a Pathan bullet zipping past one's head was likely to teach even the most careless the elementary principles of fieldcraft, the importance of cover and of surprise. But, with two honourable exceptions – Tim Moreman and Alan Warren – the younger generation of military historians has largely ignored the Frontier as a field for study, for reasons which it would be interesting but unrewarding to explore. The present volume may, I hope, tempt other serious historians to feed in this very fruitful field, as well as remind the British public of an important, fascinating and not ignoble chapter in its history.

Brian Robson
Hove, England

Introduction

In the eighty years between 1838 and 1919 British forces invaded Afghanistan on three occasions. In 1838 and 1878 both the causes and courses of events followed similar lines. Both wars were inspired by British fears of Russian imperial expansion from Central Asia through Afghanistan into India, the linch-pin of the British Empire. On both occasions the British suffered major military disasters and when they finally withdrew they left behind them a situation largely indistinguishable from the *status quo ante bellum*.[1]

The third Anglo-Afghan war, the subject of the first half of this book, followed a quite different pattern. This was a war of Afghan aggression; the British invasion followed a series of Afghan incursions on to British territory, and the subsequent British counter-invasion was limited to an advance of some thirteen miles. For the British it was a wholly unexpected war, and even now the Afghan motives remain to some extent unclear. In contrast to 1838 and 1878, it lasted only a matter of weeks, although the repercussions on the tribes on the British side of the border were more profound and are the subject of the second part of this book.

For a variety of reasons, this third Anglo-Afghan war has some claim to be the least-known of all British imperial conflicts, even among military historians. It has attracted few historians, partly, one suspects, because it was overshadowed as far as India was concerned by the tragedy of Amritsar only weeks before, partly because the apparent results of the war were minimal, and partly because events on the world stage, such as the Bolshevik Revolution, the Paris Peace Conference, and the economic and political reconstruction of Europe after the First World War, dwarfed what appeared at the time no more than a glorified Frontier campaign; for some weeks after the war had started, Edwin Montagu, the Secretary of State for India, was anxious to be assured, if possible, that it could be regarded indeed as no more than a Frontier incident and dealt with accordingly.[2] A leading participant, Sir Hamilton Grant, characterised it as 'the most meaningless, crazy and unnecessary war in history'.[3]

It came out of a clear blue sky as far as the Indian Government was concerned. In March 1919 the viceroy, Lord Chelmsford, discussing the impending retirement of the Chief Commissioner of the North-West Frontier Province, assured Montagu that events in Kabul following the murder of the Amir Habibullah were unlikely to have any immediate repercussions on India.[4] Four days before hostilities broke out, Chelmsford assured the Secretary of State that all was quiet on the North-West Frontier.[5]

That profound misreading of the situation was due partly to arrogance and partly to ignorance. Afghan grievances and the Afghan Army were not regarded by British officials as sufficiently serious to pose a threat of war. It was an attitude, no doubt, unconsciously coloured by the emergence of Britain as a victor in the recent World War. The new Amir, Amanullah, had made it clear in his first communication to the Viceroy in March 1919, announcing the murder of his father, Habibullah, and his own accession to the throne, that his immediate and dominant objective was to make Afghanistan completely free and independent; what that meant, as Indian officials were well aware, was the abandonment of British control of Afghan external relations which had been the price of Abdurrahman's accession to the throne in 1880. Habibullah had sought the same concession at the end of the First World War as a reward for his helpful neutrality during that war, and Chelmsford had been sympathetic. For Amanullah, by no means secure on the throne, freedom from British control was essential to shore up his position in Afghanistan. He was by no means the first, or the last, ruler to embark on a risky external adventure in order to distract attention from difficulties at home.

The British attitude was based equally on ignorance. The Indian Government maintained an Agent (the Vakil) at Kabul who was the channel of communication back to Delhi, just as the Afghan Vakil was the channel back to Kabul. The British Vakil was nevertheless carefully circumscribed in where he could go, who he could see and what information he was given. Although he maintained his own network of informers, he was not privy to the innermost councils of the Amir. Moreover, communication from Kabul was primarily by messenger, so news was always several days old. On one occasion, at least, a communication from the Vakil did not get through at all because the messenger was waylaid and murdered. Thus, even after the war was several weeks old, British officials were not clear as to the reasons for it or the Afghan objectives.

As it happened, Amanullah's communication was not answered until the end of April 1919 and the reply carefully ignored the question of the control of Afghan external affairs. The delay was a clear breach of diplomatic etiquette and it convinced Amanullah that the British had no intention of giving up control and recognising Afghanistan independence. There was some excuse for the delay. The Indian Government was preoccupied with the aftermath of the World War; the Indian Army, in particular, was in a state of some disorganisation, with many units still overseas, while those units in India were having to cope with disbandment, demobilisation and long-delayed leave. Above all, the Government was faced with large-scale civil unrest throughout India, and especially the Punjab; Amritsar was only weeks away. Amanullah, however, had announced publicly his intention of seeking full Afghan independence; he could not accept delay or rejection without serious risk to his own position. It can therefore be argued that, if the Afghans were guilty of the first overt acts of war, the real responsibility for the war lay at the British door.

On a global, and even on an imperial scale, the ensuing war was indeed a relatively small affair. The fighting lasted barely a month, and within three months peace terms had been signed. Casualties on the British side were roughly equal to those of a quiet day on the Western Front. Yet hostilities embraced the whole of the North-West Frontier of India, from Chitral in the north to Baluchistan in the south, and involved the mobilisation and deployment of several hundreds of thousands of men. Moreover, on the British side, the war had stirred up widespread tribal insurrection which took many months to subdue. In the case of Waziristan, it led to a punitive campaign which was perhaps the most serious ever fought on the Frontier and one in which the Indian Army faced humiliating defeat, leading to serious requests for the use of poison gas as the only way of retrieving the critical situation.

The campaign in Waziristan, which must properly be considered the last act of the Third Afghan War, was significant for three other reasons. It was the first major occasion on which the British had had to come to grips with the new situation created on the Frontier by the advent, on a large scale, of the modern, breech-loading, magazine rifle, firing smokeless powder. Despite the deployment of virtually the full range of up-to-date military technology on the British side, the early defeats and subsequent hard fighting made it clear that the balance of military advantage was now more even than it had ever been; success would depend critically upon discipline and thorough individual training. These were not new lessons, but they had acquired a criticality previously absent.

The second area of interest lies in the major change in Frontier policy which the events of 1919 forced upon the Indian Government. Ever since the British had come face to face with the problem of the Frontier tribes in 1849, it had been accepted policy that the major fighting tribes – Buners, Swatis, Yusufzais, Mohmands, Mahsuds and Wazirs – could only be administered at arm's length, by tacitly recognising their independence and by not interfering with them all the time they stayed within the limits of their territory. The issue on which almost all administrators and soldiers agreed was that a permanent military presence inside tribal territory was not a feasible option. From time to time, the maintenance of this policy involved punitive expeditions to deal with tribal incursions – 'butcher and bolt' or 'burn and scuttle', as it came to be known. The frequency of these expeditions, their cost and the ephemeral effect involved had not so far produced a serious alternative. The Waziristan campaign of 1919–20 led to a major reversal of this policy as far as Waziristan, for long the hot-bed of the Frontier, was concerned. The announcements in November 1919 of the intention to construct a network of permanent roads in tribal territory and the occupation of Ladha in March 1920 as a permanent base for a brigade of troops signalled the biggest change in Frontier policy in seventy years.

The third area of significance was the arrival of the aeroplane as a major factor in Frontier warfare. Before, it had been an item of interest, of marginal utility and uncertain potential. When the Derajat Column dispersed in April 1920, it had become accepted doctrine that no major operations could sensibly take place without the availability of air support. Air power would not guarantee success but it would hopefully prevent defeat. Beyond that, the events of 1919–20 helped to secure the future of the Royal Air Force as an independent Service.

It has sometimes been argued that Amanullah and the Afghans were the real victors of the war despite their total military defeat. The peace terms signed at Rawalpindi in August 1919 imposed no territorial losses or financial reparations upon Afghanistan, and the only obvious gain on either side was the abandonment of British control of Afghanistan's external relations. To that extent, Amanullah had gained what he set out to achieve, and the victory celebrations in Kabul, if they seemed hollow to British eyes, were not entirely without foundation.

The British did not go away empty-handed; the treaty of Rawalpindi and the subsequent treaty of friendship signed in Kabul in 1921 meant that, for the first time since the 1830s, they could look forward to peaceful co-existence with Afghanistan and to the disappearance of the Russian menace which had overshadowed British rule in India. The speed with which the British forces had mobilised and crushed the Afghans made it clear that the British were not about to surrender India and that Indian independence, when it came, would not be won by military means. The point was not lost on the politicians in India.

But there was a downside also. The formal peace with Afghanistan did not necessarily mean that Kabul would totally abandon all intrigues among the tribes on the British side of the border. For this and other reasons, the remaining years of British rule in India were marked by almost continuous instability among, and operations against, the tribes.

A word needs to be said about the relations during the war between the Viceroy and the Indian Government and the Home Government, in the form of the Secretary of State and the India Office. Formally the Indian Government took its policy directions from the Secretary of State, who in turn reported to the Cabinet. Significant political, military, financial and economic decisions were all subject to the Secretary of State's covering approval, and all important papers were automatically copied to the India Office. Day-to-day communication was normally by telegram (signal), and formal submissions and despatches were now relatively rare. The Viceroy and the Secretary of State also maintained a private correspondence, as did senior officials.

In the first half of 1919 Montagu was preoccupied with the Paris Peace Conference where he led the Indian delegation and was extensively involved in other matters such as reparations.[6] It is clear that, even allowing for personalities, Chelmsford seized the opportunity to exercise a high degree of independence. The pace of events made it difficult in any case for London to maintain close control of the war. But it is equally obvious that Chelmsford was determined to exert maximum control over decision-making, even to the extent of deliberately ignoring Montagu's wishes. He authorised Grant to sign the Rawalpindi peace treaty even though Montagu had repeatedly reminded him that matters of peace and war were for the Cabinet.[7] Similarly, he authorised Grant to sign the letter relinquishing British control of Afghan external affairs by the device of giving Montagu an impossible deadline.

Despite their scale, the Third Afghan War and the campaign in Waziristan are of interest and importance for a number of reasons and they have some resonance today. Hence this book.

Notes

1 The best modern account of the first Anglo-Afghan war is J A Norris, *The First Afghan War 1838–1842* (Cambridge, 1967). For the second Anglo-Afghan war see Brian Robson, *The Road to Kabul: The Second Afghan War 1878–1881* (London, 1975, 2nd edn 2003, paperback edn 2007).

2 Secretary of State to Viceroy, No. 1137, 17 May 1919, BL MSS Eur 264/19, No. 533.

3 *The Times*, 28 July 1919.

4 Chelmsford to Montagu, No. 238,4 March 1919, BL MSS Eur 264/10, No. 252.

5 Chelmsford to Montagu, No. 505-5, 28 April 1919, L/MIL/17/5/4057, Appendix 13.

6 Margaret Macmillan, *Peacemakers: the Paris Conference of 1919 and the Attempt to End War* (London, 2001).

7 See Chapter XI passim.

Glossary and Abbreviations

badal	blood vengeance
badragga	tribal escort, safe conduct
bhusa	chopped straw
daman	plains leading up to hills
dara	pass
durbar (darbar)	council, e.g. in durbar; the Durbar
fakir	holy man
firman (farman)	public notice; proclamation
gasht	lightly armed patrol (also used as a verb)
ghar	mountain peak
ghazi	Muslim fanatic
Ghilji (Ghilzai)	member of one of the two great Afghan confederations of tribes, the other being the Duranis
jagir	assignment of land; land revenue
jihad (jehad)	literally 'strong action', commonly used to denote a religious war, analogous to a crusade
jirga	assembly of tribal elders or representatives
kach (kats)	alluvial plain on the edge of a stream
kafila	trading caravan or convoy (see also powindah)
khassadar	tribal armed levy employed by government mainly to protect and patrol roads
kot	walled village
kotal	pass
lac (lakh)	100,000
lashkar	tribal army or raiding force
malik	headman; tribal elder or representative
malmastia	hospitality
maulvi	Muslim priest or learned man
mullah	one who leads prayers as a teacher
nala (nullah)	ravine or shallow stream bed
nanawati	shelter; asylum
narai	pass
Pakhtu	'hard' form of Pashtu (qv)

xvii

Pakhtunwali	Pathan code of conduct, based upon the three principles of badal (qv), malmastia (qv) and nanawati (qv)
Pashtu	the 'soft' form of the Pathan language
Pashtun (Pathan)	generic name for the mountain tribes of the North-West Frontier and adjacent Afghanistan (Pathan is the Indianised version)
powindah	nomad, frequently a Ghilji (qv) from Afghanistan
raghza (rogha)	plateau on the edge of a valley
sangar	stone breastwork or defence
serai (sarai)	walled enclosure, with buildings, forming an inn or resting place for travellers
sepoy	infantry soldier
sowar	cavalry trooper or horseman
spin	white
tangi	gorge; defile
toi	stream
tor	black
warn	Waziri equivalent of kach (qv)
Zai	son, thus Muhammadzai (son/s of Muhammad)
AHQ	Army Headquarters India (Simla)
BL OIOC	British Library Oriental and India Office Collections
BP	Papers of Brigadier-General G M Baldwin
Chelmsford	Papers of Lord Chelmsford (BL Mss Eur 264)
CinC	Commander in Chief, India
FPPS	Foreign and Political Department Proceedings Secret
GOC	General Officer Commanding
Grant	Papers of Sir Hamilton Grant (BL Mss Eur)
HQ	Headquarters
LI	Light Infantry
L of C	Lines of Communication
Molesworth	G N Molesworth, *Afghanistan 1919* (London, 1962)
NAM	National Army Museum
NWFP	North-West Frontier Province
Operations	*Operations in Waziristan 1919–20* (Calcutta, 1921, official history)
Rees	Diaries of 2nd Lieutenant Douglas Rees, 3/34th Pioneers (NAM 6706–21)
RFA	Royal Field Artillery
RGA	Royal Garrison Artillery
Ross	Diaries of Colonel Harry Ross, 103rd Light Infantry (NAM 8004–40)
Salmond	Papers of Sir John Salmond (RAF Museum, Hendon, B2690)
Third Afghan War	*The Third Afghan War 1919: Official Account* (Calcutta, 1926)
Watteville	H de Watteville, *Waziristan 1919–20* (London, 1925)

Part One

THE THIRD AFGHAN WAR

I

An Uneasy Peace: Anglo–Afghan Relations: 1881–1919

(Map 1)

> The genesis of the Third Anglo–Afghan War must be found in the development of Afghan nationalism and the rising social and political expectations in the country.
>
> Vartan Gregorian

Early on the morning of 22 April 1881, the last British troops in Afghanistan left Kandahar after handing over the keys of the city to the new Amir (Abdurrahman)'s representative, Hashin Khan. Five days later, the troops crossed the new border into India. The Second Anglo-Afghan War was over. It had lasted two and a half years.

The war had arisen out of British fear of a Russian advance on India via Afghanistan and from a perception that the Amir, Sher Ali, was becoming a client of the Russians. The fear of a Russian advance was not entirely without foundation. Periodically throughout the 19th century, Russian officers had entertained the vision of just such an invasion, and the temptation had grown as the Russian empire in Central Asia had crept ever closer to the northern Afghan border. In the summer of 1878, at the height of the Near Eastern crisis, Kaufman, the Governor General of Russian Turkestan, had set in motion three columns towards Afghanistan.[1] Whether or not that was simply a negotiating ploy in the negotiations which were then reaching crisis point in Berlin, the fact remained that, coincidentally, a Russian mission under General Stolietov was on its way to Kabul with the draft of a Russo–Afghan treaty. That was in very distinct contrast to the repeated refusal over the years of Sher Ali to receive any form of British envoy. When, therefore, in September 1878, Sher Ali forcibly turned back a formal British mission under Sir Neville Chamberlain, war became inevitable.[2]

Militarily, it had been a British success, against a weaker, ill-organised opponent. Sher Ali had fled from Kabul at the beginning, with the object of seeking refuge in Russia. His successor, his son, Yakub Khan, had lasted long enough to sign a peace treaty but within months had been forcibly deposed by the British and sent into exile in India, on suspicion of complicity in the murder in Kabul of the British envoy, Cavagnari, and the massacre of his escort. That had left the British with no credible alternative, political solution except a policy of despair – the breaking up of the kingdom into its constituent parts, retaining Kandahar in British hands, and leaving the rest to whoever could establish himself there. Given the original motive behind the war, it was an ironic result but it cloaked the fact that the British had never controlled more than a relatively small part of Eastern Afghanistan; Herat and Afghan Turkestan, with Bamian and Central Afghanistan, had remained wholly outside British influence or control.

From this depth of political poverty, the British authorities had been rescued by the re-appearance in February 1880 of Abdurrahman, the son of Sher Ali's brother, Afzal. Abdurrahman had been in exile in Russia since 1868; his re-appearance in Afghan Turkistan immediately attracted support from Afghans who wanted an end to the chaos and confusion caused by the British occupation. As he moved slowly and deliberately towards Kabul, pacing his advance shrewdly, the Indian Government realised that the balance of political advantage was swinging in his favour and that he, rather than the British, could soon be in a position to dictate terms.[3] It was imperative to attempt to reach agreement with him, both to solve the political impasse and to salvage something from the costly campaign before he became too strong.

In the spring of 1880, therefore, negotiations were begun to recognise him as Amir of Kabul. But his underlying ambition – to re-establish the kingdom of his grandfather, Dost Muhammad, had been underestimated. There were powerful voices in Calcutta and London who argued on strategic and political grounds for British retention of Kandahar, but the crushing defeat at Maiwand, in southern Afghanistan, in July 1880 at the hands of Abdurrahman's nephew and rival claimant, Ayub Khan, tipped the balance. When the British evacuated Afghanistan in April 1881, it was on the tacit understanding that Abdurrahman was free to attempt the unification of the whole country. It would not be the Afghanistan of his grandfather because the British, for strategic reasons, annexed the Kurram valley (covering the southern route to Kabul, which Roberts had followed in September 1879), as well as retaining Pishin and Sibi, the districts encompassing Quetta and the Bolan Pass and the southern route into Afghanistan.[4]

Of equal long-term significance was the fact that Abdurrahman had been forced to accept as a condition of the Amirship that his foreign relations would remain under British control. He had no wish to go on his travels again. Twelve years in Russia had persuaded him that, as between the two imperial powers, the friendship of the British was likely to be less onerous and more profitable than that of the Russians. The British by their action in 1878 had made it clear that they would not tolerate anything else. He had in any case enough on his plate in bringing the outlying areas of

Afghanistan such as Herat and Afghan Turkestan under his control, in subduing his turbulent subjects and in creating a centralised, unified state, without indulging in intrigues with the Russians.[5]

Nevertheless, if he was content to accept British protection, that did not mean that he did not retain significant grievances. He resented the loss of Pishin, Sibi and the Kurram, all held by his grandfather. He chafed under the humiliation of having Afghan external relations controlled by the British, and the Durand agreement of 1893, which delimited the frontier between India and Afghanistan, was disputed by Abdurrahman in several places, notably in the Khyber Pass.[6] Moreover, he was conscious that as the ruler of all Afghans, he was the leader of the Pathan tribes on both sides of the border. While his relations with the Government of India remained basically peaceful, he did not miss an opportunity to tweak the lion's tail by intriguing among the tribes on the British side of the frontier – for example, in Chitral on the death of Aman-ul-Mulk (see Chapter III), and in Waziristan.

The British were well aware of these intrigues but they were content to deal with them on a discreet, local basis. They had more important matters to worry about. The Russian threat had not evaporated with the conclusion of the Second Afghan War; indeed, it took a new and potentially more dangerous turn in the 1890s with Russian penetration southwards across the Pamirs.[7]

Abdurrahman died in 1902 and was succeeded by his son, Habibullah. He shared many of the characteristics of his great father – he was shrewd, hard-headed and realistic, although he lacked the cruelty and black humour of Abdurrahman. He did, however, share the grievances of his father, most particularly, over British control of his external relations. So long as that remained, Afghanistan could not consider itself independent and freely open to foreign investment. The anti-British faction in Kabul, which had been kept under tight control by Abdurrahman, gradually began to re-emerge under the looser rein of Habibullah and, from the Indian Government's standpoint, it became desirable to arrive at a more formal basis of understanding with the new Amir. He declined to come to India but agreed to accept a British mission, led by Sir Louis Dane at the end of 1904.

Dane found that the Amir was impressed by the recent Japanese victories over Russia in the Far East and was insistent that Afghanistan should be treated as an independent country like Japan. Nevertheless, Dane succeeded in concluding a treaty in March 1905 which retained British control of Afghan external relations and the continued exclusion of other foreign missions, in return for an increased subsidy of 18 lacs of rupees (about £180,000 then) and the right to import arms through India. Two years later, Habibullah visited India and declared his intention of remaining in peace with the British. Any goodwill that this engendered was rapidly dissipated by the Convention signed in the same year by Britain and Russia, regulating their different spheres of influence in Asia. In the case of Afghanistan, the British agreed not to occupy any part of Afghanistan so long as the Amir continued to abide by the 1905 treaty, while the Russians agreed to deal with Afghanistan only through the British.

From the British point of view, this removed a major threat but, by what seems now a major political and psychological blunder, based on arrogance, the Amir was not consulted. Consequently, deeply angered, he refused to accept the existence of the Convention and its terms. Despite this and despite the political difficulties that it created for him in Kabul, Habibullah maintained peaceful, if not friendly, relations with the Indian Government down to 1914.

Before 1914 Germany had no clear policy towards India although some German officials had had hopes of a Muslim rising in India, linked to the pan-Islam movement centred upon the Sultan of Turkey, as the nominal head of all Muslims. Suspicion of the Muslim community, going back to the Mutiny, was also deeply ingrained in many Indian officials and soldiers.

With the outbreak of war, India became of direct interest to Germany as a possible means of embarrassing and weakening the British. The immediate initiative, however, was taken by two Indian students living in Germany, Abinash Battacharya and Virendranath Chattopadhyaya, who got in touch with the German Foreign Office. An Indian Committee was formed within the Foreign Office with the object of stimulating a national uprising in India. It was shortly joined by another revolutionary, the Maulvi Barakat Allah (or Barakatullah). He and another revolutionary, Har Dayal, nourished ideas of an armed invasion from Afghanistan. At the beginning of 1915 Germany established links with the Ghadr revolutionary movement established pre-war on the west coast of Canada and the USA.

With the entry of Turkey into the war in November 1915, new possibilities opened up – in particular, the establishment of land communications with Afghanistan, across Turkey. A year earlier, Enver Pasha, the Turkish Minister of War, had assured the German ambassador in Constantinople, von Wangenheim, that Habibullah was enthusiastically pro-Islam and ready to attack India. In August 1914, therefore, the German Foreign Office began to assemble a mission to Afghanistan, which in due course came under the command of a German Army officer, Oskar von Niedermayer, who had travelled extensively in the Middle East and India. A second mission, consisting of two Indian revolutionaries, Barakat Allah and Kumar Mahendra Pratap, the deposed ruler of a minor Indian state, and some Indian Army deserters was despatched in April 1915, under the supervision of a German diplomat, Werner Otto von Hentig, and accompanied by a Turkish officer, Kasim Bey. It clearly made little sense to have two separate missions traipsing across Persia and the two were combined under the effective leadership of von Niedermayer.[8]

In Kabul, Habibullah was under increasing pressure to seize the opportunity from factions within his own court to declare war on Britain. A moderate, pro-Turkish party was led by his son and heir, Inayatullah, while a conservative, clerical and strongly anti-British party was led by the Amir's brother, Nasrullah. Finally, there was a modernist, nationalist party, led by Mahmud Tarzi, who was owner of Kabul's only newspaper, the *Siraj-al-Akhbar*,[9] and related to the Royal family. In parallel, a group of Indian revolutionaries, led by the Wahabi leader, Obeidullah Sindhi,[10] reached Kabul with the object of seeking Afghan support in instigating a revolution in India. The pressure increased when the German mission reached Afghanistan in August 1915.[11] Pratap brought with him three illuminated addresses to the princes of India, promising German support for Indian freedom, as well as a letter from Bethman Hollweg, the German Chancellor, to the Amir, promising him India as far south as Bombay if he would join the war against the British.

Habibullah was now under intense pressure to declare war on the British and the Russians, and he made this clear in secret correspondence with the Viceroy, Hardinge. He therefore played for time. He did not give the German mission an audience until the end of October 1915 and there then ensued a long delay, during which Niedermayer and Hentig concluded that the mission was at an end and that they should return home. But Habibullah did not wish to abandon all leverage on the Indian Government and at the end of December he informed the mission that he was prepared to enter into a treaty to declare war on India, in return for a German guarantee of Afghanistan's territorial integrity, a seat at any subsequent peace conference between the Powers, £10,000,000 in cash, 100,000 rifles and 300 modern guns and ammunition. Nasrullah assured Niedermayer privately that if Afghanistan could be adequately rewarded then an agreement was likely. Niedermayer, encouraged, cabled Germany asking for the despatch of £1,000,000 and a substantial quantity of arms, and then set about organising and training an Afghan army of 70,000 and encouraging agitation among the tribes on the British side of the frontier, with limited success.

From the German point of view, the prospect of an invasion of India and internal revolution there was well worth the Amir's demands. But the collapse of Persia and its effective partitioning between Britain and Russia caused Habibullah to draw back. In January 1916 he announced in durbar that Afghanistan would remain neutral. In March he told Niedermayer that Afghanistan would only enter the war on two conditions – that there should be an internal revolt in India and that an army of at least 20,000 German or Turkish troops would be deployed to attack the British in

Baluchistan, the southern invasion route into India. These conditions were so manifestly incapable of being carried out that Niedermayer and Hentig drew the obvious conclusion and left Afghanistan.

The Amir was too shrewd to abandon all forms of pressure on the British. A German rear party lingered on in Herat until October 1917 and an Afghan emissary arrived in Kermanshah in December 1916 but, true to form, with no powers to negotiate. In Kabul, Habibullah was content to have the Indian revolutionaries declare a Provisional Government of India, with Pratap as President and Barkat Allah as Prime Minister. Their adherents in Kabul were few. Obeidullah Sindhi was made Home Minister and occupied himself with organising 'the Army of God' to liberate India.[12]

By thus playing both ends off against the middle, Habibullah had succeeded in keeping Afghanistan out of the war. But in doing so he had angered powerful forces in Kabul, notably the anti-British party led by Nasrullah, the Commander in Chief (Nadir Shah), and the dowager Queen, Amanullah's mother. Moreover, he had incurred personal unpopularity through his incessant philandering. He had squandered much of the British subsidies and was unable to buy support. In 1918 he was forced to call a national assembly to explain his policy. He might still have survived if the British had been prepared to give him the reward to which, not unnaturally, he felt entitled.

His neutrality had been of immense help to Britain and India, preoccupied as they were with a World War, and Habibullah felt entitled to expect his reward in the form of complete independence from British control. The vexed question of the control of foreign policy was raised by Habibullah in a letter to the Viceroy on 2 February 1919. He considered that Afghanistan must now be regarded as free and independent in every way and entitled therefore to send a representative to the peace negotiations at Versailles. If, however, Britain would obtain from the Conference recognition of 'the absolute liberty, freedom of action, and perpetual independence of the Sublime Government of Afghanistan from further interference, damage and loss', he would waive his right to send a representative.[13] Chelmsford was sympathetic; as he pointed out to Montagu, the Secretary of State, it was inconceivable that Britain would ever go to war with Afghanistan on this issue and there seemed little point in clinging to a right which was never likely to be enforced and thus alienating Habibullah.[14]

There were contrary views in both New Delhi and London and the matter was clearly regarded as of no great weight; at the beginning of 1919, Roos-Keppel, ailing and anxious to get home on leave, assured Chelmsford: 'Everything on the frontier is so extra-ordinarily quiet that it is safe to prophesy a quiet summer.' Even allowing for his anxiety to get home, it is inconceivable that an experienced official like Roos-Keppel would have made such a rash prophecy if he had anticipated the slightest problem with Kabul. Thus, no reply had been sent to Habibullah's request when the matter was resolved by his murder on the night of 19/20 February 1919 while on a hunting trip at Jalalabad. An Afghan colonel was subsequently made the scapegoat and executed but it was patently clear that the real instigators lay elsewhere.[15] Nasrullah, who was almost certainly deeply involved, immediately had himself proclaimed Amir, and Inayatullah, Habibullah's eldest son and nominated successor, was forced to acquiesce. Nasrullah had miscalculated. While he and the Court were at Jalalabad, his nephew, Inayatullah's younger brother, Amanullah,[16] was in Kabul, close to the real levers of power. He immediately assembled the leading political and military figures and had himself proclaimed Amir. He was supported by the army which was angry over the murder and suspected that Nadir Shah was implicated. Faced with this coup, Nasrullah and Inayatullah gave way and recognised Amanullah as Amir.

The confused sequence of events which followed Habibullah's murder formed an unstable basis for Amanullah's rule. He was in debt for support to the army and to the anti-British parties, and his action in calling a popular assembly to back his accession had aroused public expectations. He sought to placate the army with a pay increase and by exiling Nadir Shah to command the forces in the distant province of Khost, on the border with the Kurram; Saleh Muhammad was made Commander in Chief in his stead.

Amanullah had come to power on a wave of Afghan nationalism, which he helped to promote. It had been fanned by anti-British elements, by Turkish and German activities, and by the presence of the Indian revolutionaries in Kabul. It was further stimulated by the limited incursion into representational government reluctantly introduced by his father. In this situation, Amanullah probably had little alternative but to ride the wave and hope to control it. In fact, it substantially chimed with his own sympathies. He had long determined to get rid of British control in any form, and make Afghanistan completely independent. In writing to the Viceroy on 3 March 1919, three days after acceding to the throne, formally notifying the death of his father and his own accession, he made his attitude quite clear:

> Nor let this remain unknown to that friend [the Viceroy] that our independent and free Government of Afghanistan considers itself ready and prepared at every time and season to conclude, with due regard to every consideration for the requirements of friendship and the like, such agreements and treaties with the mighty Government of England as may be useful and serviceable in the way of commercial gains and advantages to our Government and yours.[17]

A week or so later, he issued a firman to the people of Afghanistan:

I have placed the Crown on my head in the name of intergrity and of the free and independent administration of the internal and external affairs of Afghanistan. I also give you the good news that you are a free nation. You are not under the protection or supervision of any foreign power.[18]

At his first Durbar on 13 April 1919, he rubbed home the point further:

I have declared my country entirely free, autonomous and independent, both internally and externally. My country will hereafter be as independent a state as other states and powers of the world are. No foreign power will be allowed to have a hairsbreadth of right to interfere internally and externally with the affairs of Afghanistan, and if anyone does I am ready to cut its throat with this sword.

Moreover, he specifically asked the British Agent (the Vakil) in Kabul (Saifullah Khan), who was present, to note what he said: 'O Safir, have you understood what I have said?', to which the Agent replied that he had.[19]

He followed this up by appointing an ambassador to Bokkhara and announced his intention of sending an envoy to Persia. His new Commissary (Minister) for Foreign Affairs was Muhammad Tarzi of whom Hamilton Grant wrote:

His influence on foreign policy can only be anti-Christian, anti-British and directed towards a close union with Turkey.[20]

Amanullah's claims could hardly have been telegraphed more clearly, but there seems to have been a disposition on the part of both the Indian and British Governments to treat them as little more than posturing for an Afghan audience and that as soon as Amanullah was firmly in control matters would settle down as before. Chelmsford wrote to Montagu that the Amir would have to establish himself firmly in Kabul before he could be in a position to trouble the British: 'We have very little knowledge of Amanullah as a man, but what we have is to the good, and he is reported to be friendly and well-disposed to us.'[21] London was equally complacent: 'We may, I hope, find him as staunch a friend as his father.'[22] At the beginning of March, in reply to a query from Montagu, Chelmsford wrote:

I do not feel that circumstances warrant or are likely to warrant our keeping Roos-Keppel out here. Recent events in Afghanistan may probably lead to dissensions in Kabul but even if such dissensions react in a way directly affecting us there is very little likelihood that such consequences will ensue in the immediate future or that much influence over the course of events could be exercised by Roos Keppel... the sooner Grant gets into the saddle the better.[23]

Unfortunately, in breach of protocol, Amanullah's letter was not replied to immediately. There was discussion between New Delhi and London about how precisely to deal with the Amir's overt claim to complete independence and whether the Amir could be addressed as 'His Majesty'. The Viceroy did not reply to the letter until 15 April 1919[24] and George V not until 1 May 1919. How far the delay in replying was a serious determinant in Amanullah's actions is debatable; clearly it did nothing to weaken his resolve or to quieten the anti-British elements.

Whether or not Amanullah was actuated also by a fear of renewed British expansion consequent upon its victorious emergence from the First World War, as has been argued,[25] is problematical. Other commentators have suggested that he had decided, as other rulers had done before him, to embark on a popular external venture in order to harness political and religious forces, and to consolidate his support at home. A similar view was taken by the Indian authorities:

It is clear that the people's profound dissatisfaction with Amanullah's enquiry into Habibullah's murder and suspicion of Amanullah's own complicity are the real cause of Amir's anti-British policy. Finding his position untenable and encouraged by grossly exaggerated accounts of disturbances in India, Amanullah has been driven to avert rebellion against himself by proclaiming jehad and promising easy conquest of India.[26]

That may well have entered into his calculations but it does less than justice to his passionate desire to see Afghanistan completely independent, a desire bolstered, if anything, by the emergence of other, new and independent states after 1918. That desire would seem to have been the real driving force behind his actions.

Whatever the precise motives, the gamble of a war against the British had some elements in its favour. In the first place, there was the intense Muslim feeling aroused by the defeat and humiliation of Turkey. In India the Government was acutely nervous about the attitude of the large Indian Muslim population and particularly about the loyalty of the large (40%) Muslim component of the Indian Army.

Secondly, Amanullah was well informed about the dangerous internal situation in India, where the war had produced explosive pressures. Shortages of food and goods, caused by war-time mobilisation and accentuated by the enlistment of large numbers of men for the Indian Army, had led to massive increases in prices. Since 1914 the official price index had virtually doubled, food grains had gone up by 93%, imported goods by 190% and Indian-manufactured goods by over 60%.[27] To finance the war, taxation had gone up by 40% and wartime controls and transport shortages had restricted the development of Indian exports. High prices, especially for foodstuffs, increased taxation and shortages inevitably hit the poorer classes hardest. On the political front, wartime sacrifices had increased the pressure for early Home Rule and at Lahore in 1916 the Congress Party and the Muslim League had signed an historic pact to demand early progress to responsible government. In the Punjab, the embers of the Ghadr conspiracy still smouldered and in Bengal, the pre-war terrorist movement retained powerful roots. Finally, the war had shattered belief in British invincibility.

At the beginning of 1919 these factors combined to produce a wave of serious rioting and destruction, particularly in Western India. It was particularly extreme in the Punjab, where it led to the tragedy of Amritsar and to the proclamation of martial law in April 1919. Throughout India, feelings were exacerbated by the passing of a draconian Sedition Act (the so-called Rowlatt Act) which provided for internment without trial and the suspension of trial by jury. Within a year, Gandhi was to harness these elements in his Non Cooperation movement, presenting the Indian Government with the most serious threat to its rule since the Mutiny.[28]

The Indian Government was ill-placed in 1919 to deal with this internal upheaval. The civil police suffered like the rest of the population from the rise in prices of foodstuffs. They were underpaid and under pressure and morale was not high. The Army in India was also at an unprecedented low ebb as a result of the war. Its best regiments were either still overseas or at home suffering the loss of trained men from demobilisation or long-deferred leave. What remained in India was largely new units, containing poorly trained, young recruits. The British element, fixed pre-war at one third of the total, was now only about a quarter,[29] and of that there were only eight pre-war regular infantry battalions; the rest were Territorial battalions, anxious about getting back to civil employment (see Chapter II).

Amanullah was well informed on the Indian situation, even if his agents, such as the Afghan Postmaster (Ghulam Haidar) at Peshawar, tended to exaggerate the likelihood of an uprising. Thus on 7 May 1919 Ghulam Haidar assured the Amir that there were thousands of Hindus and Muslims in India ready to give their lives for the Amir and that the Indian Government had insufficient troops to handle a rising.[30] But senior British officials and commanders took an almost equally serious view.[31]

Nevertheless, if the odds were as favourable for Amanullah as they were ever likely to be, they still amounted to a considerable gamble. On any rational calculation, his own forces were inadequate for the task of defeating the Army in India. That Army was still more than double its pre-war numbers; if necessary, the British could be expected to pour troops into India to retain it, as they had done in the Mutiny, only sixty years before. Moreover, while the internal situation in India was serious, it still lacked the organisation and the degree of popular support to turn it into a national uprising. Few Indian politicians relished the idea of liberation by a horde of Afghan tribesmen. The conservative elements of Indian society, led by the princes, continued to support the British; even the ancient Yakub Khan, exiled in India for forty years, offered his support to the Viceroy, possibly sniffing a faint chance of reinstatement in Kabul.[32]

The crucial element for Amanullah was therefore the attitude of the cis-border tribes.

They had been deeply stirred by the entry of Turkey into the War against the British and they had provoked a major expedition against them at the height of that war.[33] They were better armed than they had ever been and the events of 1897 had shown what could be achieved if their efforts could be properly coordinated. Therein lay the difficulty. The tribes were notorious for their independence and unreliability. A simultaneous uprising of all the tribes was in practice impossible to organise and coordinate. What Amanullah could hope for was that a declaration of war, followed by some initial success, would ignite a general tribal uprising on at least the scale of 1897–8.[34] Such an uprising, coupled with widespread agitation in India, would present the British with a military problem which could force their acquiescence in Afghan demands. The vigorous support of the cis-border tribes was therefore the key to Afghan actions. The Indian authorities saw it the same way:

> The tribal offensive was, in fact, the basis of the whole plan; and the line of action to be taken by the Afghan Army depended entirely on the extent to which the tribes consented to cooperate and on the subsequent success of their operations. Their best and only chance of success lay in securing the co-operation of the tribes and in coordinating their efforts. The looseness of our political control over a large portion of the border territory made it a promising field for such activity.[35]

If, therefore, in retrospect, Amanullah's gamble seems a desperate one, it did not necessarily appear so at the time.

In the early part of 1919, Amanullah issued a firman to the tribes on both sides of the border, calling attention to the unrest in India, and calling on them to be ready to support uprisings in India when the moment came.[36] In a more practical effort to enlist tribal support, Afghan agents were busy all along the Frontier in the early part of 1919, promising support from the Amir and distributing gifts of rifles and ammunition. The efforts to enlist the aid of the tribes, like so much of the Afghan planning, were uncoordinated and the results would prove disappointing, except in Waziristan.

What precisely were Amanullah's objectives in launching a war with

India, and how realistic were they? The objectives were never fully spelled out and it may well be that Amanullah and his advisers never formulated a clear-cut set of objectives. Much depended upon success in raising the tribes and upon the development of the situation in India.

Given the disparity in the strengths and resources of the two countries, it had necessarily to be a war of limited objectives, although the possibility of triggering a mass rebellion in India may well have been a glittering fantasy in some Afghan minds. Amanullah had, however, inherited three basic objectives from his father and grandfather and all three were within the bounds of practicability in 1919.

The first was the rectification of the Durand line in Afghanistan's favour, particularly in those places such as the Khyber where the line remained undemarcated. The second objective was the recovery of territory and influence over which Afghanistan had exercised sway before the outbreak of the Second Anglo-Afghan War in 1878. This included Pishin, Sibi, Khelat and the Kurram; although Waziristan had never been under the direct control of Kabul, Amanullah nevertheless believed that the Wazirs and Mahsuds would welcome some or all of it, particularly Wana, coming under Afghan suzereignty. The recovery of Peshawar, the old summer capital of the Amirs, lost to the Sikhs in 1834 and inherited by the British in 1849, had been a dynastic ambition since the time of the great Amir, Dost Mahomed, but it seems unlikely that Amanullah saw it now as a realistic ambition. How far the British tribes concerned would have welcomed the exchange of British for Afghan rule is problematical but the ties of blood and religion were strong and their acquiescence was a reasonable assumption.

But the objective on which Amanullah had clearly set his heart was regaining control of Afghan external affairs and making Afghanistan fully independent.[37] In that, also, he was following the aspirations of his predecessors; it was the banner under which he fought the war. Nothing could be better calculated to unite all sections of Afghan society. Habibullah had agreed only reluctantly in the treaty of 1905 to accept continuation of British control of his external affairs, in return for an increased annual subsidy of 18 lacs of rupees. The exigencies of war between 1914 and 1918 had forced the British tacitly to relax their control but there remained many senior officials for whom British control was a cornerstone of their policy:

> our control of Afghanistan's foreign relations has been so long a fundamental principle of our Afghan policy that it requires an effort of mind to conceive of our willingly consenting to any diminution of it.[38]

What British officials overlooked or misjudged was the link between

Amanullah's determination to regain control of his country's foreign relations and his longer-term aim of national regeneration, both social and economic. For that, he would need help from other countries, and he needed to be able to negotiate with completely free hands.

If Amanullah's objectives were reasonably discernible, his preparations for war were oddly uncoordinated. His regular troops were in the process of assembling for operations; in the central reserve of his best troops, held at Kabul, had not been deployed, either on the central (Khyber) front or at Kandahar. The initial thrusts in Chitral and in the Kurram lacked coordination and weight, the occupation of Wana was not followed by any further progress in Waziristan, the fortress of Spin Baldak opposite New Chaman was left entirely unsupported, and no serious attempt seems to have been made to exploit opportunities in the Thob. Only in Khost was the local commander, Nadir Shah, ready for a serious, planned offensive; elsewhere, commanders gave the impression that they were working to no overall strategic plan. Only in respect of raising the British tribes had Amanullah taken serious steps.

To prepare the ground, Amanullah had summoned the chiefs of the transborder tribes to Kabul to explain his decision to go to war and to urge them to be ready to assist. To ensure their cooperation he despatched money and ammunition across the border. Using the members of 'The Provisional Government of India' he made contact with the revolutionaries in India, assuring them of his support and distributing judicious sums of money to finance their activities.

He had some hopes of outside assistance. A mission was despatched to Bokhara to seek the Emir's help, as a fellow Muslim and hitherto a pawn in the Great Game between Russia and India. The Emir, however, was grateful to the British for recent support against the Bolsheviks and therefore declined to help.[39] Amanullah had some hopes of Bolshevik support,[40] and at various times throughout the war rumours abounded in Kabul and Herat of assistance from the Turks, the Germans and even the Austrians. In the confused post-war world of 1919 stranger things were happening. But none of this possible support was in place before Amanullah set the war in motion; none of it was forthcoming after the war started. What is not clear is whether the faults in Amanullah's planning were due to the relatively primitive nature of his bureaucratic machine, or whether internal pressures hurried him into war before he was ready.

It is just conceivable that Amanullah was playing a more cynical game – that he was using the war and likely defeat to discredit the anti-British elements, tame the Army and consolidate his own position. On this basis, any gains that he might conceivably pick up would strengthen his position while defeat would discredit the war parties and weaken the position of the Army. On this basis, war was for him a positive sum game. These considerations may not have been entirely absent from his mind although it is perhaps fanciful to assume that they were a major determinant in his actions. In the upshot, he obtained from the war that which he had set his heart on.

The war came with remarkable speed and caught the Indian authorities napping. As we have seen, Chelmsford did not expect trouble with Afghanistan.[41] Five days before the first overt hostilities, he was able to assure Montagu that on the North-West Frontier, all was quiet.[42] The Army was taking no extraordinary precautions; block leave was being granted to units and plans were in hand for the normal move of units up to the hills for the hot weather.[43]

At the beginning of May Amnullah issued a public firman, saying that, although he had no right to interfere, he believed that the peoples of India, Hindu and Muslim, had been badly rewarded for their loyalty during the war, and were justified in rising against the British. Because he was afraid that the disturbances in India might spread into Afghanistan, he had sent the Commander in Chief, Saleh Muhammad, with troops, to the eastern frontier.[44] On 2 May Chelmsford reported that Saleh Muhammad had arrived at Dakka with an escort of two companies of infantry and two guns; the firman could be viewed simply as an attempt by the Amir to fish speculatively in troubled waters and Roos-Keppel took the view that the despatch of Muhammad Saleh was a natural precaution against Afghan agitation over the findings of the Habibullah murder enquiry.[45]

More disturbing developments followed rapidly. Saleh Muhammad was quickly followed to Dakka by another 2,000 regular troops; another 1,500 men were despatched to Kandahar and 2,000 to Khost to join Nadir Shah. The Afghan Postmaster at Peshawar was summoned to Kabul and given copies of a proclamation for distribution in India, calling on all Muslims to assist Afghanistan in a war against the British.[46] From Dakka Saleh Muhammad moved on to Bagh, in what the Indian Government regarded as Indian territory, although at this point the Durand Line had never been formally demarcated. The springs at Bagh provided the water supplies for the British post at Landi Kotal. Farther south, in the Kurram, Afghan regulars and Jaji tribesmen were reported to be erecting fortifications on the Peiwar Kotal.

The first overt act of hostilities came on 3 May when a party of the Khyber Rifles, escorting a convoy through the Khyber Pass to Landi Kotal, was turned back by picquets of armed tribesmen under a notorious raider, Zar Shah. Later the same day five unarmed labourers working on the water supply for Landi Kotal were killed by Zar Shah who claimed he was acting on the orders of the Afghan Commander in Chief. Bagh village and the ridge behind were then occupied by Afghan troops and next day (4 May) the water supply to Landi Kotal was cut. Chelmsford reacted by sending a message to Amanullah, asking him to arrest Zar Shah and to repudiate the firman as a forgery.[47] On the 5th, however, more Afghan regulars arrived at Bagh and the British authorities reacted by sending reinforcements to Landi Kotal.

At this stage the Indian authorities were still anxious to treat these as low-level frontier incidents. Roos-Keppel, by no means anxious to have his leave interfered with, recommended the immediate despatch of a force to expel the Afghans from the Bagh springs – not to do so immediately would create a bad impression among the tribes, while prompt action might put an immediate end to any more extended Afghan action.[48] Chelmsford concurred and telegraphed the Secretary of State the same day:

> I have ordered overwhelming force up in order that an excuse may be found for peaceful retirement.[49]

By 6 May, however, the Indian authorities were in possession of information that left little room for doubt. An informer on the staff of the Afghan Postmaster revealed that the Afghans planned to attack on three main fronts – via the Khyber (under the direct command of Saleh Muhammad), from Khost (under Nadir Shah) and from Kandahar (under Abdul Qaduz, the Prime Minister). The attacks were to be launched simultaneously within the next ten days, and would be accompanied by carefully orchestrated riots in India designed to tie up British troops.[50] On 5 May Army HQ at Simla ordered the suspension of all demobilisation, disbandments and reductions; mobilisation of all units on the Frontier, together with the 2nd (Rawalpindi) Division followed.[51] On 6 May the Indian Government issued a formal declaration of war, thus giving the Afghans the pretext for claiming later that the British had started the war.

Chelmsford had reason to be aggrieved that his officials had persisted in their complacency and had seemingly failed to heed the warning signs or to take precautionary action:

> You may ask why we have not had better information. I can only answer that I do not believe that Amanullah himself knew until the last moment that he was going to embark on this enterprise... If the military here have not been living in a fool's' paradise we ought to have hit the enemy very hard in a day or two. I have laid stress on overwhelming force as we cannot afford to have an initial reverse.[52]

The question was indeed a very pertinent one. The British maintained an Agent (the Vakil) in Kabul precisely to obtain and pass on news to Simla; he in turn maintained a network of informers. Even if, as appears to have been the case, the Afghan Government carefully restricted his activities and fed him only that news which it wished him to have, there was ample evidence available to the Indian Government on Amanullah's determination to achieve full independence for Afghanistan.

The Amir had gone out of his way, both in correspondence with Chelmsford and in his initial address to his Durbar, to make sure the message got through. If, therefore, the Indian Government was caught unawares, it must be ascribed to a certain patronising arrogance on the part of officials, coloured in Roos-Keppel's case by deep dislike of the Afghans. There was clearly a tendency to treat the Afghans as children whose squabbles in their own backyard did not need to be taken too seriously; moreover, the idea that Afghanistan, with its relatively poorly trained and equipped army, should venture upon a full-scale war with the British in India must have seemed preposterous to experienced officials. Thus, the initial tendency was to regard the Afghan incursion at Bagh as no more than a minor incursion along a stretch of disputed frontier. It should be noted also that the Government of India was preoccupied with the serious unrest in India itself, which culminated in the massacre at Amritsar on 13 April 1919. A war with Afghanistan at this time would be a serious distraction and it may therefore be that an element of wishful thinking coloured officials' perception of the Afghan situation.

Notes

1   For a survey of early Russian projects for the invasion of India see H S Edwards, *Russian Projects against India, from Czar Peter to General Skoboleff* (London, 1885).

2   For a detailed history of the Second Afghan War see Brian Robson, *The Road to Kabul: the Second Afghan War 1878–1881* (London, 1975, 2nd edn 2003, 2007).

3   Lytton to Cranbrook (Secretary of State for India), 12 April 1880, quoted in Betty Balfour, *The History of Lord Lytton's Indian Administration 1876–1889* (London, 1890).

4   Under Article 9 of the Treaty of Gandamak 1879, Pishin and Sibi were to be administered by the British and any surplus of revenue over expenditure was to be remitted to the Amir. They were formally annexed in 1887.

5   His sardonic gallows humour and his implacable will are vividly portrayed in Kipling's short story *The Amir's Homily* and his two poems 'The Ballad of the King's Jest' and 'The Ballad of the King's Mercy'. Kipling saw him at close quarters in Rawalpindi in 1885 during the Amir's visit to the Viceroy.

6   In 1919 there were still some gaps and some disputed areas – for example, in the Khyber where the Afghans regarded the Line as passing through Landi Khana, whereas the British believed it ran through Torkham, five miles farther west.

7   See, for example, the very revealing conversations which Captain Cobbold had with Russian officers on the Pamirs in 1898: Cobbold, *Innermost Asia: Travel and Sport in the Pamirs* (London, 1900). For a well-researched and very readable general survey of Anglo-Russian rivalry in this area, see Peter Hopkirk, *The Great Game* (London, 1990); also G J Alder, *British India Northern Frontier 1865–1895* (London, 1965). As late as 1940 defences were being built in the Khyber against a possible Russian invasion, following the German–Soviet Pact of 1939, and some of the anti-tank blocks are still there.

8   For a convenient general account of German policy see Strachan, *The First World War*, Vol 1,770–2, 798–80; for more detailed accounts see Barooah, *India and the official Germany* and Sareen, *Indian revolutionary movements abroad* (1905–1921). For the Ghadr movement see also Popplewell, *Intelligence and Imperial Defence* and T G Fraser, *The Intrigues of the German Government and the Ghadr Party against British rule in India* 1914–1918 (PhD thesis, University of London, 1974).

9   Literally *Light of the News*, founded by Tarzi in 1911. It was later re-named *Aman-i-Afghan*.

10 The Wahabis were a fundamentalist Muslim sect which originated in Arabia around 1860. Suppressed in India, a small colony, sometimes known as the Hindustani Fanatics, had found a base on the Frontier at Sitana, which had led to the hard-fought Ambeyla campaign of 1864. Thereafter they continued to create agitation among the tribes. Obeidullah himself was a Sikh who had converted to Islam.

11 For an account of the journeyings and travails of this mission, see the useful account in Hopkirk, On Secret Service East of Constantinople (Oxford, 1995); see also Ker, *Political Trouble in India*, 302. For an example of the addresses sent to the princes, see that sent to the Maharajah of Jhodpore: C(helmsford) P(apers)/52.

12 It included twelve field marshals, forty-eight generals, but only two captains and one lieutenant and no other ranks: Petrie, *Communism in India*, 48.

13 Viceroy to Secretary of State for India (Montagu), No. 154-S[ecret], 11 February 1919, CP/l0, No. 194.

14 Heathcote, 169.

15 Maffey came to the conclusion later that two factions within Kabul were responsible for the murder:
(a) Amanullah and his mother, the Ulya Hazrat, who resented Habibullah's refusal to accept Amanullah as his heir;
(b) Nadir Shah and his brother, Shah Wali Khan (known as Sar-Saros), who were angered by Habibullah's desire to take a girl who was already betrothed within their family and that the actual killing was done by Wali Khar, private letter from Chelmsford to Montagu, 20 August 1919, MSS Ear D 523/9.

16 He was originally known as Ain-ud-Daulah, taking the name Amanullah on his accession.

17 Viceroy to SofS, No. 298-S, 11 March 1919 – CP/10.

18 AGG Baluchistan (Dobbs) to Foreign Secretary, 22 March 1919 – Foreign and Political Proceedings (hereafter FPP), June 1919 (CP/55e).

19 British Agent, Kabul to Deputy Foreign Secretary, 16 April 1919 – ibid, No. 154.

20 Quoted in Heathcote, 171. Tarzi was married to a Turkish princess and was Arnanullah's father-in-law.

21 Viceroy to SofS, 5 March 1919 – Heathcote, 170.

22 SofS to Viceroy, 26 March 1919 – Heathcote, 171.

23 Viceroy to SofS, No. 238, 4 March 1919 – CP/10, No. 252. Roos-Keppel who was retiring was to be succeeded by Sir Hamilton Grant, then Foreign Secretary.

24 Viceroy to Amanullah 15 April 1919, No. 142 – FPP, June1919, No. 142 (CP/55e).

25 For example, by Adamec, ibid, 109.

26 Viceroy to SofS, No. 572-S, 5 May 1919 – CF/b, No. 523.

27 Judith A Brown, *Modern India: The origins of an Asian democracy*, 188–90.

28 For the internal security situation in India in 1919, see Popplewell, chapter 12 and passim.

29 On 1 February 1919 the total strength of British units in India was 76,908, of whom 15,186 were non-effective, mainly sick – Viceroy to SofS, No. 234, 1 February 1919 – CF/10, No. 244.

30 Text in Private Secretary to Roos-Keppel to Deputy Foreign Secretary, No. 1154-S. 16 May 1919 – FPP August 1919, p 61. The Central Intelligence Department of the Indian Government had for some time been intercepting the Afghan mail – FPPS August 1919, 37.

31 Cf Dyer's motivation at Amritsar only three weeks before the outbreak of the war with Afghanistan.

32 Viceroy to SofS, No. 801-S, 4 June 1919 – CP/10, No. 746.

33 See Chapter XIII.

34 For the 1897–8 uprising, see Michael Barthorpe, *The Frontier Ablaze* (London, 1999).

35 *Despatch by His Excellency General Sir Charles Carmichael Monro on the Third Afghan War* (Simla, 1919), para.21.

36 Text in Adamec, 111.

37 It seems to have been overlooked that the 1905 treaty referred at one point to 'His Majesty, the *independent* King of Afghanistan and its dependencies' (author's italics).

38 Note by Denis Bray, Secretary to the Government of India in the Foreign Department – quoted in Adamec, 105.

39 *Baluchistan Force Daily Intelligence Summary No. 37*, 14 June 1919.

40 Ditto, No. 41, 18 June 1919; No. 5,27 June 1919.

41 See note 22 above.

42 Viceroy to SofS, No. 505-5,28 April 1919 – AHQ War Diary 19 April to 15 May 1919 (L/MIL/17/5/4057).

43 By the beginning of May the hot weather moves had been suspended at Peshawar because of the internal security situation there – Lt. Col. Eric De Burgh, *Personal reminiscences of the commencement of the Third Afghan War* (NAM 6505-55-2).

44 Text in Roos-Keppel to Foreign Secretary, No. 1238-R, 4 May 1919 – CP/551, No. 5.

45 Viceroy to SofS, No. 439-S, 2 May 1919 – CP/10, No. 494.

46 Viceroy to SofS, 6 March 1919, No. 579-S – CP/10, No. 522.

47 Viceroy to SofS, No. 558-S, 6 May 1919 – ibid, No. 521.

48 Roos-Keppel to Foreign Secretary, 5 May 1919 – L/MIL/17/5/4057, Appendix 89.

49 Viceroy to SofState, No. 475, 5 May 1919 – CF/b, No. 573.

50 Viceroy to SofS, No. 582-S, 7 May 1919 – CP/10, No. 533.

51 AHQ War Diary for period 19 April to 15 May 1919, Appendix 35 – L/MIL/5/4057.

52 Private letter from Chelmsford to Montagu – quoted in Heathcote, 178.

II

The Battlefield and the Antagonists

(Maps 1, 2, 3, 6, 7, 9 and 10)

From Chitral in the north to New Chaman in the south, the Indo-Afghan frontier ran for roughly 500 miles as the crow flies. But the frontier twists and turns, for the most part through mountainous country, so that the actual length was nearer 800 miles, although in 1919 some of it was still not accurately delineated.

The mountains which separate central Afghanistan from the plains of northern India are essentially a southward-trending offshoot of the eastern Hindu Kush. It is continued southward by the Safed Koh, the hills of Waziristan and the Suleiman range, finally dying away in the coastal ranges of the Mekran coast. To the east of the mountains, in India, the Indus river provided a natural barrier and defence against invaders coming down from the mountains. But only a handful of routes existed through the mountains capable of taking large bodies of troops and wheeled artillery. Of these the most important was that from Kabul through the Khyber (Khaibar) Pass, debouching on to the plains of India at Jamrud, only nine miles from Peshawar, the capital of India's North West Frontier Province and the main military base in north-west India. This was the traditional route used by almost all the invaders of India except Alexander.[1]

Next in importance was the route from Kandahar, Afghanistan's second city, over the Khojak Pass to Quetta and then down the Bolan Pass to the plains of Sind and the Indus. Separated from the Khyber by the formidable mass of the Tirah, the heartland of the powerful Afridi tribe, is the Kurram Valley which provides a not too difficult route from Kabul over the Shutagardan Pass, entering the valley over the Peiwar Kotal Pass and then down the valley of the Kurram river to Thal, at the base of the valley, whence an easy road connects Thal to Kohat and Peshawar. This was the route taken by Roberts' army in its advance on Kabul in September 1879. A less easy route, also used by Roberts in the spring of 1879, entered the valley roughly half way down, from the Afghan province of Khost.

Two other routes provide commonly used entry points into India from Afghanistan. The first ran from Ghazni, eastwards along the Tochi river, which forms the northern boundary of Waziristan, exiting from the hills at Bannu. The second route ran from Ghazni south-eastwards, along the Gomal river, which formed the southern boundary of Waziristan, ultimately reaching the Indus at Dera Ismail Khan. These were the traditional routes of the great Ghilzai (Powindah) caravans each spring and autumn. In the far north, Chitral could be entered comparatively easily from Afghanistan via the Kunar river valley, but there was then no easy route southwards into the plains of India.

Thus the nature of the country effectively split the theatre of operations into five main areas – Chitral, the Khyber, the Kurram, North and South Waziristan, and Baluchistan – with a sixth possible area, the Zhob, which links Waziristan and Baluchistan.

There were no railways in Afghanistan. On the Indian side, Peshawar was the railhead for a broad-gauge (5 foot 6 inch) railway from the Punjab.[2] Kohat was also reached by a broad-gauge railway, whence a narrow-gauge (2 foot 6 inch) railway ran to Thal. In Waziristan, Bannu and Tank were reached by narrow-gauge lines which connected to the main Indus Valley broad-gauge at Man, on the east bank of the Indus. In Baluchistan, a broad-gauge line ran up the Bolan Pass to Quetta, and then on to a railhead at New Chaman, where material was kept to enable the line to be extended to Kandahar whenever necessary; a narrow-gauge line extended a short way into the Zhob, to Hindubagh. The Indus Valley Railway constituted the main artery behind the possible fronts, linking Peshawar and New Chaman.[3]

The only fully metalled road in the area ran through the Khyber from Peshawar but, except for the routes into Chitral, all the routes contained stretches which were traversable by motor and wheeled vehicles. In general, however, this was an area for pack animals – camels, ponies, donkeys and mules.[4]

Communications, in terms of rapid deployment, reinforcement and supply, clearly favoured the British. Distance did not clearly favour either side except on the Khyber front where the area of fighting was 180 miles from the main Afghan base at Kabul but only ten miles from Peshawar. In the south Kandahar and Quetta were about the same distance (circa seventy-five miles) from the frontier, although Quetta was connected by rail. In the Zhob and the Kurram, distances favoured the Afghans, as they did very markedly in Chitral.[5]

The communications advantages on the British side were heavily offset by the handicap of the massive administrative 'tail' which the post-war Indian Army dragged behind it – a complication from which the Afghan army suffered much less, and the tribesmen not at all. Not for them the massive panoply of workshops, supply sections, veterinary hospitals, sanitary sections, bakeries, butcheries, lithographic and printing sections which the modern Indian Army required to function. In terms of speed of operational movement, Afghan regulars and tribesmen had the advantage.

Climatic conditions were severe for both sides but especially for European troops. The hot weather season of 1919 on the Frontier was exceptionally severe; temperatures in the tents at Dakka and Landi Khana reached 125°F. At night the temperatures dropped sharply; variations of 80°F between day and night temperatures were not uncommon; at New Chaman, in May 1919, cases of sunstroke and chilblains were admitted to hospital on the same day.

At the beginning of hostilities in 1919 the regular Afghan army comprised twenty-one regiments of cavalry, seventy-eight battalions of infantry and 280 breech-loading guns. Just under half of these units (five regiments of cavalry, thirty-five battalions of infantry, and 107 guns) were stationed on the frontier with India. What was effectively the strategic reserve (seven and a half regiments of cavalry, twenty battalions of infantry and 108 guns) was kept at Kabul. In general, these units were the elite of the army and better equipped than those on the frontier. The remainder of the army was stationed in Herat and Afghan Turkestan and was in practice not available for use on the eastern frontier.

Less than half of the infantry had modern small-bore, repeating rifles although the percentage was higher in the units in the east; the remainder had single-shot Martini-Henrys or even Sniders, largely supplied originally by the British. The cavalry were equipped with rifle and sword but were mounted on ponies averaging only 14 hands; they were thus unsuitable for shock action and could best be regarded as mounted infantry. The artillery used in 1919 consisted of 10cm Krupp howitzers, 75mm Krupp pack (mountain) guns and some older 7-pounder mountain guns. The machine guns were antique Gardners, with multiple barrels actuated by a hand lever, obsolete in the British services for more than twenty years. Taken as a whole, the Afghan troops were ill-trained and lacked manoeuvrability. There was no trained staff and only at Kabul had any attempt been made to organise self-contained brigades. Generally speaking, units were under strength and some regiments drafted in tribesmen to make up numbers but this accentuated the overall lack of training and manoeuvrability. All men had a parade uniform but only the Kabul units had a regular service uniform of khaki cloth; elsewhere the men tended to campaign in their local dress over which equipment and a round fur hat were worn. But if to Western eyes the Afghan army looked a rag-tag and bob-tail lot, the men themselves could be expected to fight stoutly, in conditions which favoured them.

In addition to the regular troops, there were some 10,000 khassadars (tribal levies or militia) who wore no uniform, carried Snider rifles and were employed on road protection, general police work and revenue and customs duties. They were distributed in small parties and their military effectiveness was probably less than the trans-border tribesmen on whose assistance Amanullah clearly depended.

The only arsenal in Afghanistan was at Kabul, able to produce guns, rifles, shells, small-arms ammunition, boots, clothing and general equipment in sufficient quantities for normal peace-time needs. Fuses for shells and cordite, however, had to be imported. A factory for making black powder for the Sniders and Martini-Henrys existed at Bawali, near Jalalabad. There was little organised or vehicular transport but there were plenty of camels available for quick impressment for military use. Along the main roads, there were state granaries every twelve miles or so. Stocks varied according to ease of supply; along the Kabul–Dakka road supplies were believed to exist for 12,000 men for two days at every stage; in the remoter areas, stocks were believed to be correspondingly larger. Food was not likely to pose a campaigning problem but ammunition might do so if the war went on for very long.[6]

The Afghan regular army was clearly incapable of taking on the British by itself. Amanullah depended for success upon the active support of the Pathan tribes on both sides of the Durand Line whom he had been wooing for some months, providing them with money and ammunition.

Afghans and Pathans shared a common semi-mythical ancestry.[7] Indeed, the tribes were accustomed to talk of themselves as Afghans, although the Afghans tended to be plains dwellers whereas the Pathan tribes were overwhelmingly hillmen. There was a pecking order even among the tribes in terms of their fighting quality. Few would dispute the preeminence of the Mahsuds as the most formidable adversaries although some might argue for the Afridis or Mobmands. But they tended to share the same broad characteristics – hardy, implacable in their vengeance, tactically sophisticated, fiercely Muslim, fiercely independent and hostile to all authority. They lived by a common, relatively rigid code of behaviour, Pakhtunwali, the chief elements of which were badal (blood vengeance), malmastia (hospitality) and nanawati (asylum). All of these elements combined to produce a character which Elphinstone described with a touch of admiration thus:

> Their vices are revenge, envy, avarice, rapacity and obstinacy; on the other hand, they are fond of liberty, faithful to their friends, kind to their dependents, hospitable, brave, hardy, frugal, laborious and prudent; they are less disposed than the nations in their neighbourhood to falsehood and intrigue...[8]

Some might raise an eyebrow over the last clause, but essentially Elphinstone's description embodies the main tribal qualities even though the different tribes embodied them in varying degrees. Inhabiting for the most part hill country of low fertility from which it was hard to scratch a living, they had for centuries been accustomed to raiding down into the plains of India or levying tolls on travellers through their lands. They had been a thorn in the side of the British authorities since 1849 when the British had inherited the problem from the Sikhs, as the long list of punitive expeditions testifies.[9] At the height of the First World War, the Government of India had still been forced to mount two major campaigns – against the Mohmands in 1916 and the Mahsuds in 1917. At the southern end of the front, in Baluchistan, the Pathan tribes, such as the Achakzais and Kakars, had been largely tamed in 1880 at the end of the Second Afghan War and were less formidable although always open to temptation. The Baluch tribes, such as the Baluchis and Brahuis, are not Pathans and were not a significant factor in the calculations.

For the British, given the extensive rail network, the availability of motor transport and a large arms industry created by the First World War, supply was not likely to be a serious problem, except on a very localised scale. Nor was the number of troops available in itself a serious problem.

Between 1914 and 1918 the combatant strength of the Indian Army had expanded to nearly four times its pre-war strength.[10] In particular, the number of infantry battalions had gone up from 139 to 280. Thus, although many of the pre-war battalions were still overseas or being repatriated or on long-delayed leave, there was still the equivalent of the pre-war army available in India. The problem lay in the quality of the troops, and especially of the infantry on whom the bulk of the fighting would inevitably fall.

The majority of the new battalions had been raised in 1917 or 1918. The heavy call for recruits had involved a lowering of standards which therefore laid extra emphasis upon the level of training, especially when pitted against such formidable enemies as the Pathan tribesmen on their own ground. In the confusion of repatriation, demobilisation and disbandment, the depots had found it hard to cope with the training of new recruits as well. In the battalions themselves, there was a distinct shortage of experienced officers, British and Indian, and NCOs because the enormous war-time expansion, as well as casualties, had greatly diluted the pre-war cadres. The junior officers and NCOs were overwhelmingly wartime recruits themselves, lacking in knowledge and experience, and in the case of the British officers, lacking fluency in the language. In consequence, that intimate bond of trust and influence that is the basis of all good regiments had had little chance to develop. Most of the new battalions were destined to disappear by 1921, and in some cases, even earlier; only ten would survive into the post-war regular army.[11]

The history of the 3/34th Sikh Pioneers provides a striking example of the confusion which reigned at this time. Raised in September 1918, it was too late to see active service overseas and was reduced to a cadre of eighty men in March 1919, prior to disbandment. Because of the disturbances in the Punjab, it was expanded to war establishment in April 1919 but reduced again to cadre in May 1919. It was again raised to war establishment in June 1919 because of the Third Afghan War, largely with drafts from the 1/34th, the 2/34th and the 1/23rd Sikh Pioneers, the balance being made up of ex-soldiers and raw recruits. It was then given four weeks to be ready for active service. In the campaign in Waziristan, the battalion did well, remaining in Skeen's Striking Force throughout; its performance was probably due largely to having a fairly high proportion of old soldiers. The 3/34th may have been an extreme example but many of the wartime battalions probably had not dissimilar experiences. It was finally disbanded in 1921.[12]

The situation was scarcely any better among the British battalions. Since 1858 the proportion of British to Indian soldiers had been fixed at 1:2 and this proportion had been carefully maintained; in 1914 there were roughly 75,000 British to 155,000 Indian soldiers. But the war had seen most of the regular British battalions drawn off to other theatres; only eight regular battalions had been left in India, all located near the Frontier, together with two regular cavalry regiments.[13] Territorial battalions had replaced the departed Regular battalions but in lesser numbers so that with the expansion of the Indian Army the 1:2 ratio had had to be abandoned. In May 1919 considerable numbers of British soldiers were in the transit camps awaiting repatriation and demobilisation. When the Third Afghan War broke out, they were hastily formed into five Special Service Battalions but they arrived too late to have any significant impact on the fighting and they were equally hastily disbanded.

In terms of equipment, the technology of the 1914–18 war had of course had a significant effect on the Army in India. The Lewis light machine gun, the hand grenade, the use of heavy machine guns as a form of artillery, the introduction of the armoured car and the use of motor transport had greatly increased the fighting power of the troops and, on the face of it, significantly shifted the balance of advantage against the tribesmen. The artillery had perhaps improved the least. Field and horse artillery was of relatively little use on the Frontier, partly because the flat trajectory of their guns was not best suited to mountain country and partly because the large teams of animals required to draw the guns and limbers was an encumbrance in that landscape. The mountain artillery available consisted of a 2.75 inch gun, firing a 12 pound shell out to a maximum range of 5,800 yards at maximum elevation, and some older 10 pounder guns, introduced in 1903, with a primitive form of rope recoil, and an effective range of just over 4,000 yards. Both these guns, carried on mules, were extremely mobile but not particularly accurate and, with relatively primitive recoil systems, a slowish rate of fire. What was needed was a light howitzer which could be carried on mules, with a high trajectory enabling shells to be dropped behind the crests of hills and into dead ground, giving the tribesmen no shelter from its fire. In fact, a new 3.7 inch quick-firing howitzer, meeting these requirements and firing a 20 pound shell out to a range of 6,000 yards, was being introduced but only one battery (No. 6 Battery, RGA) was available in India in 1919 and the only ammunition available for it as yet was a high explosive shell; the lack of a shrapnel shell was a serious handicap in Frontier warfare. A small number of 4.5 inch howitzers, firing a 35 pound shell out to 7,300 yards and weighing only 8cwt, were available. This had been one of the most successful guns in 1914–18, but it could not be broken down for transport on animals and was therefore limited to roads suitable for wheeled traffic. It was used with some success in the Third Afghan War but was not used because of its lack of mobility in Waziristan in 1919–20.[14]

The ultimate weapon on the Frontier continued to be the high velocity rifle and that was only as good as the man wielding it. That basic fact was to be brought home through bitter experience in the months ahead.

The Royal Air Force had arrived on the Frontier in 1916, in the Mohmand campaign of that year. Most of the capabilities of air power – in particular, bombing, ground support, reconnaissance, artillery spotting and communications – had been worked out on the Western Front between 1914 and 1918. They had yet to be worked out in the very different and more difficult conditions of the North-West Frontier. In May 1919 the only aircraft immediately available on the Frontier was 31 Squadron at Risalpur, east of Peshawar, equipped with BE2C aircraft of limited performance[15] and a flight of 114 Squadron at Quetta, similarly equipped.

Despite all the calls for Indian troops overseas and the ever-present demands of internal security, coupled with the confusion caused by demobilisation and leave, Army Headquarters at Simla, under the Commander in Chief India (General Sir Charles Monro), was still able to deploy very large forces for the Frontier. In Baluchistan, Lieutenant General Wapshare, with his HQ at Quetta, commanded the Baluchistan Force, comprising the 12th Mounted Brigade, the 4th (Infantry) Division and the Baluchistan Area troops – in total, eight cavalry regiments, eighteen infantry battalions, six batteries of artillery, two armoured car companies and three machine gun companies.[16] Wapshare also commanded the forces in East Persia but these played no part in the operations against the Afghans.[17]

The remainder of the front, from the Gomal northwards to Chitral, came under General Sir Arthur Barrett, an officer of immense Frontier experience, commanding Northern Army. For the ensuing operations the troops were grouped as the North-West Frontier Force, under Barrett, with his HQ at Peshawar. The Force consisted of the 1st and 10th Cavalry Brigades, the 1st and 2nd (Infantry) Divisions, the Waziristan Force of two infantry brigades, the Kohat Brigade, Peshawar Area, the Chitral and Malakand Garrisons and the Northern Lines of Communications troops, in all, ten cavalry regiments, fifty-five infantry battalions, the equivalent of twenty-three batteries of artillery, seven armoured car companies and ten machine gun companies or squadrons.[18]

With engineers and signallers, the fighting troops totalled some 75,000 men. Behind them was an enormous ancillary 'tail' – transport units of every kind, from railways to bullocks, medical units and field hospitals, butcher and bakery units, ordnance parks, lithograph sections, sanitary and veterinary units, workshops, etc. These exceeded by two or three times the numbers of fighting men so that the forces deployed in 1919 exceeded in total the pre-war strength of the Indian Army. By contrast, when Roberts marched from Kabul to Kandahar in August 1880 with a force of 10,000, every unit had been a fighting unit, and signallers, medical facilities, butchers and bakers, farriers, etc. had been found from the units, the only 'tail' being several thousand hired animals and drivers.[19] It is a vivid illustration of how complex Frontier warfare had become in forty years.

Notes

1   Alexander had used a route north of the Khyber, following the Kabul river.
2   There was no railway through the Khyber until November 1925.
3   For the Frontier railways, see P S A Berridge, *Couplings to the Khyber* (Newton Abbott, 1969).
4   For comparative purposes, a camel was assumed to be able to carry 440 pounds, a bullock or mule cart 600 pounds, a Ford Van 800, a narrow-gauge train 300 tons and a broad-gauge train 900 tons. One division required 300 tons of food and stores per day or the equivalent of 45,000 camel loads. *The Army in India and its Evolution* (Calcutta, 1924), Appendix XI, 224.
5   For details of communications on both sides, see the useful table in *Third Afghan War*, 3.
6   For details of the Afghan Army see *Third Afghan War*, 22–4.
7   The best modern analysis is Sir Olaf Caroe, *The Pathans* (London, 1958). Caroe has shown that even if the tribal genealogies are largely mythical, they do correspond closely to present-day tribal relationships and explain a number of puzzles and ambiguities. The Pathan tribes share a common language albeit in 'soft' form (Pashtu) and 'hard' form (Pakhtu), the former spoken north of the Khyber, the latter south of it.
8   Mountstuart Elphinstone, *An Account of the Kingdom of Caubul* (London, 1815).
9   *Frontier and Overseas Expeditions from India*, 6 vols (Calcutta, 1907–10).
10   Combatant strength in 1914 was 155,423; in November 1918 573,484, *Army in India*, Appendix VII, 219.
11   2/6 Jat LI, 2/23 Sikh Pioneers, 3/39 and 4/39 Garwhal Rifles, 2/41 Dogras, 2 Guides, 2/56 Punjabi Rifles, 2/67 Punjabis, 2/124 Baluchistan Infantry, 1/50 Kumaon Rifles.
12   Diaries of Second Lieutenant Douglas Rees, 3/34 Pioneers (6 vols.), NAM 6706–21.
13   2 Somerset LI, 2 N Staffords, 1 Yorkshire, 1 Royal Sussex, 1 Durham LI, 1 South Lancs, 2 Liverpool, 1 Duke of Wellingtons; King's Dragoon Guards, 21st Lancers.
14   For details of these weapons see Brigadier-General C A L Graham, *The History of the Indian Mountain Artillery* (Aldershot, 1957), Appendix V, and IV Hogg and L F Thurston, *British Artillery Weapons and Ammunition* 1914–18 (London, 1972).

15 A two-seater reconnaissance/light bomber, maximum speed 72 mph, ceiling 10,000 feet, armed with one to four Lewis guns and (if flown solo) up to 230 pounds of bombs, J M Bruce, *The Aeroplanes of the Royal Flying Corps* (Military Wing) (London, 1982), 354–69

16 There is no published history of the Machine Gun Corps during its brief history from 1915 to 1922. The precise organisation of the different types of unit in India post-war is not easy to establish. Machine Gun Companies had sixteen Vickers guns and were carried on lorries or animals. Armoured Motor Batteries were equipped with three armoured cars, each carrying a Vickers gun. Motor Machine Gun Batteries carried Vickers guns mounted on motor cycles. Light Car Patrols had six Ford Model T-mounted guns. After 1922, the armoured cars were absorbed into the Royal Tank Corps and the machine gun companies into the infantry battalions. See also Dolf L Goldsmith, *The Grand Old Lady of No Man's Land: the Vickers Machinegun* (Coburg, Ontario, 194).

17 Wapshare's main claim to fame was that he commanded 27 Infantry Brigade in the debacle at Tanga on 4 November 1914. *Military Operations, East Africa* Vol. I August 1914–September 1916 (HMSO, 1941), 75–107.

18 *Third Afghan War*, Appendix I, 137–60. (Note: '6 May 1924' is a misprint for '6 May 1919'.)

19 Robson, op cit, 212.

III

The Invasion of Chitral:
May–July 1919

(Map 2)

The dominant note of Chitral is bigness combined with desolation; vast, silent mountains cloaked in eternal snow, wild glacier-born torrents, cruel precipices, and pastureless hillsides where the ibex and the markhor find a precarious subsistence. It takes time for the mind to recover from the depression which the stillness and the melancholy of the giant landscape at first compel. All colour is purged away by the sun-glare; and no birds sing. Life is represented by great eagles and vultures, circling slowly or poised aloft, and by the straight business-like flight of the hawk. The dull ceaseless roar of the distant river changes, whenever you listen fixedly, to a sound as of supernatural voices, shrieking in agony, but too remote for human sympathy.

Robertson, Chitral

Chitral is, in essence, a narrow amphitheatre, roughly 180 miles long, surrounded on all sides by mountains, rising in places to over 20,000 feet; Tirich Mir, the highest, is over 25,000 feet and was not climbed until 1950. To the north lie the Pamirs and the narrow Wakhan panhandle, artificially created in 1895 to separate Russia from India; to the north-west and west, the Hindu Kush, separating Chitral from Badakhshan, the northernmost province of Afghanistan and from the Afghan province of Kafiristan (Nuristan);[1] to the south, the Hindu Raj range separates Chitral from India, while to the east, the Shandur range separates Chitral from the Kashmir province of Gilgit.

The floor of the amphitheatre, some 11,000 feet above sea level, is formed by the valley of the Chitral (Kunar) river, which rises in the Pamirs as the Yarkhun, and is joined by the Turikho and the Tirich rivers to form the Mastuj river, which becomes the Chitral below the capital town of Chitral;[2] the Chitral eventually flows out of the south-west corner of the country into Afghanistan and joins the Kabul river at Jalalabad, which then flows eastwards past Peshawar to join the Indus at Attock. The numerous rivers and streams, which all flow ultimately into the Chitral,

31

dictate the local topography and provide the main arteries of communication. In 1919 the easiest way into Chitral by road was from Afghanistan, by way of the Kunar valley. From India the route ran from Nowshera across the Malakand Pass, up the Swat valley to Dir and then across the Lowarai Pass (10,250 feet) into Chitral. This was the route followed by Sir Robert Lowe's relief expedition in 1895 and is about 200 miles.[3]

From Badakhshan, the Dorah (15,000 feet) and Baroghil (12,000) Passes provide access but only the Dorah was suitable for significant bodies of troops and then only with animal transport. From Gilgit, a difficult road crosses the Shandur Pass (12,400 feet) but was not suitable for wheeled artillery. In winter snow obstructs the passes and Chitral was then virtually cut off for four months.[4] Even in summer only the Kunar, Gilgit, Dorah and Malakand routes were really practicable for substantial bodies of troops or wheeled artillery. Despite Robertson's somewhat bleak picture, the Chitral valley is frequently very beautiful and there are patches of highly fertile soil which produced rice, cereal and fruit of all kinds. In 1919 the population was about 90,000. The valley floor is seamed with streams coming down from the surrounding mountains and flowing into the Chitral river. Tactically, the fighting tended to be determined by possession of the bridges – rickety affairs, often made simply of plaited twigs and timber, easily destroyed but relatively easy to replace.

Logically and geographically, Chitral was a part of Afghanistan from which however it was separated by ethnicity and history. The Chitralis are a mixed race, the result of successive waves of invaders from north and west, a fact reflected not only in the number of tongues and dialects spoken in the country but in the main language, Khowar, which contains words from languages as apart as Sanskrit and Turki. A major part of the population were Sunni Muslims, like their Afghan and Pathan neighbours, but there were substantial numbers of Shiahs of the Ismaili sect, whose spiritual head was the Aga Khan to whom the Chitralis regularly sent their tithe (nazarana) of gold and precious stones.[5] The Chitralis are hardy mountaineers, excellent shots and devoted to polo. George Robertson, who knew them as well as anyone and had had good reason to distrust them, described them more or less unflatteringly:

There are few more treacherous people in the world than Chitralis, and they have a wonderful capacity for coldblooded cruelty, yet none are kinder to little children or have stronger affection for blood and foster relations when cupidity and jealousy do not intervene. All have pleasant and ingratiating manners, an engaging lightheartedness, free from all trace of boisterous behaviour, a great fondness for music, dancing and singing, a passion for simple-minded ostentation, and an instinctive yearning for softness and luxury, which is the main spring of their intense cupidity and avarice. No race is more untruthful or has a greater power of keeping a collective secret. Their vanity is easily injured, they are revengeful and venal, but they are charming, picturesque and admirable companions. Perhaps the most convenient trait they possess so far as we are concerned, is a complete absence of religious fanaticism.[6]

The Chitralis believed that their land was peopled by fairies and goblins and monsters of all descriptions, good and bad,[7] and they delighted in such tales. Perhaps in consequence, they had never had a reputation as first-class fighting men comparable to that of the Pathan tribes surrounding them, but in 1919 they performed stoutly enough. The Kalash valleys, running westwards from the Chitral valley, are inhabited by the Kalash (or Kafirs) who still practise their own form of animistic religion.

The British connection had started in 1885 when Colonel (later Sir) William Lockhart was sent to examine the passes of the Hindu Kush to see whether, as Biddulph had reported in 1874, the Baroghil Pass provided a practicable route for a Russian invasion. Lockhart was able to report that only the Dorah Pass was of strategic importance, and in 1888–9 Colonel Algemon Durand was sent to conclude an agreement with the ruler (Mehtar) of Chitral, Aman-ul-Mulk ('the Great Mehtar'), who undertook to watch the passes from the north and north-west and to exclude strangers, in return for which the British agreed to protect Chitral and to provide an annual subsidy. Aman-ul-Mullc ruled with a rod of iron for thirty years and was feared and hated by his subjects. When he died in 1892 dynastic anarchy followed. His second son, Afzal-ul-Mulk, seized the throne but was murdered by his uncle, Sher Afzal, an Afghan protege. He in turn was deposed and forced to return to Kabul by Aman-ul-Mulk's eldest son, Nizam-ul-Mulk, who asked for a British officer to be posted to Chitral.

Surgeon Major George Robertson, then resident at Gilgit, proceeded to Chitral, to find that Nizam-ul-Mulk had in turn been murdered by yet another son of Aman-ul-Mulk, Amir-ul-Mulk, at the beginning of January 1895. He was regarded as weak, unstable and unfriendly to the British; moreover, in the wings, the Amir of Afghanistan was plotting with Sher Afzal and Umra Khan of Jandol, the powerful and ambitious ruler of Dir and Bajaur, who was fishing in the pool of trouble.[8] Robertson's escort was increased by some 400 Kashmiri troops just in time to confront Sher Afzal, who had re-appeared from Kabul, determined to press his claims. Robertson found himself besieged in the fort at Chitral and his defence, largely conducted by Captain Charles Townsend,[9] was a minor Victorian classic and the relief, effected by a column from Gilgit, closely followed by another column under Sir Robert Lowe from Nowshera, which had fought its way northwards across the Malakand Pass and up through Swat, was Boy's Own Paper stuff. A 12-year-old son of the Great Mehtar, Shuja-al-Mulk, was installed as Mehtar under British protection.

Although the Russian threat might appear to have been nullified by the Anglo–Russian Convention on the Pamirs of 1895, there was evidence to the contrary and argument raged in London and Calcutta about whether the British should withdraw from Chitral. Rosebery's Liberal Government decided to withdraw but it fell shortly afterwards and Salisbury's Conservative government decided to stay. A British garrison of two battalions of infantry (reduced in 1899 to one), a section of mountain artillery and a section of Sappers and Miners was now located there. That necessitated the maintenance of a chain of fortified posts from Nowshera across the Malakand Pass, through Chakdara and Dir, to Chitral. The price to be paid was the fear and hostility of the Pathan tribesmen of Swat and Bajaur, which burst out in the great Frontier uprising of 1897.[10]

Chitral was a popular posting for British officers, despite the fact that it was cut off for four months in the winter. It offered unrivalled opportunities for shooting and fishing, as well as winter sports, and its isolation meant that units were free from the petty bureaucratic irritations of the plains. In 1919 the garrison consisted of a weak infantry battalion (the 1/11th Rajputs, 450 strong), a section (two guns) of the 23rd (Peshawar) Pack Battery and a section of the 2nd (Madras) Sappers and Miners. The 1/11th had served in Mesopotamia during the war and, like all regular battalions, it was low in numbers because of long-delayed leave and demobilisation. In addition, there were the Chitral Scouts, a part-time force of 1,000, under the Assistant Political Agent, Chitral, armed only with rifles but highly mobile.[11] Finally, the Mehtar had a bodyguard of some 2,000, only 150 of whom had even Martini-Henrys, the remainder only matchlocks or flintlocks.

From an Afghan point of view, Chitral must have appeared a tempting and easy morsel to bite off, and one which the British, preoccupied elsewhere, might not fight too hard to defend. If Amanullah could seize Chitral, then the Indian Government might think the trouble involved in regaining it not worth the effort. It was a gamble which must have appeared easy and well worth taking.[12]

News of the hostile Afghan moves in the Khaibar at the beginning of May had reached Chitral by telegraph and on 5 May Major Reilly, the Assistant Political Agent in Chitral,[13] learned of the Afghan deployments on the borders. He immediately mobilised three companies of the Chitral Scouts; three days later, having received from the Mehtar news of an intercepted firman (proclamation) by the Amir, calling on all Chitralis to assist in expelling the British, he ordered the mobilisation of the rest of the Scouts, sending one company down the east bank of the Chitral river to Galopach, thirty miles from Chitral and some ten miles from the border with Afghanistan, to watch Afghan movements. Scout patrols were also sent west on to the border with Kafiristan to watch for enemy movements there. Lieutenant Colonel Sambourne-Palmer,[14] commanding the Rajputs and the British garrison, had already begun to prepare defences round the main garrison post at Kala Drosh, ten miles south of Chitral, to cover the capital and to provide a central base for operations elsewhere in the country.

On 12 May Reilly learned that the Afghans had occupied Arnawai, in the extreme south-west corner of the country and just inside the Chitral border. On the night of 13/14 May he had news that 300 Afghan irregulars had occupied Dammar Nissar, on the east bank of the Chitral, only some two miles south of the Scout company at Galapach. What appeared to be a beacon fire on the Patkun Pass, from Kafiristan, north-west of Dammar Nissar, appeared to indicate that the Afghans were invading from that direction as well (although the report turned out to be false). Reilly therefore moved with two companies of Scouts and 120 of the Mehtar's men to Mirkhani, just above Galapach, from where he could watch both the Patkun Pass and any Afghan advance up the east bank of the river.

At Mirkhani he found that the enemy was moving north up both banks of the river and that the company at Galapach was falling back in face of superior numbers. Without hesitation, Reilly took the initiative. He sent a Scout company, with some of the Mehtar's men, across to the west bank of the river and advanced himself down the east bank, picking up the company from Galapach en route and re-occupying Galapach. From there he opened fire against the Afghans in Kauti on the west bank, Under this fire and that of the west bank company, the Afghans retired, leaving a standard behind. Reilly then pressed on to attack Dammar Nissar, the Afghans there retreating towards Barikot (Birkot) and Arnawai. He then occupied a defensive position astride the river at Galapach and Kauti. For the moment the Afghan incursion had been repulsed, with some thirty Afghans killed and forty wounded but no British casualties. It was quite literally first blood to the British, and there was the added bonus that the Scouts had fought well. But it had been a tentative thrust by the Afghans who had not yet begun to deploy their main strength.

The passes from the Wakhan and from Badakhshan to the north-west were still blocked by snow and it was clear that for the moment a further Afghan threat must come from Kafiristan and the Kunar valley. Sambourne-Palmer, having finished the defences at Kala Drosh, now decided to take the initiative and take the fight to the remaining Afghan forces concentrated near Arnawai in the south-west of the country. Reinforcements had brought them up to a strength estimated at 600, with four guns – roughly a battalion group and equal in numbers to the British garrison. With the Scouts, however, the British were numerically superior and it was obviously a sensible moment to try to expel the invaders before the Afghans could deploy all the forces at their disposal.

The Afghans held a strong position at Arnawai, with their left resting on the Bashgul stream, north-west of Arnawai, and their right on a hill (Hill 3700) a mile east of Arnawai. Sambourne-Palmer's plan was surprisingly elaborate and his readiness to divide his forces argued a high degree of confidence. He moved in four columns from Mirkhani on 21 May. The first column consisted of a company of Scouts, 1,000 of the Mehtar's men and some Kafirs who had come across the border. It was commanded by Nasr-ul-Mulk, the Mehtar's eldest son, [15] and it was ordered to cross the Chitral, cross the Patkun Pass and then move down the Istor valley to its junction with the Bashgul. Then, leaving fifty men there to guard the bridge over the Bashgul, to push on south to occupy the heights on the west side of the Afghan base at Birkot. The second column, of two companies of Scouts, [16] under Lieutenant Bowers of the Scouts, was to move straight down the west bank of the Chitral and seize the bridge over the Bashgul where it joined the Chitral. A force of 300 Chitrali irregulars was to maintain contact between these two columns by moving down the watershed separating the Istor from the Chitral.

The main (or Mobile) column under Sambourne-Palmer himself, was directed down the east bank of the Chitral to capture Arnawai; it consisted of two companies of Scouts under Reilly, the 1/11th Rajputs minus one company, the two mountain guns and the Sappers and Miners. The fourth (or left) column of three companies of Scouts under Captain Crimmin[17] was to move in a wide semi-circle south-eastwards from Dammar Nissar to come in on the Afghan right flank. It was a bold plan in the circumstances and it illustrated the peculiar difficulties of manoeuvring in a country where the only routes ran along streams or river valleys. All the columns were to be in place by 23 May. The distances were not great as the crow flies – Mirkhani to Arnawai was about sixteen miles, and the column under Nasr-ul-Mulk had about twenty-four miles to cover. But the paths were narrow and easily obstructed.

Nasr-ul-Mulk encountered no problems and by the 22nd he was in position west of Barikot; the same night he managed to cut the bridge across the Kunar linking Barikot with Arnawai. The defenders of Arnawai were thus isolated from their reinforcements. Bowers similarly encountered no difficulties and was in position on the 22nd, having linked up with Nasr-ul-Mulk.

The main column, however, was held up on the 22nd by a broken road, but Reilly pushed on with the Scouts to Lambabat, four miles from Arnawai. Next day (23 May) Sambourne-Palmer moved on but was again held up by a broken bridge five miles from Arnawai, but Reilly again pushed on and came into contact with the enemy just north of Arnawai at about 0600 hours. Crimmin's column then came up on his left as resistance began to stiffen. The mountain guns came into action from a position near Lambabat, firing at close on maximum range, at around 0740 and a company of the Rajputs, with the regimental scouts, was ordered to attack the ridge on Reilly's right. The remainder of the Mobile Column then began to move forward and Afghan resistance began to crumble. Sambourne-Palmer ordered another five platoons of the Rajputs forward to assist Reilly. Stubborn resistance by a party of twenty-five Afghans ensconced in some rocks was eliminated by bombing. By midday the Afghans had begun to set fire to Arnawai but their resistance did not cease until 1630 hours, when the survivors were in full retreat southwards to Asmar. Over on the west bank of the Chitral, Bowers and Nasr-ul-Mulk had captured Barikot which was then thoroughly looted by the Chitralis and Kafirs.

The troops on the east bank were withdrawn into bivouac that evening on a plateau north-east of Arnawai. The withdrawal was marred only by a party of Afghans who had remained in hiding and now opened fire, wounding Sambourne-Palmer. They were bayoneted by the Rajputs. All told, the Afghans were estimated to have lost 250 men and thirty-five prisoners, as well as four guns (only two of which were breech-loaders) and large stocks of ammunition. British casualties in what had been a well-managed affair totalled sixteen killed and forty-eight wounded, half of which fell on the Scouts who had borne the brunt of the action and fully demonstrated their worth.

Encouraging as this little action had been, it had involved only a small part of the Afghan forces – more formidable forces were gathering at Asmar and the snows were beginning to melt in the passes from Badakhshan. The indications were that the tiny Chitral garrison would soon face threats from at least three directions. Sambourne-Palmer decided in these circumstances not to attempt to follow up his victory by invading Afghan territory but to pull back to Kala Drosh to await the next enemy move. On 1 June he learned that the Afghans had concentrated three battalions and a cavalry regiment at Saq, twelve miles south of Arnawai. Moreover, like vultures gathering around a potential feast, some 6,000 tribesmen from Dir had gathered east of Arnawai to await events.

After dark on 1 June Sambourne-Palmer's force began to retire in the same order they had come and by the same routes, leaving their campfires burning to deceive the tribesmen. All four columns were back at Mirkhani on 4 June. The main body went on back to Kala Drosh, intermediate defences being constructed *en passant* at Galatak, half way to Kala Drosh. A force of 400 Scouts and 400 of the men, with two Lewis guns, was left at Mirkhani to observe Afghan movements.

Events now took an unexpected turn. Although, as we shall see, the Amir had agreed to an armistice on 3 June (news of which would appear not to have reached Sambourne-Palmer until some time later), the Afghan commander, presumably keen to avenge his defeat and to punish those Kafirs who had gone over to the British side, refused to suspend hostilities. In Badakhshan five or six battalions were concentrated at Faizabad, with detachments in Wakhan, threatening the Baroghil and Manjan passes into Chitral. At Asmar, the Afghan commander, Abdul Wakhil Khan, had assembled seven battalions and a force of Mohmand and Bajauri tribes-men and was threatening to invade again. Finally, to the south-east of Chitral, in Swat, a firebrand, the Sadozai Mullah, was trying to assemble a force of Yuzufzai tribesmen to attack the post at Chakdara, a vital link in the line of communication to Chitral. If these threats had materialised, then the Chitral garrison would have been in serious difficulties. The only immediate reinforcement available was two battalions of infantry and two mountain guns of the Kashmir State forces at Bunji, thirty-five miles south-east of Gilgit and roughly 240 miles from Chitral via the difficult road which Kelly's force had had to take to relieve Robertson in 1895. The 16th (Infantry) Division, which was responsible for controlling Swat and the route from the south, had been diverted to the Kurram and Kohat (see Chapter VIII).

Luckily, the Sadozai Mullah was unsuccessful and the threat from Badakhshan fizzled out. But Abdul Wakil Khan was made of sterner stuff. He reached Barikot on 23 June and Afghan irregulars occupied Arnawai again. On 24 June a battalion occupied Dokalim, just inside Chitral terri-tory while Abdul Wakil with three battalions and some 1,500 irregulars moved northwards from Barikot, inside Afghan territory, to punish the Kafirs for having sided with the British. From Kafiristan he could readily turn east and invade Chitral. By the 29th he was at Lutdeh, due east of Chitral. To counter this threat, two companies of Scouts and two weak companies of the Mehtar's bodyguard were concentrated at Ayun, where the confluence of the Bumburet and Rumbur streams offered the most likely lines of advance from Lutdeh. Two companies of Scouts were sent to Shogkot, a dozen miles north of Chitral, on the Chitral river, to watch for an Afghan move through the Dorah or Zidig (Samanak) Passes in Badakhshan and then down the Lutkho valley to Shogkot. Three compa-nies watched the passes over the Pamirs and Wakhan.

There was little else that Sambourne-Palmer could do for the moment except wait and watch. He had the advantage of operating on interior lines, but his force was too small to cover adequately all possible lines of attack. A successful defence would depend upon early intelligence and rapid movement, the classic solution.

On 16 July a small party of Afghans crossed the Zidig Pass and threat-ened an advance down the Lutkho but they retired shortly. Almost simul-taneously, on 17 July, another force of 400 Afghan regulars and 400 irregu-lars crossed the Shawi Pass and moved down the Bumburet valley. They were attacked by one of the Scout companies from Ayun and retired after driving off cattle and burning huts along the valley. By now the Afghans had occupied all the passes from Kafiristan.

Possibly under orders from Kabul, where the Amir was anxious not to jeopardise the armistice, Abdul Wakhil changed his strategy, keeping his regulars out of Chitral but encouraging the surrounding tribes to attack the British. In Bajaur he was able to persuade tribesmen under the Mullah Shah Badshah to seize the Lowarai Pass and threaten the Scout post at Ziarat. On 24 July Lieutenant Bowers, with two companies of Scouts from Mirkhani, attacked the Nullah and forced the tribesmen to retire into Dir having lost fifteen killed and some forty wounded; they dispersed a few days later. Bowers lost three wounded.

The last move in this little campaign was the arrival of an Afghan force of 100 cavalry, 800 infantry, six guns and two machine guns at Topkhana, ten miles west of the Dorah Pass. Three days later this force began to retire northwards to its own cantonments. The signing of the peace treaty on 8 August put an end officially to the campaign in Chitral. But the local Afghan commanders continued to make aggressive moves and small-scale fighting went on long after the peace treaty had been signed at Rawalpindi. Arnawai and Dokalim were not handed back by the Afghans to the Mehtar until January 1922.

The campaign had been a testimony to Afghan miscalculation and lack of coordinated planning. The outbreak of war in the Khyber came at a time when the passes into Chitral were still largely obstructed by the winter snows and when the local Afghan commander had not deployed his considerable preponderance of forces. In consequence, the initial Afghan thrust up the Kunar valley was weak and uncoordinated, and was easily contained and then picked off by the small British force. By the time that Abdul Wakhil had assembled something like his true strength and was in a position to invade Chitral through the western passes, the war was effectively over. The poor Afghan timing had played into British hands in another, equally vital way. With the concentration of tribesmen in Swat and Dir and the activities of the Sadozai Mullah, a major tribal uprising in Swat and Bajaur hung in the balance. An initial Afghan success in Chitral would almost certainly have provided the necessary catalyst. An attempt then to relieve the garrison in Chitral from Peshawar and Nowshera would probably have precipitated a general rising on the lines of that in 1897. Preoccupied with operations in and around the Khyber and the Kurram and in Baluchistan, the British would then have faced a very serious problem indeed.

The success of the defensive operations in Chitral must therefore have come as a distinct relief to AHQ India. Sambourne-Palmer and Reilly between them had conducted an able campaign with limited forces and their operations might serve as a lesson in how to conduct effective operations with a small force on interior lines. Not the least of their achievements had been to obtain the enthusiastic support of the Mehtar. The Chitral Scouts, in particular, had brilliantly fulfilled the role for which they had been created; their effectiveness and dependability would contrast sharply with the collapse elsewhere of the Khyber Rifles and the North and South Waziristan Militias (see below). The Mehtar in due course received the title of 'His Highness' and his salute was increased to eleven guns.[18] Sambourne-Palmer received a CBE, which seems less than he deserved, and retired, still a lieutenant colonel, in 1921. Reilly received no overt recognition of his efforts; he went on to be Deputy Commissioner of Bannu and then Kohat, retiring in 1927.

It had been, perhaps, the last truly Victorian campaign, before the internal combustion engine radically transformed the face of frontier warfare.

Notes

1   For centuries it was called Kafiristan (Land of the Kafirs) and was so shown on British military maps in 1919. The Kafirs are a mysterious race, often pale skinned and in consequence sometimes believed to be descended from the Greeks of Alexander the Great's army. Their religion was (and is still in Chitral) a mixture of animism, fire and ancestor worship. In 1896 Abdurrahman forcibly converted those in Afghanistan to Islam and renamed the area Nuristan (Land of Light). Kipling's story *The Man Who Would Be King* is set in Kafiristan.

2   In 1919 it was called the Chitral river until it reached the Afghan border, when it became the Kunar, which flows into the Kabul river near Jalalabad. In some modern guide books it is called the Kunar from the capital, Chitral, southwards. I have preferred to call it the Chitral while it is in Chitral as that is how it was shown on 1919 maps.

3   Today the road from India is traversable by motor vehicle.

4   'Virtually' because the main passes are practicable by small parties through extreme exertion. Robertson crossed the Shandur in January 1895 and Sher Afzul (see below) crossed the Dorah in the same month.

5   The Sunnis call them 'Maulais' a corruption of the Arabic phrase 'Mulahid-ul-Millat', meaning 'extinguishers of the Faith'. They are the descendants of the feared 'Assassins' of the Middle Ages; for a vivid account of that notorious sect see Freya Stark, *The Valley of the Assassins* (London, 1934), 159–61 and passim.

6   Robertson, *Chitral: The Story of a Minor Siege* (London, 1898), 9–10.

7   For the entertaining tale of the Boghazoo, a gigantic, deadly frog, see C Chenevix Trench, *The Frontier Scouts* (1995), 220.

8   Umra Khan had laid claim to the territory of Asmar but under the Durand agreement it had been awarded to Afghanistan, turning him into a bitter opponent of the British and a source of turbulence in the region until 1895, when he disappeared from the territory. Robertson, passim.

9   See Biographical Notes. He is best known to history as the defender of Kut during the First World War. He was nicknamed 'Alfonso' because of his penchant for singing 'The Spaniard that blighted my life'. For the siege of Chitral see Robertson, op cit, and John Harris, *Much Sounding of Bugles: The Siege of Chitral 1895* (1975). Harris argues that Captain Campbell, rather than Townsend, was the real director of the defence.

10   Barthorpe, op cit.

11   The Scouts, raised in 1900, were embodied for one month's training a year.

12   The account here is based upon Sambourne-Palmer's official report, *Report by Lieutenant-Colonel F C S Sambourne-Palmer, commanding Chitral Force, on*

Operations in the Chitral Area (Simla,1919) – (L/MIL/17/13/65). This forms the basis of the account in the official history, *The Third Afghan War: Official Account* (Calcutta, 1926).

13 Noel Edmund Reilly, posted to Chitral in 1915. He came under the Political Agent for Dir, Swat and the Malakand.

14 Frederick Carey Stukely Sambourne-Palmer; commanded 1/11th Rajputs (later 10th Battalion, 7th Rajput Regiment) 1916–20.

15 He succeeded as Mehtar in 1940.

16 Thomas Ivan Bowers, seconded to 1/11 Rajputs from 9 Bhopal Infantry, who had arrived only days before.

17 Charles Clarence Crimmin, seconded to the Scouts in 1918.

18 Roos-Keppel to Reilly, No. 1911-R, 10 July 1919–FPP, September 1919 – L/MIL/17/13/65, No. 662.

IV

Operations in the Khyber:
6-12 May 1919

(Maps 3 and 4)

It was to be expected that the main Afghan thrust would be through the Khyber Pass. At Bagh the Afghan forces were only some twenty-five miles from Peshawar, the capital of the North-West Frontier Province and the main British military base for the Frontier since 1849. Peshawar also had an historical resonance for the Afghans as it had once been the Afghan summer capital until it was lost to the Sikhs in 1834, and Dost Muhammad had spent much time, energy and treasure in trying to recover it.[1] The arrival of Afghan forces outside Peshawar would be a propaganda coup of the highest importance.

In Ningrahar, the Afghan province which included the approaches to the Khyber, the Afghans were estimated to have fourteen battalions of infantry, one battalion of pioneers, one and a half regiments of cavalry and forty-four modem guns, with their main base at Jalalabad. In reserve at Kabul, 108 miles from the frontier, along the best road in Afghanistan, there were estimated to be a further eleven battalions of infantry, five and a half regiments of cavalry and forty guns. These were the elite troops of the Afghan Army, better manned, equipped and organised than the remainder of that army; they constituted, in effect, the strategic reserve.[2]

By the evening of 6 May the Afghans had concentrated three battalions and two guns at Bagh, some two and a quarter miles as the crow flies from the advanced British post at Landi Kotal. A further five battalions, 200 cavalry and six guns were at Dakka, some ten miles back. The fort at Landi Kotal lies well above the floor of the valley and effectively guards the western end of the pass; but its water supply came from springs in the Tangi nullah, a mile and three quarters west of the post. Both the springs and the pumping station, roughly mid-way between the springs and the fort, were by now in Afghan hands.

The forward Afghan positions lay on high ground roughly two and a quarter miles west of the fort, in a horseshoe. The main body was concentrated on the Khargali ridge, a few hundred yards in rear. A force of some 350 Afghan infantry with two guns had occupied the two commanding heights of Tor Tsappar and Spin Tsuka, four miles due north of Landi

Kotal. From here the Afghans had moved south to seize the Asa (Ash) Khel ridge, a mile north-east of Landi Kotal. The British post was thus under threat from west and north.

It is impossible now to discover precisely what the Afghan commander, Muhammad Anwar Khan, had in mind. His forces were inadequate to seize Peshawar, where the British commander, General Sir Arthur Barrett, could, over a period of some days, concentrate twenty-three battalions of infantry, six regiments of cavalry, and eleven batteries of artillery, plus another four battalions of internal security troops.[3] But the occupation of Landi Kotal would enable the Afghans effectively to hold the pass, from which it might be extremely difficult and time-consuming to evict them. More importantly, such a move was likely to bring about a tribal rising on a large scale. North of Landi Kotal, the Mohmands and Shinwaris could advance rapidly across the Mullagori plain to Peshawar. South of the Khyber the even more formidable Afridis might be tempted out of their fastness in the Tirah. At Peshawar, there were revolutionary elements whom the Amir had been assured would rise against the British. There was therefore much to play for, but it required speed of action on the Afghan side.

Landi Kotal was held initially by two companies of Indian infantry, a section (two guns) of mountain artillery and a section of Sappers and Miners, hastily rushed up from Peshawar by lorry the day before; they were supported by 500 of the locally recruited Khyber Rifles, about whose steadiness in the circumstances there was bound now to be some doubt.[4]

The suddenness of the Afghan invasion caught the authorities at Peshawar somewhat on the hop. The disturbances in the Punjab in the early part of 1919 had had an unsettling effect on the inhabitants of the city and throughout April there had been a steady growth in agitation, with increasingly large public meetings aimed at promoting Hindu–Muslim unity against the British. Behind these meetings Afghan influence was undoubtedly at work through individuals such as the Afghan Postmaster,[5] but since there was as yet no violence no direct action had been taken against them. Military officers believed that Sir George Roos-Keppel, the Chief Commissioner of the North-West Frontier Province, was deliberately playing down the situation because he was due to depart on leave to England at the beginning of May and did not wish to jeopardise it. But both civil and military intelligence were uneasy and the Deputy Commissioner, Major Keen, took a more anxious view than Roos Keppel and maintained close touch with the Divisional staff.[6] Some precautions were therefore put in hand; the annual rotation of troops to the hills for the summer was suspended, military staffs were placed on 'Stand to' and plans were drawn up for a cordon of troops to be placed round the city in event of emergency. The fact that General Sir Frederick Campbell, commanding the 1st (Peshawar) Division, was allowed to depart for

Bombay and relinquish command to a temporary successor, Major General Fowler, on 27 April suggests nevertheless that war was not regarded as imminent.[7]

There was no shortage of troops in and around Peshawar. The striking force immediately to hand was the 1st Division and the 10th Cavalry Brigade; the 1st Cavalry Brigade was at Nowshera, only some twenty-five miles away, and farther back in reserve, at Rawalpindi a hundred miles away, was the 2nd Division. All these places were connected by the broad-gauge railway. Moreover, in addition, there was an internal security force of two battalions of infantry, an armoured car brigade and some mountain artillery at Peshawar. The problem, as so often in the Army in India, was a shortage of transport.

On 3 May news reached Peshawar of the murder of the five labourers near Landi Kotal and Afghan belligerence on the actual boundary line, and next day the Chief Commissioner asked for a small column of infantry to be held in readiness to proceed to Landi Kotal. Significantly he asked that the officer in command should be junior to the commander of the Khyber Rifles, who came directly under him; in this way he clearly hoped to retain control of the situation. All units in the Division were placed on full alert and warning telegrams despatched to Chitral, the Malakand and Abbottabad (HQ of 3 Infantry Brigade). When news of the Afghan seizure of Bagh reached Peshawar on 5 May, the force being held in readiness, consisting of one company 1/15 Sikhs, one company 1/9 Gurkhas, a section of Sappers and Miners and two 3.7 inch howitzers of No. 6 (Mountain) Battery RGA, was hastily despatched in 30-cwt lorries. Because the howitzers were on trial, there was only a limited supply of ammunition and there were no mules or pack saddlery for them. The force reached Landi Kotal without incident the same day. With its arrival the immediate crisis was over and the Afghans had lost an excellent chance of causing serious embarrassment.

The move of the Somersets was not without incident and even humour. Because of the shortage of lorries, the Somersets had to leave one platoon behind. To make matters worse, No. 8 Battery had filched three more lorries than it was entitled to, supposedly to carry ammunition; when they arrived at Landi Kotal they were found to be loaded with barrels of beer. One can imagine that there was much chortling among quartermasters. The column travelled in sixty-seven lorries with their hoods up to conceal the troops, and reached Landi Kotal without incident at 1000 hours on 7 May.[9] The speed of this reinforcement was the first solid demonstration of British technological superiority.

Roos-Keppel, who wanted a quick, crushing victory, was keen to exploit the advantages of air power:

There will shortly be a big collection of troops and tribesmen at Dakka... We can use aeroplanes to smash up their encampment at Dakka. We have twenty four aeroplanes here, and an attack on Dakka and possibly on Jalalabad from the air would not only take the heart out of the Afghans but would give all those who are at present half hearted a very good excuse for pulling out.[10]

Landi Kotal was now solidly held by an infantry battalion, the equivalent of a mountain battery, and 500 Khyber Rifles. A reconnaissance on the morning of 8 May to a hill aptly named Pisgah, some two miles north-west of Landi Kotal, disclosed Afghan regulars building defences less than a mile away. Other Afghan troops were at work farther to the north towards Tor Tsappar and Spin Tsuka. To the south-west, Afghan tents were clustered round Bagh.

Fowler's problem was not so much the assembly of adequate numbers but the speed with which they could be assembled, which was dictated by the water supplies at Landi Kotal. With the main supply in Afghan hands, the only available water was an 80,000-gallon tank in Landi Kotal fort and some 6,000 gallons a day from some other springs. With limited supplies of water it was essential to conduct operations speedily even if only limited forces were immediately available. Fowler decided to attack next day, using his 1st Brigade (Brigadier General Crocker). The remainder of that brigade, consisting of 1/15 and 1/35 Sikhs and 1/9 Gurkhas, plus 1/11 Gurkhas from 2 Brigade, together with 77 (Howitzer) Battery RFA,[11] two troops of 30th Lancers from the 10th Cavalry Brigade and No. 263 Machine Gun Company, began to arrive at Landi Kotal during the afternoon of 8 May. That evening, Crocker had just over five battalions of infantry at Landi Kotal, with artillery and heavy machine gun support. In the circumstances the British had reacted quickly, probably more quickly than Muhammad Anwar Khan had expected.

Now that the numerical balance of regular forces had shifted against him, Muhammad Anwar Khan could not hope to seize the Khyber; his hopes of success hung on a major tribal uprising, combined with an insurrection in Peshawar itself. Tribal rebellions by their very nature were unpredictable; it was impossible to know when or how or where the tinder might ignite, or how far and fast it might spread. To check a possible incursion of Mohmands and Shinwaris across the Mullagori plain north of Landi Kotal, the 1st Lancers, from the 1st Cavalry Brigade, were moved from Peshawar to a position on the Shahgai Ridge some twelve miles north-west of Peshawar and north of Jamrud.

For the British, it was essential to deter a tribal outbreak by swiftly expelling the Afghan invaders and Fowler now had enough troops at Landi Kotal to attempt this. Crocker, in local command, deployed 1/35 Sikhs, 1/9 Gurkhas and some of the Khyber Rifles in covering positions on the ridges north and north-west of Landi Kotal, ejecting the Afghans from the Asa Khel ridge in the process. As an attacking springboard, he occupied Suffolk Hill (Point 4147), a mile south-west of Landi Kotal and a mile and a half from Bagh, commanding the road from Jalalabad and the Tangi springs.

Round Bagh and on the Tor Tsappar and Spina Tsuka positions the Afghans had now concentrated five battalions and a battery of artillery, and it had to be assumed that other forces would be moving up from Jalalabad. Having detached the 30th Lancers, the machine gun company and a section of 3.7 inch howitzers to reinforce the picquet line north of Landi Kotal, Crocker was left with three infantry battalions (Somerset LI, 1/15th Sikhs, 1/11th Gurkhas), a field battery and No. 8 Mountain Battery, RGA; in reserve he had 2/123 (Outram's) Rifles, who had made a slightly risky night march through the Khyber, plus a field company of the 1st (Bengal) Sappers and Miners. Behind him, 2 Brigade had been ordered up by rail from Nowshera, its guns and transport following by road; 3 Brigade was ordered to concentrate at Kacha Garhi, while the 1st Cavalry Brigade was ordered up from Risalpur to act as a general reserve and to watch the Mullagori plain.[12] Troops from the internal security forces were deployed to protect the airfield at Risalpur, the Peshawar waterworks at Bara, the viaduct linking Bara with Peshawar, and the MT lines, since there was information that agitators in the city had promised the Afghans that they would destroy aircraft and mechanical transport as a preliminary to an uprising.

At Landi Kotal, Crocker was now committed to attacking a roughly equal Afghan regular force entrenched round Bagh. His plan was to seize a prominent feature (Bright's Hill),[13] half a mile ahead of Suffolk Hill and then to advance westwards to retake the water supplies and then eject the Afghans from their positions in and behind Bagh. There was nothing much wrong with the plan except that Crocker did not have sufficient force in terms of artillery support and infantry to carry it out. He was a British Service officer with not a great deal of Frontier experience and he may have underestimated his opponents. He was subject also to pressure from Roos-Keppel who, having misread the situation earlier, was now anxious for a quick termination of the war. With hindsight, Crocker had deployed too much of his force into covering positions to the north and north-west of Landi Kotal to watch the Afghan forces there, leaving himself in consequence with too small an attacking force. He would have done better to withdraw a battalion from the covering force to strengthen the attack, accepting the risk involved, which in practice turned out to be negligible.

The attack began at dawn on 9 May; it consisted of two battalions only (1/15 Sikhs and 1/11 Gurkhas), the Somersets being retained on Suffolk Hill. Bright's Hill was quickly taken by a company of the Sikhs, the day time Afghan garrison having not yet arrived. The remainder of the attacking force then pushed on uphill towards the Afghan outpost positions round Bagh, against gradually increasing Afghan opposition reinforced from the main positions on Khargali Ridge. By 0800 it was clear that the attack had stalled; it lacked adequate weight and the available covering fire from the two batteries, firing at near extreme ranges from positions close to Landi Kotal, was too thin to carry it forward. Fowler now ordered Crocker to stand fast until the remainder of the Division could reach Landi Kotal. The two attacking battalions were forced to dig in about 900 yards short of Bagh; the only tangible gain had been the recovery of the Tangi springs, which relieved the concentration problem at Landi Kotal. The Somerset LI on Suffolk Hill had scarcely fired a shot and the troops occupying the covering positions north and north-west of Landi Kotal had not been engaged at all. It was not an auspicious beginning.

The obsolete BE2Cs of the RAF had not participated in direct support of the troops, apart from some reconnaissance. But they had struck a telling blow by attacking the Afghan concentration at Dakka, as Roos-Keppel had urged. They interrupted Afghan officials distributing rifles, blankets and other supplies to insurgent tribesmen. Some twenty-five people were killed and Government buildings, including Saleh Muhammad's HQ, were hit; the Governor of Jalalabad lost a foot. When the Afghan officials emerged from shelter it was to find that the tribesmen had taken the opportunity to decamp with the rifles and supplies.[14] It was a telling psychological blow and retrieved something from a day which had not gone well for the British.

The concentration of the 2nd Brigade at Jamrud had been interrupted by events in Peshawar. Investigations by the Criminal Investigation Department of the police had shown that the Amir's Postmaster in Peshawar, Ghulam Haidar, was conspiring with the Indian Revolutionary Committee there to raise a mob of 8,000 – tribesmen, Afghan subjects, Hindu revolutionaries and criminal elements from the bazaars – to attack the Civil Lines, the military cantonment, the radio station and the railway station, and to seize the city, as the start of a general insurrection.

Writing to the Amir on 7 May, Ghulam Haidar gave an optimistic account of British weakness and insurrectionary strength:

Hearing that the [Afghan] Post Office was to be searched I ordered armed resistance, as the whole of my correspondence went against the British. If necessary, I would begin a Holy War in Peshawar. Hearing of this, about 8,000 Peshwaris, both Hindus and Moslems, came to help me. That night 2,000 villagers from outside offered their assistance. I said that I would invite them when the time came. Sikh regiments have assured Hindus that they look on Moslems as brethren, and will not fire on them. The [Indian] Government has not sufficient troops in India and often moves about one regiment consisting of 2 or 3 companies to make a display. In spite of many telegrams sent by the Chief Commissioner no regiments have arrived by train. British subjects will not supply recruits. There are disturbances throughout India, and troops, if sent from England, will not arrive in time. It has been given out at a public meeting that the Amir and Ghazis are ready to help Indians, and if war is delayed the [Indian] public will be displeased with the Amir. The assembly cried with one voice that they could not forget the oppressions and tyrannies of the British Government. If after selected leaflets have been circulated and three Sipah Salars [Corps Commanders] have been appointed the Amir refrains from invading India, Hindus and Moslems will be much displeased. It is not expedient to delay and give the English time to collect troops.[15]

The rising in Peshawar was timed for 8 May.

To a confidant, Ghulam Haidar imparted the information that the Amir's strategic plan was to attack on three axes – through the Khyber on Peshawar, under the CinC, Saleh Muhammad, down the Kurram valley, under Nadir Shah, the former CinC and against Quetta under General Abdul Qudus, the Prime Minister. All this information was duly passed on to the British authorities by an informant. Clearly, the most immediate threat was in Peshawar and Roos-Keppel therefore issued orders on 7 May for the city to be surrounded and the ringleaders seized.

Five battalions of infantry were nominally allotted for internal security in the Peshawar area but only two were actually in Peshawar. The remaining two battalions of 2 Infantry Brigade, coming up from Nowshera, were therefore detrained at Peshawar on the morning of 8 May and, with the King's Dragoon Guards, were to carry out this operation. To this force was added two armoured car batteries, which were part of the Peshawar area internal security force. The whole was placed under Major General Climo, commanding 2 Brigade.

The city of Peshawar extended roughly south-west to north-east for a distance of some two miles. It was surrounded by a high wall, with a perimeter of about five miles, pierced by sixteen gates. The main railway line from the Punjab and Delhi ran along the northern edge. Climo deployed his force in four columns along the line of the railway, each column consisting of infantry and cavalry, the 1st and 4th columns being preceded by an armoured car company whose task was to patrol the south-easterly wall. The columns began their march round the city at 1400 hours when, it was calculated, most of the inhabitants would be resting. As each gate was reached, a small detachment of cavalry was left to hold the gate and to prevent egress until the following infantry came up, which then left a detachment to hold the gate securely. Within eleven minutes, the cavalry had seized every gate, and within forty-four minutes each gate was securely in the hands of the infantry and the city effectively sealed off.

Roos-Keppel then announced that until all thirty-three wanted men had surrendered or been handed over, no one would be allowed to enter or leave the city, and that, if necessary, he would cut off the water supply. No one doubted his resolution and by sunset Ghulam Haidar and twenty-two revolutionaries had surrendered; nine had already left the city. The threat of an uprising was over and the city remained secure for the rest of the war.

Peshawar was now handed over to the care of 6 Brigade, from the 2nd Division at Rawalpindi. The two infantry battalions of 2 Brigade (2 North Staffordshire Regiment and 2/11 Gurkhas), with the remaining two sections of No. 6 Mountain Battery RGA and No. 285 Machine Gun Company, left Peshawar next morning (9 May) by train for Jamrud and thence on foot through the Khyber Pass to Landi Kotal which they reached on the morning of 10 May, although not without incident. A mile beyond Jamrud they were fired upon by Afridis who had penetrated the Khyber Rifles' picquets supposed to be guarding the route. Climo, a very experienced Indian Army officer, distrusting the Rifles, then picqueted the heights through the pass with his own troops. It was the first hint of disloyalty among the Rifles although there had been some uneasiness about the obvious strain on their loyalty as they were overwhelmingly recruited locally. Behind 2 Brigade, 3 Brigade, under Major General Skeen, another very experienced Indian soldier, was moving up; its HQ, together with 4/3 and 2/1 Gurkhas, reached Landi Kotal early on the morning of 11 May, relieving 1/9 Gurkhas as Fowler's reserve and freeing that battalion to assist in the attack the same day.

Peshawar was now a beehive of activity, with units arriving from all parts of northern India. Communications were overloaded and units were arriving before notification of their coming. Transport was so short that even the first-line requirements of the 1st Division could not be met and there were no stores or ammunition dumps, no accommodation and very few staff officers to deal with the situation. The Afghan advance had very obviously caught the British authorities on the hop and for the moment there was chaos. A panic message from the Superintendent of Police at Mardan, the home of the Guides, that the 3rd Guides had mutinied and seized the magazine, fortunately proved false.[16]

Major General Fowler, GOC 1st Division, had arrived at Landi Kotal on the evening of 9 May to assess the situation. He was not impressed. The Afghans were holding their positions with great confidence; more ominously, the hills to the south were covered with tribesmen, carefully watching events and a picquet of the Khyber Rifles had deserted with their rifles. Fowler knew that he could not risk a further check and decided to take over command himself. With the additional two battalions from 2nd Brigade and the impending arrival of another two battalions from the 3rd Brigade, he decided to launch a major attack on 11 May.

He had available at Landi Kotal eight infantry battalions, a field battery (No.77), a mountain battery (No.8), a section of 3.7 inch howitzers, and two machine gun companies (263 and 285), with a total of twenty-two Vickers guns – he thus now had the overwhelming force which he had originally been instructed to assemble to expel the Afghans. He left only one battalion (1/35 Sikhs) in the covering positions north of Landi Kotal, another (1/9 Gurkhas) in reserve at Landi Kotal, and a third (the Somersets, with one section of 263) to occupy a position ('Rocky Knoll') some 500 yards south-west of Bright's Hill whence it could bring rifle and machine gun fire on to the right-hand Afghan positions, Fowler's chosen point of attack. Two battalions (1/15 Sikhs and 1/11 Gurkhas) were still in position below the Afghan positions following the attack on 9 May. The remaining three battalions (North Staffords, 2/11 Gurkhas and 2/123 Rifles) would carry out the main attack. The howitzer battery and two sections of machine guns would fire on the right-hand Afghan positions; the mountain battery and a machine gun company would cover the rest of the front, leaving the 3.7 inch howitzers to engage targets of opportunity. It was a well-designed attack, with a properly thought-out fire plan. Nevertheless, the Afghan positions were strong and the terrain difficult and exhausting.

The Somersets, having one company supporting 1/35 Sikhs and two companies left on Suffolk Hill, were down to barely two companies (roughly 200 men),[17] had some difficulty reaching their position. At one point the ascent was too steep for the mules carrying the Vickers guns and they had to be manhandled up. The Somersets were not in position when the main attack started, but the delay did not affect the outcome. The main attack went smoothly. The North Staffords crossed the start line just after 0830 and, with frequent pauses because of the heat and steepness of the terrain, seized the right-hand Afghan positions at the point of the bayonet. The 2/11th Gurkhas, moving rapidly over easier ground, burst through the Afghan centre, capturing the Afghan guns and bayoneting the gunners.[18] They then pressed on to take the Khargali Ridge ahead of them. The 1/11th Gurkhas now advanced and seized Bagh village and the positions on the Afghan left flank.

The troops were too exhausted to mount any sort of pursuit but the RAF proceeded to bomb and machine gun the retreating enemy. Fowler established a line of outposts along the line of the original Afghan positions covering Bagh, while the remainder of the troops camped round the village, except for the 1/15th Sikhs who had been in position west of Landi Kotal since 9 May and who were now relieved and sent back to Landi Kotal for a rest.

It had been a neat, workmanlike plan and the troops had carried it out with great dash. The coordination of the artillery and machine guns and the infantry attacks had been particularly noteworthy. The moral effect of what would turn out to be the decisive action of the war was not lost on the tribesmen. In assessing Fowler's success, it is worth noting that he had available two of the original eight regular British battalions left in India. The official history paid tribute to Climo's careful training of his brigade and certainly the contrast between their performance and that of some of the Indian battalions in Waziristan later was very marked. British casualties totalled eight killed and thirty-one wounded, almost all from the North Staffords, illustrating the severity of their task. Throughout the day there had been sniping from the surrounding hills, causing a number of casualties.

Afghan losses were put at 100 killed and 300 wounded, plus five guns and an ancient machine gun. As in Chitral, there had been a curious hesitancy about the Afghan effort. They had not fought badly, but from the initial occupation of positions round Bagh they had fought without initiative. No attempt had been made to concentrate the forces in Ningrahar, no attempt had been made to seize Landi Kotal on 6 and 7 May when the British garrison was at its weakest, and perhaps most strikingly of all, no attempt had been made to eject the two British battalions dug in below the Afghan positions after the action on 9 May. There was from the British point of view the makings there of a first-class disaster if the Afghans had seized the opportunity. If the explanation for this Afghan inertia was not simply an absence of leadership and planning, it could only have been that the Afghans counted on their initial advance provoking a major tribal uprising which would do the Afghan Government's work for it.

Fowler now had the great bulk of his division concentrated at Landi Kotal and on 12 May Crocker conducted a careful reconnaissance of the remaining Afghan positions on Tor Tsappar and Spin Tsuka. They were found to be strongly fortified and manned by some 800 men. No clear advantage was seen in attacking such positions and the troops were withdrawn. The Afghans defeated by Fowler had retired on Dakka, some twenty-five miles to the west, where they were bombed by the RAF again, whereupon they retired in some haste towards Jalalabad, leaving their camp and equipment to be pillaged by the local Mohmand tribesmen, an indication of which way the wind was beginning to blow.

The Amir was already beginning to regret his actions, it would seem, because on 10 May he had written to the Viceroy, criticising the arrest of his Postmaster at Peshawar, claiming that he had moved troops to the frontier solely to prevent the disturbances in India from spreading into Afghanistan, and reiterating his regret that the British would still not formally recognise Afghan independence:

> The doors of calamity may not be opened upon the world because a demand for justice is right.[19]

The Indian Government retaliated with leaflets dropped by the RAF, couched in the same flowery, Persian style. 'O brave and honest people of Afghanistan' it began, and then went on to state that the Afghan army had been defeated and its guns captured by the vanguard of the huge army being assembled even now by the British. In familiar fashion, it then sought to drive a wedge between the Amir and his subjects:

> Will the peoples of Afghanistan allow this inexperienced youth, false to the memory of his martyred father, false to the interests of his country, false to the dictates of the Holy Koran, to bring calamity upon the brave people and fair country of Afghanistan? God forbid.[20]

It was all very unscrupulous but the British clearly won that propaganda battle.

Dakka was now the obvious next step for the British, with Jalabad and perhaps Kabul beyond. Dakka offered ample space for the concentration of a large force, as well as a landing ground for the RAF. From there a relatively short advance would bring them to Jalalabad. To remain stationary at Landi Kotal would allow the Afghans to regroup and would have a bad effect on the tribes, who were still wavering. Accordingly, Fowler received orders on 12 May to open the road from Landi Kotal to Dakka to allow a cavalry force to pass through to occupy the Dakka plain. The cavalry force was to consist of the 1st Cavalry Brigade and the 30th Lancers, under Brigadier General G M Baldwin, commanding 10th Cavalry Brigade at Risalpur.[21]

Notes

1   See J A Norris, *The First Afghan War* (Cambridge, 1967), passim.

2   For these estimates, see *Third Afghan War*, map facing page 1.

3   *Third Afghan War*, Appendix I, 142–8.

4   In fairness to the Khyber Rifles, their record of service and loyalty since their foundation as the Khyber Jezailchees in 1878 had been a proud one – see Chenevix Trench, 8–12.

5   The Afghan official maintained at Peshawar to handle mail to and from Kabul.

6   Roos-Keppel was a Frontier officer of enormous experience and legendary influence among the tribes. If he took a more sanguine view, it may simply have been a case of 'familiarity...'

7   The Peshawar Division had no Intelligence staff of its own, the staff officer in charge of Intelligence coming directly under Army Headquarters. The Division therefore relied for local intelligence on Roos-Keppel and his staff. The result was not entirely happy. According to de Burgh, the acting GSO1 at Divisional HQ, military officers were discouraged from visiting the Khyber Pass, needing a pass signed by the Political Agent to do so. Work on communications and water supplies between Jamrud and Landi Kotal was also outside the military jurisdiction, the military Chief Engineer reporting for this purpose to the civil authorities, de Burgh, 2.

8   Molesworth. He was Adjutant of the Somersets.

9 Molesworth.

10 Roos-Keppel to Maffey, Private Secretary to Chelmsford, quoted in Heathcote, 179.

11 Six 4.5 inch howitzers.

12 This concentration was apparently ordered on local initiative, Army HQ's intervention being limited according to de Burgh to a 'futile' order to await a new concentration plan being despatched 'by post' – de Burgh, 4.

13 Named after Sir Robert Onesiphorus Bright who had commanded the Khyber Lines of Communication Force in the Second Afghan War in 1879–80 – see Robson, 163–5 and passim. 14 Heathcote, 182–3.

15 Third Afghan War, 29–30.

16 De Burgh, 5.

17 Molesworth, 49.

18 *Third Afghan War*, 34, indicates that it was 2/123 Rifles, passing through 2/11 Gurkhas, who captured the ridge. But the map opposite page 33 and eyewitness testimony makes it clear that 2/11 Gurkhas occupied the ridge in the first instance – see *The Bugle and Kukri* (the journal of the 10th Gurkhas), Vol. 5, No. 6 (1986–7), 65.

19 Text in CP/10, No. 656.

20 Text in CP/55f, No. 143.

21 Baldwin's precise orders and the reason why he was put in over the head of 1st Cavalry Brigade's commander, Davies, are examined in the Annex to Chapter V below.

V

The Occupation of Dakka:
13 May–8 August 1919

(Map 5)

The road from Landi Kotal to the entrance to the Dakka plain is dominated by hills coming down close to the road on either side, which required picqueting all the way. The forces available for this task comprised 2 and 3 Infantry Brigades, with Divisional troops and Khyber Rifles, the whole under the immediate command of Skeen, to whom this type of operation was second nature.

Early on 13 May 2/123 Rifles, with the two 3.7 inch howitzers, occupied Hill 3618, some two miles from Landi Kotal, commanding the western exit from the Khyber Pass, without opposition, in order to protect the line of advance from an attack from the remaining Afghan positions north of Landi Kotal. At the same time, Skeen's covering force assembled between Landi Khana and Michni Khandao fort. The vanguard under Climo consisted of a composite battalion from 1 Brigade and 1/35 Sikhs, No.285 Machine Gun Company (minus two sections) and No.8 Mountain Battery. It was to undertake the actual task of picqueting along the road. The main body under Skeen, consisting of 1 Yorkshire Regiment, 4/3 Gurkhas, 77 Battery, the remaining two sections of No.285 Machine Gun Company and 250 Khyber Rifles, would clear away opposition along the road, leaving it clear for the cavalry to advance to occupy Dakka. Each picquet consisted of an officer and six to thirty men, but it had to be supported by a covering party while it climbed up to its allotted position and fortified itself within a stone sangar. When the main body had passed, the picquet could be withdrawn and would then join the rearguard. It was an operation which required speed, timing and strict adherence to procedure, particularly in the withdrawal, and it was very expensive in manpower.[1]

At 0600 Climo's advanced guard crossed the frontier at Torkham, thirteen miles from Landi Kotal, becoming the first British troops to enter Afghanistan since 1881. The small Afghan garrison at Haft Chah, five miles beyond Torkham, hastily abandoned the post, leaving behind 30,000 rounds of .303 ammunition. At this point, Climo had advanced about thirteen miles but had used up all his infantry; 4/3 Gurkhas had to be sent up from Skeen's main body. By 1000 the entrance to the Dakka plain had been reached, virtually without opposition, and the road was now open for the cavalry to pass through.

Baldwin's force had concentrated at Jamrud. Between there and Dakka, a distance of thirty-three miles, the only place where the horses could be watered, apart from the small stream by the road at Ali Masjid, was three long stone troughs midway between Landi Kotal and Landi Khana. It was assumed that watering from these troughs would take an hour. A supply of fodder in lorries would follow the force to Dakka.

Baldwin reached Landi Kotal at 0930 but the watering arrangements proved faulty. Instead of an hour, it took three hours for the bulk of the force to water and it was not ready to move on until 1230.[2] To try to regain momentum, Baldwin sent forward an advance guard of one cavalry regiment, two horse artillery guns and the supply convoy, escorted by an armoured car battery; the main body following on as soon as all the horses had been watered. Just after mid-day, Baldwin's leading troops were entering the Dakka plain. On the whole, it had been a reasonably expeditious advance and uncontested.

The first view of the DAKKA plain is not exhilarating; an arid stony waste surrounded on three sides by barren rocky hills, with a group of mud buildings near the river constituting the village of LOE DAKKA, and excepting for one small clump of trees at SIRIKH DAKKA, there is hardly a tree on the right bank of KABUL river. In the distance the crumbling walls of ROBAT fort and SHERABAD cantonment do not add beauty to the outlook.[3] Across the KABUL river, over which no bridge existed, the village and trees of LALPURA village added a touch of colour to an otherwise depressing scene. This first impression was fully borne out by later experiences, when the heat and dust alike were found to be abominable and the only redeeming features proved to be the bathing in the river and the absence of mosquitos. Nobody who has once ever been to DAKKA ever evinces any desire to revisit that delectable spot.[4]

The plain measures roughly four miles by four miles and is cut up by innumerable shallow, dry watercourses, which offer good cover for infiltration. To the north the plain is bounded by the Kabul river – wide, generally shallow, broken up into numerous channels beyond which lies Lalpura, the Mohmand capital. To the west, the road to Basawal and Jalalabad exits through a pass in the Khurd Khaibar hills which sweep round to the south-west and south in a horseshoe, ending some 500 yards from the river, at a point about a mile due west of Loe Dakka village and Baldwin's camp. This end of the horseshoe is dominated by two hills – Stonehenge (later Somerset Hill) and Sikh Hill, from which the camp was within artillery and rifle fire. (Baldwin's choice of camp site, close to Loe Dakka, and his action in not putting out picquets on the hills to the west and south-west, was subsequently severely criticised by Fowler, Barrett and Monro, and led to Baldwin's early retirement. The arguments are by no means clear-cut, and, together with other criticisms of Baldwin's dispositions, are examined in the Annex to this chapter.)

As soon as Baldwin's force was established and the MT convoy unloaded, Skeen's force withdrew to Landi Khana and Landi Kotal, leaving Baldwin for the moment isolated. The reason for this apparently dangerous with-drawal was that old bane of the Indian Army – a severe shortage of trans-port. The 1st Division had not yet received all its first-line transport[5] and there was not enough available to supply the troops beyond Landi Kotal.

On 14 May Baldwin was joined by Crocker, with two infantry battalions of his 1st Infantry Brigade and the 30th Lancers. There were now three brigadiers on the spot – Baldwin, Crocker and Davies (commanding 1st Cavalry Brigade), a situation open to confusion. At the same time, HQ 2nd Infantry Brigade moved up to Landi Khana where it was better placed to undertake the picqueting of the road to Dakka. Some limited local cavalry patrolling took place on 14 and 15 May within the Dakka plain. It did not penetrate the Khurd Khaibar hills and no signs of any enemy were discov-ered. RAF reconnaissance flights towards Basawal also saw nothing. To the south, a party went up on to Stonehenge but unaccountably returned without leaving a picquet there, even though it dominated the camp, at a range of some 2,300 yards.[6] At Landi Kotal, Fowler, apparently uneasy about the lack of information about hostile forces and any reaction from the direction of Jalalabad, issued orders to Baldwin on the evening of 15 May to push a reconnaissance through the Khurd Khaibar pass, towards Basawal, thirteen miles to the west.[7]

The next day, 16 May, proved to be very busy. The remaining two battal-ions of the 1st Brigade, with No. 8 Mountain Battery, reached Dakka and Crocker assumed command there; Baldwin was ordered back to Peshawar under a cloud. Fowler arrived with this reinforcement and, disapproving of the siting of the camp, ordered it be moved next day to a new position some two miles farther west, between Robat fort and the Sherabad can-tonment. He also gave orders for picquets to be placed on the hills to the south and west to screen the camp and to give early warning of any enemy advance from that direction. He then returned to Landi Kotal. His tactical instincts were sound but he was just too late.[8]

At 0530 that morning the reconnaissance ordered on 15 May had left camp. It was commanded by Colonel Macmullen, commanding 1/15 Sikhs and consisted of three squadrons of the King's Dragoon Guards, 1/15 Sikhs, one section (two guns) M Battery RHA and one section of No.15 Machine Gun Squadron.[9] Macmullen sent the infantry forward to occupy the pass through the Khurd Khaibar hills, placing the horse artillery guns near the Robat fort to support the infantry; two troops of

the King's Dragoon Guards were sent to reconnoitre the Sherabad cantonment, a large walled enclosure.

Macmullen was a careful and experienced Frontier officer. Leaving
one company of 1/15 Sikhs on the pass to cover his withdrawal, he
moved in bounds, cavalry covered by infantry and supported by the
guns and machine guns. Just beyond the pass was the large village of
Girdi, not marked on British maps, from which a hot fire was opened on
Macmullen's troops. The village was captured fairly easily by 0930, but
as the troops continued the reconnaissance westwards they came under
artillery and rifle fire from a ridge west of the village; enemy troops were
soon working their way round the southern flank of Macmullen's force,
in an effort to cut him off. It was clear that Macmullen had bumped into
a substantial body of Afghan troops. He was now six miles from camp
and it was time to retreat; he had, in any case, fulfilled his basic objective
of locating the enemy. He began to retire at 1045 and was immediately
closely followed up by the Afghans in increasingly large numbers. It was
touch and go whether the troops could reach the pass before being cut off
– 'the retirement was somewhat uncoordinated and disorganised' admitted Macmullen.[10] Once the troops came under the cover of the infantry
company which he had prudently left on the pass, he was able to conduct
an ordered retreat; covered alternately by the infantry and the cavalry, and
supported by the guns. Even so, he came under very strong pressure from
the enemy who by 1230 were within 300 or 400 yards of the guns, close to
Robat fort. To relieve the pressure, Macmullen ordered a squadron of the
KDGs under Captain W R. F Cooper to charge the enemy, which he did
with success, inflicting heavy losses on those Afghans who stood to fight.[11]
It was the last mounted charge of British cavalry in India. By 1300 hours
the force had reached camp which was now under fire from the hills to the
west and south-west.

Macmullen assumed that it was his reconnaissance which had stirred
up the Afghans; in fact, he had bumped into a force of some 3,000 regulars,
with seven guns, on its way to reoccupy Dakka. In his covering note to
Macmullen's report,[12] Barrett expressed the view that the force sent out
was too small and that the Khurd Khaibar pass should have been secured
by troops sent out from camp. That reads very much like hindsight. As
a result of Macmullen's skilful handling, the force had exactly fulfilled
its reconnaissance purpose, with minimal casualties. Barrett, aware that
aerial reconnaissance had reported no signs of the enemy, warned that too
much weight should not be placed upon negative reports from aircraft;
experience was to show that tribesmen, in their dust-coloured clothes,
were difficult to spot among the hills.

Fowler left Dakka at 1300 hours, totally unaware of the fighting in
which Macmullen was engaged. He had spent the morning with Crocker,
discussing the precise location of the new camp site and successfully

distracting the latter's attention in the process.[13] By early afternoon, the camp was under heavy fire from artillery and rifles established on the hills forming the eastern end of the horseshoe, some 1,700 yards from the camp, which was without any natural line of defence. Men and horses were in the open and casualties would mount unless something was done to dislodge the enemy. The 2nd Battalion Somerset LI and the 1/35th Sikhs, just arrived from Landi Kotal, were hastily despatched to hold positions west and south-west of the camp, and two squadrons of the 1st Lancers were sent towards the Ghori Ghakai pass, some two and a half miles south of the camp, to prevent the enemy tribesmen working their round to the east of the camp. That temporarily stabilised the position, although sniping continued throughout the night and succeeded in stampeding many of the horses. British casualties on the 16th had numbered ten killed and eighty-nine wounded, a relatively severe loss.

Despite the availability of air reconnaissance, the British had been surprised. The victory at Bagh and the uneventful advance from Landi Kotal to Dakka had perhaps induced a slight sense of over-confidence and this was compounded by the initial siting of the camp. Crocker had available four infantry battalions (Somerset LI, 1/15 and 1/35 Sikhs, 1/9 Gurkhas).[14] His camp was untenable in face of the Afghan fire and he decided on a night advance followed by a dawn assault next day (17 May).

The Afghans occupied a position on the western hills spread over a length of some 4,000 yards from north to south in a rough semi-circle. At their nearest these positions were only a mile or so from the British camp round Loe Dakkh. Crocker planned to launch 1/35 Sikhs, supported by two companies of 1/9 Gurkhas, against Stonehenge (later called Somerset Hill), some 3,000 yards due west of the camp, while 1/15 Sikhs were to attack a feature called Sikh Hill, just south of Stonehenge; the Somerset LI were to remain in camp as a general reserve. The cavalry watched the right and left flanks against a possible attack by Mohmand tribesmen from across the river. As no landing ground had been laid out by the 16th, the RAF was unable to offer close support or tactical reconnaissance; and with only one, horse artillery, battery at his disposal, Crocker was severely handicapped in providing fire support to his attacking troops; he was, in any case, short of artillery ammunition. In effect, he was gambling that his infantry could attain their objectives without sustained fire support, other than machine guns.

In his subsequent report to the CinC, Barrett thought that:

Brigadier-General Crocker, when faced with a difficult situation, shewed great resolution and confidence in the superiority of his troops, which he turned to good account. His plan of attack was a very bold one, depending for its successful issue upon the timely arrival of the expected reinforcements.[15]

That seems in retrospect a surprisingly charitable judgement. In fact, the bold and impetuous Crocker was proposing to commit exactly the same error that he had made at Bagh on 9 May – attacking inadequately reconnoitred positions with inadequate forces. With his camp under fire and casualties increasing, he was clearly right to seek to eject the Afghans from the nearby hills as quickly as possible. But by failing to use the cavalry, dismounted, to protect the camp, thereby releasing the Somersets to strengthen the assault, he was repeating his earlier error. Moreover, if his plan depended upon Skeen's arrival, it would surely have been prudent to await that arrival – a delay of some hours would seem to have been well worth the increased prospect of success. Since Crocker's message, informing Fowler of his decision to attack, did not reach the latter until 0330 on the 17th, it is by no means clear that Crocker was aware of Skeen's reinforcement before he made his plans for an attack.

The initial attack on Stonehenge went deceptively well, and by 0530 the Sikhs were within 100 yards of the crest without a shot having been fired against them. The Afghans had clearly held their fire and, as the leading platoons reached the crest, they were greeted with intense rifle fire at short-range. The three senior officers were wounded and three Indian officers killed outright. The guns from camp opened fire to try to retrieve the situation, but under increasingly heavy fire the Sikhs broke and fled down the hill. One company was rallied and, with the two companies of the Gurkhas, managed to work its way back up the the hill to a position some twenty yards from the crest but could go no farther and hung on in an increasingly desperate situation. The remainder of the Sikhs huddled in some ruins at the bottom of the hill whence they were unable to move because of the Afghan fire.[16]

To the south of them, 1/15 Sikhs had run into similar problems. They had got to within 300 yards of the crest of Sikh Hill but could get no farther and there was no artillery to support them. By 0830 the two attacks were stalled and the artillery had run out of ammunition. To make matters worse, cavalry patrols reported hostile fire from the north bank of the river.

Too late, Crocker now prepared to commit his reserve battalion, but at 0915 he learned that reinforcements were on the way and he therefore suspended his attack. Three lorries arrived at 1030 with ammunition for the mountain guns and an hour later the reinforcements under Skeen began to debouch on to the eastern end of the plain.

On receiving Crocker's message at 0330, Fowler had realised at once that Crocker would need reinforcing; he may also have had some doubts as to the latter's tactical ability in view of the earlier fiasco at Bagh. Even so, he could hardly have expected Crocker to have got himself into exactly the same situation. Skeen was ordered to move at 0700 with his HQ and two battalions (1st Battalion Yorkshire Regiment, 2/1 Gurkhas) of his 3rd Brigade, together with No. 285 Machine Gun Company, the 3.7 inch howitzers (in mule carts) and a section of No. 77 Battery. The 2nd Brigade under Climo was ordered to open the road from Landi Khana to Dakka to prevent any opposition to Skeen's move.

Skeen's column reached the entrance to the Dakka plain at 1130. He was an officer of immense Frontier experience, perhaps the outstanding Frontier soldier of his generation, and fully understood the need to regain the initiative as quickly as possible. He immediately ordered the 2/1st Gurkhas and the machine guns to occupy a knoll some 1,600 yards from the enemy, whence the machine guns could bring down fire on the Afghan right flank; the Yorkshires were posted in support. The two howitzer sections were ordered to open fire on the rear of the Afghan positions, from a point close to the mouth of the Khyber.[17] He then proceeded to meet Crocker, taking over command from him at about 1230. Through a misunderstanding, the Yorkshires advanced on to the lower slopes of Sikh Hill and, mistaking them for Afghans, opened fire on 1/15 Sikhs still in position there, wounding two officers and eight other ranks. They were then hastily ordered to stand fast. Skeen's orders were issued soon after 1300:

Dakka Force Order No. 1
1 Our infantry at present engaged with enemy in positions to be pointed out to Commanding Officers.
2 Attack will be resumed as follows:
2/Somerset LI to leave present positions at 1400 and establish themselves, as first objective, on ridge now held by 1/35 Sikhs by 1430.
At 1450 howitzers will open section fire, 30 seconds, until 1530. No. 8 Mountain Battery and 'M' Battery keeping up a sustained fire along the ridge. Objectives to be pointed out to Commanding Officers. Os – on both sides of Stonehenge.
2/Somerset LI will advance on to forward slopes of Stonehenge and work up strong line to within 150 feet of summit by 1530.
At 1530, all guns will open section fire, 10 seconds, until 1540.

Timings for machine guns
No. 285 Machine Gun Company, on objectives shown,
1450 to 1500, rapid fire.
1500 to 1530, frequent bursts.
1530 to 1540, rapid fire.
Machine Gun Squadron [No. 15 Company] on objectives shown, timings as for No. 285 Machine Gun Company.
3 Advance dressing station close to Camp.
4 After gaining ridge, Somerset Light Infantry will prepare for occupation and occupy it to-night.
5 Force headquarters at present 1st Brigade Headquarters.[18]

The Somersets started at 1400 hours and moving fast, reached the remnants of 1/35 Sikhs and 1/9 Gurkhas at about 1430.[19] The remainder of the climb was extremely steep and very hot. The battalion halted, as ordered, about 100 feet below the crest, in dead ground. From there they could see 1/15 Sikhs going forward on Sikh Hill, and at approximately 1530 the Somersets sounded the charge with their buglers and climbed the last 100 feet on hands and knees. The 1/15th Sikhs appear to have reached the summit of Sikh Hill at roughly the same time.[20] By now the Afghans were streaming away rapidly, apparently demoralised by the howitzer fire landing on the slopes behind them. With some difficulty, because of the narrowness of the ridge, shallow sangars were constructed to occupy the positions gained. They would have been difficult to defend in the case of determined attack but the Afghans were engaged in retreating fast.

The ability of the howitzers to drop their shells on the rear of the Afghan positions had been the determining factor, the low trajectory of the mountain and horse artillery guns being unable to burst shells accurately on the razor edge of the ridge. It had been an expensive day, casualties on the British side amounting to twenty-eight killed and 157 wounded, the great bulk of the casualties falling on the two Sikh battalions; 1/35 Sikhs lost seven officers, two thirds of the officer strength.[21] The Afghan regular troops may have numbered as many as 3,000, with seven guns; the number of tribesmen engaged is not known. Afghan losses were put at 200 killed and 400 wounded, with five Krupp guns.

There are close parallels between these operations and those at Bagh on 9 and 11 May. In both cases, the initial attack had been made with too small a force and without an adequate fire plan, and the position had been retrieved only by using a bigger force and a proper fire support plan, under a more experienced commander. It is tempting to place the blame for the initial failure on Crocker, and certainly his tactical planning had its faults. The cavalry had been virtually spectators in this action – it was not natural cavalry country but, as the Official History suggests, they might have been used dismounted to protect the camp, thus releasing the Somerset LI to strengthen the initial attack.[22] The failure to place picquets on the hills to the west and south-west was a clear error; a reconnaissance had actually gone on to 'Stonehenge' on 15 May but had withdrawn without leaving anyone there.

But in the upshot, it was not Crocker but Baldwin who bore the brunt of subsequent criticism. Barrett wrote to the Commander, in Chief:

> It does not appear to have occurred to him [Baldwin] that, if occupied by the enemy, the ground below [the Khurd Kilaibar hills] on our side would have been untenable. If the Cavalry Brigade had shown more activity on the 14th and 15th, it does not seem probable that so large a hostile force could have collected in the neighbourhood without being detected.[23]

Baldwin was, in effect, sent back in disgrace; Molesworth met him trailing back disconsolately to Landi Khana. For an analysis of this controversy see the Annex to this chapter. Whatever Baldwin's shortcomings may have been, Barrett's subsequent endorsement of Crocker's actions surely went too far the other way. But Crocker was a British Army officer and public criticism of his performance would clearly have raised awkward questions between Simla and London.[24]

On a more positive note, the speed with which Skeen assessed the situation and issued his orders, and the succinctness and clear headedness of those orders was in marked contrast to the actions of other commanders, and revealed the qualities which made him such a distinguished Frontier officer.

Again the Afghans had missed a great opportunity; a serious assault on the remnants of the two Sikh battalions clinging desperately to Stonehenge and Sikh Hill might have inflicted a tactical disaster of the first magnitude as there was only a battalion and the cavalry in reserve and no proper defences round the camp. Once again, the Afghans had shown themselves adept at seizing tactically advantageous positions but unable to turn them to advantage. They would not get another chance in this theatre.

Notes

1 For a valuable analysis and description of picqueting and mountain warfare generally, see T M Moreman *The Army in India and the development of Frontier Warfare 1849–1947* (1998). Skeen himself wrote what was effectively the text book, *Passing it On: Short talks on Tribal Fighting on the North-West Frontier of India*, which contains a detailed description of the complex picqueting procedures. Climo also produced a book on the subject – see Bibliography.

2 It is not clear who was responsible for the blunder. It may have been another consequence of the somewhat casual way in which Baldwin's orders were issued – see Annex to this chapter.

3 Robat and Sherabad were relics of the Second Afghan War.

4 De Burgh, *Action at Dakka 16/17th May 1919*, 2 (NAM 6505-55-2).

5 First-line transport was that immediately required for a unit to move into action; 2nd line transport was the additional transport required to sustain a unit in its position i.e. rations, spare parts, ammunition, etc.

6 Molesworth, 60.

7 Telegram No. A.L-73 dated 15 May 1919, from 1st Division to Cavalry Force, Dakka – File 4683-F Operations, 8.

8 Molesworth, for one, was severely critical of the failure to picquet these hills on 15 May and blames both Baldwin and Crocker for failing to observe the elementary Frontier principle of 'all-round defence' – Molesworth, 59–60. It does seem extraordinary that it was left to Fowler to rectify the omission. But it may have been another outcome of having three brigadiers on the spot.

9 De Burgh says that a section of No.6 Battery RGA also went along – de Burgh, 4. But this is an error.

10 *Report of a reconnaissance made by a small force under Colonel Macmullen towards Basawal on 16th May 1919*, Simla, 1919 (File No. 4608-F-Operations).

11 Molesworth, arriving with the remainder of the 1st Brigade, saw lines of infantry near the Sherabad cantonment but it was only when he saw what appeared to be a squadron of cavalry charging them that he realised that the infantry was Afghan – Molesworth, 59.

12 *Report of a reconnaissance*, 1.

13 *Report on the action at Dakka on 16th–17th May, 1919*, Simla, 1919 (File No. 4683- F-Operations).

14 The individual battalions were all significantly below their authorised establishments; the actual fighting strengths on 16 May were 1/15 Sikhs 453, 1/35 Sikhs 528, 1/19 Gurkhas 335 and Somersets 412 – Crocker's report in *Report on the action at Dakka.*

15 Fowler's covering note in Report on the action at Dakka.

16 An observer noted that Afghan shells fired from an ancient gun and filled with black powder bounced along the ground before exploding, rather like a child's firework, and that one keen cricketer reversed arms and endeavoured to hit one for six – Molesworth, 61.

17 The 3.7 inch howitzers fired only a few rounds before succumbing to recoil problems.

18 Text in Skeen's report of 21 May in *Report on the action at Dakka*, 7–8, Simla, 1919.

19 Molesworth tried to get some of the Indian soldiers to join the attack but many of them were young and inexperienced and they had had to endure many hours of enemy fire in exposed positions. Not surprisingly they declined to move.

20 There is some uncertainty as to the timing of the 1/15th Sikhs' advance. Skeen's report says that the 1/15th gained their objective at 1430; Crocker's report simply says that the 1/15th advanced at 1350 and gained their objective. Molesworth claims to have seen the 1/15th begin their advance when the Somerset LI were near the crest of Stonehenge at around 1500. The official history says the Sikhs reached their objective at 1335. Evidently Macmullen used his initiative in ordering the 1/15th to advance and the going was easier than on Stonehenge. The official history timing implies that Macmullen had reached his objective at virtually the same time as the Somersets received their orders from Skeen, who was close by. On balance it seems probable that Macmullen used his initiative and began his advance as soon as he saw the Somersets begin to move, reaching his objective at around 1430, as Skeen says.

21 Many of the Afghan rifles were old Sniders, firing a clay-filled expanding bullet which inflicted horrific wounds. Molesworth came across an Indian soldier whose leg had been nearly severed by a bullet in the back of the knee – Molesworth, 69.

22 *Third Afghan War*, 43.

23 Memo. No. 1118-50-G.S. from Barrett to CinC, dated 26 May 1919 (File 4683-F Operations, 1.

24 Crocker subsequently received a CB but retired as a brigadier-general in 1920, which might suggest that the Army was not over-enthusiastic about his abilities.

Annex

The Baldwin Affair

Baldwin, with his cavalry force, occupied Dakka on the afternoon of 13 May 1919. On the evening of 15 May he was relieved of that command and returned to Peshawar early on the morning of 16 May. Less than three weeks later, on 4 June, he was relieved of command of the 10th Cavalry Brigade at Risalpur[1] and effectively retired from the army.

He was denied a court of enquiry or a court-martial; he had great difficulty in obtaining an interview with the Adjutant General India or the Commander in Chief (Monro), and even in obtaining a clear statement of the reasons for his dismissal. He had clearly become an embarrassment to the authorities. To many observers, it seemed that he had been cast as the scapegoat for the near-reverse at Dakka on 16 May, which had clearly frightened the authorities back in Simla. Baldwin himself was left to believe that personal animosities had played a significant part in his dismissal.

His treatment was in marked contrast to that of Crocker, who, having failed in two attacks (at Bagh on 9 May and at Dakka on 17 May), was nevertheless retained in command of his brigade and eventually received the CB for his services.[2]

Any analysis of the rights and wrongs of l'affaire Baldwin must logically start with the decision to summon him from his brigade command at Risalpur and appoint him to command the Dakka cavalry force over the head of Davies, whose 1st Cavalry Brigade made up the bulk of the force. Davies was junior to Baldwin,[3] but he was an experienced officer who was presumably regarded as competent to command his brigade on active service. Baldwin had, however, commanded a brigade in the 1917 Mahsud expedition, for which he had received accelerated promotion. His recent annual confidential reports had been good. That for 1917, signed by Sir Frederick Campbell, GOC Peshawar Division, included a particular comment on his fitness for a field command:

> I should say he was at his best in the field where he has shown up well as a leader in the past, to my personal knowledge. Plain spoken and practical. Is very young looking and active for his age. I have confidence in him as a Cavalry Commander who in action will do the right thing at the right time.[4]

That report was countersigned by Barrett, as GOC Northern Army, on 27 January 1918:

> A fine Cavalry leader with sound judgement and good powers of command... Fit for advancement.[5]

In his report for 1918, Campbell wrote:

> He is a capable energetic Cavalry leader. I hope some command may
> soon be found for him of a more compact and satisfactory nature
> than his present one, which is not concentrated for a great part of
> the year.[6]

In choosing him, therefore, the authorities were fully justified on grounds
of seniority, experience and competence. Barrett had even recommended
him for promotion to major general.

Baldwin having been selected, what was the precise nature of his orders
for the advance on Dakka? Herein lies a problem because his orders were,
in the first instance, given to him orally and we have only his testimony.
The main outlines, however, are reasonably clear. On 10 May he was
summoned to Peshawar from Risalpur, where he was engaged in mobilising his own brigade for active service. At North-West Force HQ he was
apparently told simply that he was 'to go to Dakka.'[7] Those orders were
countermanded by Barrett when he saw him next morning (11 May),
when he was told to take command of the cavalry force and march to
Jamrud, which he did the same day. Next day (12 May) he received North
West Force Order No. 1, signed by Loch, the BGGS North-West Force. That
instructed him to march next day to Loe Dakka, where he was to prepare
a landing ground for the RAF and to seize all boats and other means of
crossing the Kabul river. He was to open up visual means of communication with 1st Division.[8]

While at Jamrud on 12 May he had another short interview with Barrett,
who was travelling back to Peshawar after visiting operations round
Landi Kotal. Barrett then told him that the Afghans had disappeared and
that he (Baldwin) would be reinforced at Dakka within a day or two by
probably an infantry brigade.[9] Barrett also appears to have told him that
the advance was 'for political purposes'.

The sum of these orders is notable in two respects – first, there is no
information of any kind about the enemy's movements, dispositions or
estimated intentions, and second, there is no indication of what operations, if any, were to follow the occupation of Dakka. Even more importantly perhaps, there was no indication of who was to command overall
when, and if, the infantry brigade arrived.

What Baldwin could reasonably derive from these somewhat imprecise
orders was that he was required to proceed to Dakka to lay out an airfield
for the RAF and a camp to contain at least a cavalry brigade and an infantry brigade. But the general tenor of the orders suggested that there was
not likely to be any serious contact with the Afghan regular forces.

None of this in any way relieved Baldwin of the duty of taking every
precaution against hostile attack, but it may have influenced him sub-

consciously to choose a camp site on the basis of convenience rather than defence; and it may have influenced his arrangements for local cavalry patrols. But there is one further point which would have been in his mind. Cavalry can seize ground but infantry are needed to occupy it. The early arrival of the infantry brigade was therefore essential.

The charges against Baldwin ultimately fell into three categories. They were formally set out in a letter from HQ North-West Frontier Force of 22 June 1919,[10] but they were fairly summarised in Baldwin's report of 17 May 1919.[11] He was criticised for splitting up his force during the advance, and for the poor march discipline of the troops in the rear. These criticisms had been the subject of an angry exchange at the time between Baldwin and Colonel Tarver, Fowler's GSO1.[12]

To the first of these charges Baldwin had a perfect reply. He had been ordered to advance to Dakka without delay. The watering arrangements at Landi Kotal, for which he was not responsible, had been defective. Rather than delay the advance until the last horse had been watered, he had sent on an advanced guard to seize Dakka, while the remainder followed on as soon as watering was complete. Because the Pass had been declared free of the enemy and aircraft reconnaissance had shown nothing, he was justified in taking the risk in the interest of seizing his objective. As to the charge of poor march discipline, Baldwin pointed out very reasonably that it was not his brigade and he could not be held responsible for its training and discipline.

Both of these charges now seem petty and perhaps give some credence to Baldwin's belief that personal animosities were at work. Their significance lies in the bad blood which was created between Baldwin and Tarver, who was in a position to influence matters against the former.

The next set of charges related to Baldwin's initial choice of camp at Dakka. These charges were altogether more serious and more difficult to counter. They were clearly the charges that weighed most heavily with higher authority. For his camp Baldwin chose a site at the eastern end of the plain, just south of the village of Loe Dakka and close to the river, which made it convenient for watering the horses which needed an ample supply of water in the intense heat. The landing ground was laid out half a mile to the north-west of the main camp. That camp, however, was roughly 2,500 yards from the Khurd Khaibar Pass, the western exit or entrance to the plain, and some 1,200-1,300 yards from the hills to the south-west. Baldwin claimed that the site he chose was an exceptionally good one, with clear fields of fire, an absence of places where snipers could cause damage, and sufficiently far from the surrounding hills for them not to require picqueting.[13] (The sketch map which accompanied his letter of 17 May gives the distance to Somerset Hill (Stonehenge), for example, as 2,300 yards whereas the more accurate Survey of India map shows it to be rather more.) Baldwin was an experienced Frontier officer and he would have been well aware of the need to protect his camp by establishing picquets on commanding heights round it. But he was equally clear in his own mind that it would be wrong to fritter his cavalry force away in picqueting distant hills when he needed to keep it fit and ready for a further advance if necessary. His critics, led by Fowler, considered that the camp was open to attack and that the correct site was one farther west, in the lee of the hills through which the Khurd Khaibar passed, and from which the hills could be properly picqueted and the pass defended.

Fowler was, of course, speaking from the luxury of having an infantry brigade, and imminently two, available – in all, some 4,000 infantry – to do the necessary picqueting. Baldwin initially had approximately 1,500 cavalry and two battalions of infantry (roughly 1,000). Even so, Baldwin claimed to have identified the site subsequently chosen by Fowler but was unable to occupy it because of inadequate numbers.

In this welter of claims and counterclaims, it is difficult to reach a clear conclusion. The events of 16 May suggest that Baldwin's judgement as to the vulnerability of his chosen camp site was optimistic, and that the failure to guard the Khurd Khaibar was a serious misjudgement. But could he have done better with the force at his disposal? The arguments are at best finely balanced and impossible to judge at this distance in time from the place and the situation.

The third group of charges relates essentially to Baldwin's reconnaissance arrangements, and particularly to his failure to push a patrol through the Khurd Khaibar Pass to ascertain what, if anything, the enemy was doing. Here, perhaps, Baldwin was on his weakest ground. He was well aware that the basic function of cavalry is reconnaissance and, in the absence of information on the situation beyond the Pass, he was effectively blind. In his defence, he claimed to have sent out patrols which reached the summit of the western hills and reported nothing. Aeroplane reconnaissance also reported nothing stirring. But to claim, as he did, that he had received no written order to reconnoitre towards Basawal[14] but that he was about do so when Fowler intervened to order him to do so, lacks conviction.[15]

Taken as a whole, although there were grounds for criticising Baldwin's actions and judgement, the action taken against him seems harsh. Crocker's blunders seem more culpable, especially as they were repeated. But what really counts in the end is whether senior commanders retain or have lost faith in their juniors. It is here that we come back to Baldwin's belief that personalities played a major part in his treatment.

As we have seen, Baldwin had clashed with Tarver, Fowler's Chief Staff Officer, over the advance from Jamrud; Baldwin, in his own words, 'practically had to tell Tarver to "go to hell"'.[16] Clearly, Tarver would have reported the incident to Fowler with his own 'spin' on it. Fowler in turn reported unfavourably on the matter to Barrett. Baldwin believed that both Fowler and Barrett had got the wind up.[17] Whether that is true or not is impossible to determine at this distance, but it is not impossible that both commanders were anxious and tense over the advance into enemy territory. Neither had, of course, witnessed Baldwin's advance and their subsequent criticisms were clearly based upon Tarver's report. It is perhaps relevant that Barrett, Fowler and Tarver were not cavalrymen.

Fowler arrived at Dakka on 15 May and immediately criticised the choice of camp site and what he saw as Baldwin's failure to push reconnaissance patrols through the Khurd Khaibar. He gave immediate orders to shift the camp next day and for a patrol to be sent out towards Basawal at the same time.

Baldwin was relieved of his command the same evening and asked verbally for explanations. It is not clear whether this request was made to Baldwin on the 15th or 16th, but the presumption must be that it was made on the 16th, following his return to Peshawar and in the light of the Afghan advance and fighting on that day. It is important to note that Baldwin's dismissal took place before the Afghan attack, which suggests that Fowler's action was taken as a result of a loss of confidence rather than on the demonstrated results of Baldwin's 'mistakes'.

Baldwin furnished a full, written explanation to HQ North-West Frontier Force on 17 May.[18] Barrett seems to have reached a judgement almost immediately because on the following day (18 May) Baldwin received a handwritten note from the BGGS (Loch):

> I am to say that, in view of the explanation furnished by you, the Force Commander has decided not to recommend you being relieved of the command of your brigade.
>
> I am to say, however, that he is very far from being satisfied with the manner in which your advance on Dakka was carried out or with the manner in which you rested content with a few snipers holding the Khurd Khaibar Pass, taking no action to support your patrols and clear up the situation on and beyond the pass.'[19]

There was no reference to the choice of camp site. Nevertheless, the proposal to relieve Baldwin of his command and the 'facts' on which Barrett's decision was based, could only have come from Fowler, amplified possibly by conversation between Tarver and Loch. (HQ NWFF and HQ 1st Division shared adjacent headquarters in Peshawar.) What is significant about this letter is that, although not happy with Baldwin's performance, Barrett at that stage did not consider it a dismissable offence.

Eight days later, clearly on instructions from Army HQ Simla, Barrett submitted a memorandum for the Commander in Chief, reference No. 1118/50 GS, setting out very briefly what had happened at Dakka between 13 and 16 May. Barrett's comments on Baldwin were noticeably restrained:

It does not seem to have occurred to him [Baldwin] that if occupied by the enemy the ground below on our side would have been untenable. If the Cavalry Brigade had shewn more activity on the 14th and 15th, it does not seem probable that so large a hostile force could have collected in the neighbourhood without being detected.[20]

In contrast, however, Barrett is complimentary about Crocker's performance:

I consider that Brigadier-General Crocker, when faced with a difficult situation showed great resolution and confidence in the superiority of his troops, which he turned to good account.

His plan of attack was a very bold one, depending for its successful issue upon the timely arrival of the expected re-inforcements.

Less than a week after Barrett's memorandum had been received in Simla, Baldwin was dismissed from command of the 10th Cavalry Brigade. On 5 June the Chief of the General Staff replied to Barrett's memorandum, on behalf of the Commander in Chief. The CinC fully concurred in Barrett's criticisms of Baldwin's choice of camp site and his failure to secure the hills to the west and south-west of his camp, thus allowing the enemy to regroup and launch his attack on 16 May.[21] That was effectively the end of the matter for Baldwin. He stayed on in India for several months, seeking an interview with the CinC, which was eventually granted. It proved unsatisfactory. Monro was clearly not in full command of all the facts; at one point he was reported by Baldwin as saying: 'Well, Baldwin, I haven't the dossier with me but there was one thing I didn't think you were wise'.[22] This would seem to have been a reference to Baldwin's action in relieving the post at Sarwekai during the Mahsud campaign in 1917. Baldwin finally left India in 1920 and in effect was retired from the army.

He believed in retrospect that he was the victim of personal animosity on the part of Tarver, Fowler and Barrett. He had quarrelled with Tarver over the conduct of the advance from Jamrud and he believed that Tarver had got his own back. He believed that Fowler's hostility derived from the latter having had a quarrel with Baldwin's brother in France during the First World War. Barrett's attitude appeared to Baldwin to be based upon the view that he (Baldwin) had behaved rashly in 1917 when under Barrett's command in relieving Sarwekai. That, however, seems at odds with Barrett describing Baldwin in his annual confidential report for 1918 as 'a fine cavalry leader... Fit for advancement'.[23] That seems to lend some credence to Baldwin's view that Barrett had got the wind up over the reverse at Dakka on 16 May. Baldwin regarded Barrett subsequently as 'a nice man but was passed over practically in Mespot and afterwards came to India. In my opinion he was no tactician.'[24] Monro was categorised by Baldwin subsequently as utterly unfit to be Commander in Chief.[25]

How far these views were simply the bitterness of a disappointed man with a grievance is profitless to explore. It does seem that Baldwin had managed to make a number of important enemies – or perhaps rather that he lacked supporters among senior officers, despite his good annual reports. In the end it came down to the fact that he had lost the confidence of Fowler and Barrett. If that is so, then they were right to relieve him.[26] It may also be said that it was right also to relieve him of command of his own brigade because the authorities could hardly in logic retain an officer in a peace-time command who had proved unfit for an active service command.

Baldwin was perhaps unlucky. Others committed equal or greater mistakes and remained in command, and the suspicion must remain that the events on 16 May had given the authorities a scare and they had sought a scapegoat.

Notes

1 Secret telegram No. 283, 4 June 1919, CGS to General Northfront, copy in Baldwin papers (BP).

2 Crocker came under the operational command of the CinC India but under the War Office for personnel administration and disciplinary matters.

3 Baldwin had leapfrogged over Davies, who was at one time his Commanding Officer in the Guides.

4 Campbell, Peshawar,13 January 1918 – Baldwin to Adjutant General India (undated but apparently September 1919), Annex A, No. 9 – BP.

5 Ibid.

6 Ibid.

7 Baldwin to CGS India 20 June 1919, paragraph 4 – BP. This is borne out by de Burgh's recollection that Baldwin's orders were simply 'Go to Dakka' – de Burgh, op cit, letter dated 7 December 1922.

8 North-West Force Order No. 1, dated 12 May 1919 – copy in BP.

9 Baldwin to BGGS NW Force, 22 August 1919, paragraph 4 – BP.

10 Letter No. 0/1182/692 – Loch to Baldwin, 22 June 1919.

11 Baldwin to BGGS North-West Frontier Force 17 May 1919 – copy in BP.

12 Note by Baldwin dated 6 July 1928 in BP. The note is actually headed 'Note dated 5th July 1928' but it is initialled and dated 6 July 1928.

13 'The first camp selected was unsuitable' – Baldwin to BGGS North-West Frontier Force, dated 17 May 1919.

14 Basawal lies ten miles west of Dakka, on the main road to Jalalabad.

15 Baldwin to BGGS NWF Force, 17 May 1919, 3.

16 Private note by Baldwin written in 1929 – BP.

17 Private note by Baldwin – see Note 12 above.

18 See Note 11 above.

19 BGGS (Loch), NWFF, to Baldwin, dated Peshawar 18 May 1919 – copy in BP.

20 Barrett to War Section, Simla, dated 26 May 1919, reference no. 1118/50 GS/.

21 CGS India to Barrett dated 5 June 1919, reference no. 4608–1.
22 See Note 16 above.
23 See Note 5 above.
24 See Note 12 above.
25 Ibid.
26 The case of Admiral North, relieved of his command at Gibraltar in 1940 as a result of his superiors having lost confidence in him, is a relevant case.

VI

Continuing Operations through the Khyber: 17 May–8 August 1919

(Map 5)

On 18 May the main camp was moved two miles to the north-west, to a position close to the river, between the Robat fort and the Sherabad cantonment. A landing ground for the RAF had been constructed between the old and new camps but was now replaced by a second and bigger landing ground close to Robat fort. Aerial reconnaissance, limited though it was by the performance and unreliability of the BE2C aircraft available, now reduced the possibility of an unexpected Afghan attack. Attention could be given to protecting the camp on a more permanent basis, and to planning the next move.

A screen of ten semi-permanent picquets was established on the hills covering the western and southern approaches to the camp, extending from the Kabul river round to Somerset Hill (thus re-named the day after the battle); similar fixed picquets covered the road back to Landi Khana. The largest was 'Green Hill', at an elevation of 2,630 feet, at the point where the hills surrounding the camp began to trend north-westwards towards Girdi. It was built to hold 100 men. Roughly oval in shape, the dry-stone walls were 4ft 6in high, enabling a rifleman to stand and fire over it, with loopholes at ground level, to counter the usual tribal tactic of employing riflemen to keep down the heads of the defenders while an assault party of swordsmen or knife men crept up close and jumped over the wall. At each end of the sangar was a machine gun nest and in the centre a small 'keep' to contain stores, a first aid post, kitchen and signals equipment. Ground sheets were stretched inwards from the walls to provide some shelter. Intensely hot during the day, it was nevertheless cooler and relatively dust-free compared to the main camp. The other picquets, although smaller, followed the same general pattern.

Conditions in the main camp were uncomfortable. The site was ankle deep in dust, which rose in dense choking clouds to a height of fifty feet when stirred up, getting into everything – food, weapons, kit, stores, hair and nostrils. An attempt was made to reduce the nuisance by laying gravel or shale over the area but with only limited success. Equally unpleasant was the stench from rotting bodies of animals and humans. These corpses were gradually cleared away and burnt but the smell lingered on for weeks. With the stench came the flies.

To add to the discomfort, the troops were still existing on biscuit and tinned mutton which, in the prevailing heat, emerged from the tin in a semi-liquid condition. It could not be eaten cold and had to be rendered into stews and curries, assisted, when flour was available, by chapattis. An attempt to supply a cheese ration resulted in the cheese melting all over the floor of the lorry, producing 'an indifferent "Welsh Rarebit", garnished profusely with straw.'[1] Matters improved when the Mohmands from Lalpura, across the river, were allowed over to sell fruit and vegetables, eggs and chickens, and, in due course, sheep and goats. With the arrival of field bakery and butchery units the situation gradually became tolerable.[2] Medical stores were initially very short and there was no ice so that heatstroke cases could not be properly treated until, at a later stage, heat stroke stations were set up along the L of C.

Skeen now divided his troops into three forces:

Striking Force Cavalry (Striforcav)
Striking Force Infantry (Striforin)
Defsec (Line of Communication Troops).

Dakka itself was of no great strategic importance, but the advance there had had the significant benefit of keeping the Mohmands and Afridis separated. As far as the war was concerned, it was clear that the force could not rest immobile at Dakka, surrendering the initiative to the enemy. The obvious move now was an advance on Jalalabad, forty miles ahead, the provincial capital, the main military base for eastern Afghanistan and the only major town before Kabul. With the sobering experience of two previous invasions in mind, it was a move which required careful and anxious thought. Inevitably, it would suck in large numbers of additional troops and resources. Roos-Keppel, a pronounced Afghanaphobe, was in favour of annexing the whole of the province of Jalalabad to create a permanent barrier between the tribes on the British side of the Frontier and their Afghan tribal counterparts. In this he was supported by AHQ Simla and the CGS, and by the military staff at the India Office. Anglo-Afghan history suggested, however, that, far from creating stability on the Frontier, it would constitute a permanent running sore that would render the Frontier more unstable. For that reason, and because he thought that generosity promised greater dividends, Chelmsford rejected Roos-Keppel's view, but he accepted reluctantly that in the immediate circumstances there was no sensible alternative to an advance to occupy Jalalabad; as he told Montague: 'the only sound policy is to advance on Jalalabad... We shall by so doing threaten Kabul and force the withdrawal of enemy forces from our frontier.'[3]

Preparations were accordingly made to accumulate thirty days' supplies at Landi Kotal and Dakka to support an advance by the 1st Cavalry Brigade and the 1st Infantry Division. As always, the problem was a shortage of transport. Maffey, who had been appointed Chief Political Officer to the force and was at Dakka, wrote: 'The burden of everyone's song here is – Motor Transport, more Motor Transport. Is it coming from England? Can we commandeer private firms; transport from Calcutta and Bombay?'[4]

In addition to the Khyber, AHQ was having to cope with an invasion of Chitral, trouble with the Mohmands, a potentially serious threat in the Kurram, near-anarchy in Waziristan and demands for reinforcements in Baluchistan. In the Khyber, especially, supplies of grain, and chopped straw (*bhusa*) would be in short supply until the monsoon rains came in July. Foraging expeditions from Dakka brought in useful stores of grain from the surrounding Afghan villages at the expense of alienating the inhabitants who faced starvation themselves. It was already clear that the scarcity of transport would prevent the 16th Infantry Division, the designated Army reserve at Lahore, from deploying forward to release the 1st Division for the advance on Jalalabad. In face of these difficulties, the force at Dakka was not ready to advance until 26 May.[5] The actual forward movement was planned for 1 June.

In the meantime, the troops at Dakka were not short of activity. The local tribesmen had no cause to love the British. This was the third time that they had been invaded and on the two previous occasions they had suffered fairly severely both in the fighting and from the hardships which inevitably result from an invader's operations. Sniping, particularly at night, was therefore endemic. Reconnaissances beyond the camp almost invariably attracted opposition. The snipers were seldom caught and when they were, they stood a good chance of being released by the Political Officers in the interests of good relations. In these circumstances, regrettably, prisoners became a scarce commodity. The village of Girdi, in particular, appeared to be the source of much of the sniping and near it the mutilated bodies of troopers of the King's Dragoon Guards, killed in the withdrawal on 16 May, had been found. When a reconnaissance party visited Girdi on 30 May, it left behind it a number of booby traps using Mills grenades, which duly exploded with gratifying results for the troops.

The RAF had continued to bomb Afghan concentrations, including Jalalabad itself, where nearly a ton and a half of high explosive had been dropped in a single day, a very considerable feat and not without amusing results. Deputations of Afridis, present in the town to receive gifts of money and ammunition from the Amir in order to carry on the fight against the British, took advantage of the confusion to loot Jalalabad and decamp with their loot. One pilot, unable to see because of the dust, landed on what he thought was the landing strip, only to find himself on top of a dug-in tent, holding transport personnel.[6]

The advance on Jalalabad was destined not to take place. Five days before it was due to start (27 May), Nadir Shah opened fire on Thal in the Kurram. The transport intended for the Jalalabad advance was now diverted to enable 16 Division to reinforce Kohat and the Kurram. Four days later, on 31 May, the Amir asked officially for an armistice, to take effect from 3 June 1919.

It was not unwelcome on the British side. The longer supply lines which an advance deeper into Afghanistan would entail increased not only the resources required but increased the chances of a serious reverse. An advance deeper into Afghanistan would have involved the deployment of more and more resources to keep open the lines of communications and supply; longer lines of communications increased the risk of an unpleasant reverse. In 1879–80 a separate Khyber L of C force, under Major General Bright, equal in size to the main force at Kabul, had had to be created. Moreover, an advance to Jalalabad could not be an end in itself; its true strategic objective could only be the occupation of Kabul. Even the occupation of Kabul, as the British had found out in 1879, was not automatically the key to total victory. The Army in India had coped admirably with the conflict which had suddenly faced it at the beginning of May, but the strain was beginning to tell. Men and machines were beginning to run down, transport and supplies were beginning to exert an increasing strain and the CinC, Monro, was already warning that if the war continued much longer, resources available in India might be inadequate.[7] Montagu, in London, had heard disturbing rumours of 'another Messpot'.[8] Twice before, Afghanistan had proved to be India's Spanish ulcer. The request for an armistice came as a relief to both sides.[9]

But although the Afghan regular troops were no longer players in this theatre, the local Shinwari and Mohmand tribesmen continued to harass the troops at Dakka with constant sniping from the hills west and south west of the camp and from across the river. To try to put an end to this activity, Skeen set up two large-scale ambushes in broad daylight. A mile west of the Khurd Khaibar pass, the road passed between two small hills, 'Conical Hill' and 'Twin Peaks'. On 19 June a company of 1/9 Gurkhas established small picquets on the tops of these hills, concealing the remainder of the company behind the hills. The bait, 150 transport mules, then emerged to graze on the plain beyond the hills. A squadron of the King's Dragoon Guards now advanced to lure the enemy on. When the enemy took the bait and advanced in considerable numbers, the squadron retired, the mules were withdrawn to the rear, and the picquets retreated from the tops of the hills. When the tribesmen were within 200–300 yards, the picquets reoccupied their positions and the concealed platoons emerged, occupied the gap between the hills and poured in a heavy fire from rifles and machine guns. Totally surprised, the tribesmen lost ten to fifteen killed and the troops withdrew to camp without any casualties.

Infuriated, a large body of tribesmen, including Mohmands from across the river, gathered the same evening and planned an attack on the camp the following night (20 June). Forewarned, Skeen set a bigger and more sophisticated trap. At 1300 hours on the 20th, 1/9 Gurkha Rifles left camp and proceeded to occupy 'Conical Hill' and 'Twin Peaks' with three companies, leaving one company in reserve behind 'Twin Peaks'. Two sections of No. 8 Mountain Battery and a section of No. 285 Machine Gun Company then occupied the positions astride the narrow col between 'Twin Peaks' and 'Conical Hill', but out of sight of the enemy. Two companies of 1/15 Sikhs moved up in reserve behind 'Conical Hill' and finally two companies of the Somersets were deployed in reserve farther back along the road, towards the camp. The trap being set, the bait was now dangled. A squadron of the 33rd Cavalry with two sections of M Battery RHA moved across the col into the open country beyond. Coming under fire, the cavalry and guns effected what appeared to be a hasty retreat towards the river. Taking the bait again, the tribesmen came hurrying forward and were then heavily fired upon, by guns, machine guns and rifles, losing some thirty killed and twenty-five wounded; British casualties were one wounded.[10]

The tribesmen, despite their losses, were not cowed and a few days later a large party assembled on 'Crescent Hill', south of Girdi, where they were dispersed by some lucky shells from No. 77 Battery firing from near the main camp at a range of some two and a half miles.

The armistice made no difference to the discomfort of Dakka Force. The heat reached a peak and although the Kabul river rose because of the melting of the snows on the Hindu Kush and the water was icy cold, enjoyment of it was restricted by continual sniping, particularly from the Lalpura side. Sniping was supplemented by increasingly bold raids by the tribesmen. A raid in the small hours of 2 July on the Camel Camp netted the raiders a handful of beasts, and an even more daring raid in the early hours of the 9th resulted in the loss of a large tent from the RAF Landing Ground.[11] A week later, on the night of 15/16 July, the picquet on 'Black Hill', roughly 2,800 yards due west of the camp, was attacked. Meanwhile on the 12th the tribesmen had made a determined attack in daylight on a company of 2/1 Gurkhas picqueting the Khurd Khaibar pass. The attack was beaten off with the aid of artillery fire from the camp but the troops lost five killed and seven wounded and the tribesmen twenty-five killed and twenty-four wounded.[12]

An even more serious attempt was made on 23 July to ambush the Yorkshire Regiment when it moved out to picquet the hills overlooking Girdi. The tribesmen seized 'Twin Peaks' and two attempts by platoons of the Yorkshires failed to recapture it. A third attempt, reinforced by a company of 2/1 Gurkhas, also failed and it was only when the remainder of 2/1 Gurkhas, aided by fire from 77 Battery and No.8 Mountain Battery, joined in that 'Twin Peaks' was finally captured. Losses were severe on both sides, the British losing nine killed and fourteen wounded, while thirty dead were counted on the ground and their total casualties were estimated at 150.

Attempts were made to ambush the nightly snipers, sometimes with success. The most ambitious attempt to put an end to sniping was the construction of a 'flying bridge' across the Kabul river, due north of the camp, in order to place a permanent picquet on the Lalpura side to eliminate the Mohmand sniping from that side. Amid cheerful shouts of 'Go it, Oxford! Go it, Cambridge!', the troops were successfully ferried over on 25 July. A large country boat secured with a wire hawser was then moored to form the flying bridge. Sniping from Lalpura then largely ceased.[13]

The tedium and discomfort at Dakka was partially relieved on 24 July by the arrival of the Afghan delegates to the peace conference to be held at Rawalpindi. They were received by a Guard of Honour of the Somerset LI and accommodated in a tent with magnificent rugs and carpets specially sent up to Dakka for the purpose. The delegates left for Landi Kotal after only an hour and attempts by the Somersets' Officers Mess to 'acquire' a rug were unsuccessful, although some light-fingered soldier acquired the Afghan Finance Minister's hat.[14]

Peace was signed at Rawalpindi on 8 August and the chief Afghan delegate, Sirdar Ali Ahmed, reached Dakka on his return journey on 12 August, en route for Jalalabad where he happily informed a large public meeting that Afghanistan had won the war and that the British would now evacuate Dakka and pay compensation. As a piece of propaganda it was destined to run and run.

In fact, Dakka was not evacuated until 13 September; the Afghan representative did not appear on time, possibly deliberately, so that it was never formally handed back.[15] The whole force was back inside Indian territory a day later.

Notes

1 Molesworth, 75–6.
2 A particularly unpopular addition to the rations was an early form of dried potato known as Potato Meal, supplied in large tins which appeared to have contained paraffin originally. Visiting the Somersets' cook house, Fowler incautiously expressed a liking for the stuff and was promptly and courteously invited by the Cook Sergeant to 'take the whole ******* lot' – Molesworth, 86.
3 Viceroy to SofS, No. 698-S, 21 May 1919 – FPPS, August 1919, Part II, No. 253 (CP/55g).
4 Quoted in Heathcote,198.
5 *Third Afghan War*, 50.
6 Tents were normally erected over a specially dug pit, to give cooler ventilation and as a protection against sniping.
7 Quoted in Heathcote,198.

8   Montagu had heard stories about alleged deficiencies in the medical arrange-
    ments – L/MIL/17/5/4063. He was anxious lest there be a repeat of the medical
    scandals in Mesopotamia in 1915. Chelmsford reassured him that although
    some difficulties had been inevitable because of the suddenness of the war and
    the chaotic situation in India, the complaints were not on the whole justified.
    Nevertheless, Chelmsford took the precaution of ordering Malcolm Halley to
    carry out a thorough investigation after the war was over – a copy of his report
    is in MSS Eur D52319.

9   The gist of the armistice terms set out in a letter from the Viceroy to the Amir of
    2 June 1919 were as follows:
    (1) the Afghan troops to be withdrawn at least twenty miles from the nearest
        British troops;
    (2) British troops to remain where they were in Afghanistan but to undertake no
        further advance;
    (3) the RAF to have freedom of movement but would not bomb or machine gun;
        they would not be fired upon and any aircraft or crews shot down would be
        returned;
    (4) the Amir would discourage the tribes from hostilities and would give them
        no support or asylum.
    For the full terms, see *Third Afghan War*, 50–1.

10 Molesworth, 84–5 differs somewhat from the account in the official history
    (*Third Afghan War*, 73) – for example, in the positioning of 1/15 Sikhs. I have
    preferred the account in the official history which has a detailed plan.

11 Molesworth saw the tent literally 'walking' across the Landing Ground,
    lying down when the picquets opened fire, and then 'walking' off again
    – Molesworth, 89.

12 Estimates of tribal losses must be taken with considerable caution. The
    number of dead could sometimes be verified by a body count on the spot but
    figures for wounded, and by extension, deaths from wounds were impossible to
    verify. Reports by spies and tribal witnesses were seldom precise and frequently
    unreliable.

13 The picquet on the Lalpura side had the benefit of shade from trees and was
    popularly known as 'Phyllis Court', after the well-known riverside club at
    Henley.

14 Molesworth, 90–1.

15 Barrett to Army HQ, No. 0-1927-251, 13 September 1919 – L/P&S/10/870.

VII

Operations against the Afridis and Mohmands: 13 May–13 September 1919

(Map 3)

The successive Afghan defeats at Bagh and Dakka could have been expected to damp down any thoughts that the Mohmands and Afridi tribes on either side of the Khyber might have had of coming out in support of their co-religionists. But old habits die hard and, with what might seem curious timing, the British successes touched off a wave of insurrection among both tribes.

The catalyst was a dissident Afridi malik, Yar Muhammad, a turbulent character who, at one stage, had been rewarded by the Indian Government with the honorific title of 'Khan Bahadur', which he then lost for acts of rebellion. From his fort at Chora, seven miles south-west of Ali Masjid, he now sent a defiant letter to the Political Agent for the Khyber, announcing his intention of cutting communications through the Khyber. On 13 May he and his followers constructed a barricade of stones on the road which momentarily obstructed the advance of Baldwin's cavalry force. Parties of Afridis then began sniping at anything moving through the pass and cutting the telegraph wires at night.[1] More ominously, Afridis began to desert from the Khyber Rifles,[2] taking their rifles and ammunition with them. It was clearly essential to nip this incipient revolt in the bud before it spread and began seriously to threaten the operations at Dakka and beyond. The only regular British troops between Jamrud and Landi Kotal were two companies of 3/11 Gurkhas and a section of No.6 Mountain Battery, belonging to the 1st Division. In consequence, the Khyber was placed under the command of the 2nd Division,[3] and Brigadier General Christian,[4] commanding 6 Brigade of that division, was ordered to tidy up the situation. He had at his disposal two battalions of his own brigade (2/33 Punjabis and 2/8 Gurkhas [less 250 men]), 1/61 Pioneers from the divisional reserve and No.1 Armoured Motor Battery from the Peshawar internal security troops. It was not, on the face of it, a big enough force for the potentially difficult task it faced and it is curious that the other two battalions of 6 Brigade (1 Royal Sussex and 2/67 Punjabis) were not placed at his disposal from the start, especially since 1/61 Pioneers had had to be brought up from Ferozepore in the Punjab.

On the morning of 14 May the daily civilian convoy through the Khyber left Jamrud.[5] It included No.7 Combined Field Ambulance, and was escorted by 2/8 Gurkhas and reinforcements for 1st Division, consisting of 2/34 Sikh Pioneers (from the Corps Reserve at Sialkot, in the Punjab) and details for some of the other battalions in the Division. The route was to be picqueted by 1/61 Pioneers. Two miles from Ali Masjid the rear of the convoy was heavily fired on from the encircling heights and the rear guard had to be extricated by troops from Ali Masjid. The 2/34 Pioneers and the reinforcements for 3/11 Gurkhas continued on to Landi Kotal without incident, but it was considered prudent to detain the convoy itself, 2/8 Gurkhas and the remainder of the details at Ali Masjid overnight, where they were nevertheless heavily sniped.[6] Next morning the convoy, with the remaining details, moved on to Landi Kotal. Because of increasing doubts about the reliability of the Khyber Rifles, their two permanent posts between Jamrud and Ali Masjid were taken over by 2/33 Punjabis. A prominent feature 2,000 yards south of Ali Masjid, known as 'Orange Patch', which commanded the road through the pass at a distance of some 400 yards, was occupied by a picquet of 2/8 Gurkhas.[7]

For reasons which are not at all clear, that picquet was withdrawn the same evening (15 May). As it withdrew, it was attacked by a large body of Afridis, who had infiltrated along a scrub-covered valley below. It was quickly in difficulties and had to be extricated by a company of 2/33 Punjabis from Ali Masjid. The situation was clearly deteriorating, but as yet only some sections of the Afridis were involved.

Next morning (16 May), another convoy had to be passed through the Khyber and it was necessary to occupy 'Orange Patch' again. But it was now occupied by some 250 Afridis and a company of 2/33 Punjabis, with 200 men of 2/8 Gurkhas, was unable to make any progress. A reinforcement of 100 rifles of the 1 Royal Sussex and 100 rifles of 2/8 Gurkhas was rushed up from Peshawar in lorries and, with covering fire from a section of No. 6 Mountain Battery, the position was finally occupied at a cost of five dead and twenty-two wounded. It was a heavy price to pay for the blunder the previous evening. Next day the Khyber Rifles were paraded at Jamrud and told that any man who wished to leave could do so; out of 500, only 100 chose to stay. A corps with a long and proud history thus disappeared and the insurgents were the stronger by 400 trained men and their modem rifles.

The situation in the Khyber continued to deteriorate and a second brigade from 2 Division (4 Brigade, under Brigadier General Peebles[8]), was sent forward from Peshawar to clear up the situation. The Brigade[9] concentrated at Jamrud on the morning of 17 May and reached Ali Masjid, exhausted by the heat but without serious opposition, the same evening. With effectively two brigades deployed against them, Afridi agitation sharply diminished. The Afridis had in any case an alternative form of distraction in the activity developing in the Kurram Valley, on the southern borders of the Tirah.[10]

Eleven days after the declaration of war the situation on the main Khyber line of operations had stabilised. The 1st Division was concentrated on the line Landi Kotal–Landi Khana, with the advanced striking force, consisting of one and a half infantry brigades and a reinforced cavalry brigade, at Dakka. The lines of communication through the Khyber were held by one and a half infantry brigades from the 2nd Division, with reserves at Jamrud and Peshawar.

The move forward to Dakka meant that the Mohmands to the north of the Khyber were effectively separated from the Afridis to the south, but the logistic implications were formidable. Supply convoys had to be run almost every day through the Khyber to maintain the troops at Landi Kotal and beyond. There were three mechanical transport companies available; the remainder of the transport consisted of pony, mule, bullock and camel units, all of which had to carry their own fodder.

To ease the strain, work was started on an aerial ropeway from Jamrud to Ali Masjid and then on to Landi Kotal. It consisted of rope cables suspended from iron lattice pylons, the supplies being carried on open trays suspended from the cables every fifty yards – in effect a sort of horizontal, glorified ski-lift. Because it was impossible to guard every foot of the line, the tribesmen soon found places where the line ran close to the hillside, out of sight of a picquet, and proceeded to remove everything that came along. To vary the fun, the tribesmen learned to bind the ropes to the tops of the pylons with copper wire cut from the telephone and telegraph lines. When the powerful winding engines started up, the tops of the pylons, unable to withstand the strain, buckled and all activity had to stop until the pylons could be repaired or replaced. It is hard to think of a more vulnerable and expensive method of conveying supplies. Surprisingly, the supply line to the forward troops at Dakka was never seriously interrupted, an unexpected bonus for the British and a serious setback for the Afghans. The rapid deployment of strong forces to Ali Masjid and Landi Kotal played a powerful part, but it seems probable that the threatened loss of tribal allowances because of bad behaviour played an equally important part.[11]

Attention now shifted to the Mohmands. Scarcely less troublesome or formidable than the Afridis, they had been the subject of a blockade only three years earlier, and a barbed wire barrier, the 'Mohmand Blockade Line', was still in existence.[12] The Mohmands had yet to show their hand, but no one expected them to refrain from fishing in an increasingly troubled pool.

It was an obvious pool for the Afghans to stir and a small force of two battalions, with six guns, entered Mohmand country on 14 May.[13] By 19 May they had reached Galanai, eleven miles from the nearest point of the Blockade Line and less than twenty-five miles from Peshawar to the south-east. Few Mohmands had joined at this stage; the majority of the 4,000 tribesmen who had joined were Bajauris, from the territory immediately to the north of the Mohmand country.

There were insufficient troops now in Peshawar to handle this potentially serious threat so 44 Brigade, from 16 Division, in Army Reserve at Lahore, was ordered up to Peshawar by rail, arriving on the evening of 20 May.[14]

From the troops now available, two columns were formed to confront the Mohmand threat. The first column,[15] under the commander of 44 Brigade, was sent to Shabkadr, in the centre of the Mohmand Blockade Line, to where it was believed the Afghans were headed. The second column[16] went to Michni, at the southern end of the Line. Beyond burning some empty towers on the Line, the tribesmen showed little activity and soon dispersed when their food ran out. The Afghan regulars then retired to their original bases on the Kunar river, sixty miles from Peshawar. Both columns were withdrawn on 25 May and were back in Peshawar by the 30th. That was effectively the end of a serious Mohmand threat and of Afghan hopes of a major tribal uprising north of the Kabul river. The rapid deployment of troops along the Khyber line had successfully kept Afridis and Mohmands apart and, left on their own, the Mohmands were clearly not prepared to try conclusions again so soon after the blockade three years earlier.

It was not the end of trouble on the Khyber line. Between Landi Khana and Dakka, two systems of picqueting were in force to protect the road. From Dakka back to a point near Haft Chah, Dakka Force maintained a system of permanent picquets; from Haft Chah back to Landi Khana 2 Infantry Brigade operated a system of temporary picquets which were withdrawn when the daily convoy had passed. It was a system very liable to attack. On 24 May the battalion picqueting the road from Landi Khana to Haft Chah was 2 North Staffordshire Regiment, one of the eight Regular battalions left in India in 1914. The first four picquets were posted without trouble but the fifth picquet, west of the road, was suddenly fired upon as the leading men approached the crest of the hill. Four men were killed or mortally wounded instantly and a fifth seriously wounded. The remainder of the picquet, assisted by a section from the covering reserve below on the road, counter-attacked and seized the crest. The tribesmen then retired, coming under fire from the picquet already in position to the south. They finally sought shelter on a high hill from which they were evicted by shells from a section of No.6 Mountain Battery which had been despatched from Landi Khana as soon as the trouble was reported. British losses were four killed and two wounded; the tribesmen, a party of Shinwaris under the notorious Zar Shah, were believed to have lost sixteen killed and wounded. It was a classic example of the ability of the tribesmen to spot a fleeting tactical opportunity; but it was also a good example of well-trained troops responding quickly and skilfully. Thereafter the system of temporary picqueting was abandoned and replaced by permanent picquets. There was no further trouble on this section of the road apart from occasional sniping.

Even more than the Mohmands, the British authorities feared a major uprising by the Afridis. Perhaps the largest fighting tribe on the Frontier and, apart from the Mahsuds, the most formidable, their almost impenetrable heartland of the Tirah hid within it some of the most beautiful country on the Frontier. As a tribe they were more prosperous than most; they found ready employment in the Army and Khyber Rifles and as traders in Peshawar and elsewhere, and much of the Tirah was very fertile. No one assumed that the bitter fighting in 1897–8, in which the Tirah had been penetrated for the first and only time by the British, had tamed the Afridis or that they had lost their predatory characteristics. The failure of Afghan attempts to stir up open rebellion on a large scale and the absence of serious trouble on the line of communication from Jamrud to Landi Kotal were therefore very significant bonuses for the Indian Government.

It was too much to expect that this situation could last indefinitely. Unrest among the tribes had many strands – the defeat of Turkey, the unrest in India proper, a feeling that the British were not as firmly seated as they had been, an appreciation of the weakness of the Indian Army in terms of training and experience, ties of kinship with the Afghans, and, of more immediate consequence, the virtual disbandment of the Khyber Rifles which threw up 400 trained Afridi ex-soldiers, armed with modern rifles and large stocks of ammunition – all of which reinforced their natural aggressiveness based on cultural history and a spirit of mischief. For an Afridi or Mohmand probably nothing surpassed the satisfaction of scoring off the troops.

Throughout June and the early part of July 1919 there were signs of growing unrest among the Afridis. Its focus appeared to be Chora, the home of Yar Muhammed, some seven miles south-west of Ali Masjid. In the middle of July large bodies of Afridis were gathering in the Bazar valley farther south and it was concluded that some sort of attack on the road in the vicinity of Ali Masjid was being planned. On 17 July Major General Dobell, commanding 2nd Division which was responsible for the Khyber, took the serious step of closing the pass to all animal convoys. Mechanical transport was allowed to proceed only after armoured cars had patrolled the road from Jamrud to Ali Masjid and pronounced it clear. These precautions were just in time because next day the Afridis launched a concerted attack on the picquet posts between Bagiari, just inside the Pass, and Ali Masjid, about four miles farther on,[17] with the obvious aim of completely blocking the pass and cutting the British line of communication to Landi Kotal and Dakka. These posts were manned by 2/67 Punjabis from 6 Infantry Brigade.[18]

The Afridi plan was cleverly worked out and wrong-footed the British brigade commander at Ali Masjid. At about 0630 parties of tribesmen began to lay down a heavy fire on the picquet posts around Fort Maude and Shagai, between two and two and three-quarter miles as the crow flies from Ali Masjid but perhaps four miles by road. Under cover of this fire, a party of 300–400 tribesmen, including many in the uniform of the Khyber Rifles, attacked the 'Barley Hill' picquet, 1,000 yards south of Fort Maude, held by an Indian officer, and thirty men of 2/67 Punjabis. The attack was beaten off and at about 0800 the officer commanding at Fort Maude took the opportunity of a lull to send up reinforcements of men and ammunition. The OC 2/67 Punjabis, on a tour of inspection, had by now reached Ali Masjid and immediately asked Brigade for artillery support before hurrying back to Shagai by which time all the picquets from Shagai to 'Orange Patch' were under rifle fire and more Afridis were moving down the valley from Chora.

While there was no shortage of units at Ali Masjid, the topography made for difficulties. The main body of troops, comprising 1 Royal Sussex, 2/33 Punjabis, one company 1 South Lancashire Regiment, two companies 2/8 Gurkhas and No.3 Mountain Artillery Brigade (Nos. 3 and 4 Batteries) were located on a flat piece of ground about three quarters of a mile south of Brigade HQ in Ali Masjid fort. A telephone line connected the two but this was frequently cut at night and had to be repaired each morning. It was not until 0940 that orders were issued for two guns of No. 4 Mountain Battery, escorted by a company of the Royal Sussex, to move to 'Orange Patch' and for two guns of No.3 Battery, escorted by a company of the South Lancashires, to move down to Shagai. The two detachments moved off at about 1030 hours. The two guns of No.4 Battery opened fire from 'Orange Patch' at about 1100 at a range of 4,000 yards, but the gunners had difficulty in distinguishing friend from foe since many of the attackers on Barley Hill were in the khaki uniforms of the Khyber Rifles. Fire was therefore suspended after only a few rounds.

The guns of No. 3 Battery came into action at Shagai at 1145, just too late to prevent the 'Barley Hill' picquet from being overwhelmed by the attackers; seventeen men and thirty rifles were captured. By good fortune the first round fired from Shagai scattered the tribesmen and the seventeen prisoners managed to escape. Nevertheless, 'Barley Hill' had been taken – from there rifle fire could be brought down on Fort Maude, less than 1,000 yards away, on the road through the pass. Accordingly, at about 1430, 200 men of the Royal Sussex and 2/8 Gurkhas, with two machine guns, were despatched to Fort Maude in the lorries of a returning convoy from Landi Kotal, and they recaptured 'Barley Hill' later that afternoon. But honours remained with the tribesmen. The British response had been slow and fumbling. It would appear that the British commander had expected the main attack to concentrate on 'Orange Patch' and it was some time before it was realised that 'Barley Hill' was the main focus. Because No. 3 Mountain Brigade near Ali Masjid was within range of 'Barley Hill', the guns could have opened fire from there rather than from 'Orange Patch' and Shagai and it may be that the separation of the main Brigade HQ at Ali Masjid from the Mountain Brigade HQ hindered clear communication. Finally, the skill with which the tribesmen, who numbered in total about 6,000, laid down covering fire on all the posts from Ali Masjid southwards undoubtedly distracted the British command. On a lighter note, the ex-Khyber Rifles who captured 'Barley Hill' used a captured heliograph to call up Ali Masjid to announce their success. Casualties on the British side were nine killed and twenty-five injured; tribal casualties were estimated at fifty killed and sixty wounded, but these figures may over-estimate their losses.

Still full of fight, the tribesmen attacked a number of picquets, north, south and west of Ali Masjid, the same evening. The barbed wire surrounding the 'Orange Patch' picquet, held by thirty men of the Royal Sussex, was penetrated three times, but the attackers were expelled with bayonets and grenades. Its loss would have been a serious tactical blow as it commanded the road at a distance of only 600 yards.

On the following day (19 July) a strong colunm[19] under Major General Shepherd,[20] commanding 5 Infantry Brigade of 2nd Division, left Jamrud with orders to unblock the pass. It reached Fort Maude at 0900 without serious incident and convoys were then able to flow freely. Ali Masjid was reinforced with No. 60 Battery RGA, equipped with tractor-drawn 6 inch howitzers (the heaviest guns seen on the Frontier), the remainder of the South Lancashires, 2/35 Sikhs and No. 11 Company 1st (Bengal) Sappers and Miners.

There were no further attacks on the picquets in this area but Yar Muhammed of Chora, the primary source of all the trouble within the pass, was owed a reckoning. In the meantime, Afridis from the eastern Tirah, facing Peshawar, had seized the opportunity of the general unrest to raid deep into the more settled area of the Kajuri plain, south-west of Peshawar. The raiding continued throughout May and June 1919 and was not noticeably affected by the armistice with the Afghans which came into effect on 3 June.

The Kajuri plain was a favourite hunting ground of Afridi gangs. Roughly eighteen miles square and lying at the base of the hills forming the eastern wall of the Tirah, there were no roads across it and its numerous dry, shallow watercourses provided excellent cover for raiders intent on penetrating the gardens and orchards on the western outskirts of Peshawar city. A successful minor operation on the night of 6/7 June 1919, against the village of Badber, due south of the city, on the road to Kohat, netted a number of bad characters and weapons but the Afridis simply shifted their base of operations to the Besai ridge, a spur running out from the eastern Tirah hills into the Kajuri plain, roughly south of Jamrud. Any form of frontal pressure simply forced the raiders back into the Tirah where they could not be followed.

The plan decided upon was therefore to deploy an infantry cordon on a six-mile line roughly south from Kacha Garhi as far as the Bara river, and then use the cavalry operating on a parallel line south of Jamrud to drive the raiders into the arms of the infantry. The cavalry consisted of the 23rd Cavalry (Frontier Force), the 30th Lancers, a squadron each of the 12th and 17th Cavalry and two armoured car batteries; the infantry comprised 3/39 Garwhal Rifles, the 1 South Lancashires, 2/35 Sikhs and 3/5 Gurkhas. A reserve of 2/4 Border Regiment, an armoured car battery and three sections of field artillery was located at Bara fort, in the south-eastern corner of the area, on the direct road back to Peshawar. The troops took up their planned positions without serious difficulty early on the morning of 21 May, but the cavalry drive netted only thirty men, who claimed to be members of the South Waziristan Militia returning from leave. Frustratingly, a large body of 200–300 armed men was seen south of the Bara river, just outside the area of the drive. It was engaged with machine gun fire at a range of 1,500 yards by the armoured car battery at Bara fort, but the raiders rapidly went to ground in the network of dry watercourses and were not seen again. The area in which the large gang was seen had originally been included in the operational plan, but had been excluded at the request of the Chief Commissioner (Roos-Keppel).

The raiding went on unchecked and in July reconnaissance located a body of 500 tribesmen on Karawal Hill, due west of Bara fort, just outside the area of the 'drive' in May. The continued presence of this party led to a decision to attack it on 22 July. The two columns employed, from Kacha Garhi and Bara, comprised the 30th Lancers, 23rd Cavalry, two armoured car batteries, 3/5 Gurkhas, two companies 2/35 Sikhs and two sections of field artillery. The cavalry, moving in from north, east and south, managed ultimately to clear the hill but failed to trap the tribesmen. In their retreat, they came under fire from the armoured cars who had managed to get into position three miles west of Karawal. Casualties were negligible, but the operation had not been particularly successful. Nevertheless, raiding gradually died away, largely because the Afridis were anxious to get home to plough their fields in readiness for the spring sowing.

The long-delayed attack on Yar Muhammad took place on 18 September after careful preparation.[21] Chora fort lay in a deep valley surrounded by mountains and the approach required careful planning, not least because any penetration of the Tirah risked major trouble with the Afridis. Moreover, any mishap in that country could easily lead to disaster against a tactically sophisticated foe like the Afridi. The use of heavy artillery to reduce the fort necessitated the construction of a road three miles long, which followed the alignment of a mule track from the Khyber river, a mile south of Ali Masjid, south-westwards to a point a mile from the Chora Kandao (Pass), which was itself about two and a half miles from Chora fort. From this point the 6 inch and 4.5 inch howitzers would bombard the fort at ranges of between 6,500 and 7,500 yards. The preparation of this road in itself militated against surprise other than in the timing.

The whole operation was under the command of Brigadier General G A H Beatty,[22] commanding 6 Brigade of 2nd Division. The force employed comprised an advanced guard of No. 4 Mountain Battery RGA (minus one section), 222 Machine Gun Company (minus two sections); a main body comprising 1 Royal Sussex (minus two companies), 2/67 Punjabis, the remaining section of No. 4 Mountain Battery, a section of No. 222 Machine Gun Company, No. 11 Field Company RE, two sections of 74 Battery RFA (4.5 inch howitzers), and miscellaneous details; and a rear guard of the South Lancashires, behind which came the two tractor-drawn 6 inch howitzers of 60 (Heavy) Battery RGA, escorted by a platoon of 2/33 Punjabis. A flank guard of 2/33 Punjabis protected the flanks of the column.

The operation was planned in four phases:

Phase 1 concentration of the force one mile east of the Chora Kandao Pass;
Phase 2 approach march and bombardment, timed for 0830;
Phase 3 occupation of Chora by 0945;
Phase 4 destruction of fort at 1400, and retirement.

The RAF was to bomb the fort at 0600 and then commence registration of the target for the artillery at 0615. It was expected that the principal problems would be the passage of the heavy guns and the withdrawal in the afternoon. In fact, the operation passed off without any serious hitch.

The force moved out at midnight on 17 September and by 0345 the advanced guard had reached the point from which the howitzers were to open fire. Pushing on, it quickly dispersed a small body of tribesmen on the Chora Kandao and by 0600 had reached the hamlet of Sara Garhi one and a half miles east of Chora. No.4 Mountain Battery now opened fire on Sara Garhi and Chora, while the RAF bombed Chora fort. The bombing had little effect and one aircraft was shot down and the pilot and observer captured. The heavy guns, as expected, had difficulties getting over the road and one 4.5 inch howitzer broke down, but the remainder were apparently in position by 0645. They were scheduled to open fire at 0830, the 6 inch howitzers from a position about a mile short of the Chora Kandao, at a range of 7,600 yards, the 4.5 inch howitzers at 6,600 yards and the 3.7 inch guns of 4 Mountain Battery, from a position near the village of Sara Garhi, at a mere 1,500 yards.

Sara Garhi was captured at 0720 and the guns opened fire ten minutes early at 0820.[23] Despite the failure of the aircraft's radio in assisting registration of the artillery targets, the bombardment seems to have been extremely effective, the two 6 inch scoring eleven direct hits. The fort was occupied at 0945 and work began at once on laying the demolition charges, the fort being protected on all four sides by the infantry. The charges were exploded at 1400 but twelve failed to go off because of defective fuses. The replacement charges were exploded at 1530, completely levelling the fort. The retirement began immediately and was not followed up by the tribesmen. By 1815 all troops had crossed the Chora Kandao; the whole force was back within the outposts of Ali Masjid by 2200. Casualties totalled six killed and seven wounded, the majority of these occurring when a party of Indian soldiers and followers was examining an unexploded RAF bomb.

The success of the operation was due to careful reconnaissance and planning. The successful deployment of the 6 inch howitzers was particularly noteworthy.

Officially the war had been over for some weeks but the destruction of Chora can reasonably be regarded as effectively the end of the campaign along the Khyber line.

Notes

1 The Afridis had a very long history of turbulence and aggression. Their mountain fastness of the Tirah, immediately south of the Khyber Pass, had only once been fully penetrated by British troops, in 1897–8, in a campaign of exceptional severity, in which honours were by no means all on the British side – *Overseas and Frontier Expeditions*, Vol. II. For a very useful general account, see Michael Barthorpe, *The Frontier Ablaze* (London, 1998).

2 The Khyber Rifles, a full-time militia, raised in 1878, during the Second Afghan War, as the Khyber Jezailchees, mainly from Afridis. It remained loyal during the Tirah campaign of 1897–8 and the 1908 expedition against the Zakka Khel (Pass) Afridis.

3 HQ at Rawalpindi, under the command of Major General Sir C M Dobell.

4 Gerard Christian.

5 Jamrud to Ali Masjid is eight miles, and to Landi Kotal a further ten miles. The convoy would normally have gone straight through to Landi Kotal, the western exit from the pass.

6 The convoy would have camped on the floor of the pass which is some 400 feet below the fort of Ali Masjid.

7 Orange Patch Ridge was subsequently re-named Sussex Ridge and is so shown on the map in *Third Afghan War*, opposite page 43. Third Afghan War, 43 describes it as south-west of Ali Masjid but it is actually due south.

8 Evelyn Chiapini Peebles.

9 1 Durham Light Infantry, 1/33 Punjabis, 40 Pathans (the famous '40 Thieves'), 2/54 Sikhs, No. 2 Mountain Artillery Brigade RGA (minus two sections), a battery of No. 1 Armoured Motor Brigade and one section No. 222 Machine Gun Company.

10 See Chapter VIII.

11 Monetary allowances were paid to the tribes, ostensibly to keep the pass open, in reality, as a form of *danegeld*.

12 It consisted of a double apron of barbed wire, some fifteen miles long, with watch towers at 400-yard intervals. It was manned by the Mohmand Militia, created for the purpose in 1917.

13 One battalion, the Turki, was considered to be in a fair state of training and discipline; the other, the Wardaki, was regarded as little more than a tribal rabble. The whole force was estimated at not more than 1,200. *Third Afghan War*, 43.

14 An interesting illustration of the strategic value of the Indian railway system as Lahore is roughly 250 miles from Peshawar. 44 Brigade comprised 1/1 Kent Regiment (a Territorial Army battalion), 1/30 and 2/30 Punjabis and 1/6 Jats.

15 Comprising 44th Brigade minus one battalion (1/1 Kent Regiment, 1/30 and 2/30 Punjabis), one squadron 23rd Cavalry F.F., half squadron 30th Lancers, two armoured car batteries and 16th Brigade RFA (minus 1 battery). Note: *Third Afghan War*, 48 refers to the 19th Lancers, instead of the 30th; the 19th Lancers did not take part in the war.

16 Half squadron 30th Lancers, 1/6 Jat Light Infantry (from 44 Brigade) and two machine gun sections.

17 The scale on Map 2 in *Third Afghan War* is inaccurate by a factor of about four.

18 These posts were of two kinds: brick-built blockhouses, of which there were six, including Fort Maude, Shahgai, Ali Masjid and Sam Browne, and open sangar-type posts, protected by barbed wire, of which there were nine. (Forts Maude and Sam Browne were named after prominent generals of the second Afghan war.)

19 1 squadron 30th Lancers, 74 Field Battery RFA (minus one section), No. 222 Machine Gun Company, No. 1 Armoured Car Battery, 1/61 Pioneers, 2/61 Pioneers (minus two companies) and 3/39 Garwhal Rifles.

20 Seymour Hubert Shepherd.

21 *Report by Major General Sir C. M. Dobell, Commanding 2nd (Rawalpindi) Division, on the operations on 18th September 1919, resulting in the destruction of Chora Fort, 20th September 1919* – L/MIL/17/14/7.

22 Guy Archibald Hastings Beatty.

23 Dobell's Report says 0820; the official history says 0840. If the guns were in position by 0645, then it seems more likely that they would open fire early rather than late. The point is not important.

VIII

The Kurram

(Map 6)

The Afghan invasion through the Khyber posed the most direct threat to Peshawar and the North-West Frontier Province. It brought with it the spectre of a large-scale rising of the Mohmands and Afridis such as had stretched British resources to the full in 1897–8. An almost equally potent threat lay in an Afghan attack though the Kurram.

From the base of the valley at Thal the Kurram Valley points like a giant thumb north-westwards towards Kabul. From the head of the valley, sixty-five-miles from Thal, a relatively easy road ran over the Peiwar Kotal and the Shutagardan Pass to Kushi, whence Kabul was only forty-four easy miles away, along the Logar Valley. This was the route taken by Roberts in September 1879 in his advance on Kabul.[1] Conversely, an Afghan invader reaching Thal then had an easy road eastwards along the Miranzai Valley to the important post of Kohat from where it was only thirty miles over an easy route to Peshawar. The Kurram was inhabited by the Turis, separated from the other neighbouring Pathan tribes by the fact that they were Shiah, not Sunni, Muslims.[2] In consequence, they had suffered a good deal at the hands of Kabul and in 1860 had petitioned to be taken under British rule. The Kurram came under British administration in 1879 as a consequence of the Treaty of Gandamak, under which the British paid over any net surplus revenue to the Afghan Government. It was quietly annexed in 1887.

The administrative centre of Northern (or Upper) Kurram was at Parachinar, a cantonment built by Roberts in 1879, fifteen miles west of the Peiwar Kotal. In 1919 it was the headquarters of the Kurram Militia, formed in 1892 and composed mainly of Turis. It was similar in organisation, function and equipment to the other militias, with a strength of 1,346, including two troops of mounted infantry and two obsolescent 10-pounder mountain guns carried on mules or camels.[3]

The great stronghold of the Afridis, the Tirah, lay north of the Kohat–Thal road and east of the Kurram valley itself. The exceptionally predatory Zaimukhts occupied the angle just north of Thal, the administrative centre of Lower Kurram. West of the Kurram, on its flank, lay the Afghan province of Khost, with its capital, Matun, occupied briefly by Roberts in the spring of 1879. The Kurram was therefore vulnerable to an Afghan attack from two directions – from Khost, or from Kabul, over the Peiwar Kotal. To that had to be added the threat, from the Tirah Afridis and from the so-called Pass Afridis, who controlled the Kohat Pass over which the road from Peshawar to Kohat ran. Of at least equal importance was the fact that Thal was only twenty-five miles north of Bannu, the administrative capital of northern Waziristan. An Afghan thrust from Khost might therefore link up with a rising of the Tochi Wazirs; it was known from intelligence sources that Amanullah was aiming at such a combination.

The Afghan commander in Khost was Nadir Shah, the former Commander in Chief of the Afghan Army. He was an energetic, aggressive soldier and he had something to prove as a result of his exile from the seat of power at Kabul. In due course, he would become Amir. He was reported to have at his disposal sixteen battalions of infantry, two battalions of pioneers, four regiments of cavalry and some sixty guns.[4] It was the most compact and formidable of the Afghan armies. Its main base was at Ghazni, with a detachment on the Peiwar Kotal and the main striking force at Matun, just over the border from the Kurram, on the Kaitu river which flowed due east to join the Kurram river, just south of Thal. To oppose this threat, Major General Eustace, commanding Kohat Area and L of C, which included the Kurram, had available four battalions of infantry, a regiment of cavalry, three armoured cars and a mountain battery, together with the Kurram Militia.[5]

From Khost, Nadir Shah had three possible lines of attack – over the Peiwar Kotal and down the Kurram valley to Thal, due west from Matun direct on Thal, and south-east to the Tochi valley and then on to Bannu. From Thal he could move east to Kohat and then north on Peshawar by which time he might expect to have the Afridis with him. From Bannu he could move eastwards towards the Indus at Dera Ismail Khan or northwards again on Thal; either way he could then expect to have the Wazirs and probably the Mahsuds with him.

Given these options of the Afghan commander, the textbook British strategy would have been an offensive-defence in the form of a forestalling attack on Matun. There were alas not enough troops and transport immediately available for this strategy to be followed. (From subsequent events, one might also doubt whether Eustace was the man to carry it out.) Failing an offensive against Khost, there was little option but to carry out an aggressive defence based on interior lines. Eustace therefore reinforced Parachinar with a battalion of infantry and a squadron of the 37th Lancers, while relying on the Kurram Militia to observe Afghan movements and to try to identify the direction of an Afghan thrust.

In the fortnight after British mobilisation, a further three battalions arrived at Kohat, together with HQ 60th Infantry Brigade from Army

Reserve at Ambala and No. 22 Motor Machine Gun Battery from Rawalpindi. On 22 May the troops were distributed as follows:

at Parachinar
   one squadron 37th Lancers
   two sections (four guns) 28 Mountain Battery
   No. 22 Motor Machine Gun Battery
   1/57 Rifles
   3rd Guides Infantry;
at Thal
   HQ 60 Infantry Brigade
   one squadron 37th Lancers
   one section 28 Mountain Battery
   1/109 Infantry
   3/9 Gurkhas;
between Thal and Kohat
   3/8 Gurkhas;
at Kohat
   two squadrons 37th Lancers
   23 Mountain Battery
   1/151 Sikh Infantry
   2/26Punjabis
   4/39 Garwhal Rifles.

The forces in the Upper Kurram, at Parachinar, were under the command of Brigadier General Fagan, while Eustace, based at Thal, commanded directly the troops in Lower Kurram.

Whether Eustace was right to concentrate roughly a third of his troops as far forward as Parachinar is a matter of judgement. The Peiwar Kotal was perhaps the least likely Afghan line of attack and an Afghan thrust eastwards from Khost on Thal would cut Eustace's force in half. If the Afghans did invade by the Peiwar Kotal, there was time and space in which to move troops up from Thal. On the other hand, the effect on the surrounding tribes of being seen in effect to give up defending the Upper Kurram might well have been out of all proportion to the tactical gain.

Major Dodd,[6] commanding the Kurram Militia, had, as early as 2 May, established a picquet at Ghundi Khel east of the Peiwar Kotal, to watch that pass, and another at Shinghak, on the Kurram river, to watch any movement from Khost.[7]

On 14 May information was received that Nadir Shah had arrived at Ali Khel, between the Shutagardan and the Peiwar Kotal, and Dodd moved out from Parachinar with 450 Militia infantry, fifty mounted infantry and two guns, and camped near the Peiwar. The rumour was false, but Dodd remained close to the pass. The post at Lakka Tiga, on the border with

Khost, about half way down the Kurram valley, was also reported under threat and a force of 200 Militia infantry and sixty mounted infantry, under Captain Champion,[8] moved there but found no signs of Afghan movement. These rumours may have been part of an Afghan deception plan, but they are more likely to have been stimulated by Nadir Shah's movements towards Matun.

On 22 May Nadir Shah left Matun and moved south-eastwards, down the Kaitu river, apparently in the general direction of Bannu. It was a clever move because it still left unclear whether his objective was actually Bannu or whether he intended to branch north-east towards Thal. Either way, his move caused excitement among the Wazirs, which was no doubt a part of the Afghan plan. Two days later (24 May) it was learned that he was moving on Spinwam, a North Waziristan Militia post, roughly half way between Bannu and Thal. His ultimate intention was still unclear, but Spinwam was evacuated on 25 May and the garrison withdrawn to the Tochi Valley, closely followed up by Wazirs in large numbers. Concurrently, the Militia posts along the Tochi Valley, west of Miran-Shah, were withdrawn to the latter place (see Chapter XV). The news of Nadir Shah's movements and the withdrawal of the posts created unreliability among the Wazirs in the North Waziristan Militia and 150 were found to have deserted with their weapons during the withdrawal. (Subsequent developments in both South and North Waziristan are dealt with in Part Two of this book.)

Nadir Shah occupied Spinwam on 25 May with 3,000 Afghan infantry, nine guns and a large body of tribesmen from Khost and Waziristan. He was equidistant now from Thal and Bannu. From Bannu a small force of all arms moved out to Kurram Garhi, four miles from Bannu, to watch the exit of the Kaitu river; to the north Eustace reinforced the garrison at Thal with 1/151 Sikhs, 4/39 Garwhalis and a section of 23rd Mountain Battery, bringing the garrison there up to four infantry battalions, four guns, two 3-inch trench mortars, a squadron of cavalry and a company of 1st (Bengal) Sappers and Miners. Eustace himself took command at Thal and an inner and an outer line of defences was constructed, the inner line covering the fort, railway station and Civil Rest House, the outer line forming a perimeter at a distance of very roughly 1,200 yards round the post.[9] In concentrating on Thal, Eustace was deliberately leaving Kohat virtually unprotected. It was a slightly risky strategy, but in the circumstances the correct one since Eustace could reasonably expect Kohat to be reinforced from Peshawar and the Army Reserve.

Thal lies at the confluence of three streams – the Kurram river, coming in from the north-west, the Sangroba, coming in from the north-east, and the Ishkalai, coming in parallel to the Sangroba, some 1,800 yards farther south. The military post, containing the fort, the railway station and the Civil Rest House, lies on a plateau at the confluence of the Sangroba and Ishkalai Nala about 100 feet above them. Almost opposite, on the north

bank of the Sangroba, was a Militia fort and the village of Thal, about
half a mile from the main post. The railway and the road to Kohat run out
north-eastwards, following the line of the Ishkalai Nala. To the west, Thal
is dominated by an isolated hill, Khapianga, 800 feet above the Kurram
river, while to the north, the peak of Khadimakh marks the border with
the Zaimukhts. The water supply for the post came from a well in the
Sangroba Nala, from where the water was pumped up to the post some
300 yards away. Clearly, the water supply was a potentially critical weakness in the defence, particularly in the hot weather.

Nadir Shah ended all uncertainty by appearing before Thal on the
morning of 27 May, setting up his HQ and main camp at Yusaf Khel, on the
Kurram river, some three miles from Thal. His artillery, consisting of two
10cm howitzers and a number of 7.5cm guns, opened fire the same day
from positions on Khapianga and Yusuf Khel. Thal village was occupied
by Afghan infantry, while hostile tribesmen occupied the lower slopes of
Khadimakh, as well as hills due south of Thal. He had achieved a stunning
strategic surprise; he had cut off the garrison in the Upper Kurram, he had
forced the evacuation of the western half of Waziristan and he now had
the opportunity to overwhelm Thal before reinforcements could arrive,
having a local superiority in artillery and men over Eustace.

The Afghan 10cm howitzers, firing at ranges of up to 5,500 yards, significantly outranged Eustace's mountain guns and proved both accurate
and destructive. Attempts by two aircraft of the RAF to bomb the Afghan
artillery positions were only temporarily effective. On the night of 28/29
May the Militia fort on the north bank of the Sangroba was abandoned
and the enemy, occupying it, was now in a position to threaten the water
supply. As an emergency measure, large pits were dug and lined with tar-
paulins to act as reservoirs. The following night (29/30 May) the Afghans
attacked the picquet on 'Picquet Hill', 1,500 yards south of the fort, on the
edge of the plateau. It was beaten back by the garrison of 1/109 Infantry,
but the following morning (30 May) the Afghans managed to place a
7.5cm gun on a height 3,000 yards due south. While not completely cut off
– the railway and the Kohat road were still open, even if threatened – the
garrison at Thal was in a perilous situation. The Afghan artillery was causing very serious damage, food supplies were running low and the water
supply was threatened. Relief was essential.

Nadir Shah's invasion and the threat to Thal put an end to any thoughts
of a move on Jalalabad from Dakka – the 16th Division (Army Reserve)
and all available transport was needed in the Kurram. Thus, in addition
to his other strategic successes, Nadir Shah had halted the invasion of
Afghanistan and in doing so reversed much of the effects of the Afghan
defeats in the Khyber.

Reinforcements began to flood into Kohat, the first units arriving on 28
May. The 45th Infantry Brigade from Peshawar arrived the next day and

HQ 16th Division (Major General Beynon) arrived from Lahore on 30 May. By 1 June twelve battalions of infantry, two batteries of field artillery and two units of heavy machine guns, together with a company of Sappers and Miners, had reached Kohat. From these and the troops already there a relief force was hastily organised. It was to be commanded by Brigadier General Dyer, whose 45th Infantry Brigade would form the core of the relief force. Barrett's instructions were simple: 'I want you to relieve Thal,' he told Dyer. 'I know you will do it if any man can.'

Six weeks earlier Dyer had been responsible for the 'massacre' at Amritsar, the event which was to be the turning point for British rule in India. Public criticism of this shocking event was beginning to rise but when Dyer, very properly, mentioned it to Eustace, he was told not to worry because if his action was to be disapproved he would have been told of it before. Eustace was disastrously wrong but he could be forgiven for assuming that, under the normal military principle of mitigation, Dyer would not have been placed in an important operational post if he was still under threat of serious disciplinary action.

Dyer was, in fact, a thoroughly competent and experienced Frontier soldier and in 1916–17 he had conducted a highly successful, if little known, campaign in Eastern Persia.[10] He was known to be bold, aggressive and daring, and, as Barrett had recognised, no better commander could have been found for this task.[11]

The 'Thal Relief Force' concentrated at Togh, thirty-three miles west of Kohat, on 31 May and began its march the same day.[12] Dyer had lashed trees to some of his lorries in the hope that the dust would give the impression of a large artillery force.[13] The road from Kohat to Thal is dominated by the Samana ridge to the north, the southern boundary of the Afridi stronghold of the Tirah. Dyer was conscious of the threat posed by the tribesmen on the ridge and decided that the best way of keeping them quiet was a rapid advance on Thal.[14] Only the assumed urgency of the situation at Thal could have justified the decision to march when many of the men had not had any food or water, and in intense daytime heat.[15] Not surprisingly, the men fell out in scores and had to be picked up by the ambulances following. Dyer marched most of the way at the head of the column. The force staggered into the village of Darsamand, only nine miles from Thal, the same evening. From here Dyer was able to signal his advance to Thal by heliograph to Fort Lockhart on the Samana ridge which then radioed the message on to Thal. One must assume that through civilian sources Nadir Shah was also aware of Dyer's progress.

Dyer moved off next morning at 0500 and two miles from Thal, on the RAF landing ground there, he was met by Eustace's Staff Officer, Major Wylly,[16] who was able to give him a detailed description of the Afghan dispositions. North of Thal, a body of some 3,000 tribesmen was holding Thal village and the lower slopes of Khadimakh; behind them, Orakzai and Zaimukht tribesmen from the southern half of the Tirah watched and waited to see which way the wind would blow. An even larger body of tribesmen from Khost, and Wazirs from British India under Babarak Zadran, was occupying the hills south of the Ishkalai Nala. The main body of Afghan regulars, with most of the artillery, was west of the Kurram river, on Khapianga and at Yusuf Khel, Nadir Shah's main camp. Thal was thus effectively surrounded on three sides and the only way in – or out – was by the route that Dyer had followed. The Afghan forces were estimated at 3,000 regulars and some 9,000 tribesmen.[17]

Dyer immediately appreciated that Nadir Shah's regulars and guns could not easily support Babarak Zadran's men south of Thal because the Thal river lay between. He therefore decided to attack Babarak Zadran first. To mask his intentions he opened fire with 89 Battery and the Frontier Garrison Artillery both on Thal village and on the tribal positions to the south. The 1/69th Punjabis, supported by 3/150 Infantry, were ordered to seize Hill 2637, south of the Ishkalai Nala and on the right flank of the Khost and Wazir tribesmen. The attack was continued by 1/25 London, 2/41 Dogras, a section of 23 Mountain Battery and a half section of 57 Company, 1st Sappers and Miners. By 1600 hours Hill 2637 was in Dyer's hands and the rest of the attacking force had reached a position within a mile of Thal fort. Startled by the speed of the attack and the accuracy of the artillery fire, the tribesmen rapidly dispersed. Leaving half of 3/150 Infantry to hold Hill 2637, the remainder of the troops were withdrawn to camp which was set up close to the Kohat road, two miles from Thal. No. 89 Battery set up position close to Thal fort and opened fire on the Afghan artillery on Khapianga, which was quickly silenced. Dyer could do no more that night, but already he had transformed the situation. Nadir Shah, presumably surprised by the speed and vigour of Dyer's movements, failed to react.

Next morning (2 June) Eustace handed over command at Thal to Dyer and returned to his HQ at Kohat. Dyer now deployed 1/151 Infantry and 3/9 Gurkhas from the original Thal garrison, with 1/25 London and 2/41 Dogras in support, to attack the tribal gathering on the southern slopes of Khadimakh. In the course of the attack, Dyer received a letter from Nadir Shah, saying that he had been ordered by the Amir to suspend hostilities, and asking for an acknowledgement; he clearly knew of the armistice before Dyer. The latter's rather grandiloquent reply has gone down into Indian Army legend: 'My guns will give an immediate reply, and a further reply will be sent by the Divisional Commander, to whom the letter has been forwarded.'[18] Nadir Shah had already begun to act on his letter, even before Dyer saw it; his regular troops were already in full retreat, and were quickly followed by the tribal gatherings. The Khadimakh slopes were occupied for a loss of only five wounded, the RAF bombing and machine gunning a gathering of Zaimukhts to the north. Dyer now rested his infantry in view of the intense heat, but sent his armoured cars and the 37th Lancers squadron along the west bank of the Kurram[19] to harass the retiring Afghans while two sections of 89 Battery took up position at Mulla Rasul, a mile and a half west of Thai, to speed the retreating enemy with a few well-placed shells on Nadir's camp at Yusuf Khel.

The siege had been lifted and it now remained to tidy up. On 3 June a column left Thai at 0700 to occupy Nadir Shah's former camp at Yusuf Khel. It was littered with stores and ammunition, abandoned in haste, but when a working party went out next day (4 June) it found that the locals had been there before and had removed virtually everything of value. Any plans to pursue Nadir back to Matun were nullified when Dyer received official notification of the armistice which had come into force on 3 June.

The armistice did not preclude the punishment of those Wazirs who were British subjects, and on 4 June a column set out to destroy the Wazir village at Biland Khel, three and a half miles south of Thai, which had been a focus of hostility. The attempt had to be abandoned because the Kurram river was in spate but a renewed attempt next day succeeded. Three companies of infantry surrounded the village, blew up the six largest towers and removed as much grain and bhusa as the camels could carry. Significantly, the force was not followed up when it retired although it lost two men wounded from long-range sniping.

In the aftermath, Eustace came under severe criticism. Fitzpatrick, writing to Barrett, detailed three areas in which Eustace appeared to have fallen short:

(a) he had made no plans against a possible attack on Thal;
(b) he had not organised the defence of Thal itself;
(c) he had made no plans to cooperate with Dyer when the latter arrived.

The CGS felt that Eustace was not adequate for an independent command in the field; Barrett was therefore asked to recommend a successor and to consider the question of Eustace's future employment, if any.[20]

Nadir Shah had missed the best Afghan opportunity of the war. His opening moves, which had brought him to Thal by routes not hitherto considered feasible for large forces and artillery, had kept the British command on the back foot. No plans had been made to defend Thal and the hastily fortified perimeter was too large for the garrison, which consisted largely of young, inexperienced units. A determined, coordinated attack might well have overrun the garrison and given the Afghans a stunning coup. That would almost certainly have brought about a general rising of the Orakzais, Zaimukhts and Afridis, as well as Wazirs and Mahsuds – even Peshawar might have been threatened. With Thal in Afghan hands, Pagan at Parachinar would have been effectively cut off from any reinforcement.

Nadir seemed reluctant to hazard his infantry and relied upon his artillery to batter the Thal garrison into surrender. Given time and the threat to the water supply, that might just have worked but time was what he could not sensibly rely upon. He exhibited once again that curious Afghan reluctance to push home a clear advantage, noticed before at Bagh and Dakka. It did not, however, prevent him claiming a victory or having a statue erected in Kabul which included a symbolic chained lion. Nor did it prevent him becoming Commander in Chief and War Minister again. In truth, he had scored the nearest thing to an Afghan success in the whole war.

Whatever his other failings, Dyer had shown himself an able tactician and commander. He had driven his troops hard in the initial stages but they had responded well and his success was undoubtedly the most important, as well as the most dramatic, of the war. Amritsar and ill-health put an early end to his career. But for that, he would almost certainly have gone farther and he deserves to be remembered for his victory at Thal. Casualties among the garrison during the siege amounted to twelve killed and eighty-two wounded, a tribute to the destructiveness of the Afghan artillery and a pointer perhaps to the way in which the siege might have gone but for Dyer's relief.

While attention had necessarily been focused on the situation round Thal, events had been moving in Upper Kurram. There four groups of Afghan regulars and tribesmen threatened invasion. On the Peiwar Kotal a force of 2,000–3,000 regulars, with four mountain guns and two machine guns, backed up by 1,000–2,000 tribesmen, were being watched by 400 of the Kurram Militia. At Kharlarchi, ten miles to the south, where the Kurram river enters the valley from the west, 100 Afghan regulars and 900 tribesmen, with a mountain gun and a machine gun, were being watched by 200 Militia. At Ghoz Garhi, six miles farther south, and well within British territory, a body of 800 Maqbil tribesmen had assembled, while, finally, another thirteen miles to the south, at Lakka Tiga, 400 Afghan regulars with two mountain guns, and supported by some 1,600 tribesmen, faced 280 Militia, including eighty mounted infantry.[21] Faced with these enveloping threats, Fagan's strategy was to keep his regular troops concentrated at Parachinar, ready to strike at any Afghan advance while using the Militia to watch the frontier. At Parachinar he had one squadron 37th Lancers, three sections (six armoured cars) No. 22 Motor Machine Gun Battery, two sections (four guns) 28 Mountain Battery, and two battalions (1/57 Rifles and 3 Guides Infantry), together with 400 Kurram Militia. A further 240 Militia manned the chain of posts down the valley, connecting Parachinar and Thal.[22]

On 26 May, the day before Nadir Shah appeared before Thal the Afghans made their first move. Using the route down the Spingawi Pass, east of the Peiwar Kotal, which Roberts had used in 1878, they attacked villages at the foot of the Kotal but were driven back into the hills by the Militia, assisted by the armoured cars. Next day, Fagan received a telegram from Kohat, telling him of Nadir Shah's arrival before Thal and warning him that the small force of 1/109 Infantry at Alizai had been ordered into Thal leaving behind only fifty men of the Militia. Fagan immediately despatched 200 Guides Infantry in lorries, with two armoured cars to reinforce Alizai and sent a letter by despatch rider to Kohat, proposing that he should now operate via Lakka Tiga against Nadir Shah's line of communication back to Matun; his despatch rider, however, was stopped by enemy forces on the road and turned back. Nevertheless, a small column of Militia mounted infantry from Lakka Tiga succeeded in ambushing one of Nadir Shah's convoys returning to Matun, killing nine of the escort. Local hostility and a shortage of supplies forced the column to return before more damage could be done.

Although there appeared to be no overall coordination of the Afghan forces threatening the Upper Kurram, Fagan faced a rapid succession of immediate threats. On 28 May the Afghan forces at Kharlarchi surrounded the Militia post there but the Militia, reinforced from Parachinar by two troops of the 37th Lancers and two armoured cars, succeeded in repulsing the enemy who left nineteen bodies on the ground; the cavalry and armoured cars were withdrawn to Parachinar the same evening to enable Pagan to reconstitute his central striking force. The reinforcement sent to Alizai was withdrawn to Parachinar at the same time.

It was a prudent precaution because Pagan now faced his most serious threat – an invasion via Lakka Tiga which threatened to cut the Kurram in two at its narrowest point. The Afghan plan was to link up with the hostile Orakzais and Zaimukhts whose border came down close to the Kurram river, only fifteen miles or so east of Lakka Tiga. Aided by Jaji tribesmen from the Afghan side of the border, who had long-standing feuds with the local Turis, the Afghan commander managed to assemble a force of some 3,000 men with five guns. Despite the enormous disparity of forces, Lieutenant Beamish[23] with 200 of the Militia at Lakka Tiga, was ordered to attack the Afghan force. Manoeuvring skilfully and with great determination, he managed to stall the Afghan attack until the armistice brought formal hostilities there to an end. In its way it was one of the most remarkable achievements of the war. It was also fortunate for Pagan as he was simultaneously faced with an incursion of Orakzais who, under the mullah Mahmud Akhinzada, attacked the post of Badama, some three and a half miles east of the main Kurram road, twenty miles south-east of Parachinar, on 29 May. Deprived of Afghan support by Beamish's gallant action, the Orakzais were driven back into their hills by a force of Kurram Militia collected by an Indian officer, Subadar Gul Khan, and aided enthusiastically by local Turis.

Heartened and relieved by Dyer's success, Pagan could now take the offensive with an attack on the Afghan forces near the Peiwar Kotal and an attack on the Afghan gathering near Kharlarchi. He then intended to strike at Nadir Shah in his retreat from Thal. The attack at the Peiwar Kotal was cancelled because of a miscalculation over distances, and Nadir Shah's retreat was so precipitate that there was no opportunity to intercept him.

The attack at Kharlarchi proved highly successful. On the evening of 2 June Dodd left Parachinar with two troops 37th Lancers, two armoured cars, a section 28 mountain Battery, one company 3rd Guides, a mounted infantry troop of the Militia and 100 Militia infantry with two trench mortars. The force reached Kharlarchi, ten miles away, the same evening under cover of darkness. The 3rd Guides immediately occupied a ridge just west of Kharlarchi and 1,100 yards from the Afghans who were at Amir Thana, north-west of Kharlarchi. At dawn on 3 June the mountain guns opened fire and under cover of their fire the trench mortars were installed some 500 yards from the Afghan position in Amir Thana fort.[24] The Kurram Militia then attempted to scale the walls of the fort, unsuccessfully, but at 0900 the Afghan garrison surrendered. The cavalry and mounted infantry then pressed forward to Mir Kalai, one and three quarter miles farther west, where they managed to surprise the Afghan brigadier and the rest of his force, who fled precipitately. It was a resounding little victory and the Afghans lost an estimated sixty killed, thirty-two bodies being counted on the ground; British losses amounted to two killed and five wounded. Six Jaji villages inside Afghanistan were burned in retribution before Dodd withdrew to Parachinar the same, evening. The following day (3 June) two armoured cars and seventy of 1/57 Rifles in lorries succeeded in reaching Thal without opposition.[25]

Despite the armistice on 3 June, which stipulated that all Afghan forces must withdraw a distance of twenty miles from the nearest British forces, the Afghan forces on the Peiwar Kotal, under Shah Mahmud, a younger brother of Nadis Shah, did not withdraw and on 5 June actually launched an attack on the village of Teri, just below the pass. It took two days of fighting to drive the Afghans back. Beynon, who had succeeded Eustace, addressed a very sharp letter to Shah Mahmud, reminding him of the terms of the armistice and threatening to attack him within forty-eight hours unless he withdrew. Shah Mahmud apologised for the attack but still did not withdraw. Beynon, nevertheless, was refused permission to attack because of the armistice.

That concluded formal hostilities against the Afghans in the Upper Kurram. But the long delay between the armistice on 3 June and the signing of a formal peace on 8 August unsettled the tribesmen who were led to believe that the Amir did not intend to end the war but was merely playing for time before resuming hostilities. The tribesmen could therefore see no point in desisting from trouble and a series of attacks against British posts in the Kurram continued until peace was actually signed and notified early in August.

Although the British could take comfort from the fact that the Kurram had been successfully defended and its territorial integrity fully preserved in face of very superior numbers, it had been a fairly close-run thing. Nadir Shah's dramatic appearance before Thal and the events in the Upper Kurram showed that, with a more carefully coordinated strategic plan, the outcome of the war need not have been as one-sided as it turned out. As it was, the campaign in the Kurram had left the British facing the necessity of a major campaign in Waziristan.

Nevertheless, the British could take comfort from the splendid perform-ance of the Kurram Militia. Like the Chitral Scouts, it had performed to perfection the tasks for which it had been designed. As in Chitral, the policy of recruiting only from local tribes of proven loyalty had been fully vindicated; it had evident lessons for the reconstitution of those militias such as the Khyber Rifles and the Waziristan Militias which had collapsed under the strain of war.

While Fagan had been fortunate in his subordinates, he had neverthe-less shown himself a courageous and competent commander. It would be hard to find a better conducted small campaign than that fought in the Upper Kurram.

Notes

1 For a fuller description of the Kurram and of Roberts' advance, see Robson, 80 and 122–6.
2 The schism between Sunnis and Shiahs arose in the first instance from the dispute over the Prophet Muhammad's successor. The Sunnis believe that his successors were to be temporal leaders, chosen by election from the Quresh tribe; the Shiahs believe that the successors were to be spiritual leaders and that the first was Ali the cousin and son-in-law of the Prophet. But over the centuries, the schism has acquired a deeper and more complex doctrinal overlay. The Turis had the reputation of being somewhat fanatical. In 1860 they had actually petitioned to be taken under British protection against their Afghan and Pathan neighbours.
3 Chenevix Trench, 72.
4 *Third Afghan War*, 25, Map 1.
5 On 6 May 1919 Parachinar was held by the Militia, the Miranzai valley posts by 3/8 Gurkhas, and Kohat by the 37th Lancers, No. 4 Armoured Motor Battery, 28 Mountain Battery, 1/57 Rifles, 3/9 Gurkhas and 1/109 Infantry. For subse-quent build-up, see *Third Afghan War*, 52–4.
6 Percival Charles Russell Dodd, 31st Lancers, seconded to Kurram Militia.
7 This was the route taken by Roberts when he entered Khost in the spring of 1879; the route was therefore known to be practicable for troops and guns.
8 Frederick Walter Champion, seconded to Kurran Militia 1917.
9 *Third Afghan War*, Map 13.
10 He had served in Burma 1886–7, on the Hazara Expedition of 1888, the relief of Chitral in 1895, in Waziristan in 1901–2 and against the Zakka Khel Afridis

in 1908. For his campaign in Persia see the official history, Brigadier General F J Moberly, *Operations in Persia 1914–1919* (reprinted HMSO, 1978), and Dyer's own account, *Raiders of the Sarhad* (London, 1921).

11 There is evidence, however, that Dyer was beginning to suffer from a degenerative disease which would kill him in a few years' time.

12 The Force consisted of one squadron 37th Lancers, 89 Battery RFA, four 15-pounder guns of the Frontier Garrison Artillery, from Kohat, dragged by lorries, one section 23 Mountain Battery, an armoured car battery, 1/25 London Regiment, 2/41 Dogras, 1/69 Punjabis, 3/150 Infantry, 250 men 1/57 Rifles and one company 2/4 Border Regiment – in total, about 3,000 men; *Third Afghan War*, 59.

13 The trick worked because Nadir Shah, watching through binoculars, protested: 'In the name of God, we have the whole artillery of India coming against us.'

14 *Report by Brigadier-General* R. E. H. Dyer CB, *Commanding 45th Infantry Brigade, on the operations for the relief of Thal May–June 1919* – L/Mil/17/14/65 (hereafter cited as Report).

15 On 13 June an observer recorded a daytime temperature of 120° Fahrenheit in the shade – Ian Colvin, *The Life of General Dyer* (London, 1929), 218.

16 Guy George Egerton Wylly, VC DSO, late Guides.

17 *Report*, 3.

18 *Third Afghan War*, 61.

19 *Third Afghan War*, 51, has this force advancing along the left (or east) bank, but this makes little sense because Nadir's troops and his artillery were west of the Kurram river, i.e. on the *right* bank.

20 CGS to Barrett, 19 June 1919 – L/MIL/17/5/4060, Appendix 115.

21 Figures for the Afghan forces are as reported by the Political Agent, Major Heale – for these and the British forces, see *Report by Brigadier-Genera B. A. Fagan CMG, DSO, on events between 27th May and 3rd June 1919 in and around Parachinar*, Case No. 4847-F – Operations (Simla, 1919).

22 300 ex-Militia sepoys had been temporarily recruited to carry out depot duties at Parachinar, thus releasing the rest of the Militia for active operations.

23 Richard Percival Beamish, 22nd Punjab Infantry, seconded to Kurram Militia. Unaccountably, he was not decorated.

24 This appears to be the first use of trench mortars on the Frontier. They were not a success because of defective propelling cartridges.

25 Fagan's Report is a singularly bald document, differing only in minor details from the account in *Third Afghan War*, 52–70, which is presumably based on it. Where the two differ, I have chosen to use the *Report* as having been written closer to the events.

IX

Operations in Baluchistan

(Maps 7 and 8)

Over the centuries the road from Kandahar, the second city of Afghanistan, over the Khojak Pass to Quetta, then down the Bolan Pass to the Indus and the plains of India, has been second in importance only to the road through the Khyber Pass as a gateway into India. In particular, it was the route followed in reverse by the British when they invaded Afghanistan in 1838 and 1878. As a result of the latter war, the districts of Sibi and Pishin, as well as the state of Khelat, had come under British rule and the boundary with Afghanistan had been fixed at New Chaman, only seventy miles from Kandahar, over easy country. The main British base was at Quetta, sixty-five miles behind New Chaman. In the 1880s a broad-gauge railway had been built up the Bolan Pass to Quetta and on to New Chaman, where rails were stockpiled to extend it on to Kandahar if ever required.

Despite its traditional strategic importance, the Bolan Pass route was an unlikely axis of invasion by the Afghans in 1919. Quetta was strongly held by the 4th Division, and the railway enabled it to be reinforced from India quickly. By comparison, Kandahar was connected to New Chaman only by an indifferent cart road which would take infantry the best part of a week to traverse. Kandahar itself was some 325 miles from Kabul, the nearest source of major reinforcements; in 1880 it had taken Roberts three weeks to march from Kabul to Kandahar and, given the state of Afghan roads and the scarcity of wheeled transport, it was not likely to take much less in 1919.[1] Even if the Afghans succeeded in reaching Quetta, there were no obvious strategic targets within easy reach.

If the Afghans did decide to invade, then a capital defensive position existed on the Khwaja Amran range of hills, nine miles south-east of New Chaman. Wapshare decided to strengthen his covering troops at New Chaman and to concentrate as large a force as possible at Kila Abdullah, nine miles south of the Khojak Pass through the Khwaja Amran. In Baluchistan, the administrative boundary coincided with the international boundary; there were no awkward semi-independent tribes in between. To create insurrection, the Afghans would need to invade Baluchistan; even then the tribes who might be prevailed upon to attack the British, such as the Achakzars and Kakars, were not comparable in fighting quality with the Pathan tribes farther north. They would be an embarrassment rather than a menace.

Per contra, a significant and readily accessible Afghan target in the form of the fortress at Spin Baldak lay just across the frontier from New Chaman. India did not however have the immediate resources available to advance on Kandahar, and two previous British occupations had found occupying Kandahar a good deal easier than staying there.

In May 1919 the forces in the Afghan province of Kandahar were put at between one and five regiments of cavalry, eight to sixteen battalions of infantry and thirty-one to forty-four guns,[2] the major part of which were at Kandahar. No long-range aircraft were available for reconnaissance, but intelligence reports indicated that up to 15 May none of the troops at Kandahar had been pushed forward to the frontier. It was believed from other intelligence that some 1,500 reinforcements under Abdul Qudus, the Prime Minister, had left Kabul but could not reach Kandahar until 16 May at the earliest.[3] The British had available in Baluchistan the 12th Mounted Brigade and the 4th Infantry Division – in all, three cavalry regiments, ten battalions of infantry, one Machine Gun Company, one field battery and two mountain batteries. On garrison duty in the Zhob there was a further mountain battery, an armoured car battery, a regiment of cavalry and two battalions of infantry[4] On the outbreak of the war, all of these forces were brought together as the Baluchistan Force, under Lieutenant General Wapshare, who gave up command of 4 Division to Major General Woodyatt, previously commanding in Waziristan.[5]

Wapshare's main claim to fame was that he had briefly taken over the ill-fated Indian Expeditionary Force B after the debacle at Tanga, in East Africa, in November 1914. Meinertzhagen, his Intelligence Officer then, described him as 'a kindly old gentleman, nervous, physically unfit and devoid of any serious military knowledge'.[6] It is difficult to believe that garrison life in India since then had wreaked any great change.

He had on paper, at least, an adequate defensive force and one which was certainly qualitatively superior. But he had a large area to cover. In addition to Baluchistan proper, he was responsible for the Zhob, the area lying between Baluchistan and Waziristan, its northern border being the Gomal valley. It was hilly, barren country, of no economic or strategic importance and since it had been occupied in the 1880s by Sandeman it had given little trouble apart from the occasional banditry. But it was occupied by a number of Pathan tribes – notably the Sherannis, the Achakzais, the Mando Khel and the Kakars – who could be expected to take advantage of any opportunity presented by British distraction else where. The border with Afghanistan was highly porous and an Afghan tribal invasion from that quarter would be easy, as well as contagious.

Wapshare had been ordered to show a bold front. He concluded that it would be strategically unsound to reinforce the Zhob, despite the obvious danger, and decided instead to concentrate a force to capture Spin Baldak, some 6,000 yards north-west of New Chaman, guarding the main road to Kandahar.[7] It was reputed to be the second strongest fortress in Afghanistan and it was assumed that its capture would have a significant effect on Afghan morale, as well as disrupting any Afghan invasion plan and keeping the Zhob quiet.[8] Using the railway network, Wapshare could concentrate a striking force at New Chaman before the Afghans could reinforce Spin Baldak.

Wapshare's judgement was endorsed by Army HQ and he was ordered to keep his striking force concentrated at New Chaman. Dobbs, the Agent to the Governor General in Baluchistan, was in favour of an advance on Kandahar; he believed that the capture of Spin Baldak alone would create only a temporary impression:

'we should make speedy efforts to make real advance on Kandahar.'[9]

Wapshare's strategy was clearly correct in the opening phases, although it could be argued that he and Army HQ were too complacent about the Zhob and slow to reinforce it when resources became available. The Afghans reacted sharply to the loss of Spin Baldak and the effect in the Zhob was contrary to what had been expected. On the whole, the southern (Baluchistan) front gave AHQ and the Indian Government no serious anxiety throughout the war.

Even so, when the war broke out, substantial reinforcements began to pour into Baluchistan. Between 14 May and 7 June, a further two field batteries, a machine gun company, two regiments of cavalry and six battalions of infantry reached Baluchistan.[10] By 26 May, therefore, Wapshare was able to concentrate at New Chaman two regiments of cavalry, a squadron and a company of the Machine Gun Corps, a field battery of 18-pounders, a battery of 4.5 inch and 5 inch howitzers, plus six infantry battalions and two field companies of Sappers and Miners.[11] Given the demands for troops and transport elsewhere, the scale of reinforcement for Baluchistan now appears excessive.

The fort at Spin Baldak (Map 8) lies at the south-western end of a ridge running north-east for some 1,200 yards. The ridge had three prominent knolls. Some 500 yards from the fort was Hill A, the highest, rising 200 feet above the surrounding plain. Three hundred yards closer to the fort was Hill B; closest to the fort was 'Tower Hill' (shown in the plan in the official history as Hill C).[12] 'Tower Hill' was crowned with a row of three towers connected together, and to the fort, by a wall which acted as a covered way.

The fort itself was a relatively old-fashioned, square structure, with an inner and outer wall, and massive semi-circular bastions at each corner. The outer walls were 250 yards square and twenty-five to thirty feet high. Gun platforms had been prepared on Hills B and A, connected by trenches and sangars, but no guns had been mounted and there were none in the fort. The garrison was estimated, accurately, at 500–600 regulars. On the south and west sides of the fort were large walled gardens, and just north of the western garden was a small walled serai.

The task facing Wapshare was one with which Wellington would have been entirely familiar and the plan of attack was appropriately straight-forward.[13] The cavalry was deployed in two bodies north and north-west of the fort to prevent the garrison escaping. 57 Brigade, under Brigadier General Gordon, composed of 1/4 Royal West Kent, 1/129 Baluchis, one section 270 Coy MGC and 73 Field Coy 3rd (Bombay) Sappers and Miners, was to attack along the ridge from the north-east. When the three hills had been captured, further orders would be issued for the assault on the fort proper.

11 Infantry Brigade, under Major General Hardy, comprising 1/22 Punjabis, 1/4 Gurkhas, one section 270 Coy MGC and 24 Field Coy 3rd Sappers and Miners, was to advance astride the main road to Kandahar and occupy the walled gardens and the serai; fresh orders would then be issued for the assault on the fort. The 18 pounders were to fire a creeping barrage along the ridge to cover the advance of 57 Brigade; the howitzers were to fire on the towers on 'Tower Hill' and the fort itself. They were to be deployed astride the road from New Chaman, some 3,000 yards south east of the fort. The General Reserve, consisting of the Duke of Wellingtons, 2/10 Gurkhas (less one and a half companies), one troop 42nd Cavalry, one company 2/23 Sikh Pioneers, two sections 24 Field Company and the remainder of No. 270 Company MGC, was stationed just behind the guns. The plan provided for a flag of truce to be sent forward three quarters of an hour before zero hour (0800), inviting the Afghan Commander to sur-render. The timing of the attack was dependent upon the arrival of the howitzers to create the necessary breaches in the walls of the fort. They arrived on 26 May[14] and the attack took place next day.

The cavalry left camp at New Chaman at 0430 on 27 May and reached their positions without opposition. The infantry and artillery moved out an hour later and were in position between 0630 and 0730. Hardy duly sent forward the flag of truce but its purpose appears not to have been understood by the Afghans who opened fire on it. The normal Afghan procedure in such circumstances would seem to have been to send for-ward a mullah with a copy of the Koran and it is extraordinary that this procedure was not apparently known to Wapshare, his staff or his politi-cal adviser. If it had been, much unnecessary bloodshed could have been avoided.

As it was, the guns opened fire promptly at 0800. The 57 Brigade attack, with 1/4 RWI (leading, was quickly in difficulties, making slow progress through the deep, sandy soil. Gordon tried unsuccessfully to delay the barrage and it had to be repeated. Even so, the Royal West Kents were held

1. Ali Masjid. Fort on hilltop in middle distance, temporary camp in foreground. (NAM 47062)

2. Ropeway transit system at Landi Kotal; note the fragile nature of the piers. (NAM 98073)

3. Dardoni camp, taken in 1924. (NAM 98083)

4. Afghan nomads photographed in Spring 1919, part of the George Grantham Bain Collection. (LOC)

5. The flying bridge at Dakka. (NAM 6511-111-133)

6. 'M' Battery Royal Horse Artillery in action at Dakka.
(Illustrated London News Picture Library)

7. The Kurram valley, with what would appear to be a tribal khassadar in the foreground. (NAM 98084)

8. General view of Thal from the east, showing the fort (left centre) and the village (right centre), with railway in the foreground. (NAM 98082)

9. Spin Baldak, looking west. (NAM 96900)

10. Spin Baldak – towers on Hill C and covered way. (NAM 96901)

11. The outer wall of Spin Baldak, showing the damage caused by British artillery and aerial bombardment. (Illustrated London News Picture Library)

12. Arrival of the Afghan peace delegation at Dakka on 24 July 1919. (NAM 24271)

13. Skeen *c.*1923. (National Portrait Gallery)

14. A typical Mahsud. (NAM 6510-220-25)

15. Skeen and staff 1919 (back row, from left) Lt JC Brommage (ADC), Maj Daddings (DAGMS), Capt Nicholls (Surveyor), Maj SM Cookson (DADST), Flt Lt Kerley (RAF), (middle row) Lt Col Hughes (CRE), Lt Col JH Keogh, (CRA), ?, Hastings, ?, Lt Spurling (ADC), Capt Murray Stewart (geologist) (front row) Lt Col Steel (ADS&T), Col Stoddard (ADMS), Skeen, ?, Maj ECW Conway-Gordon. (NAM 23849)

16. Transport in the Tank Zam (NAM 99810)

17. Mandanna Hill (middle distance, left centre), taken from east bank of Tank Zam (foreground). (NAM 96904)

18. Wana fort and surrounding plain (NAM 6510-220-66)

19. The Barari Tangi. (NAM 98080)

20. Flathead Left – on horizon, left centre. (NAM 96899)

21. Interior of a picquet post (sangar). (Courtesy of Somerset Military Museum Trust) (NAM 60338)

22. Kaniguram from the south. (NAM 98085)

up for two hours by a handful of men occupying the sangars on Hill A. By contrast, the 11 Brigade attack went well. The 1/4th Gurkhas captured the southern gardens by 0845 for the loss of one man wounded. On their left, 1/22 Punjabis had rather more difficulty breaking into the western gardens; nevertheless they were in control by 0930 and two platoons, with a Lewis gun, seized the serai without opposition. The fort was now under intense rifle and machine gun fire from a range of 200 yards, as well as heavy shelling from the howitzers, and some of the garrison attempted to escape northwards. They were not intercepted by the cavalry posted for that purpose. Through faulty staff work, no clear locking point or boundary had been agreed between the two forces and the fugitives escaped between them. An obvious and natural boundary would have been the point at which the main Kandahar road crossed the Kadanai river, northwest of the fort.

By 1000 hours the guns had opened two breaches in the wall on 'Tower Hill' and seriously damaged the southern face of the fort. 11 Brigade was ready to assault the fort but the RWK had not yet taken Hill A. At 1020, therefore, Wapshare ordered the Duke of Wellington's to advance and seize the orchards immediately south of 'Tower Hill', with a view to seizing 'Tower Hill' thereafter. By 1110 the orchards had been seized and reconnaissance showed that the towers on the hill had been heavily damaged. The south side of the hill, although very steep, was considered practicable for an assault. At 1145 Wapshare ordered the battalion to assault the hill after a barrage from the 4.5 inch howitzers. The assault was launched at 1157 and fifteen minutes later 'Tower Hill' was in the battalion's possession even though, in places, the men had had to climb up on their hands and knees. By now the RWK had taken Hill A but were held up by Afghans dug in on Hill B, who were also firing upon the Duke of Wellington's on 'Tower Hill'. By 1400 the right-hand companies of the Duke of Wellington's had occupied Hill B which was then handed over to 57 Brigade.[15]

Meanwhile the left-hand companies of the Duke of Wellington's had got into the fort and begun to clear the north, east and south sides, linking up with 1/4 Gurkhas, who had forced an entry through a breach and a drainage hole in the south wall, and by 1/22 Punjabis, who had climbed the walls. By 1345 the fort was in British hands, and by 1715 the bulk of the troops were on their way back to New Chaman. Total British casualties amounted to eighteen killed and forty wounded. The Afghans appear to have lost at least 200 killed, including their commander, Colonel Daud Shah, as well as 186 prisoners.[16] The garrison had numbered 500, armed only with single-shot Martini-Henry rifles[17] – in the circumstances, they had fought gallantly, if unnecessarily.

It had been a neat and creditable little action on the British side, with an agreeably eighteenth-century flavour about it; a Peninsular veteran would have been quite at home. It was marred only by poor staff work and by the 'sticky' performance of the Royal West Kents. They were a war-time battalion, shipped out to India at the end of 1914 to release a regular battalion. It had been on internal security duties until moved to Quetta in 1918. It had seen no active service of any kind and lacked operational experience and the necessary training.[18] It is reasonable to assume that the men were anxious to get home to re-establish themselves in civilian life, and therefore lacked something in aggressiveness. The Duke of Wellington's, by contrast, was one of the eight pre-war regular battalions retained in India in 1914. Although 'milked' of experienced officers and men for other, wartime, units, it still retained a core of professional soldiers and strong regimental pride. With hindsight, Wapshare might have been better advised to have used them in the original assault, and to have left the West Kents in reserve, but that would have meant introducing a new battalion into the brigade on no very obvious grounds.

The fort and the ridge were left in Gordon's hands, with a garrison consisting of the RWK, the Baluchis, a squadron of the 25th Cavalry, the two field companies, a section of the MGC company and two 5 inch howitzers. Water proved a problem since the existing channel was too dirty to use. Water was initially brought in by camel until the channel had been cleaned out. Even then the supply remained inadequate until a water main was laid from New Chaman in July.

The loss of Spin Baldak was a serious shock and humiliation to the Afghans and they showed every intention of attempting to get it back. On 31 May Abdul Qudus reached Kandahar and two days later he was at Mel Karez, thirty-two miles from New Chaman, with a force estimated at one cavalry regiment, five battalions of infantry and ten guns, together with a tribal force of perhaps 9,000 men. Qudus must have been aware that peace feelers had already gone out from Kabul, but he seemed determined to avenge the humiliation of Spin Baldak. Since any attempt to advance into Afghanistan was ruled out, Wapshare had no option but to stand strictly on the defensive and to put New Chaman into a state of defence. A line of defences was constructed round the town to include the railhead, the native bazaar and the two forts. It was a necessary measure because, despite the signing of the general armistice on 3 June, Abdul Qudus refused to withdraw the stipulated twenty miles from the nearest British troops, and instead occupied Murgha Chaman, five miles north-east of Spin Baldak, cutting off the garrison's water supply. A cavalry force sent out on 12 June discovered that Murgha Chaman was occupied by 3,000 Afghan regulars and tribesmen, and was forced to withdraw. Another Afghan force was established on the Takht, six miles north-west of Spin Baldak.[19] The deep anger of the Afghans over the loss of Spin Baldak and the delay in the Afghan peace delegates reaching Dakka suggested that hostilities might be renewed at any moment.

British forces continued to pour into Baluchistan; between 19 June and 4 July another six battalions of infantry, a regiment or so of cavalry; an armoured car battery and a battery of field artillery arrived, together with two field companies. The Indian Government was, however, getting stretched for troops and three of the battalions and the cavalry were Indian States Forces units.[20]

By the middle of July the Afghan forces round Murgha Chaman and on the Takht were put at four cavalry regiments, ten battalions of infantry and thirty-eight guns, supported by 6,000 tribesmen; Wapshare was refused permission to attack this menacing concentration 'unless the military security of his force was threatened'.[21] With peace in the balance, the Indian Government was not anxious to risk further hostilities. Attacks continued, however, on British patrols round New Chaman, and the Achakzais, taking advantage of the situation, attacked troops guarding the Khojak Pass railway tunnel. The Afghan threat could not be ignored indefinitely and on 20 July Brigadier General O'Grady was ordered to assemble a force at Kila Abdullah[22] to attack the enemy force at Murgha Chaman. The attack was cancelled when news was received that the Afghan delegation had at last reached Dakka, en route for the peace talks at Rawalpindi.

This anomalous and unsatisfactory situation, half peace and half war, continued in Baluchistan until peace was signed on 8 August. Spin Baldak was handed back on 14 August and hostilities were finally over. If the Afghans had achieved nothing else, they had successfully diverted nearly two divisions of troops and a mass of transport which could have been more usefully employed elsewhere. Moreover, the British had suffered serious embarrassments in the Zhob.

Notes

1   For a detailed description of these routes see Robson, op cit.
2   Official estimates of Afghan strength differ widely. *Third Afghan War*, 98, gives one cavalry regiment, eight infantry battalions and thirty-one guns. Map 1 in that volume, however, shows three regiments of cavalry and thirteen battalions of infantry. Monro's *Despatch* (see note 7), paragraph 69, gives five, sixteen and eleven batteries of artillery. If nothing else, these estimates suggest a rather alarming lack of accurate intelligence.
3   A deserter subsequently reported that Abdul Qudus had left Sherpur (the cantonment outside Kabul) with four battalions of infantry, thirteen troops of cavalry, each 100 strong, eight field and eight mountain guns, and four elephants – L/MIL/17/5/4060. Appendix 310.
4   *Third Afghan War*, Appendix I, 155–60. A further two squadrons of cavalry and the equivalent of two battalions of infantry were employed guarding the road and rail links into southern Persia and played no part in the war.
5   For both officers, see Biographical Notes.
6   Richard Meinertzhagen, *Army Diary* 1899–1926 (Edinburgh, 1960), 109.
7   Monro, *Despatch*, paras 70–1.

8 Ibid, para 77.
9 AGG Baluchistan to Foreign Secretary, No. 185-L, 21, May 1919 – FPPS August 1919, Part II, No. 257. This may reflect Dobbs' assessment of Wapshare.
10 *Third Afghan War*, 107.
11 25th Cavalry (less one squadron), 42nd Cavalry, 92 Squadron and 270 Company Machine Gun Corps, 102 (Field) Battery and 1107 (Field) Batteries RFA, 1 Duke of Wellingtons, 1/4 Royal West Kents, 1/22 Punjabis, 1/4 and 2/10 Gurkhas and 1/129 Baluchis, 24 and 73 Field Companies 3rd (Bombay) Sappers and Miners.
12 *Third Afghan War*, Map 21, 101.
13 *11th Infantry Brigade Order No. 1*, dated 26 May 1919.
14 *Report on the action at Spin Baldak 27th May 1919* (Simla, 1919) – L/MIL/17/14/67.
15 *Operations against Spin Baldak, 27th May 1919* – Duke of Wellington's Regimental Archives, Halifax. I am indebted to Major Harrap, the Regimental Secretary, for the opportunity to consult this document. For an eyewitness account of the regiment's action, see E C B 'Chaman and Spin Baldock (sic), 919', in *The Iron Duke*, Vol. 8 No. 23 (1932), 204–6.
16 Casualty figures – *Third Afghan War*, 103.
17 *Baluchistan Force Intelligence Summary No. 23, 31 May 1919*.
18 It was not, strictly speaking, a Territorial battalion, having been formed from war-time volunteers, with a leaven of officers and men from the pre-war 4th (Territorial) Battalion – C T Atkinson, *The Queen's Own Royal West Kent Regiment 1914–1919* (London, 1924), 68–9.
19 On 19 June the Afghan forces in the Takht–Murga Chaman area were put at two cavalry regiments, ten infantry battalions, fourteen field and twelve mountain guns, plus 5,000–10,000 irregulars (i.e. tribesmen), *Baluchistan Force Intelligence Summary No. 42, 19 June 1919*.
20 Alwar and Nawanagar Lancers, Jind, Nabha and Kapurthala Infantry.
21 *Third Afghan War*, 108.
22 Twenty miles south of New Chaman, on the road to Quetta.

X

Operations in the Zhob

(Map 9)

The territory known as the Zhob, named after its principal river, lies north-east of Quetta and forms the link between Waziristan and Baluchistan (Pishin) to the south-west. The Gomal river marks the boundary between the Zhob and Waziristan and its valley was a major trade route for the great nomadic caravans (kafileh) which moved down each spring from Ghazni to the Indus and the plains of India, returning each autumn. The Zhob had been under British administration only since 1890 when Sir Robert Sandeman moved northwards through the country, reaching agreement with the aggressive Pathan tribes who inhabited the sparsely populated area, roughly twice the size of Wales.

The country is basically rolling desert but with occasional hills, bounded on the east by the Suleiman range of mountains, an offshoot of the Hindu Kush, whose highest peak is the Takht-i-Suleiman (the 'Seat of Solomon'). The principal feature is the Zhob river which flows north-east across the territory, joining the Gomal at Khajuri Kach, some sixty-five-miles west of Dera Ismail Khan. The main Pathan tribes were the Kakars, who inhabit the centre of the territory, with the Mando Khel and Sherranis to the north-east and the Musa Khel to the east. Wazirs from the north and Achakzais from the east contributed to a fairly turbulent population. Like some of their major brethren to the north, the inhabitants of the Zhob found it difficult and unrewarding to try to scratch a living from the soil and found it easier to plunder caravans and raid into the settled districts east and south of them. While not formidable in numbers, the size of the country made it difficult to control them. The Zhob Militia, some 1,800 strong, had been formed as the Zhob Levy Corps in 1890 to fulfil this policing role. It was organised on much the same lines as the other militias, with both infantry and mounted infantry sections, and was recruited from local Pathans, Pathans from farther north such as the Orakzais, Brahuis (who were not Pathans but desert dwellers from south-west of Quetta, with a good fighting reputation), and even Ghilzais from Afghanistan. The headquarters was at Fort Sandeman, in the Zhob valley, 160 miles north east of Quetta and some fifty miles south-west of Khajuri Kach.[1]

Communications in 1919 rested mainly on the circular road which ran from Quetta east and north to Fort Sandeman, whence it doubled back along the valley of the Zhob river to Hindubagh, about sixty miles north east of Quetta. Hindubagh was connected by a narrow-gauge railway to the broad-gauge railway and Quetta. Loralai, 100 miles east of Quetta, on the main road to Fort Sandeman, was the other principal post in the area.

In May 1919 the Zhob was lightly held by regular troops. At Loralai were the 3rd Skinner's Horse and 2/11 Rajputs, most of whom were dispersed in small detachments along the southern loop of the road. From Fort Sandeman, 3/1 Gurkhas manned posts along the northern loop, while 1/5 Light Infantry were at Harnai, on the broad-gauge railway, due east of Quetta.

It was not considered very probable that the Afghan Army would invade the Zhob as it led to no major strategic objective except possibly Dera Ghazi Khan, on the Indus, opposite Multan. The commander of Baluchistan Force (Wapshare), responsible for the Zhob, and Army HQ had agreed that the Zhob should not be reinforced pending a possible Afghan advance from Kandahar aimed at Quetta. But it was considered prudent to cover the two most likely invasion routes into the Zhob – first, from the north-west, from Khost via Gul Kach (on the Gomal), towards Fort Sandeman and secondly, from Kamr-ud-Din Karez, sixty-four miles west of Fort Sandeman and roughly the same distance north of Kila Saifullah on the western loop of the main road, thus threatening both the Upper and Lower Zhob.

On 20 May spies reported that four Afghan battalions were only some thirty miles from Kamr-ud-Din Karez. Accordingly, 1/5 Light Infantry (who were replaced at Harnai by 2/15 Sikhs) and two squadrons of 3rd Skinner's Horse were moved to Kila Saifulla; No. 281 Machine Gun Company was moved from Harnai to Loralai and drafts were despatched to Fort Sandeman to bring 3/1 Gurkhas up to strength. The Afghan concentration proved to be a rumour and the column at Kila Saifullah was dispersed. Nevertheless, it was clear that available troops were stretched very thin, especially if the local tribesmen were to rise.

It was, in fact, from Waziristan that trouble first appeared. The evacuation of Wana and the Gomal posts, Russell's epic retreat, and the dissolution of the South Waziristan Militia in May 1919 is properly part of the Waziristan campaign and is dealt with in Chapter XV, below. But the last stages of Russell's retreat were into the Zhob and were assisted by the Zhob Militia; that in turn proved to be the catalyst for widespread disturbances throughout the Zhob.

When the news of Russell's retreat from Wana reached Fort Sandeman it was immediately realised that the Upper Zhob would soon be up in arms. At Fort Sandeman 3/1 Gurkhas were pulled in to man perimeter defences round the fort, and orders were hastily issued to evacuate all posts on the road between Fort Sandeman and Murgha Kibzai, forty miles to the south, and to concentrate their garrisons at Fort Sandeman. Such an obvious defensive move would have been a clear signal that the British were losing their grip on the country, and would have provided an immediate incentive for widespread rebellion. Fortunately, the order was cancelled before it could be carried out. Even so, the Sherannis inhabiting the country immediately north-east of Fort Sandeman began to rise and on 2 June cut the telegraph wires south of Sandeman. Desertions of Kakars and Mando Khel from the Zhob Militia increased. On 3 June Captain Yule, the Assistant Political Officer,[2] left Fort Sandeman with a force of Militia mounted infantry to escort the wounded of the South Waziristan Militia (including Russell) to Loralai. At Lakaband, twenty-five miles from Sandeman, ambulances were waiting and Yule was able to communicate with Quetta and give a full report of the situation in the Upper Zhob, including the unpleasant news that all the Kakars and Mando Khel in the Militia had deserted, and that the Militia post at Manikwha, twenty-four miles north-north-east of Fort Sandeman, had surrendered to a large party of Sherannis without firing a shot. The men manning the post were all Ghilzais from Afghanistan and their explanation was that the Sherannis had put a charm on their rifles, which would not fire!

In the Upper Zhob, the situation was now utterly confused; rumour and counter-rumour flourished and on the British side no one seems to have had any clear idea of the situation – in particular, no one knew where serious local tribal opposition could be expected. In such circumstances, even a slight error of judgement could bring serious consequences.

On 5 June a party of some 220 reinforcements for 3/1 Gurkhas arrived at Zarozai, nine miles south of Lakaband. The bulk of the men were young recruits of six to eight months' service from the 10th Gurkhas' depot at Maymo, in Burma. They were under the command of 2nd Lieutenant Thatcher,[3] who had no Gurkha officers with him and only a handful of NCOs. Between Loralai and Zarozai they were joined by a small party of Gurkhas returning from leave and courses, under Second Lieutenant Allinson.[4] The lack of Gurkha Officers and NCOs meant that the men could not be organised into platoons or companies.

At Lakaband, Yule had received orders to rendezvous with Thatcher's party and to escort them back to Fort Sandeman. He had been told, incorrectly, that Kapip was in rebel hands and that accordingly the posts at Babar and Gwal, north of Lakaband, had been abandoned.

Yule met Thatcher's party at Adozai, five miles north of Zarozai, on 6 June. Judging that the direct road from Lakaband to Sandeman was now likely to be blocked, Yule decided to cut across country to join the western road into Fort Sandeman, entailing a march of some thirty-seven miles. At Zarozai Thatcher's party transferred its baggage from carts to donkeys in preparation for the journey across country. Yule marched from Zarozai on the evening of 6 June, across broken and arid country, at the height of the hot weather. By 1000 the next morning (7 June) the donkeys were becoming exhausted and their loads were transferred to the mules of the Zhob Militia. A halt was made at Sabakzai and the march resumed at 1800 hours that evening. By now the Gurkha rearguard was beginning to straggle and it was replaced by Militia mounted infantry. By 2300 hours the party had reached Mina Bazar, still twenty-two miles from Fort Sandeman. The party moved on at 0600 on 8 June, reaching Arzanzai at 0900 where they found water. Many of the young recruits were exhausted and had to be put on whatever animals could be made available after abandoning the rations. By 1200 on 8 June the column had reached the plain twelve miles south of Fort Sandeman. The men had had no food since the previous evening and little water, and were all close to exhaustion. The party clearly needed help and attempts were made to communicate with Sandeman by heliograph but these were frustrated by low cloud. Yule therefore sent a mounted orderly into the fort to request help, including carts to carry in the more exhausted men. It may be assumed that the progress and condition of the party was under close observation from the local tribesmen.

The march continued at a slower and slower pace; by 1730 they were some six miles from the fort, having taken five and a half hours to cover around six miles.[5] At this point, when the column was almost within sight of the fort and succour, large numbers of tribesmen appeared, holding two hills immediately ahead of the column, through which the road to Sandeman passed. Yule sent forward his mounted infantry, supported by those Gurkhas still on their feet. The left-hand hillock was quickly seized but the attempt to seize the right-hand hill failed. A Gurkha flank guard which had been put out on the right flank got into serious difficulties and was badly mauled. The remains of the column was now concentrated on the left-hand hillock where it was joined by fifty men of 3/1 Gurkhas under Lieutenant Campbell,[6] who had been despatched from Fort Sandeman in response to Yule's urgent message. A further reinforcement of fifty men of the Zhob Militia, under Lieutenant Hawkes, arrived at around 2030.[7] Under the protection of these reinforcements the survivors of the column straggled into Fort Sandeman late that night.[8]

Campbell had returned to Sandeman only after being assured that all the wounded and stragglers had been accounted for. In fact, Allinson and a small rearguard were missing; their bodies were discovered next morning on a low hill, six miles south of the fort, where they had made their last stand. By the time that Campbell reached Fort Sandeman it was already dark and clearly the survivors were in a state of confusion. The failure to pick up Allinson's party is therefore understandable if tragic. In retrospect, given the disturbed state of the country, it seems a major blunder to have allowed Thatcher's party to have proceeded beyond Lakaband without providing a much stronger escort.[9] Worse was to follow.

Hitherto, Sandeman had had to endure only a little sniping but the disaster to Thatcher's party encouraged the tribesmen to loot and burn the bazaar and to fire on the bungalows and picquets, retiring in daytime to the hills south of the post. On 10 June a party of the Zhob Militia attacked these hills under cover of heavy machine gun fire and drove the tribesmen out. Thereafter matters quietened down and on 11 June a force of 200 infantry marched out from Sandeman and successfully relieved the garrison of Kapip. The column was attacked on its return journey but beat off the attack without casualties. At the same time a small force from Sandeman relieved and reinforced the garrison of Musa Khel, east of Zarozai.

The situation was clearly deteriorating. Wana Wazirs, Sherannis, Kakars and Mando Khel had all been involved in the series of attacks. Quetta now concentrated a force under Brigadier General H de C O'Grady, commanding 10 Infantry Brigade, to relieve Fort Sandeman. It comprised the Patiala Lancers, 3/124 Baluchis (minus two companies), 1/5 Light Infantry and a section of No. 285 Machine Gun Company. It began its advance from Murgha Kibzai on 16 June and reached Kapip three days later. It encountered no significant opposition – the tribesmen had wisely absconded with their loot. The force remained at Kapip, eight miles east of Sandeman, because the water supplies at Sandeman were inadequate for a brigade strength reinforcement.

As the neighbourhood seemed to have quietened down and Fort Sandeman itself was no longer in danger, it was decided to withdraw part of O'Grady's force to Loralai, leaving the Patiala Lancers, 3/124 Baluch and a section of No. 38 Mountain Battery at Lakaband to escort convoys between Lakaband and Babar, where they would be met by escorts from Sandeman.

The retiring troops (1/5 Light Infantry, a section of No. 38 Mountain Battery and the section of No. 285 Machine Gun Company) marched from Kapip to Sandeman where they were joined by 200 rifles of 3/1 Gurkhas and 100 Zhob Militia, under Captain A W Woodhead,[10] which was to meet an 'up' convoy at Babar. The combined force, escorting surplus civilians from Sandeman, marched on 4 June, taking the western road. The retiring troops and civilians reached Mina Bazar on 5 July where news was received of a large body of Kakars who had been raiding south of Murgha Kibzai and were believed to be heading in the direction of Mina Bazar with their loot. An ambush was mounted south of Mina Bazar on the night of 5/6 July by a party of 1/5 Light Infantry. At 0200 the raiders were intercepted and fled, leaving behind four camel loads of cloth. On the 7th the troops cut across country to join the eastern road, reaching Zara on 8 July. At Loralai, O'Grady handed over command in the Zhob to Brigadier General E S Gale.[11]

Meanwhile, Woodhead's party had left the main body on 5 June and cut across to the eastern road, reaching Babar the same day. Here it took over the 'up' convoy and began its march back to Fort Sandeman the following day. Beyond Kapip the road ran through a defile which was blocked by a force of some 200–300 Sherannis. Woodhead managed to fight his way through against fierce opposition and finally reached Fort Sandeman late on the evening of 6 July; he had lost three killed and twenty wounded, including Woodhead himself.

The Zhob was still in a thoroughly unsettled state with bands of insurgent tribesmen roaming at will. While a permanent camp was being constructed at Lakaband for the Patiala Lancers and 3/124 Baluchis, the force occupied a temporary site two miles to the north-west. This was fiercely attacked in the small hours of 14 July by a large force of Kakars and Wazirs. They were beaten off, and then routed by a counter-attack. But the forces in the Zhob were too thinly spread, and disaster against tribesmen operating on their own ground, and able to pick the time and place for an ambush, was an ever-present possibility.

The next 'up' convoy should have left Lakaband for Fort Sandeman at 0600 on the morning of 14 July. It was delayed by attacks on the camp at Lakaband and by doubts as to whether it should go at all in view of the recent troubles round Sandeman and the attack on the previous convoy at Kapip. It eventually left at 1300 hours,[12] escorted by 191 men of 3/124 Baluchis, under Captain A W Goolden,[13] but with no cavalry or mounted infantry. The convoy was to be handed over to an escort from Sandeman at a point two miles north of Babar and roughly sixteen miles from Sandeman.

The convoy reached Dewal, some ten miles north of Lakaband, on the evening of the 14th. On the morning of the 15th, leaving forty men under Lieutenant Daws,[14] at Dewal, Goolden moved off for Babar, seven miles beyond Dewal. At Babar, he learned that a body of some 200 tribesmen had been seen in the vicinity. In the first of a number of critical decisions, he decided to leave the slow-moving bullock carts under guard at Babar and to press on with the faster mule carts. With the detachments left at Dewal and now Babar, the escort was down to fewer than 120 men. At 1030 Goolden reported by telephone that he was under attack half a mile beyond Babar by a large force of Wazirs (subsequently estimated at 800–900). He pressed on to the agreed meeting point at milestone 98 but there was no sign of the escort from Sandeman. At 1127 Goolden reported that he was retiring on Babar. From the accounts of survivors, the thirty-three mule carts and their drivers stampeded in panic and the convoy and its escort reached Babar in a state of complete confusion. Goolden apparently attempted to re-form the whole convoy, before retiring on Dewal. It proved impossible to get the bullock carts organised in face of increasingly heavy fire from the tribesmen. Goolden now made his second critical decision. He divided the remaining escort, leaving the larger part (two Indian Officers and eighty-seven men) at Babar to guard the bullock carts while he, with the rest of the escort (now down to some sixty men) and such of the mule carts as could be rounded up, retired on Dewal. He presumably counted on the troops left at Babar being relieved by the escort from Sandeman while at Dewal he could pick up Daws and his men. It proved a disastrous decision.

Under overwhelming attack, in bare, open country, Goolden's party was destroyed, Goolden himself being killed two and a half miles from Dewal. If he had reached that place, he would not have found Daws because that officer, warned of what had happened by fleeing mule carts, had abandoned his tents and transport and retired to Lakaband. At Lakaband, the commander, Captain Munn, sent out a party to try to rescue Goolden's party but it became clear that it had been destroyed. The troops were recalled to Lakaband where Munn abandoned his tented camp and moved into the fort, police station and serai, which he fortified.

The party left at Babar managed to beat off repeated attacks until relieved that night by the missing escort from Fort Sandeman. That escort, consisting of 225 men of 3/1 Gurkhas, seventy-five men of the Zhob Militia, with two guns of 38 Mountain Battery, had been delayed in starting and did not leave Sandeman until 0900. It reached Babar late in the afternoon, after a march of some seventeen miles in the full mid-day sun, in face of some considerable opposition. The whole force then encamped at Babar for the night.

Next morning (16 July) local inhabitants reported all clear and the whole party, now encumbered with casualties among the original garrison of eighty-seven men, moved out for Kapip, at the late hour of 1100. The force was under the command of Captain Copland, 3/1 Gurkhas,[15] who picqueted the road ahead as far as Kapip but at around 1600, a mile beyond Kapip, the force was ambushed in the same defile where Woodhead had run into trouble on 6 July. Copland tried strenuously to force a way forward but was unable to do so in face of overwhelming numbers of tribesmen occupying the hills on either side of the defile. He was killed in the fighting and command devolved on the only surviving officer, Second Lieutenant Gilbert.[16] The end was not far off: 'as it grew darker, whistles were blown by the enemy who, at this signal, rushed the convoy in overwhelming numbers; fierce hand to hand fighting ensued and the escort hopelessly outnumbered was swept away'.[17] Both guns were lost and the survivors made their way in twos and threes back to Sandeman. The gallant Gilbert remained on the ground with a small rearguard of Militia until 0115 and then made his way back to Sandeman where he arrived at 0900 on 17 June. Subsequent intelligence revealed that Copland had been attacked by a force of some 2,000 Wazirs, Sherannis and Ghilzais from Afghanistan. Goolden and Copland lost between them four officers and forty-seven men killed, and one officer and sixty-seven men wounded, some twenty-two per cent of the troops engaged. Tribal losses are not known but are unlikely to have been significant.

This was a stunning double disaster, coming so soon after the disaster to Thatcher's party. As before, the root cause was the lack of intelligence about the size and nature of the tribal insurrection which had swept over the Zhob. In consequence, the authorities at Quetta had not grasped the extent of the opposition. The incursion of Wazirs, Suleman Khel Ghilzais from Afghanistan and the local tribes such as the Kakars and Sherannis had produced a situation for which the existing garrisons in the Zhob were inadequate. British control had virtually disappeared and what was left were a series of isolated posts under continuous threat of attack. With two divisions available and more troops arriving daily,[18] it should have been possible, in the aftermath of Spin Baldak, to reinforce the Zhob. Of particular significance was the inability to provide aerial reconnaissance; there were only five obsolete aircraft from 114 Squadron available and these were deployed at Quetta and New Chaman.[19]

The double disaster was compounded by decisions taken on the ground. It was unfortunate that Goolden's force included no mounted troops which could have been used to provide him with better information about the opposition. By electing to leave forty men at Dewal and another eighty-nine at Babar to protect the bullock carts, he was left with a third of his original with which to push through with the mule carts to the rendezvous. In effect, he was gambling on the escort from Sandeman being at the rendezvous on time. When it failed to appear, he was in an almost hopeless situation. His subsequent decision to retreat on Dewal, given the opposition swarming round him, was clearly a mistake, made worse by Daws' precipitate decision to abandon Dewal and retire to Lakaband. If Goolden had stood firm at Babar until relieved by the Sandeman escort, then the combined force of some 450 men would have stood a good chance of fighting its way through to Sandeman. Of critical importance was the late departure of the Sandeman escort. As subsequent events showed, it would have been able to relieve the pressure on Goolden's party and prevent his retreat. As frequently happens in war, one faulty decision led to a chain of errors which resulted in disaster.

Quetta was now forced to accept, belatedly, that the Zhob had to be reinforced. The necessary reinforcements were calculated at one cavalry regiment, three battalions of infantry, a battery of artillery and a machine gun company. To meet this need, No. 37 Mountain Battery was sent from Army Reserve at Rawalpindi, and 1/97 Infantry, 1/153 and 2/153 Infantry were ordered up from India. The machine gun company was improvised from guns held at Quetta. The infantry could not arrive in the Lower Zhob until the beginning of August so a section of No.38 Mountain Battery from Quetta, a company of 2/11 Rajputs from Loralai and the newly arrived 16 Rajputs were sent to Murgha Kibzai.

Fort Sandeman was rationed until 8 August and it was decided not to run another 'up' convoy until conditions had improved. Foiled in this,

4,000 tribesmen collected on 28 July to lay siege to Fort Sandeman. Siege warfare demanded a discipline and an ability to plan ahead which tribal forces rarely possessed. A bombing raid on their camp by an aircraft from Quetta helped to accentuate tribal disunity and the gathering began to disperse after a week. The 3/1st Gurkhas were relieved at Sandeman by 1/97 Infantry on 19 August and that was effectively the end of a serious threat in the Upper Zhob.

Action now shifted to the Lower Zhob where a force of rebellious tribesmen, including deserters from the Militia, gathered north of Hindubagh. A force of Jhind Infantry[20] sent out from Hindubagh on 14 July proved incapable of attacking the tribal positions and had to retire to Hindubagh. It was decided to replace the Jhind troops with 2/15 Sikhs from Quetta, where they had arrived at the end of May. Before this could happen, the local Extra District Commissioner, who was presumably aware of the debacle eight days earlier, took out an escort of Jhind Infantry on 22 July to destroy two towers in the hostile village of Urgas, three miles north of Hindubagh. The force was attacked by a large body of tribesmen, and the under-trained and ill-disciplined infantry got out of hand and fired off all their ammunition. Eventually, the survivors reached Hindubagh protected by a party of 3rd Skinner's Horse. The Jhind Infantry lost one British officer and fourteen other ranks killed, and one British officer and twenty-one other ranks wounded. The same evening Hindubagh came under fire all night and the railway station was burned. The situation was not cleared up until the arrival at Hindubagh of 1/102 Grenadiers and two sections of No. 19 Motor Machine Gun Battery (armoured cars) from Quetta, followed by No. 11 Armoured Motor Battery and a squadron of the Alwar Lancers from Kila Saifullah. It was not until Karezgi, just west of Hindubagh, was occupied and garrisoned, that the fighting round Hindubagh died away.

This was effectively the end of the war as regards the Zhob. What remained were several months of fighting to suppress the tribal insurrection.

With hindsight, Quetta had been slow to grasp the situation in the Zhob and equally slow to reinforce the area when additional troops became available. Proportionately more casualties were suffered in the Zhob than in any other theatre.

Notes

1 For the Zhob Militia, see Chenevix Trench, 12; 43–6.
2 Robert Abercrombie Yule, commissioned 1898, joined Indian Political Service 1905.
3 Allan Frank Beauchamp Thatcher, commissioned 1914 into the Somerset Light Infantry, transferred to 10th Gurkhas 1917. No Frontier experience.
4 Gordon Allinson, 1st Gurkhas. The precise numbers in his party are not clear but were probably not more than twenty.

5 The official history says six miles – *Third Afghan War*, 113. The regimental history of the 1st Gurkhas says eight.

6 James Whittaker Campbell, 3/1 Gurkha Rifles.

7 C E Hawkes. There are discrepancies in the precise lime of Hawkes' arrival. The official account gives the impression that Campbell and Hawkes had arrived at roughly the same time – *Third Afghan War*, 113. The history of the 1st Gurkhas states that Hawkes was not sent out until 1930.

8 *Third Afghan War*, 113, gives the casualties as twenty-seven killed and six wounded; the War Graves Register records twenty-eight dead, which, with Allinson, gives a total of twenty-nine killed. Similarly, regimental accounts give a total of seventeen.

9 For a useful account of this unhappy affair see 'The Young Soldier's Battle', by D W Harding in *The Bugle and Kukri*, Vol. 5, No. 12 (1993).

10 Alexander William Woodhead, 3/1 Gurkha Rifles.

11 Ernest Septimus Gale.

12 *Report by the General Officer Commanding Baluchistan Force on the operations in the vicinity of Lakaband, Kapip, Fort Sandeman on 13th–18th July 1919* (Simla, 1919) – L/MIL/17/14/70. Third Afghan War, 118, gives the departure time as 1130. Whether the late departure had any effect on subsequent events, however, is doubtful.

13 Alexander Wood Goolden, 3/124 Baluch. Commissioned 1916, transferred to Indian Army 1917.

14 Harold Alfred Daws, North Staffordshire Regt, attached 3/124 Baluch.

15 Reginald Wallace Copland, 3/1 Gurkha Rifles.

16 Victor John Gilbert, Royal Artillery, attached No.38 Mountain Battery.

17 Reports by GOC Baluchistan Force, op cit. – Gilbert's Report, 6.

18 See Chapter VI, Notes 3 and 4.

19 AHQ War Diary for 1–15 July 1919 – L/MIL/17/5/4061, 31.

20 Troops from Jhind (in the Punjab) had served in the Second Afghan War and had, in consequence, been selected to become Imperial Service Troops, i.e. trained and equipped to regular Indian Army standard, with British officers in command but paid for by the ruler of the state.

XI

Peacemaking

Within a few days of the war starting, there were indications that Amanullah was regretting having unleashed a whirlwind. On 10 May he replied to Chelmsford's letter of 3 May, complaining about the arrest of the Afghan Postmaster, explaining that his troops had been mobilised only to prevent the disaffection in India spreading into Afghanistan, and complaining that the British were still not prepared to recognise Afghanistan's independence:

> I hope that friend [Viceroy] will use his best and well-meaning endeavours to avert this very grave and dangerous state of affairs with great prudence, by abolishing tyrannical laws and recognising the absolute independence, equal rights and freedom in all respects of the Government of Afghanistan... so that the doors of calamity may not be opened upon the world for it is right to demand right and it is not right to shed blood without right in the path of right.[1]

The same day the British Vakil (Saifullah Khan) had a talk with the Afghan Minister of Foreign Affairs, who admitted that the Amir had made a great mistake in starting the war. Saifullah Khan reported that the Minister was terrified of the RAF bombing and that he (the Vakil) had urged the Minister to secure the withdrawal of the Afghan troops and to seek peace.[2]

Three days after the British victory at Bagh, on 14 May, the Afghan CinC (Saleh Muhammad) wrote to the British Agent in the Khyber, blaming the British for starting the war and accusing them of causing heavy casualties among civilians 'by throwing bombs from aeroplanes'; because, however, the Viceroy had sent the Afghan Vakil to the Amir, seeking peace, Afghan troops had been ordered to suspend hostilities pending further orders.[3] By the time his letter reached the British authorities, British troops had occupied Dakka; Roos-Keppel was in favour of ignoring the letter, arguing that the Amir would seriously treat for peace only when the British reached Kabul – in the meantime the letter could be usefully publicised to the tribes.

On 20 May the Afghan Vakil (Abdur Rahman) wrote to the commander of the British forces at Dakka, saying that he had seen the Amir and was authorised to arrange peace negotiations.[4] Saifulah Khan was now reported to be on his way from Kabul with peace proposals.[5] Roos-Keppel, who was an Afghanophobe, believed these overtures to be false and recommended their rejection; in his view, efforts should be made to speed up the proposed advance on Jalalabad.[6] Roos-Keppel's view gained some substance from the fact that hostilities still continued in Chitral, and Nadir Shah was about to launch the most serious Afghan attack of the war, from Khost. These overtures, if not coordinated by the Amir, were clearly known to him, and were clear evidence that he wanted peace. It was becoming evident that the RAF bombing was now a serious factor – by the end of May, a ton of bombs a day was being dropped, mainly on Jalalabad, and against this considerable onslaught the Afghans had no effective defence. While both Montagu and Chelmsford had sought assurances that civilians would not be attacked, it was inevitable that, given the primitive equipment available and the difficult operating conditions, civilians would suffer casualties. It was impossible to persuade the Afghans that this was not deliberate.

Preparations continued for an advance on Jalalabad, scheduled for 1 June. Peace, however, was already in the minds of the authorities in London and Simla. On 17 May Montagu had telegraphed anxiously to Chelmsford, asking if hostilities had actually gone beyond what might be regarded as ordinary Frontier incidents and asking whether Saleh Muhammad's letter could be used to secure peace and the withdrawal of troops on both sides. He wished to have more information about the background and nature of the war since the matter would have to be considered by the Cabinet.[7] He was also anxious about the advance on Jalalabad; he impressed on Chelmsford the necessity of ensuring that there was ample transport available; with Jalalabad secured, it should then be possible to open serious peace talks.[8] A careful explanation from Chelmsford served to calm nerves in the India Office,[9] but Montagu could be forgiven for his anxiety; he was deeply engaged in the Paris Peace Conference and British resources were widely stretched – in Russia and the Middle East, as well as in Germany and Ireland and elsewhere.

The bombing raid on Kabul on 27 May was probably the real catalyst.[10] On the following day, the Amir wrote to Chelmsford, seeking peace.[11] It was by no means the letter of a defeated, supplicant foe. He began by rehearsing the now familiar argument that he had sent his troops to the Frontier to protect Afghanistan from the disturbances in India, and that they had occupied only territory which they regarded as theirs.[12] It was the British who had declared war. But because the Viceroy had chosen to send a conciliatory letter via the British Vakil, he (the Amir) had sent the Vakil back with an offer to negotiate; hardly had the Vakil started, however, when the British bombed Kabul, causing great panic and much damage:

> It is a matter for great regret that the throwing of bombs by Zeppelins on London was denounced as a most savage act and the bombardment of places of worship and sacred spots was considered a most abominable operation, while now we see with our own eyes that such operations were a habit which is prevalent amongst all civilised people of the West.

Nevertheless, he had ordered his troops to suspend hostilities pending the start of peace talks; he proposed that 'some personage on your illustrious Government and some on behalf of our Sublime Government may be selected and nominated to assemble at Landi Kotal or Peshawar to discuss matters and conclude an honourable and dignified peace for both parties'.

Despite its military successes, the Indian Government was keen to end the war. Resources to sustain war on five fronts were becoming stretched; Waziristan was in open insurrection and would require a major expedition in due course; and a massive outbreak of cholera along the frontier was threatening to overwhelm medical resources.[13] Montagu had heard rumours of 'another Messpot'.[14] There was another, hidden reason. At the Peace Conference in Paris the major powers had been deeply concerned about the spread of Bolshevism; indeed the minor powers had used this to extract concessions.[15] The fear of it spreading to the masses in India was a perpetual nightmare to the Indian authorities who were spending much time and resources in tracking Bolshevik agitators and preventing the ingress of Bolshevik material.[16] By appealing for Bolshevik support the Amir had touched a very sensitive nerve.

In his reply of 3 June, Chelmsford welcomed the proposal for an armistice but refused to accept responsibility for the war.[17] He offered to stop the bombing immediately provided that Afghan troops were withdrawn to a distance of twenty miles from the nearest British troops, that there was a cease-fire on all fronts and that the Amir would inform the tribes that he had sought peace. The Indian authorities considered that Landi Kotal or Peshawar was too close to the Frontier and would give too much of an impression that the Amir was treating on equal terms; Chelmsford therefore insisted on Rawalpindi. But he ordered a cease-fire to come into immediate effect on the British side.

In London the mood had swung quickly from anxiety to triumphalism. Montagu complained to Chelmsford that he should have been consulted about the terms of the reply of 3 June and reminded him that peace terms were a matter for the Cabinet. Clemency could be mistaken for weakness and he therefore expected to be consulted closely about the final settlement; in the meantime, nothing must be done to limit the freedom to impose terms on the Afghans.

Montagu, fresh from the delights of imposing peace terms on the Germans, was clearly in no mood to be conciliatory to the Afghans. He was not happy about the speed with which Chelmsford had embraced the Amir's offer of peace; he had been expecting news of an advance on Jalalabad, rather than an armistice. In particular, he thought the Amir's letter, with its refusal to accept responsibility for the war and its telling thrust about bombing, impudent. He felt that Chelmsford had been over eager:

> It seems to me that you should have summoned him to appear to learn your terms and not to negotiate peace.[18]

The Chief of the Imperial General Staff (Sir Henry Wilson) was also keen on an advance to Jalalabad:

> Our advance to Jalalabad will probably knock the bottom out of the whole thing and incidentally do an infinite amount of good to our prestige in Mesopotamia, Persia and Trans-Caspia.[19]

But it is fair to say that neither could have fully understood the pressures which faced the Indian Government.

Chelmsford took an early opportunity to warn Montagu of the consequences of attempting to impose harsh terms on the Afghans:

> We must plainly warn His Majesty's Government if there is any idea of imposing drastic conditions or exacting heavy reparations, that for that purpose we must indefinitely continue war and at least advance and occupy Kabul and Kandahar. Result would probably be chaos and disappearance of all stable Government, thus giving door to Bolsheviks... we must be prepared to deal with general frontier conflagration with its inevitable reaction on India... There is really no half way house between policy of complete subjugation of Afghanistan and policy of attempting to establish mutual trust and really friendly relations.[20]

If aerial bombardment had played an important part in the overtures for peace, it had also had a peculiar significance for the Royal Air Force. Strategic bombing had been seized upon by the founders of the fledgling Service as a means of justifying its separate existence. The First World War had finished too early for the concept to be properly demonstrated. The raid on Kabul, therefore, was eagerly seized upon by the RAF as proof of the value of the concept. Trenchard, the Chief of the Air Staff and the driving force behind strategic bombing, went so far as to congratulate Halley, the pilot, on winning the war single-handed. Even Roos-Keppel, not given to enthusiasms, went so far as to say that without it he doubted whether the Army would have been in a position to advance. Monro, in his Despatch, emphasised the major importance of the air contribution.[21]

In agreeing to an armistice, Chelmsford had made it conditional upon substantive peace negotiations taking place without delay. In insisting on Rawalpindi as the venue, he had to some extent met Montagu's criticisms. The Amir seemed intent on justifying Montagu's attitude. He replied on 11 June to Chelmsford's letter of 3 June.[22] He claimed grandiloquently that the Afghan nation had repeatedly been a cause of destruction and ruination to any foreign power on its sacred soil (a not-too subtle reference to the previous Anglo–Afghan wars); that the present war had created a mood of national regeneration in Afghanistan and that it was now a nation in arms. Consequently, as the people were in effect the Army, he could not pull back his troops without literally shifting the population, which was impossible. From this ingenious but not very promising beginning, he went on to say that nevertheless he would agree to peace talks in Rawalpindi and that he would name his representatives in due course; they would be ready to leave on 27 June.

Amanullah's bold front was not entirely hollow. In Chitral, the Kurram and Baluchistan, the Afghan commanders had not withdrawn as stipulated and showed every sign of reluctance to end hostilities. Even where the Afghan regulars had suspended action, local commanders such as Nadir Shah and Abdul Quduz continued to incite the tribesmen to keep up their attacks on the British troops. Nadir Shah had been hailed as a victor in Kabul, where in due course a statue would be erected to him. Both he and Abdul Quduz were playing a deeper game, aiming at the throne of Kabul. The latter had already put out feelers to the British for a separate peace in return for British support in a bid for the throne. Nadir Shah would eventually succeed to that throne in 1929 after Amanullah had been forced to flee. It would have been surprising if the latter was totally ignorant of these machinations and this knowledge probably underpinned his defiant attitude to Chelmsford.

Despite his promises, there was no sign of the Afghan delegation. By 20 July Chelmsford had lost patience. He informed Montagu that if no satisfactory letter or a delegation had not appeared within two days he intended to resume hostilities without notice.[23] Fortunately, the following day Maffey, the Chief Political Officer to Barrett, reported that a letter had arrived for Chelmsford from the Amir, telling him that the Afghan delegation would arrive at Dakka on 24 July but without an escort.[24] The delay had encouraged the tribes to believe that the Amir was playing a waiting game and that at a suitable moment he would renew the war. He gave substance to that belief by issuing a proclamation calling on the tribes to be ready to renew the war if the peace terms at Rawalpindi were unsatisfactory.[25] While this was probably mere bombast, he could scarcely have done less without losing face among the tribes.

The Indian Government had thus a double incentive to conclude peace quickly – to ease the economic and military strain, and to prevent the Afghan Government from continuing to keep the tribes in a ferment. There was, however, a deep division between London and Simla over the peace terms to be offered to the Afghans. The Indian Government, faced with deep political and economic strains within India, was anxious to conclude peace on terms which would restore good relations with Afghanistan and relieve India of worry on that score. Chelmsford had long believed that this could best be achieved by giving up British control of Afghan external affairs; he had been prepared to do this for Habibullah. He believed that a generous peace treaty would powerfully contribute to stability on the Frontier; he could see no point in hanging on to a control which was increasingly unlikely ever to be enforced and was merely a growing irritant to Afghans. Not all his officials were prepared to take such a radical step and others, particularly among the military, were keen to annex Afghan territory to improve India's strategic position. The CGS (Kirkpatrick) wanted to annex Dakka, Khost and the area north of New Chaman.[26] Sir Edmund Barrow, the Military Adviser at the India Office wanted to go even further and annex as far as Jalalabad and the Kunar river, and to insist on the Afghans withdrawing permanently from Kafiristan.[27] Chelmsford believed that Roos-Keppel would like to have seen all Afghanistan conquered:

> He [Roos-Keppel] is confessedly an Afghanophobe. He hates the Afghans, and, I think I may say with confidence, he would like to see Afghanistan thoroughly conquered.[28]

While there is no evidence that Montagu sympathised with these extreme views, he was keen to take a stern line with the Afghans:

> The Afghans at the Peace Conference should be made to understand clearly that we regard them as in a position tantamount to defeat, and that the terms of peace will be prescribed by us and not by them.[29]

He considered that the terms should include continued control of Afghan foreign policy, the forfeiture of all arrears of subsidy, the permanent withdrawal of the Afghan Postmaster from Peshawar and a period of six months' probation before the peace treaty was ratified. He made it clear that he expected to be closely consulted during the negotiations; the final terms would have to be approved by the Cabinet.

Chelmsford, as the man on the spot, was not to be deflected from his views as to the desirability of generous terms. The draft treaty which he sent back to Montagu followed closely the terms of the final treaty but made some concession to Montagu's views, particularly on the arrears of subsidy and the period of probation.[30] It included alternative versions of Article V – the original providing for British troops to stand firm at Dakka and elsewhere until the Afghans had demonstrated their good faith, the alternative providing instead for Afghan acceptance of the Durand Line as the permanent frontier and for British demarcation of the disputed boundary west of the Khyber.

Predictably, the draft terms did not commend themselves to Montagu. He put forward tougher alternatives.[31] These were patiently dissected by Chelmsford in his reply three days later.[32] Montagu did not press the matter further although he still expected to be consulted about, and to approve, the final terms. A few days later, he approved Grant's negotiating position at Rawalpindi but he wished him to make clear to the Afghans that 'in a word, we and not he [the Amir] are the victors'.[33]

Chelmsford had chosen Sir Hamilton Grant, a previous Foreign Secretary and Roos-Keppel's designated successor, to lead the British delegation at Rawalpindi.[34] Roos-Keppel, who was sick and on the point of retiring, was deliberately excluded, because of his anti-Afghan views.[35] Grant was convinced that Amanullah would not surrender his demand for Afghan independence, and that the alternative was a resumption of the war, with the daunting possibility that the tribes might then decide to come out in full support of the Amir. The Afghan delegation reached Rawalpindi on 26 July. It was led, somewhat curiously, by Ali Ahmad, the Minister for Home Affairs, rather than by Muhammud Tarzi, the Foreign Minister. Grant's initial impression was not particularly favourable:

> a vain, hot-headed, blustering, florid man whose temper may at any moment make him impossible.[36]

There was an early skirmish. The Amir had originally proposed to send an Afghan escort of thirty cavalry and fifty infantry, but he had been forced to drop this gesture. Now Ali Ahmad protested over the restrictions placed on the delegation's movements and about the refusal to provide an armed escort when he ventured out in Rawalpindi.[37] He threatened in consequence to boycott the talks. Grant called the bluff by offering to facilitate the delegation's immediate return to Afghanistan, pointing out that this would result in an immediate resumption of hostilities. There would be other minor pieces of friction but Grant, who had been part of the Dane Mission in 1905 and was well aware of Afghan sensitivities, went out of his way to smooth ruffled feathers, going so far as to hold one session in Ali Ahmad's house, a gesture which was much appreciated. It helped that Grant was fluent in both Persian and Pashtu, well-versed in the Pathan love of argument and able to swap quotations with the best of them. In consequence, while there was much sharp cut-and-thrust, the negotiations were remarkable for their relative harmony.

It soon became clear that the Afghan delegation's instructions were to accept the terms already communicated to the Amir if nothing better could be obtained. Fortified by this, the British team (essentially Grant and Maffey) were determined to permit no substantive amendments to what had been proposed. Negotiations therefore proceeded briskly. The first of six formal meetings was held on 28 July and the treaty was signed on 8 August.

Ali Ahmad opened with a shrewdly judged argument. Just as Britain had defeated Germany by mobilising all its national resources, so Afghanistan was preparing to do the same, on a wave of national regeneration. If, by chance, Afghanistan fell to the Bolsheviks, then the British Raj in India would inevitably follow. It was not entirely a hollow threat. Even before the war had started, the Amir had written to Lenin, seeking friendly relations and claiming to espouse the principles of equality and the peaceful union of all peoples.[38]

Grant affected to dismiss any such threat:

How can a state ruled by an autocratic king, and supported by an aristocracy of great and highstanding land owning Sirdars like Your Excellency, amalgamate and work in sympathy with a violent rabble, who hold that Kings must be murdered, that monarchies must be abolished, that aristocracies must be abolished and that all property must be common, even women... the Bolsheviks certainly have one doctrine which many people – perhaps Afghanistan – share and that is that the British Empire must be destroyed. But I do not think that the Bolsheviks will throw away the rest of their doctrines for this alone, and I believe that if Afghanistan trusts to this she will be making a great mistake.

Ali Ahmad replied that the British would be wise to have some anxiety about Bolshevism which had already brought down many European powers. Grant countered this by saying that it was an ideology alien to Indian society, a view which was backed up by the Indian members of the British delegation.

This exchange showed that the Afghans were both quick-witted and well-informed, and the duelling continued at this high level, with honours by no means one-sided.

The Afghans then moved on to the question of money. Ali Ahmad claimed that the British had promised Habibullah a grant of four crores of rupees[39] as a reward for his neutrality in the First World War but only one crore had been paid. Grant asked innocently if he was perhaps thinking of the £4M included in the abortive Afghan–German treaty, a copy of which he would be happy to lend Ali Ahmad. Ali replied angrily that if that was the British attitude, then it was a pity that Afghanistan had not signed that treaty. When Grant expressed gratitude for Habibullah's neutrality, he was sharply reminded that the British had shown their gratitude by bombing Habibullah's tomb at Jalalabad.

The arguments continued over the Amir's insistence that he should be addressed as 'His Majesty',[40] the accidental bombing of Habibullah's tomb, and the suggestion that Waziristan should be ceded to Afghanistan.

The arguments could have been carried on indefinitely, but the British were anxious to begin returning troops to their peace-time locations and to ease the economic burden of the war. From the Indian Government's point of view, the longer the talks went on the greater the chance of London interfering. Since it was clear that the Afghans had no option but to sign, Grant issued an ultimatum on 1 August; unless peace was concluded immediately, the war would be resumed in fourteen days' time. To meet what was clearly at the centre of the talks, he was prepared to agree to recognise Afghan control of its external affairs; in return, the Durand Line must be accepted as the permanent frontier, Indian agitators and foreign agents must be expelled, the British Vakil must have full liberty of movement, and Afghanistan must refrain from intriguing among the British tribes.

These conditions were accepted by the Afghan delegation on 4 August, subject to three conditions – first, that the treaty should be concluded with 'the Afghan Government', rather than with 'the Amir' as hitherto; second, that any reference to 'unprovoked aggression' by the Amir should be deleted; and lastly, that there should be an amnesty for all the tribes. Grant accepted the first demand reluctantly, rejected outright the third, and agreed to meet the second point by the use of the phrase 'in view of the circumstances which gave rise to the war'.

Grant sidestepped the basic issue of Afghan control of its external affairs, by claiming somewhat casuistically that as the war had automatically cancelled all previous treaties, British control no longer existed; there was therefore no need to refer to it in the treaty. But he agreed to confirm this as the official British view in a letter attached to the treaty.[41] Thus, finally, Grant surrendered the power which had been the bedrock of British policy vis à vis Afghanistan since 1880.

The treaty was signed on 8 August 1919.[42] Reactions to it varied widely in London, Simla and Kabul. London was unhappy about both the conduct of the negotiations and the outcome. Montagu was particularly unhappy about Grant's letter. He had seen it in draft and had immediately telegraphed back his objections. He regarded the letter as either pointless or as making a major change which the home Government had previously refused to agree to. He thought it highly unsatisfactory that the British had been forced to fight an expensive war, which had left much unfinished business with the Frontier tribes, and yet the letter gave away the basis of British security.[43] His irritation was hardly assuaged when he was told that it had been impossible to hold the letter back because the Afghans had already seen it in draft and to have withdrawn it would have led to the collapse of negotiations and the resumption of the war.

He was even more irritated by the fact that, despite clear instructions, the treaty had been signed without either his or the Cabinet having had an opportunity to consider it.[44] Faced with a fait accompli, he took his revenge by refusing to grant honours and awards for the war.

The London *Times* was ferocious in its criticisms: Grant was 'not well fitted to parley with Afghans or anybody else upon a war issue'. The Afghans had gained exactly what they wanted. They had 'unquestionably won the peace and so the war'. The real truth is that the Government of India muddled the campaign and muddled the peace.'[45]

In Simla, Chelmsford regarded the treaty with satisfaction:

While we realise that we have embarked on the nature of an experiment we ourselves believe that in the end it may well prove more satisfactory and successful than the old arrangement... we feel confident that, if due allowance is made for this [Afghan sensitivities] there is every chance that they will eventually seek our advice of their own accord in essential matters.[46]

Grant expressed the same confidence rather more cynically:

Liberty is a new toy to the Afghan Government and they are very excited and jealous about it... Later on, if we handle them well, they will come to us to mend their toy when it gets chipped and broken.[47]

To Dobbs, the Foreign Secretary, he wrote:

I am convinced that the Afghan Government, from self-interest and possibly from a revival of former sentiment, will wish to retain our friendship. Their initial acts and omissions may be open to criticism but they know best how to manage their fanatical, ignorant, credulous, mercurial countrymen – and if one leaves them alone they will in due course return to the fold.[48]

In Kabul the treaty was hailed as a victory. Afghanistan had surrendered no territory or incurred any reparations: on the contrary, it had achieved its primary aim of securing the surrender of British control over its external affairs. At long last it could claim to be fully independent. In this light, there was some truth in *The Times*' bitter comment that the Afghans had won the peace and therefore the war. That remained the Afghan view.

If Afghanistan could claim the most obvious gain, Britain had not come away empty-handed. It had, in fact, made three major gains – first, in securing Afghan recognition of the Durand Line as the permanent frontier; second, in securing the right to demarcate the line west of the Khyber; and, lastly, in securing what seemed likely to become freedom from the ever-present menace of Afghan hostility. The Rawalpindi treaty needs, in fact, to be seen as only the first step in a three-stage process of peace-making. In accordance with Article 4, a further Anglo–Afghan conference took place in Mussourie in the spring of 1920,[49] which in turn paved the way for a treaty of perpetual friendship signed in Kabul in 1921.[50]

There remained one further task. Immediately after the treaty had been signed in Rawalpindi, Maffey, as Chief Political Officer to the North-West Frontier Force, carried out the task of demarcating the boundary west of Landi Kotal. The task was completed and approved by the Indian Government by the end of August 1919. Unsurprisingly the line followed closely that which the British had always claimed.[51]

Annex A

Treaty of Rawalpindi, 8 August 1919

Treaty of Peace between the Illustrious British Government and the Independent Afghan Government, concluded at Rawalpindi on the 8th August 1919, corresponding to the 11th Ziqada 1337 Hijra.

The following Articles for the restoration of Peace have been agreed upon by the British Government and the Afghan Government.

Article I From the date of the signing of this Treaty there shall be Peace between the British Government on the one part and the Government of Afghanistan on the other.

Article II In view of the circumstances which have brought about the present war between the British Government and the Government of Afghanistan, the British Government, to mark its displeasure, withdraws the privilege enjoyed by former Amirs of importing arms, ammunition or warlike munitions through India to Afghanistan.

Article III The arrears of the late Amir's subsidy are furthermore confiscated and no subsidy granted to the present Amir.

Article IV At the same time the British Government are desirous of the re-establishment of the old friendship that has so long existed between Afghanistan and Great Britain, provided they have guarantees that the Afghan Government are on their part sincerely anxious to regain the friendship of the British Government. The British Government are prepared, therefore, provided the Afghan Government prove this by their acts and conduct, to receive another Afghan Mission after six months for the discussion and settlement of matters of common interest to the two

Governments and the re-establishment of the old friendship on a satisfactory basis.

Article V The Afghan Government accept the Indo–Afghan Frontier accepted by the late Amir. They further agree to the early demarcation by a British Commission of the undemarcated portion of the line west of the Khyber, where the recent Afghan aggression took place, and to accept such boundary as the British Commission may lay down. The British troops on this side will remain in their present positions until such demarcation has been effected.

Annex B

Grant's letter, 8 August 1919

You asked me for some further assurance that the Peace Treaty which the British Government now offers contains nothing that interferes with the complete liberty of Afghanistan either in internal or external matters.

My friend, if you will read the Treaty carefully you will see there is no such interference with the liberty of Afghanistan. You have told me that the Afghan Government are unwilling to renew arrangements whereby the late Amir agreed to follow unreservedly the advice of the British Government in regard to his external relations. I have not therefore pressed this matter, and no mention is made in the Treaty. Therefore the said Treaty and this letter leave Afghanistan officially free and independent in its internal and external affairs.

Moreover this war has cancelled all pre-war Treaties.

Notes

1 FPPS August 1919, Part II, No. 249.
2 Viceroy to SofS, No. 684-S, 19 May 1919 – CF 10, No. 630.
3 FFPS, August 1919, No. 54.
4 Ibid, No. 251.
5 Viceroy to SofS, No. 702-S, 21 May 1919 – CF 10, No. 646.
6 Ibid, 21 May 1919, No. 255.
7 SofS to Viceroy, No. 1137, 17 May 1919 – CF 10, No. 533.
8 SofS to Viceroy, No. 1223, 23 May 1919 – CF 10, No. 557.
9 Viceroy to SofS, No. 698-S, 21 May 1919 – CF 10,.No. 644.
10 For a description of the raid see Group Captain Robert ('Jock') Halley, 'The Kabul Raid', *Aeroplane*, 1974. There was only one suitable aircraft in India and it is doubtful if it could have carried out a second raid.
11 Amir to Viceroy, 28 May 1919 – text in Viceroy to SofS, No. 786-S, 1 June 1919 – CF 10, No. 726. Adamsec gives the date of Amanullah's letter as 24 May, as does Gregorian, but the reference to the Kabul raid makes that obviously wrong.

12 A reference to the disputed area between Torkham and Landi Kotal, where the Durand Line had never been formally demarcated.

13 *Third Afghan War*, Appendix XI.

14 A reference to the medical scandal in Mesopotamia in 1915.

15 Margaret Macmillan, *Peacemakers: The Paris Peace Conference and the Attempt to End War* (London, 2001).

16 Popplewell, op cit, passim.

17 Text in Viceroy to SofS, No. 793-S, 2 June 1919 – CF 10, No. 733.

18 SofS to Viceroy, No. 7617, 5 June 1919 – CF 10, No. 617.

19 Wilson to Sir William Robertson, 5 June 1919 – Wilson papers, 2/IA/19 – Imperial War Museum.

20 Viceroy to SofS, No. 837-S, 9 June 1919 – CF 10, No. 768.

21 Monro, *Despatch on Third Afghan War*, para. 17.

22 Amir to Viceroy 11 June 1919 – text in Viceroy to SofS, No. 881-S, 15 June 1919 – CF 10, No. 804.

23 Viceroy to SofS, No. 1086-S, 20 July 1919 – FFFS, September 1919, No. 721.

24 Maffey to Foreign Secretary, No. 12.M.M, 21 July 1919 – ibid, No. 727.

25 FFFS, September 1919, 40–1.

26 'Strategical considerations affecting the alignment of the North-West Frontier of India', 17 June 1919 (with covering note by Monro) – L/F&S/10/809.

27 Memorandum dated 26 July 1919 – L/F&S/1O/807.

28 Heathcote, 101.

29 SofS to Viceroy, No. 10591 19 June 1919 – CF 10, No. 672.

30 Viceroy to SofS, No. 954-S, 29 June 1919 – CF 55h.

31 SofS to Viceroy, 7 July 1919 – ibid, No. 647.

32 Viceroy to SofS, No. 1014-S, 10 July 1919 – CF 55i. No. 665.

33 SofS to Viceroy, 16 July 1919 – ibid, No. 678.

34 The other members were Maffey, the Director of Military Operations (Brigadier F J Moberley), Nawab Shams Shah (representing the Muslim interest), and Baba Gurbaksh Singh (representing the Hindu and Sikh interest).

35 He seems to have taken his exclusion philosophically, realising that his views and Chelmsford's were poles apart, and being convinced that the Amir was only playing for time.

36 Grant to Foreign Secretary, No. 11-F-C, 26 July 1919 CF 55i, No. 766.

37 The account of the negotiations given here is based upon the verbatim English record in Grant's two telegrams to the Foreign Department dated 6 August 1919 – CF 55j, Nos 862 and 905.

38 Chelmsford had already relayed this intelligence to Montagu – see 'Hostilities with Afghanistan', *Parliamentary Papers* (*East Indies* [*Afghanistan*]) 1919, 18.

39 A crore is 100 lacs or 10 millions, roughly equal in 1919 to £1M.

40 It is curious that both sides seemed to have forgotten that this form of address had been used in the 1905 treaty without comment.

41 See Annex B.

42 See Annex A.

43 SofS to Viceroy, 8 August 1919 – CF 55j, No. 847.

44 SofS to Viceroy, 1 August 1919 – ibid, No. 876.

45 *The Times*, 30 October 1919.

46 Viceroy to SofS, No. 1157- 8 August 1919 – CP 55j, No. 852.

47 Quoted in Heathcote, 103.

48 Grant to Foreign Secretary, No. 108-P.C., 6 September 1919 – L/P&S/10/807.

49 For the Mussourie talks see the verbatim record in CP 55m.

50 For the Kabul negotiations see Dobbs' report in L/P&S/10/961; the text of the treaty is in L/P&S/10/955.

51 CP 55j, No. 954.

XII

Reflections

The genesis of the Third Anglo–Afghan War must be found
in the development of Afghan nationalism and the rising social
and political expectations in the country.

Vartan Gregorian

'But what good came of it at last?
Quoth little Peterkin: –
'Why, that I cannot tell,' he said.
'But 'twas a famous victory.'

Robert Southey, 'After Blenheim'

Viewed from this distance in time, the Third Afghan War must appear to
have been one of the most absurd and unnecessary wars that Britain (and
India) has ever been involved in. It was a war started by the Afghan ruler
in response to pressures which he had in part instigated and over which
he had little control, and in an attempt to bolster his own political stability. Logically, it was not a war which he could hope to win unless it was
supported by a general rising of the cis-frontier tribes. When that failed to
materialise the war was over within a month although, true to its untidy
origins, the embers of tribal warfare which it had stirred up continued to
smoulder for many months and the situation in Chitral was not finally
resolved for three years.

No single action in the war involved the use of more than the equivalent
of two brigades. Yet the effort required of the Indian Government was
immense. At its height, the Army in India was forced to deploy nearly
350,000 men and 158,000 animals, the equivalent of some eight divisions,
with another two in reserve[1] and the repercussions were felt all over India.
The cost to the Indian taxpayer was put at some £7M[2] and battle casualties
on the British side amounted to some 250 killed and 650 wounded. But
there were nearly 57,000 sick, with 1,000 deaths, mainly from cholera.[3]

That was not the full extent of the cost to the Indian treasury. There
remained the necessity of a major campaign against the Wazirs and
Mahsuds of Waziristan to punish them for the outrages throughout 1919

which had had to go unpunished while the Indian authorities were preoccupied with the war. Longer term, the war had stirred up unrest among the tribesmen on the British side of the border which would result in almost continuous military operations throughout the '20s and '30s.

No precise figures exist for the cost of the war for Afghanistan. Much of the fighting was done by the Afghans' tribal allies and casualty estimates given in the official history do not distinguish between Afghan regulars and tribesmen, many of whom were British subjects anyway. British estimates of enemy battle casualties in the principal actions give a total of some 600 killed and 1,000 wounded[4]; subsequent deaths from wounds are impossible to calculate but are likely to have been proportionately higher than on the British side because of the inferior medical facilities available. Casualties among the Afghan civilian population from bombing and disease are equally impossible to calculate. It seems likely that Afghan and tribal losses were roughly double those of the British. For comparison, the British losses were approximately those of a quiet day on the Western Front. What can be said with some confidence is that casualties were not a major factor in Amanullah's decision to end the war.

What can be said with a higher degree of certainty is that the financial cost for the Afghans was only a fraction of that for the British – partly because the number of troops and supplies involved was very much less, partly because the Afghan army operated on spartan principles and did not carry round with it the administrative 'tail' which British armies post–1918 had acquired, partly also because the British had used much of the expensive hardware developed in the First World War. By contrast, the Afghans had deployed only a handful of elderly field and mountain guns and a few ancient machine guns, but no mechanical transport or aircraft. Overall, the financial cost to the Afghan Government was not serious, especially when balanced against the clear political gain.

The British had deployed most of the advanced technology of the First World War – the armoured car, motor transport, the Lewis and Vickers machine guns, the 4.5 inch howitzer, the Mills bomb, barbed wire; the major exception was poison gas for which there had been no serious need. In the end, it had turned out to be a rather old-fashioned war, largely decided by men armed with rifles and bayonets and swords; there had even been a cavalry charge and the storming of a fortress in true Peninsular style. Above all, it had been decided by the traditional factors of discipline, leadership and training.

Aircraft had, for the first time, been used on the Frontier in some numbers and, although they had demonstrated their potential in the close support role, they had not had a major impact in close support of ground forces; that would have to await the campaign in Waziristan at the end of the year when better machines were available. The surprising development had been the effectiveness of strategic bombing of Jalalabad and, ultimately, Kabul, against which the Afghans had no defence. Even Roos-Keppel waxed enthusiastic and went so far as to say that without it he doubted if the Army could have been in a position to advance beyond Dakka. The CinC (Monro) emphasised the major importance of the RAF's contribution in his despatch on the war.[5] For the RAF it was a matter of great significance. Strategic bombing had been espoused by the fledgling RAF as a means of justifying its separate identity, but there had not been time to demonstrate its efficacy in the First World War. The raid on Kabul, in particular, was therefore seized upon by RAF commanders as proof of the concept. Trenchard, the Chief of the Air Staff, and a driving force behind strategic bombing, went so far as to congratulate the pilot who bombed Kabul on winning the war single-handed, and that was not entirely exaggeration. Within months aircraft would become a necessity in Frontier warfare.[6]

Militarily, the war had taught few new lessons but it had raised one or two new tactical problems for the British. Mechanical transport had proved its great value in its ability to move supplies and men quickly, and it had proved surprisingly capable of handling the unmetalled roads of the Frontier; towards the end of the war there had been a continuous demand for more such transport and new uses for it had developed. But as always in the Indian Army it was in short supply; it was entirely British-manned; on the outbreak of the war it was some twenty per cent below establishment.[7] It had also raised a difficult new tactical problem in how best to protect mechanised convoys moving at speeds beyond the protection of the foot soldier and even mounted cavalry. It was a problem which was to defy solution for the next twenty years; as late as 1937 there would be a major disaster to a motor convoy.[8] The Russians would encounter similar problems seventy years later.

The armoured car had proved valuable wherever it could operate, but the limits of its operating capability and its precise role alongside horsed cavalry remained to be determined.

Overall, the war had demonstrated once again the importance of a high standard of individual and unit training, and the importance of mobility and communications. It was clear, for example, that the use of mobile, ground-based radio would be of increasing importance; a handful of sets had been deployed but too few and too unreliable to affect tactical thinking significantly. On the logistical side, it was apparent that motor-transport was the key to the future and that meant in turn more and better roads, with implications for tribal societies. Similarly the railway system, particularly in its reliance on narrow-gauge systems in the forward areas, needed substantial expenditure; the completion of a railway through the Khyber in 1926 was the first result.

These lessons would gain added sharpness in the Waziristan campaign which followed. There was, however, nothing really revolutionary in these lessons. The radical change in Frontier warfare had started before 1914 with the use among the tribesmen of the small-bore, breech-loading, magazine rifle, firing smokeless powder.[9] While it had made its appearance among the tribes before 1914, the World War had greatly increased the availability of such weapons and the tribesmen had not been slow to seize on the tactical possibilities. Again, this would be demonstrated more vividly in Waziristan a few months later.[10]

Faced with an unexpected war on widely separated fronts, at a time of considerable economic and internal political upheaval, the Indian Government and the Army had reacted with commendable speed and force. It had repulsed the Afghan regular forces on all fronts and on the Khyber front it was deep into Afghanistan, preparing for an even deeper advance. The lesson had not been lost on the wavering Frontier tribes and the danger of a major uprising of the Afridis, the Mohmands, the Shinwaris and others had been averted. Only in Waziristan and the Zhob had there been serious tribal hostilities and these had owed little to Afghan support or coordination. The armed support of the major tribes on the British side of the Frontier had been an essential element in the Afghan plans; the failure of the tribes to rise had effectively doomed the Afghan invasion.

Despite the reality of his military defeat, Amanullah was quick to assume the role of victor. Foreign missions, including one from the new Bolshevik regime in Russia, appeared in Kabul, and Afghan envoys took up residence in Bokhara and Moscow. In 1928 the Amir even made a grand tour of the Middle East and Europe, during which he was received by King George V. The bubble burst shortly after his return. His extensive programme of radical social and religious reform aroused deep antipathy among the mullahs and the conservative majority of his subjects. He was forced to abdicate in 1929 and, after a period of anarchy, he was succeeded by the so-called 'victor of Thal', Nadir Shah.

No war is entirely pointless and if the Third Afghan War seemed more pointless than most, it nevertheless gave each of the combatants what they wanted – for the Afghans full independence and, for the British, a fixed frontier and the prospect of a permanent peace. The tragedy was that neither objective required a war to achieve it.

Notes

1 Monro, *Despatch*, paras 5 and 28.
2 This was borne by the Government of India.
3 Monro, *Despatch*, para. 17; *Third Afghan War*, 128.
4 *Third Afghan War*, passim.
5 Monro, *Despatch*, para 31.
6 For a more detailed analysis of air power on the Frontier see Chapter XXIV below.

7   Monro, *Despatch*, para 3.
8   In the Shahur Tangi, in Waziristan, in April 1937 – see *Official History of the Operations on the N.W. Frontier of India* 1936–7 (Delhi, 1943).
9   T R Moreman 'The Arms Trade and the North-West Frontier Pathan Tribes 1890–1914', *Journal of Imperial and Commonwealth History* (1994), 187–216.
10 T R Moreman, *The Army in India and the Development of Frontier Warfare, 1849–1947*, 103–32, is a valuable analysis of the tactical experience of the Third Afghan War and the subsequent Waziristan campaign although primarily concerned with the latter. De Watteville is equally, if not more, valuable although written with a narrower focus. Neither is concerned with the wider political background and consequences.

Part Two

WAZIRISTAN

XIII

The Land and the People

(Map 10)

The core of the Frontier problem was Waziristan.

Chenevix Trench, The Frontier Scouts

One may liken the Mahsud to a wolf, the Wazir to a panther. Both are splendid creatures; the panther is slyer, sleeker and has more grace, the wolf-pack is more purposeful, more united and much more dangerous.

Sir Olaf Caroe, The Pathans

No area of the Frontier has been more turbulent than Waziristan and no tribes more aggressive or dangerous than the Wazirs and Mahsuds who inhabit it. It is not a large area; from its northern boundary, along the Tochi Valley, to the southern boundary along the Gomal, it measures about sixty miles; from Tank or Bannu westwards to the Afghan border about eighty miles. The core of Waziristan is contained within a square roughly fifty miles each way. It is exceptionally difficult country, composed of a tangle of rocky mountain ridges, which rise gradually from the Administrative Border[1] towards the west where the peaks of Pir Ghal and Shuidar reach a height of 11,000 feet; Kaniguram, the Mahsud 'capital', stands at 6,600 feet. The mountains are seamed with river valleys and streams, mainly dry except in the rainy season. Where the rivers cut through mountain ranges there are narrow defiles (tangi), classic places for ambush and exception- ally dangerous and difficult to penetrate. Like much of the Frontier, the soil is generally poor and difficult to work, offering only a bare livelihood. Occasionally, patches of flat alluvial plain along the rivers (kach) offer some degree of fertility and the areas round Makin and Kaniguram are relatively fertile. Much of the landscape is bare and stony, but with some patches of trees at the higher altitudes. Apart from Kaniguram, there were in 1919 no towns or large villages; instead, topography and ethnicity produced large numbers of tiny hamlets. There were no roads in Central Waziristan. Lightly armed troops such as the Militias could move, with difficulty, across country; regular formations and transport were confined

147

to the river valleys. Campaigning was impossible in the summer because of the intense heat; the best campaigning season was from November to May, despite the bitterly cold weather, with rain and snow. The cold had the advantage that the tribesmen could not sleep out at night and sought refuge in their villages or caves. The early summer when the snow melts and creates rushing torrents in the dry river beds is the time when the tribesmen are busy harvesting their crops and reluctant to take time off to campaign.

The poverty of the country meant that for centuries the Mahsuds and Wazirs had earned a living by raiding the settled, prosperous areas to the east, along the Indus, and by preying on the great Ghilzai trading caravans (kafileh) which moved down each year from Afghanistan, along the Gomal Valley into India. Its economic poverty, the difficulty of the topography and the aggressive nature of its inhabitants meant that no conquerer had ever considered it worthwhile to attempt to conquer Waziristan. In consequence, Mahsuds and Wazirs remained fiercely independent.

The river valleys offered in 1919 the only avenues of penetration through, and into, Waziristan. In the north, the Tochi Valley offered a relatively easy way westwards for some fifty miles, as far as Maizar; a tributary, the Khaisora, ran roughly parallel to it, some ten miles to the south, as far as Razani. In the south, the Gomal offered a relatively easy route to Wana. This was the main route of the kafileh in spring and autumn. At Khajuri Kach the Zhob river diverges south-westwards, forming the route into the Zhob district. The Tank Zam, running diagonally north-west from Tank, provided the only real access into the heart of Waziristan at Makin and Kaniguram; a tributary, the Shahur Zam, diverged westwards just beyond Jandola and offered a relatively direct route in Wana, except for the fearsome defile of the Shahur Tangi. But it lay in Mahsud territory and most traffic to Wana preferred to take the longer route along the Gomal and Wana rivers.

Although there were no metalled roads in 1919, the road along the Tochi was motorable in stretches and suitable for wheeled vehicles such as carts and artillery throughout. The Tank Zam, from Tank to Jandola was similarly open to wheeled traffic; beyond Datta Khel and Jandola entry into Waziristan was by pack animal only. In 1860 Chamberlain had marched from Jandola to Makin, and out, via Razani and the Khaisora valley, to Bannu; in 1881 Kennedy's and Gordon's columns had, between them, covered the same route. If a central road was ever to be built in Waziristan, linking north and south, Bannu and Tank, that was the obvious line to be followed.

Four tribes inhabited Waziristan – the Daurs, the Bhittanis, the Wazirs and the Mahsuds, all Muslim and all speaking Pashtu, the soft form of the Pathan language.[2] The Daurs inhabited the Tochi valley close to Bannu; they gave little trouble and were not considered in the same league as fighting men as the other tribes although they could be stirred up, as 1936 was to prove. The Bhittanis lived on the eastern fringes of Waziristan between Dera Ismail Khan and Bannu, straddling the Administrative Border. Known as 'the Mahsuds' jackals',[3] they were unlikely to cause trouble on their own but, as their sobriquet implied, were not above joining in whatever profitable trouble there was. It was the Wazirs and, above all, the Mahsuds who formed the real problem.

The Wazirs (more accurately, the Darwesh Khel) were divided into two main branches. The Utmanzai (or Tochi) Wazirs, as their name implied, lived along the Tochi and Khaisora valleys, as far west as the Afghan border – some of them indeed migrated in summer across the border into Afghan Khost. The Ahmadzai (or Wana) Wazirs lived round Bannu and Wana. In 1919 the Wazirs' fighting strength was estimated at just over 25,000.[4] They were among the most aggressive and formidable fighting men on the Frontier but they were more dispersed than the Mahsuds, and the Tochi Wazirs, in particular, were within range of the troops based on Bannu, so that, taken as a whole, the Wazirs were marginally less formidable than the Mahsuds. From the British point of view, their saving grace was that they were not natural allies of the Mahsuds, and were frequently at odds with them.

The Mahsuds constituted the core of the Waziristan problem. Man for man, they were probably the most formidable fighting men on the Frontier. Never conquered, fiercely independent, their fighting skills honed by centuries of raiding, they inhabited the most impenetrable part of the country. They referred to themselves as 'Dre Mahsud' (Three Mahsuds), referring to the three divisions of the Alizai, Bahlolzai and Shaman Khel. In 1919 their total fighting strength was put at just over 11,000[5] and it was strengthened in due course by the presence of many hundreds of deserters from the North and South Waziristan Militias.

McMunn described the Mahsuds as 'Arrogant, pig-headed, faithless, three-cornered, attractive, jaunty, soldierly'.[6] The Mahsuds themselves might not have disagreed entirely with that assessment. Despite their less attractive characteristics, they had been enlisted in small numbers into the Indian Army before 1914. In that war their performance had been patchy; some had fought well, many had deserted rather than fight against the Sultan of Turkey, the head of the Muslim faith. They had also been enlisted into the two Militias, where they had acquired an unsavoury reputation for murdering their officers.[7] But many British officers found them, as a race, attractive and this may, on occasion, have led to a false sense of security.

Both Wazirs and Mahsuds were supreme warriors on their own mountain sides – highly mobile, immensely hardy, excellent shots, and tactically astute. Accustomed to exist on meagre rations, and encumbered only with a bag of food, a rifle, knife and a handful of cartridges, they were able to move across country at a pace which even the most agile regular troops found it impossible to match. Equally, they could watch patiently for hours for the slightest error or weakness. Treachery was a basic part of their armoury, assisted by the ability to melt instantaneously back into their role of innocent farmer. Only the fittest and most highly trained regular troops could be expected to meet them on roughly equal terms. A pamphlet issued by HQ Waziristan District in 1924 after the campaigns of 1919–21 distilled the Army's experience:

> The Mahsud or Wazir is an expert at attacking convoys or small detachments and is assisted by the nature of his country, the ravines being narrow and winding, while the hillsides in the western tracts are often thickly covered with bushes. He attacks systematically, with special parties being told off for specific duties, such as the neutralisation of adjacent picquets by fire, supports to his advanced parties of swordsmen etc... Ambushes may sometimes open by a few shots from one side of a nullah. Untrained troops rush to cover on the side from which fire comes. This is what is waited for. Heavy accurate fire from the other bank then finishes the party.
>
> Against troops proceeding to take up position the usual plan is to ambush the leading party of the advanced guard, firing a volley and charging immediately. Knives are used to cut free rifles and equipment, and the tribesmen make off in the inevitable confusion before a counter-attack can be organised.[8]

The Achilles heel of the Wazirs and Mahsuds lay in their extreme individualism. Unlike other Frontier tribes, their maliks exercised no authority – they were essentially representatives, not leaders, and individual Mahsuds felt no obligation to honour any agreements which the maliks might have concluded on their behalf. No tribesman felt himself obliged to continue fighting if he had other, more pressing, things to do, or felt that fighting was no longer in his own personal interest. Tribal lashkars could thus disperse as quickly as they had assembled. There was little loyalty or unity between sub-sections of the same tribe and in normal times no unity between Wazirs and Mahsuds. They were the supreme pragmatists, calculating the odds instinctively, so that as soon as the opposition reached equality in mobility and fighting power, they were apt to drift away. Thus it may be argued that the real turning point of the campaign in Waziristan in 1919–20 was Skeen's audacious seizure of the Barari Tangi at the end of January 1920.[9]

The tribesmen's tactical skill was balanced by a failure of strategic thinking. In 1919–20 they got no further than opposing head-on Skeen's advance and attacking the construction of picquet posts. There was no attempt to mount a sustained attack on the British line of supply or to carry out a sustained campaign of guerrilla warfare, using their superior mobility. The line of supply to Skeen's column remained virtually untouched throughout the campaign. He was thus able to evacuate casualties, receive reinforcements and build up supplies for each succeeding step without serious hindrance. In consequence, the longer the campaign lasted the more the balance of strength and advantage moved steadily in his favour.

At the beginning of December 1919 morale among the tribesmen, particularly the Mahsuds, was very high. They had had ample opportunity to assess the state of the Indian Army. They were well aware of the political disturbances in India, and during the summer of 1919 they had inflicted a series of defeats on detachments of Indian troops, victories which had revealed the low state of training and experience among those troops. Since May 1919 Wazirs and Mahsuds had rampaged virtually unchecked over Waziristan. Moreover they were still expecting the Afghans to renew hostilities with the British and, if the worst came to the worst, they expected the Amir to obtain an amnesty for them; they had been promised as much.[10] Lastly, rather more than half of the Wazirs and Mahsuds now possessed modern magazine rifles, as well as a few captured light machine guns and very large stocks of smokeless ammunition. With the presence of numbers of trained Militia deserters, the Wazirs and Mahsuds were militarily stronger than ever before.

As in all Frontier campaigns, much depended on the British side on the close cooperation of political and military authorities. Waziristan came under the political and administrative control of the Chief Commissioner of the North-West Frontier Province, in Peshawar, who was also formally the Agent to the Governor General in Tribal Territory. Under him, detailed responsibility rested with the Resident in Waziristan, based at Dera Ismail Khan, who in turn controlled a Political Assistant for Northern Waziristan, based at Miranshah, and a Political Assistant for Southern Waziristan, based at Tank. Assistant Political Assistants at Miranshah, Sorarogha and Wana completed the hierarchy, with Assistant Political Officers and Tahsildars completing the political and administrative machinery. On active service, the military commander was accompanied by one of these officers as his Chief Political Officer; nominally, the commander exercised full political responsibility, acting on the advice of his CPO, who was normally also responsible for providing the commander with intelligence derived from native spies or agents. Because the Militias in peacetime came under the political officers rather than the Army, and as the Army did not deal direct with the tribes, there was frequently a suspicion among the military that the political officers' advice tended to be biased in favour of the tribesmen rather than the Army. Friction between soldiers and politicals was not new and had reached a peak during the Second Afghan War,[11] but it had ceased to be more than a minor irritant and it played no significant part in the operations in 1919–20.

Notes

1 The Administrative Border was the limit of direct Government administration. To the east, the ordinary Indian Penal Code applied; within tribal territory, the Frontier Crimes Regulations applied. Their markedly different provisions recognised the widely differing societies. Tribal territory was often referred to as Yaghistan (Land of the Outlaws).

2 A curious small tribe, the Urmars, live round Kaniguram. They are not Pathans and do not regard themselves as such. They stood totally aloof from the Mahsuds' aggressive activity but in an odd way seemed to run Kaniguram almost as town managers for the Mahsuds – Caroe, 23; 200–1.

3 Major General G F McMunn, 'The North-West Frontier of India Today', *Royal Artillery Journal*, October 1924, 212.

4 *Operations in Waziristan 1919–20* (hereafter referred as *Operations*), Appendix L.

5 Ibid. 187. But de Watteville puts their strength at 16,000 (including Urmars) – De Watteville, 24. Chenevix Trench puts it at 18,000 in 1900 – Chenevix Trench, 14.

6 McMunn, 221.

7 For example, Chenevix Trench, 18–24.

8 Ibid, 4 8–9.

9 See Chapter XX below.

10 The Amir had given them no overt indication that he intended to renew hostilities, and had specifically advised them to make peace with the British when he received the Wazir and Mahsud maliks at Kabul early in 1919. But Afghan troops continued to occupy Wana, Afghan agents continued to circulate among the tribes, and Nadir Shah had promised to obtain an amnesty.

11 Robson, passim. For this reason, Roberts had insisted on having full political powers.

XIV

The British and Waziristan: 1849–1919

(Map 10)

The annexation of the Sikh Kingdom of the Punjab in 1849, on the conclusion of the Second Anglo–Sikh War, first brought the British into direct contact with Waziristan and opened yet another theatre of conflict with Afghanistan. No attempt was made initially to exercise control over the inhabitants, but a chain of posts stretching from Bannu to Tank was established to protect the settled districts to the east from Mahsud and Wazir raiding. Initially, it was the Wazirs round Bannu who occupied British military attention, culminating in the murder of a British officer on his way to Kohat in 1859.

After 1859 attention shifted to the Mahsuds who had continued their traditional pastime of attacking the caravans passing along the Gomal. The first significant conflict occurred in 1860 when a body of some 3,000 Mahsuds, emboldened by a previous lack of military response, gathered to attack Tank which lies in an open plain five miles or so from the beginning of the Mahsud hills. Tank was then held by a troop of the 5th Punjab Cavalry,[1] commanded by an Indian Officer, Risaldar Sadat Khan. He immediately assembled all his outposts and some local levies, and with 158 troopers and thirty-seven levies he moved out to attack the Mahsuds, gathered at the mouth of the Tank Zam. On coming up with them, Sadat Khan ordered his force to retire in order to lure the Mahsuds from their position. When they were fairly into the plain, he turned and charged. Helpless against cavalry on open ground, the Mahsuds lost 300 killed; Sadat Khan lost one killed and sixteen wounded.

It led to the first expedition against the Mahsuds. A force of some 5,000 men under Brigadier-General Neville Chamberlain[2] assembled at Tank in April 1860 and proceeded to invade Mahsud territory by way of the Tank Zam. At Palosina, some twenty miles from Tank, the force was attacked at night; the outlying picquets were overrun and the tribesmen managed to reach the centre of the camp where for some time matters were touch-and-go. Eventually the camp was cleared and the tribesmen pursued for some three miles. They had lost some 130 killed but Chamberlain had lost thirty-seven killed and 132 wounded. It was a startling illustration of the dangerous nature of fighting on the Mahsuds' own ground.

Nine days later, the force encountered the Mahsuds occupying a formidable position blocking the Barari Tangi fifteen miles north of Palosina. The defile was blocked with trees and rocks and the sides of the defile were lined with sangars full of riflemen, with more in support. Chamberlain attacked in two columns along the heights on either side of the defile. His left-hand column was initially beaten back, the troops panicking and falling back on the reserve. The Mahsuds were in turn beaten back by the reserve who then proceeded to carry the heights. The Mahsuds offered little resistance on the right and the whole position was then taken. Chamberlain lost thirty killed and eighty-six wounded; the Mahsuds left thirty-five bodies on the ground.

The rest of the campaign produced no further upsets. The column reached Makin and Kaniguram, burned Makin and spared Kaniguram only on payment of a heavy fine. The force was then withdrawn, via Razmak and the Khaisora valley, to Bannu. The expedition had been a conspicuous success; the Mahsuds had been trounced on their own ground and their territory traversed from end to end for the first time in their history. Much had been learnt on the British side about the nature of the country and about the problems of fighting the Mahsuds. It was to be the first of many expeditions and the similarity between it and the operations of the Derajat column in 1919–20 is striking.

The 1860 expedition had no great lasting effect, nor, given the economic situation of the tribesmen, could it have been expected to. Over the next twenty years a series of minor 'butcher and bolt' expeditions followed. When in 1879 the Mahsuds raided Tank, plundered and burned the bazaar and retired with a large amount of plunder, the British were preoccupied in Afghanistan with the Second Anglo–Afghan War and unable to punish this outrage immediately. With the conclusion of the war in 1881, matters were taken in hand in Waziristan. The Mahsuds were invited to submit peacefully and to agree upon suitable reparation for all the outrages of the last two decades, on pain of a second, large-scale punitive invasion. In preparation for the almost inevitable Mahsud intransigence, a striking force of roughly brigade strength was concentrated at Tank under Brigadier General T G Kennedy, and a similar-sized reserve force under Brigadier General J J H Gordon at Bannu; both commanders had had recent operational experience under Roberts in Afghanistan. The Bannu force included the 4th Battalion of the Rifle Brigade, the first of many British battalions to experience active service in Waziristan.

The Tank column took a more southerly route to Kaniguram than the 1860 expedition, moving via the Shahur Valley. It reached Kaniguram with only one significant piece of fighting. The Bannu column moved down the Khaisora Valley to Razmak, establishing communication with the Tank column at Kaniguram. The columns then returned to their starting points. Despite the ease with which the British had again traversed their country, the Mahsuds had not been brought to a full submission and they continued to flirt with the Afghan Amir until they discovered that he had designs on their country. They then hastily submitted in full to the British authorities. An uneasy peace reigned until 1892 when the Amir again began to intrigue, sending a force of regular troops to Wana. The Amir was sternly warned off and a British force concentrated as a precaution at Khajuri Kach, on the Gomal, within easy striking distance of Wana. The Afghan troops then withdrew and in September 1892 the Amir signing an agreement relinquishing all claims on Waziristan. The border between Afghanistan and India remained unsettled until 1894 when Sir Mortimer Durand agreed a line for the frontier with the Afghan Government – the so-called Durand Line – and preparations were put in hand to mark that boundary on the ground.

In Waziristan that task fell to R I Bruce, formerly Sandeman's right-hand man in the Zhob. It coincided with an invitation from the Wana Wazirs to take over the administration of their country. Bruce's HQ was fixed at Wana and he and his escort arrived there at the end of October 1894.[3] Three days later news came in that the Powindah Mullah was fomenting trouble and planning to attack the camp at Wana. The attack came in the early hours of 3 November 1894. It was skilfully planned and, as at Palosina thirty-four years earlier, achieved considerable surprise, reaching the centre of the camp before being stopped. The camp was eventually cleared and order re-established, but the Mahsuds[4] had inflicted severe damage, killing forty-five and wounding seventy-five, and carrying off a large number of rifles; their own losses were estimated at 350 killed.[5]

Another punitive expedition was now inevitable and three brigades assembled at Wana, Jandola and Bannu in December 1894, under the overall command of Lieutenant General Sir William Lockhart, an officer of great Frontier experience. In the event, there was little fighting but Waziristan was traversed from end to end, towers and defences destroyed, and immense quantities of grain, forage and animals seized. The Mahsuds eventually accepted peace terms and the campaign formally came to an end in March 1895.

The sad rhythm of outrage and punitive expedition had now become established in Waziristan and would continue down to 1939. Given the sterility of the land and the consequent poverty of the tribesmen, it was almost impossible to see an escape. Some had tried. Macaulay[6] in 1865 had attempted to settle Mahsuds in British India but the attempt had failed in its object of giving them an economic stake outside their own country. Ten years later, the experiment was tried of paying allowances in return for free passage for the Ghilzai caravans and two years later tribal allowances were introduced. Macaulay's attempt to solve the problem had culminated in the assembly of a great Mahsud jirga at Tank but it had been pre empted by malcontents who staged the attack on the camp. Because the war in Afghanistan had prevented an immediate expedition, resort had been had to a blockade of the Mahsuds which, by lumping in the innocent with the guilty and further weakening the economic situation of the tribes, made matters worse.

In 1888 Bruce arrived as Commissioner from Baluchistan where he had been Sandeman's assistant.[7] Sandeman's success there in working through the tribal maliks, in a form of 'arm's length' administration, had led him and his supporters such as Bruce to believe that the same system could with advantage be applied, *pari passu*, to the rest of the Frontier. But it rested on two basic assumptions – that the maliks had sufficient influence and standing in their tribes to be able to make effective agreements, and secondly, upon the ability of the army adequately to police those agreements. Experience showed that neither assumption was valid in Waziristan where the maliks had little real influence and the geographical conditions made swift military action difficult. The decision to occupy Wana permanently in 1894, while broadly welcomed by the Wana Wazirs as affording them a degree of protection against the Mahsuds, was resented in equal measure by the Mahsuds, who saw immediately that its real purpose was to provide a backdoor entry into their territory.

The late 1890s were a time of policy confusion. The Sandeman remedy as applied by Bruce had not worked; a reversion to the system of paying allowances direct to the tribes had not seemed to work, either. Curzon was typically sure that he knew the real solution, but was uncharacteristically reluctant to apply it:

No patchwork scheme, and all our recent schemes, blockade, allowances etc., are mere patchwork, will settle the Waziristan problem. Not until the military steam-roller has passed over the country from end to end will there be peace. But I do not want to be the person to start the machine.[8]

Only Macaulay, thirty years earlier, had seen where the real problem lay – tribal poverty – and attempted to do something about it.

The creation of the North and South Waziristan Militias in 1899 was a step forward militarily because their mobility enabled them to deal quickly with small outbreaks, thus obviating the need for ponderous forays by regular troops.[9]

Throughout the period, until his death in 1913, the Mullah Powindah had continued actively to foment trouble, encouraging the murder of British officers and officials and culminating in a plot to seize the fort at Wana by means of a mutiny by the Mahsud company of the South Waziristan Militia. But thorn as he had been in the British flesh for more than twenty years, the Mullah had been a determined and able fighter for Mahsud independence; Caroe has suggested that in a more stable and cohesive society he might have created a coherent Mahsud state.[10]

On the conclusion of the 1894 expedition, Lockhart had recommended the stationing of regular troops in the Tochi valley, where they could be supplied easily from Bannu, maintain a calming influence on the Utmanzai Wazirs and guard a strategic route to Ghazni. In the spring of 1896 a force of one squadron of cavalry, a mountain battery and two battalions of infantry was established in the Tochi with HQ at Datta Khel. The Wazirs continued to cause trouble, culminating in an attack on a Political Officer and his escort in Maizar in June 1897. The escort, consisting of twelve sowars of 1st Punjab Cavalry (Frontier Force), 300 rifles of 1 Sikh and 1 Punjab Infantry (Frontier Force) and two guns of No. 6 (Bombay) Mountain Battery, was resting outside the village when it was suddenly fired on and then attacked in overwhelming strength. Caught at a disadvantage, the escort made a fighting retreat until relieved by troops from Datta Khel. The baggage mules had stampeded early on, taking the reserve ammunition with them, and the guns had been reduced to firing blank until that, too, gave out. It was only sheer determination that prevented total annihilation; casualties totalled twenty-three killed and thirty-two wounded, including every British officer. A subsequent punitive expedition, under Major General Corrie Bird, moved down the Tochi valley from Bannu, traversing most of the country west of Datta Khel and destroying villages in the Maizar area. The Wazirs, encouraged by the news of the great tribal outbreaks to the north, proved recalcitrant, and it was only the approach of winter and the potential loss of the spring crops which forced their surrender in November 1897.

The Mahsuds had continued to raid police and levy posts around Tank. A fine of 100,000 rupees was imposed and the Mahsud jirga was told that unless half was paid within fifteen days a blockade would be imposed. The fine was not paid and the blockade came into force on 1 December 1900.[11] To enforce the blockade, a line of posts was established between Bannu and Dera Ismail Khan, along the Gomal and towards Wana, and troops from the Zhob were moved up to form a chain along the Zhob–Waziristan border. Some eight battalions of infantry, two regiments of cavalry and four sections of mountain artillery were initially employed. Some payments of the fine were made but outrages still continued, troops and Militia were killed and rifles and mail stolen.

Originally, the blockade had been seen as a relatively cheap alternative to a punitive expedition, but after twelve months results were meagre and recourse was had in November 1901 to a number of small mobile columns. Operating southwards from Datta Khel, from Jandola along the Tank Zam, from Sarwekai and north-eastwards from Wana, the columns harassed the Mahsuds from all directions simultaneously, destroying defences, capturing men and cattle and destroying grain and crops. The columns averaged between 900 and 1,250 men, almost all infantry. Columns of this size would normally have run serious risks against the Mahsuds but the latter were unable to combine effectively when attacked simultaneously from different directions. The tribe eventually sued for peace in January 1902 after losing 126 killed, 250 wounded and 215 prisoners; 8,000 animals had been seized, sixty-four towers destroyed as well as the defences of 135 villages; British losses totalled thirty-two killed and 114 wounded. It was a sad commentary on British policy that no better method could be found to curb Mahsud intransigence.

The comparative failure of the policy was exposed when a section of the Tochi Wazirs committed a series of outrages in the area north of Bannu, necessitating an expedition against them in November 1902. In 1905 the murder of the Political Agent at Wana, and the killing of the Commandant of the South Waziristan Militia and the Brigade Major at Bannu led to the dismissal of all Mahsuds from the South Waziristan Militia. Six years later, some 2,000 Mahsuds besieged Sarwekai and two years later the posts at Spinwam and Spina Khaisora, on the Upper Tochi, were attacked.

The twenty years between the permanent occupation of Wana in 1894 and the outbreak of the First World War in 1914 marked a major strategic change in Waziristan. Largely as a result of the setting up of the two Militias in 1900, a string of posts was established along the Tochi valley as far as Datta Khel, backed up by a strong army presence at Miranshah. In the south, similarly, a line of posts was established from Tank westwards along the Gomal valley, linking up with Wana; posts were also established along the Tank Zam as far as Jandola. In effect, Mahsuds and Wazirs were now almost encircled by a cordon, supported by brigades at Bannu and in the Derajat and the garrison at Wana. Bannu and Tank, the base points of the system, were connected by narrow-gauge railway to the main Indus Valley line. The implications of these developments were not lost on the tribes; now, only towards the west, across the Afghan border, was there an easy exit.

The outbreak of war in 1914 produced a difficult situation on the Frontier for the British, partly because the Sultan of Turkey was the leader of all Muslims and partly because the Army in India was weakened by the despatch of large numbers of regular troops overseas. It was imperative to avoid hostilities so as not to divert resources more needed elsewhere. That was easier said than done in Waziristan. Raids and attacks by both Wazirs and Mahsuds did not cease simply because the British were occupied elsewhere, rather the opposite; and although the Amir Habibullah steadfastly resisted all attempts by the Germans and Turks to embroil him in the war, he could not prevent inflammatory, pro-Turkish and anti-British Muslim propaganda reaching the tribes via Kabul.[12] In March 1915 a force of some 10,000 Afghan tribesmen crossed the border from Khost and advanced on Miranshah in the Tochi valley, the HQ of the North Waziristan Militia. It was driven back across the border by a small regular force and comparative peace reigned in Northern Waziristan for another two years.

The Mahsuds were not intimidated. They were coming under the malign influence of the Mullah Powindah's son, Fazl Din, who shared his father's bitter hostility to the British. In an attempt to improve the tribal economy, the British authorities offered contracts of work to the Mahsuds for the improvement of an existing road linking the Shahur valley with the Gomal at Spinkai. The Mahsuds acknowledged that the road lay outside Mahsud territory but Fazl Din proclaimed it a breach of faith and pointed out that better roads meant easier military invasion, On 1 March 1917 he attacked the Militia post at Sarwekai with a lashkar of 2,000 men. The post was relieved after a week by the moveable column from Tank. Further trouble followed and it gradually became clear that the Mahsuds were becoming generally hostile. An attack on a convoy in the Gomal near Nili Kach on 1 May resulted in a serious reverse, the escort losing fifty-five killed and fifty-three wounded. An attempted ambush of a party of Mahsud raiders near Sarwekai on 10 May resulted in the troops and Militia losing thirty-nine killed, sixty-three wounded and seventy missing, more than half the original force. Farther north, a bold attack on the Militia post at Tut Narai, five miles south-east of Datta Khel, resulted in the loss of forty-nine rifles and 120 boxes of ammunition. A major punitive expedition now seemed unavoidable.

Because Northern Waziristan seemed to be equally disturbed, Roos-Keppel, the Chief Commissioner, proposed that one brigade should also operate from the Tochi valley, southwards into Mahsud territory. The suggestion was not adopted because it would have involved two lines of communication and extra resources. Even so, it was considered necessary to concentrate a considerable force at Bannu and Miranshah, comprising nine battalions, a mountain battery and two regiments of cavalry. This force played no part in the subsequent operations against the Mahsuds and was probably an unnecessary waste of resources.

A major expedition in Waziristan at this stage of the World War was a severe and unwelcome embarrassment to the Indian Government. Many of its most experienced troops were overseas and Indian economic and financial resources were severely stretched to maintain its large forces in Persia, Palestine, Mesopotamia and East Africa. An active blockade or a prolonged occupation of any part of Waziristan was not affordable. The alternative was a short, punishing blow where it would damage the Mahsuds most. The objective chosen was the fertile Khaisara Valley,[13] between Wana and Kaniguram. It was, in the longer term, a self-defeating policy. It worsened the Mahsud's economic position and it punished women and children by inflicting starvation on them, increasing Mahsud bitterness. No one in the higher reaches of Government had a better alternative.

The expedition was to be under the command of Major General Beynon, an experienced Frontier soldier, commanding the Derajat Brigade. His striking force of two brigades[14] was to concentrate at Wana and then strike north-eastwards into the Khaisara Valley, withdrawing to Wana on completion of the task. To operate from Wana, three weeks' supplies would need to be concentrated there, and this proved difficult, partly from Mahsud opposition and partly because the Gomal was in flood. These difficulties persuaded the higher command to abandon the Wana route and instead to concentrate the force at Jandola and advance westwards along the Shahur valley. It was calculated that this would shorten the operations by ten days. But the Jandola line was not then suitable for wheeled transport and supplies would have to be moved by camel from Tank. The Jandola line also involved the passage of the fearsome Shahur Tangi defile, which runs for three miles and would be a major problem if the Mahsuds chose to defend it in strength. By contrast, Wana could be supplied along the Gomal using wheeled transport as far as Nili Kach. As the route lay outside Mahsud territory, it was less liable to attack. The choice was finely balanced.

Tank was to be held by a battalion of infantry and a half squadron of cavalry, Jandola by two battalions of infantry, with another two battalions in posts between Tank and Jandola. Two battalions would occupy Sarwekai and another battalion occupied posts along the Gomal route to Wana, with 1,200 of the South Waziristan occupying the smaller posts along the Gomal. For the first and only time, Territorial Army battalions were to take part in operations in Waziristan, while the RAF took part for almost the first time on the Frontier.[15] For the first time also the force commander had a detailed map of his line of advance based on aerial photographs. What is striking about this expedition is the relative weakness of Beynon's force – only two regular battalions (54 Sikhs and 55 Rifles), the remainder of the infantry being Territorial or war-time Indian battalions, with two battalions of Nepalese troops.

On 29 May the Mahsuds held a large jirga at Kaniguram, at which they heard Fazl Din read out a letter from the Amir which made it clear that they could expect no support from him. In the light of that, the jirga passed a resolution that they were willing to be friends with the Indian Government and to return all stolen rifles, provided that their allowances were continued and Mahsud prisoners and detainees released. This offered the basis for a peaceful settlement, but further Mahsud attacks and raids made it obvious that the hope was an evanescent one.

The imminence of a punitive expedition must by now have become obvious as a result of the steady concentration of troops and the accumulation of supplies. Despite this or possibly because of it, attacks on troops and posts continued. On 7 June a detachment of ninety-one men of 2/1 Gurkhas, moving from the post at Zam to Khirgi, in the Tank Zam north-west of Tank, was attacked by an estimated 500 Mahsuds and lost thirty-five killed and twenty-one wounded or missing. Casualties of these proportions were a new phenomenon on the Frontier. Within a week a Wazir havildar of the South Waziristan Militia had deserted from his post, taking with him twenty-five rifles, thirteen boxes of ammunition and some hand grenades. The temperature of resistance was being steadily fanned by the Mullah Fazl Din. It was high time for Beynon to move.

It soon became apparent that the Mahsuds had assumed that, as on previous occasions, the expedition's objective would be Makin and Kaniguram. Accordingly, they had gathered in a large lashkar in the Tank Zam to oppose it. When Beynon moved out of Jandola along the Shahur on 13 June 1917, the Mahsuds were wrong-footed and took time to regroup. Beynon was therefore able to pass through the Shahur Tangi without any fighting. By the time that the Mahsuds had re-grouped to oppose him, he was already close to the Khaisara Valley and, despite heavy fighting, he was able to start the work of destruction of crops and villages. Aircraft operating from Tank had played a useful part in reconnaissance and in bombing concentrations of tribesmen.

On 25 June the Mahsuds sued for peace and Beynon was able to start his withdrawal. They were disheartened by their losses, by the unexpected striking power of the aircraft and by a clear message from the Amir that he would not send help. The Mahsuds surrendered a considerable number of rifles and prisoners, and gave hostages; the peace terms were embodied in a formal document which was carefully explained to them at a full ceremonial jirga at Sarwekai on 10 August. For their part, the maliks repeated a solemn prayer of peace before dispersing.

The expedition had been short, successful and costly – 124 killed, 272 wounded and missing, and twenty-eight died of sickness.[16] Although having had to operate at the height of the hot weather, in a notoriously unhealthy area, the troops on the whole had done well despite the presence of many young and unseasoned men.

For the next two years relative peace reigned in Waziristan but essentially there had been no change in the economic and political parameters of the situation. It remained to be seen how long the uneasy peace could last.

Notes

1 Then a part of the Punjab Irregular Force which came directly under the Lieutenant Governor of the Punjab, not the Commander in Chief India. It subsequently became the 25th Cavalry and then part of the 12th Cavalry (Sam Browne's), which was transferred to Pakistan in 1947 – Gaylor, 83–5.

2 Chamberlain had commanded the Punjab Moveable Column at the siege of Delhi in 1857, when Roberts had served on his staff. He subsequently commanded the Madras Army and rose to the rank of Field Marshal. His son, also called Neville, is credited with the invention of the game of snooker.

3   Richard Isaac Bruce (1840–1924). His escort consisted of one squadron 21st
    Cavalry, 23 Mountain Battery, 20 Punjab Infantry, 53 Sikhs (all from the Punjab
    Frontier Force – see Note 1) and 1 Gurkhas.
4   Wana is in Wazir territory but the Mahsuds actually carried out the attack, sug-
    gesting a degree of tribal cooperation.
5   *Operations*, 21–2. For a vivid account of the fighting see Nevill, 151–4. Tribal
    losses were always difficult to estimate accurately because the tribesmen always
    tried to remove their casualties. British estimates sometimes exaggerated tribal
    losses but probably equally frequently underestimated them. In particular, there
    was no way of knowing how many wounded tribesmen died of their wounds
    subsequently.
6   Major Charles Edward Macaulay.
7   See Biographical Notes and T H Thornton, *Colonel Sir Robert Sandeman*
    (London, 1895).
8   J G Elliott, *The Frontier* 1839–1947 (London, 1968), 229.
9   Chenevix Trench, passim.
10 Caroe, 404–5.
11 The effect of the blockade was to prevent the Mahsuds having any contact out-
    side their tribal area. They were thus cut off from all commerce and intercourse.
12 For an excellent account of German–Turkish intrigues at Kabul see Peter
    Hopkirk, *On Secret Service East of Constantinople* (London, 1995).
13 Not to be confused with the Khaisora Valley in Northern Waziristan.
14 43 Brigade:
        half squadron 11th Lancers
        two sections 30 Mountain Battery
        7 Company 1st (Bengal) Sappers and Miners
        1/25th London Regiment (TA)
        54th Sikhs
        1st Nepalese Infantry (Rifles);
    45 Brigade:
        half squadron 11th Lancers
        23 Mountain Battery
        11 Company 2nd (Queen Victoria's) Sappers and Miners
        2/6th Royal Sussex Regiment (TA)
        55th Rifles
        2/1st Gurkhas
        Mahindradal Regiment (Nepal).
15 They had been used for the first time on the Frontier against the Mohmands in
    1916.
16 Casualty figures in *Operations*, Appendix C, 157. Sickness rates reached 55 per
    cent for British and 42 per cent for Indian troops – mainly dysentery, malaria
    and sandfly fever but the death rate was low.

XV

Events in Waziristan:
April–November 1919

(Map 10)

While they may have been ignorant of the Amir's precise plans and the date of the Afghan invasion, both Mahsuds and Wazirs were well aware that hostilities were about to commence. Apart from the frequent and unrestricted intercourse with their brethren across the border, maliks from both tribes had been summoned to Kabul in the early spring of 1919 to receive gifts of rifles and ammunition in return for a promise to assist the Afghans in any war which might break out. A rising in Waziristan, combined with an Afghan invasion from Khost, was an obvious element in the Amir's plan. The British strategy for Waziristan was to maintain an active defence within the resources available, if necessary abandoning temporarily the westernmost Militia posts in the Tochi and Gomal valleys. It was considered that, in the event of an Afghan invasion, these posts would in all probability come under immediate siege from hostile tribesmen and resources were insufficient to relieve them. In such circumstances, the fidelity of the Militias could not be relied upon. In effect, the British authorities were planning to abandon, even if temporarily, most of the tribal territory west of a line from Miranshah to Jandola.

The regular troops available in Waziristan at the beginning of May 1919 amounted to two brigades; they were supported by the two Militias, each about 1,850 strong, and detachments of the Frontier Constabulary.[1] The 67th (Bannu) Brigade[2] was divided, with roughly half the brigade at Bannu and the other half at Dardoni (three miles north of Miranshah[3]) forming the Dardoni Moveable Column; a small infantry detachment at Kurram Garhi watched events at Spinwam and Shewa. The 68th (Derajat) Brigade,[4] with headquarters at Dera Ismail Khan (DIK), was divided between that place, Tank and Manzai, with two companies of infantry forward in the Khirgi–Jandola–Girni area. All of these troops were stationed outside the Administrative Border. The two brigades were now brought together to constitute Waziristan Force, under Major General Woodyatt, with HQ at DIK.

The outbreak of war on 6 May brought news of an Afghan troop concentration in Khost under the former Afghan CinC, Nadir Shah, and of the movement of Afghan troops towards Wana and the Upper Tochi.[5] On 21 May Roos-Keppel warned Simla that it might be necessary to evacuate Wana, Sarwekai and the posts in the Gomal if Afghan troops arrived; posts beyond Miranshah, in the Tochi valley, might have to be evacuated similarly. Orders to that effect had gone to the Political Agents at Wana and in the Tochi. In accordance with the strategy of keeping things at a low temperature and of not provoking the Wazirs and Mahsuds prematurely Woodyatt was instructed by Barrett on 22 May not to operate beyond Miranshah, or to send troops up the Gomal to Wana. On 23 May, as a precaution the commander of the troops in Bannu (Lieutenant Colonel Ross,1/103 LI) was instructed to plan for the with drawal of the Militia garrisons at Spinwam and Shewa which linked Bannu and Thai, in the Kurram.[6]

The following day the commander of 67 Brigade (Brigadier Lucas), at Dardoni, decided to take his moveable column to Mahomed Khel in order to bolster the morale of the Militia garrisons in the Upper Tochi and to exercise a calming influence on the local tribes who were becoming disturbed by rumours of an Afghan invasion. This move was promptly countermanded by Barrett, who had received information of an Afghan move on Thal or Miranshah. Lucas was ordered to bring the column back to Dardoni immediately. In the prevailing atmosphere, he decided that there was no sensible alternative to evacuating all the Militia posts in the Upper Tochi and bringing the garrisons back to Miranshah. The withdrawal on 25 May proved, predictably, difficult. There was not enough transport to bring back all the Militia stores and equipment and what could not be brought away had to be burned. Thus alerted, the tribesmen swarmed to loot the abandoned posts and to harry Lucas's column. He was forced to carry out a night march back to Dardoni and, in the confusion and darkness, ammunition camels were lost and 150 of the North Waziristan Militia deserted with their rifles and ammunition.

By the time Lucas's column got back to Dardoni in the early hours of 26 May, Nadir Shah had occupied Spinwam and the whole country round Dardoni and Miranshah, and between Dardoni and Thal, was ablaze. Spinwam and Shewa were successfully evacuated on 25 May, with the assistance of the 31st Lancers, from Bannu, and the garrisons reached Idak with the loss of sixteen men captured. But the effect of the withdrawal and of Nadir Shah's presence at Spinwam was the desertion of the Militia from all the posts between Miranshah and Bannu except for Idak and Saidgi. Lucas was effectively cut off from Bannu except by radio.

Lucas's decision, taken on his own initiative, to evacuate the Upper Tochi posts was scathingly criticised by Roos-Keppel He regarded it as disastrous: 'In one night the situation has gone from "set fair" to "stormy"'; the Government would now have to prepare for a general Wazir/Mahsud rising.[7] In England, also, the decision was heavily criticised, Curzon writing to Montagu, asking for the name of the officer responsible. Not all officers on the spot were happy with the decision.[8]

At this remove, the criticism seems overdone. If Lucas erred it was in his decision to move up to Mahomed Khel, against his instructions. His decision to evacuate the Upper Tochi posts when ordered back by Barrett was probably correct in the circumstances and only anticipated the inevitable by a day or two. Barrett's decision to order Lucas to withdraw immediately was dictated by the absence of any clear information on Nadir Shah's intentions and was equally correct. From Khost the Afghan forces could move either on Thal or Miranshah. Even when they reached Spinwam, roughly equidistant from Thal and Miranshah, on 26 May, their objective was unclear. A move on Miranshah would have found 67 Brigade dangerously split. Without reinforcement from outside it would have been very difficult to re-establish connection between the two halves and Lucas at Dardoni would have faced a very awkward situation. Even without direct Afghan intervention, the tribesmen managed to put Dardoni under siege for nine days. As we have seen, Roos-Keppel was ready to evacuate both the Tochi and the Gomal if threatened. The basic fact was that the British did not have enough troops available to maintain control of Waziristan in face of an Afghan threat. Lucas can, however, be faulted for not signalling his intentions to Peshawar in good time.

The unfortunate sequence of order and counter-order led inevitably to disorder, and to a tribal uprising stimulated by Afghan claims that the British were evacuating the country. Some officers on the spot inevitably took the view that Lucas's decision was a mistake because it was bound to stimulate the tribes and to unsettle the Militia. That this was precisely what happened is not, however, proof that the critics were right in their criticisms. It can be argued that the Afghan invasion was bound to arouse the tribes whatever happened and that in consequence desertions from the Militia were inevitable. The compilers of the official history were in two minds. On the one hand, they recorded the view that:

> The timely decision made by the General Officer Commanding the 67th (Bannu) Brigade to evacuate the Upper Tochi posts was more than justified by the subsequent events. Had the withdrawal not taken place when it did, the majority of the garrisons, thinking they had been abandoned would have deserted, and the Wazirs having risen, and being supported by the Afghans, no troops could have been spared from Dardoni to assist the loyal portions of the militia.[9]

A later judgement took a more critical line:

> Such then was the grave situation caused by a policy which had demanded hurried retrograde movements of our troops, accompanied

by the destruction of much valuable stores, without a single shot being exchanged with an Afghan tribesman or regular, thus violating with lamentable results a well-known principle in warfare against an uncivilized enemy.[10]

At the end of May, with the situation still deteriorating, Waziristan Force was removed from Barrett's control and placed directly under Army HQ at Simla. Woodyatt was moved to Baluchistan to take over the 4th Division and was succeeded by Climo, who had successfully commanded 3 Brigade in the Khyber.

With Nadir Shah at Spinwam, only sixteen miles from Bannu, the main forward supply base for Northern Waziristan, the officer commanding Bannu was in an anxious situation. He accordingly moved the major part of his troops out to Kurram Garhi, on the Kaitu river, ten miles north-west of Bannu, between it and Spinwam, to cover any advance on Bannu. Nadir Shah, however, turned north towards Thal on 26 May and Bannu was reinforced with 43 Brigade, which began to arrive on 30 May. With Bannu safe, attention could be given to clearing up the situation between Bannu and Dardoni. At Miranshah, the Wazir members of the Militia were under pressure from the Afghans to desert; Lucas had therefore reinforced the post with 300 men of 1/41 Dogras from Dardoni. Despite this, 600 Wazirs of the Militia, led by the Jemadar Adjutant and another Indian Officer, dug their way out of the post under cover of darkness on 27 May and deserted with their rifles, leaving behind the loyal Khattak elements.[11] Dardoni itself was under a loose form of siege and Saidgi was closely surrounded by hostile tribesmen. The garrisons of the small posts at Thal, Surkamar, Isha, Kajuri and Shinki had deserted, except for the Khattak elements which managed to reach Idak or Saidgi.

The relief of Saidgi and Dardoni was imperative and on 29 May a small force from Bannu[12] got through without serious opposition to Saidgi and lifted the siege. The arrival of 43 Brigade (Brigadier-General Clark)[13] transformed the situation and on 2 June a relief column under Clark moved out of Bannu. Despite Ross's misgivings, the march was relatively uneventful, apart from the squadron of the 31st Lancers managing to get to close quarters with a hostile party of Daurs outside Idak. The heat was extreme as it was now the height of the Indian summer and there were sixty-four cases of heat stroke. The uneventful march was greatly aided by the Dardoni moveable column which attacked a Wazir lashkar near Miranshah, inflicting heavy casualties. Clark halted at Idak on 3 June and sent on a convoy of supplies to Dardoni next day, thus raising the siege.

Events in the Gomal had pursued a parallel but more disastrous course. News of the abandonment of the Upper Tochi posts had reached the HQ of the South Waziristan Militia at Wana on 25 May. Plans for the evacuation of the militia posts in the Gomal, including Wana, had already been drawn up on the assumption that there was even less chance of holding them in face of a tribal uprising than in the Tochi because the number of regular troops available was even smaller. On the 25th the Political Agent for South Waziristan, Major Crosthwaite, who was at Sarwekai paying the Mahsud allowances, conferred by telegraph with the Militia Commandant, Major Russell, at Wana, and took the decision to start the evacuation of all posts west of Murtaza the following evening (26 May). The garrisons of the posts between Wana and Khajuri Kach would retire southwards into the Zhob where they could hope to find assistance from the Zhob Militia; garrisons east of Khajuri Kach would retire on Murtaza. The evacuation was likely to prove more difficult than in the Upper Tochi because the Mahsuds were more aggressive and formidable opponents than the Wazirs. Speed was of the essence.

At 1800 hours on 26 May Captain Traill, with Lieutenants Hunt and Barker and seventy men, left Wana to evacuate Karab Kot and Tanai; Lieutenant Barker was to move on to evacuate the garrison at Khajuri Kach. All would rendezvous at Moghal Kot, on the Zhob river, fifteen miles south of Khajuri Kach. Back at Wana, Russell assembled the Indian officers and announced his intention of evacuating the post immediately. Within a short time, the Wazirs and Afridis in the garrison had seized the keep, containing all the treasure, transport and 600,000 rounds of ammunition. It proved impossible to pacify them, and at approximately 2200 hours Russell moved out for the Zhob with some 300 loyal men and four British officers. The party marched all night and by 0700 next morning was approaching Toi Khula post, on the Gomal, due south of Wana. By this time the Wazirs among the party had disappeared; what was left included raw recruits and some 100 unarmed followers. Toi Khula was found to be in the hands of Wazir tribesmen who fired on the party and Russell decided to carry on to Moghal Kot, fourteen miles farther on, under constant attack. Between Toi Khula and Moghal Kot the party was joined by Traill and Hunt with the loyal remnants of the Karab Kot, Tanai and Toi Khula garrisons. For the last two miles into Moghal Kot they were assisted by Zhob Militia from that post. The party reached Moghal Kot at nightfall but stragglers continued to come in through the night. They were joined there by Barker with seven men, all that remained of the Khajuri Kach garrison.

Russell was forced to remain at Moghal Kot throughout the 28th and 29th because his men were exhausted. But the post could not feed and water Russell's party, which numbered around 300, of whom 100 were recruits and half the remainder trans-border tribesmen of doubtful loyalty. Russell arranged to leave Moghal Kot at 0630 on 29 May for Mir Ali Khel, thirteen miles to the south, where there was a strong Zhob Militia garrison; simultaneously 130 infantry and 100 mounted men of the Zhob Militia were to leave Mir Ali Khel, the infantry to halt half way to Moghal

Kot and the mounted men to push on to Moghal Kot, to arrive at 0630 to escort Russell's party. By 0830 they had not arrived and Russell was forced to begin his march. The party was immediately fired on heavily by tribes-men surrounding the post and a picquet which had been sent on ahead appears to have misunderstood its orders and, failing to come back when signalled, carried straight on towards Mir Ali Khel. All discipline was now lost and the men began to throw away their rifles and flee towards Mir Ali Khel. Attempts to rally them proved impossible. Four or five miles on, the Zhob Militia mounted party appeared and escorted the remnants into Mir Ali Khel where it was at last safe from hostile pursuit. Casualties among the other ranks were estimated at forty killed and wounded which seems a surprisingly low figure, but some men had headed east to the Derajat and it was difficult to obtain an accurate count. Of the eight British officers, five were killed, including Traill, and two (Russell and Hunt) were wounded; only Barker was unhurt.

It was one of the great Frontier feats. Official histories are not much given to purple prose but it recorded its judgement in lapidary terms:

> Regarded merely as a feat of endurance at this period of the year, the withdrawal of this party was, of itself, a fine achievement; but tak-ing into consideration the almost insurmountable difficulties which beset it on the road and the dangers through which it emerged, the exploit stands out as one of the finest recorded in the history of the Indian frontier... The steadfast fortitude of these men in circum-stances before which most would have quailed, is a stirring example of the height to which the devotion of the British officer can rise.[14]

Fewer than 600 men, mainly Khattaks, finally reported at Tank; some 1,100 had deserted and 1,200 rifles and some 700,000 rounds of ammunition were missing.[15] It was effectively the end of the South Waziristan Militia. It was formally disbanded in 1921 and subsequently re-raised by Russell as the South Waziristan Scouts. But there were no Wazirs or Mahsuds and garrisons and operational units were always mixed.[16]

The decisions which led to Russell's retreat were not universally approved:

> Thus again did we fail to realise the lessons of the past; failure to sup-port the maliks; failure to support the militias; retire from Wana, the hot bed of the Afghan intrigues of the past, and thus did we play into the hands of the Afghans and the malcontents of the tribes.[17]

Given the disastrous consequences of the decision to abandon Wana, the decision to abandon it now seems precipitate. But the civil and military authorities, faced with what seemed general insurrection and a shortage of troops, took the prudent, if over-cautious, decision in the circumstances and atmosphere of the time, and historians writing ninety years later are in no position to criticise it.

For the time being the Mahsuds and Wazirs in South Waziristan were busily occupied in looting the abandoned posts and in carrying off the plunder to their villages. Attention therefore refocused on the Tochi Valley, where Dardoni and Saidgi remained under siege.

The Tochi Valley was in a state of insurrection throughout the summer and autumn – convoys and picquets were attacked and camps continually sniped. In retaliation, columns went out to burn offending villages. Between May and the beginning of November 1919, the Tochi Wazirs and Daurs were responsible for more than fifty outrages of various kinds and inflicted casualties of forty killed or missing and sixty wounded, plus a large number of sick as a result of the troops having to operate in extreme conditions.[18] It was clear that something had to be done once the Third Afghan War was out of the way.

Matters were even worse in the Gomal. There, a large Mahsud lashkar, under Fazl Din, had invested Jandola, expecting that post also to he abandoned and hoping to profit from the loot as the Wana Wazirs had profited from the posts farther west. Lashicars and raiding parties of Mahsuds, Wazirs and Sherannis roamed the area, seeking opportunities to attack posts and villages. There were occasional British successes. On 30 May a party of Mahsuds was caught near Murtaza by a squadron of the 27th Light Cavalry and lost twenty killed and many more wounded. On 3 June a Wazir lashkar of some 400 was driven back into the hills, losing thirty men, and next day a similar-sized lashkar of Mahsuds, threatening !the post at Girni, was driven off. Jandola was garrisoned by 176 men of 76 Punjabis and had been effectively under siege since the end of May. Its water supply had been cut and in temperatures reaching 115°F the ration 'had had to be cut to two and a half water bottles per man per day for all purposes, including cooking, Even so, there was now water only until 5 June; relief was imperative. With the arrival of infantry battalions from the Tochi, Climo was able to despatch a relief force under Brigadier-General Miles from Khirgi which reached Jandola without opposition on 9 June. Early in June, despite the armistice in force since the 3rd, an Afghan force occupied Wana. Although it remained passive and appeared to be essentially a propaganda coup, the effect was to encourage the tribes in their belief that the war would be re-started shortly; that may, indeed, have been the object of the move. A bombing raid on the Sheranni village of Drazinda, the centre of a number of raiding gangs, followed by a joint operation between cavalry and aircraft, destroyed the village, captured 500 head of cattle and damped down raiding for several weeks in the area. Cholera in the latter part of June similarly reduced the activities of the British forces. But hostile tribal activity continued at a high level in the Tochi. A large lashkar of Wazirs and Mahsuds was reported to be gathering near Boya on 7 July and next day an attack was made on a Militia picquet leaving Isha. A week later, in the early hours of 15 July, a determined attack was made on the aircraft hangar outside Bannu. It was driven off and no aircraft was damaged, but it revealed the impression that air activity was having on the tribes. A fortnight later, on 29 July, a North Waziristan Militia picquet was ambushed near Kajuri, losing three killed and seven wounded, plus nine rifles. A more serious reverse occurred on 8 August when a picquet of eighty-two Punjabis was ambushed between Saidgi and Shinki by 200 Mahsuds, losing twenty killed and four wounded. Fifteen days later, on 23 August, picquets from Saidgi were again attacked by some 250 Wazirs; armoured cars from Bannu helped to drive the Wazirs off with significant casualties. But the fact that the tribesmen were continuing to operate so close to Bannu was a significant measure of their morale. *Per contra*, these engagements had raised questions about the experience and lack of training among the regular troops.

Not to be outdone, the Mahsuds, Sherannis and Wana Wazirs continued to wreak havoc in the Gomal area. Tank itself was raided on 14 and 15 August, the post at Girni was penetrated and rifles stolen on 27 August, and on 29 August a labour camp near Gambila was attacked and fifteen unarmed labourers were killed and fourteen wounded; but the raiders in the latter case were pursued and were estimated to have lost fifteen killed; another thirty were believed to have died of wounds, heat stroke or thirst.

More serious British reverses were to come in September and October as the Mahsuds and Wazirs assessed the quality of the opposition. On 19 September a patrol of the 27th Light Cavalry, supported by a party of Militia, was ambushed near Zarkani, losing six killed, five wounded, a light machine gun and nine rifles.

On 5 October a force of three troops of the Bhopal Lancers[19] and a platoon of 1/150 Infantry, escorting a telephone construction gang, was ambushed near Manjhi, in difficult country, with long grass, and largely wiped out, only a few survivors eventually reaching Manjhi. Casualties totalled twenty-eight killed, including the officer in command, and ten wounded. Worse was to come. The following day, a force of one squadron of the Bhopal Lancers and two companies of 3 Guides and 109 Infantry, left Kaur Bridge to bring in survivors of the previous day. It was ambushed in turn in broken country, losing three officers and eight men killed. Losses of these proportions were a new and unwelcome development, and were blamed on lack of experience and training. That was almost certainly true; 3 Guides was a war-time unit and 109 Infantry had not served on the Frontier before. But it should be noted that both the Guides and 109 Infantry had been on active service since May, the former in the Kurram and the latter at Kohat. It did not augur well for major operations against the Mahsuds.

The success of these ambushes encouraged a large lashkar to gather near Murtaza and to cut the water supplies to that post, Jatta and Kaur Bridge on 17 October. It then moved on to Girni and on 21 October attacked a column engaged in escorting a contingent of the Labour Corps back to Manzai. This time the lashkar lost some seventy men while British losses were six killed and sixteen wounded. The same day a lashkar of 300 Wazirs attacked a convoy near Kajuri in the Tochi valley, detaching other tribesmen to invest Shinki to prevent the garrison intervening. Troops, rushed up from Idak in Ford vans, managed to turn the tide but losses still totalled three killed and twelve wounded.[20]

At this stage, more than two-thirds of the country was in tribal control. In the Tochi Valley no post was held west of Boya; in the south Murtaza and Jandola marked the limit of British occupation, while Wana was in Afghan hands. Even within these limits no post was free from the threat of attack and no party immune from ambush. The principal instrument of control, the two Militias, had largely collapsed. Two questions therefore require some answer. First, what was the basis of the continuing tribal hostility?; and, second, why had the British not hitherto made a more determined and coordinated effort to retain or re-assert control?

The hostile tribal activities were undoubtedly dominated by the belief that the British had agreed to transfer Waziristan to the Amir within six months of the peace treaty with Afghanistan being signed. A corollary was the fact that Nadir Shah had promised that the peace terms would include a general amnesty for all who had given armed support to the Afghans.

The belief that Waziristan would be transferred to the Amir had no basis in fact, although it may well have been encouraged by the Afghans. Under pressure from the tribes, Nadir Shah arranged in October 1919 for selected Wazir and Mahsud maliks to be received by the Amir at Kabul. There the Amir distributed medals and awards to the tribesmen and to the Militia deserters,[21] and announced that peace had been signed with the British; the tribesmen should therefore now negotiate terms with the British. Despite this the maliks left Kabul in November, after interviews with Nadir Shah, apparently convinced that a resumption of the war with the British was imminent. Despite their losses, the tribes had more than held their own in the summer and autumn of 1919 and their morale and prospects had undoubtedly been raised by the signs of inexperience and lack of training in this most demanding form of warfare among the Indian troops opposed to them. The absence of British troops can only have appeared to the Wazirs and Mahsuds as a sign of the general weakness of the Indian Government.

The British military effort in Waziristan had hitherto been circumscribed by the wider problems which faced the Indian Government in 1919. Despite Amritsar, the internal situation in India throughout 1919 remained delicately poised, absorbing a significant amount of military effort. The problems of post-war re-organisation, the shortage of experienced officers and men and the consequent dependence upon young, war time battalions full of recruits, limited the effort which could immediately be deployed. Finally, although the Third Afghan War was formally over, large forces were still deployed over the rest of the Frontier and time was needed before they could be re-deployed to Waziristan and the lines of supply adjusted accordingly. A conscious decision had been made that a major punitive expedition in Waziristan would have to await a lessening of the strain elsewhere. For the political and military authorities in Waziristan it was a time of frustration as the province slipped farther and farther into lawlessness, a frustration deepened by the awareness that the task of regaining control would be made more difficult by the accession of strength which the tribes had received from the large-scale accession of trained men from the militias and the very large quantities of rifles and ammunition which had fallen into their hands.[22]

Between May and November 1919, the Tochi Wazirs and Daurs had carried out fifty raids and other outrages, carrying off huge quantities of cattle, property and money, and inflicting casualties of forty killed and missing and sixty wounded. The Wana Wazirs and Sherannis had committed thirty-two offences and inflicted casualties of fifty-five killed, eighty-three missing and 106 wounded. The Mahsuds had however topped the list: more than 100 raids and other outrages, loot amounting to 448 camels, 1,674 cattle and property valued at 35,000 rupees and casualties inflicted of 135 killed, thirty-eight missing and sixty-five wounded. In total, the British had suffered a total of some 225 killed, 126 missing and 276 wounded.[23] Waziristan Force alone suffered 139 killed and 159 wounded between August and November, a clear indication of the growing strength of tribal opposition. The losses did not stop there. Operating in the most unhealthy part of the year, sickness, including the cholera epidemic, had been high.

By October 1919 troops were beginning to become available for a major punitive expedition and consideration was being given to the future policy for Waziristan. There were, in effect, three possible policies which might be followed:

(1) to occupy the whole of the territory, right up to the border with Afghanistan, and to disarm the tribes;

(2) to retire to the Administrative Border which would be held in strength by Frontier Constabulary, Militia and regular troops to prevent any tribal incursion, in effect a sort of twentieth-century Hadrian's Wall;

(3) to establish regular garrisons within the territory, connected by a net of modern roads to enable troops to move rapidly all over the country, and thus slowly but surely bring the tribes under control.

The advantages and disadvantages of each course were manifest. The first course would entail a massive military effort and huge expenditure but would, it was assumed, solve the security problem once and for all. But success would also depend upon solving the tribes' economic problem and that would require massive expenditure also. The second course required, in effect, the abandonment of Waziristan to the tribes. It would not be cheap if it was to be effective, and would not necessarily obviate the need for the occasional punitive expedition. There would also be the possibility of an Afghan occupation of the abandoned territory which would in turn produce a major political crisis. Above all, experience from the Roman Empire onwards had shown that such a policy of strict containment simply would not work – sooner or later, the British would be forced to extend their boundaries to protect themselves against their turbulent neighbours, just as the Russians had been forced to do in Central Asia and as the British had had to do in India. The third course was the course finally adopted in the 1920s. It, too, involved massive military and financial expenditure and as it was not accompanied by an equal effort to improve the tribal economy, its success by 1939 was not easily perceived.

In October 1919 the future policy was still a subject of fierce debate, and military and financial considerations did not allow the Indian Government to look beyond the immediate necessity of restoring some sort of order within Waziristan and bringing it back to the situation immediately ante bellum. The course of action proposed by the Indian Government and accepted by the India Office[24] was in three stages: first, terms were to be offered to the Mahsuds and Wazirs. If these were accepted, then the Government intended to proceed to build within tribal territory a series of strategic roads to aid future control. If the tribes refused to accept the terms offered, then there would be an intensive bombing campaign which was confidently expected to bring submission. Should this, however, fail, then there would be a punitive expedition using four brigades. For the future, it was intended to develop advanced bases at Jandola and Razmak from which to control the centre of Waziristan.

The terms finally agreed[25] by the political and military authorities were basically the same for both Wazirs, and Mahsuds, although there were significant differences:

(1) the tribes were to be informed that there would be no cession of territory to the Amir and no general amnesty, the rumours on these points being false;
(2) all rifles, ammunition and equipment stolen since 1 May 1919 were to be handed back;
(3) 200 tribal rifles were to be handed over by each tribe as a guarantee of good faith;
(4) each tribe would pay a heavy fine in compensation for damage;

(5) roads were to be built and regular troops were to be stationed in tribal territory, as follows:

(a) anywhere along the Tochi from Bannu to Datta Khel and wherever posts had been established before;

(b) anywhere within the so-called 'Protected Area', which comprised roughly an area running westwards from Jandola along the Shahur Zam as far as the Tiarza Pass and thence north-westwards to link up with Wazir territory.

Behind (5) lay the intention to station regular brigades probably at Miranshah and Sarwekai, and to build roads from Thal (in Kurram) to Idak, from Khirgi to Tanai and Khajuri Kach, and from Khajuri Kach back to Murtaza. Later extensions would link Tanai with Wana, and Khajuri Kach with the Zhob.[26]

The detailed terms would be put first to the Mahsuds at a jirga to be assembled at Khirgi on 3 November and a reply to be submitted at Khirgi by 11 November. Terms would be put to the Wazirs and Daurs at a jirga at Miranshah on 9 November; troops would concentrate at Dana Khel to receive the reply on 17 November. In both cases, if the terms were refused, air action would commence immediately, followed in due course by a punitive military expedition in the old style. The Wana Wazirs were, for the moment, left out because they were more difficult to get at and it was undesirable to leave any considerable amount of time between a refusal of terms and the succeeding punitive operations. The timetabling of terms to Wazirs and Mahsuds was curious because it was intended in fact to deal, if necessary, with the Wazirs first, because that was considered the easier operation, and then to deal with the Mahsuds, who were considered, correctly, the more difficult proposition, both geographically and militarily. That being so, it is by no means clear why terms were presented to the Nahsuds first; no one could realistically have expected the Mahsuds to accept terms before they had seen the reaction of the Wazirs. Nor were the available resources sufficient to deal with both tribes simultaneously.

Notes

1 The Frontier Constabulary was an armed police force, under civil control, operating in the sealed area between the Administrative Border and the Indus.

2 31st Lancers, 33 Mountain Battery, Nos 5 and 6 Armoured Motor Batteries (armoured cars), 55 Field Company 2nd (Madras) Sappers and Miners, 1/103 LI, 1/41 Dogras, 2/112 Infantry, 3/6 Gurkhas.

3 Dardoni was built in 1917 as a base for regular troops because Miranshah was too small and unhealthy. But the latter remained in use as a Militia HQ.

4 27th Cavalry, 27 Mountain Battery, No. 7 Armoured Motor Battery, 75 Company Bombay Sappers and Miners, 1/76 and 1/66 Punjabis, 2/2 Gurkhas.

5 Viceroy to SofS, No. 700-5, 21 May 1919 – CF 10, No. 645.

6   GSO1, HQ 67 Brigade to Ross 23 May 1919 – Ross's diary (NAM 8004–60), 170.

7   Roos-Keppel to Foreign Secretary, No. 1461-R, 26 May 1919 – CP 10, No. 692.

8   See, for example, Ross's narrative – NAM 8004–60, 173.

9   *Third Afghan War*, 66.

10 Ibid, 68.

11 For details, see Chenevix Trench, 51–3.

12 31st Lancers, section 33 Mountain Battery and one company 103 LI, under Ross.

13 One squadron 31st Lancers, 33 Mountain Battery, 55 Rifles, 27 Punjabis, 103 LI, and a section of three armoured cars. Ross had misgivings about Clark's competence: 'I had not much faith in Br. General Clark who kept informing us that he knew nothing about hill warfare and I personally did not think he knew much about anything.' NAM 8004–60, p. 175. In the event Clark did not last long, being replaced by Brigadier-General Gwyn-Thomas (known to all as 'Tosh').

14 *Operations*, 72. Russell received a very well-deserved DSO and went on to become the Inspecting Officer of Frontier Militias, in the rank of colonel. He would rarely talk about the exploit but his experience apparently destroyed his faith in the Pathan sepoy – Chenevix Trench, 53. Russell's report is in L/P&S/11/155.

15 *Operations*, 73.

16 For the re-formation of the Waziristan Militias post-1919 see Chenevix Trench, 50–3.

17 Unnamed officer quoted in Colonel George Brown 'Notes for a brief history of Wana and the Gomal Valley' (unpublished, c.1930) – NAM 6605–24.

18 For a detailed list of outrages committed since the outbreak of the Third Afghan War, see Grant to Foreign Secretary, No. 1274-Pc, 3 December 1919 (L/P&S/10/870, No. 31).

19 These were Imperial Service troops, trained and equipped to regular standards, but paid for by the state of Bhopal.

20 Captain Andrews, Indian Medical Service, won the VC here – see Appendix 4, below.

21 300 rupees to the Indian Officers and 100 to each man.

22 On a conservative estimate, desertions from the two Militias amounted to not less than 1,500 while some 2,600 modem rifles and 800,000 rounds of ammunition had fallen into tribal hands.

23 Statistics of casualties in *Operations*, 85. 'Missing' almost certainly means 'killed' as prisoners were rarely taken. The figures do not appear to include subsequent deaths from wounds, which may have averaged five per cent.

24 L/P&S/10/951.

26 L/P&S/10/870, No. 113, dated 23 October 1919; *Operations*, Appendix E, 22. One effect of the proposed road building would be the occupation of the Shahur Zam and the Shahur Tangi, an important back door into Mahsud territory. This point would not have been lost on the Mahsuds. These proposals still did not provide, on the face of it, a direct road linkage between the Tochi and the Gomal.

XVI

Operations in the Tochi Valley:
November 1919

(Map 10)

Skeen, with Climo, perhaps the most experienced and able Frontier officer of his rank, was well aware that the state of training and experience of the troops available was well below that required for extended operations against foes as formidable as the Wazirs and Mahsuds. Grant was equally pessimistic:

> with the present quality of our troops I feel no confidence in their succeeding in such difficult country against an elusive enemy. Hence I think we should try any expedient which can obviate military operations. Untrammelled action from the air seems to offer the best hope.[1]

These doubts seem to have produced no effect. More experienced and better trained troops were not readily available. It may be also that the relatively easy victory against the Afghans had induced a degree of complacency. In view of these well-founded doubts it seems even odder that no British battalions were deployed.

At the beginning of November 1919 Waziristan Force, under Climo, had a strength of just under 30,000 combat troops and 34,000 non-combatants (followers). The striking force itself, renamed the Tochi Column, consisted of two brigades (43 and 67), comprising the equivalent of two squadrons of cavalry, a section of 4.5 inch howitzers, two mountain batteries, an armoured car battery and ten battalions of infantry, totalling 8,444 combatants, 6,464 non-combatants, 8,757 animals,[2] with a further three battalions deployed on the L of C to Bannu. It was organised in three echelons. The first echelon, under Skeen himself, was the main striking force and comprised 67 Brigade, a mountain battery, the 4.5 inch howitzers, a field squadron of Sappers and Miners, a pioneer battalion and one and a half squadrons of cavalry. The second echelon, charged with improving the route along the Tochi Valley to allow maximum use by Ford vans, comprised the armoured car battery, a field squadron, the pioneer battalion and a battalion of infantry. The third echelon had the task of safeguarding the route and collecting supplies at Datta Khel; it consisted of 43 Brigade, a half squadron of cavalry and a mountain battery (less one section).[3]

Skeen could call on air support from the eighteen Bristol Fighters of No. 20 Squadron of the Royal Air Force, distributed between Bannu and Tank, and from a detachment of nine DH9As of No. 99 Squadron and three DH10 light bombers of No.97 Squadron, both based at Mianwali, on the far side of the Indus.[4] For the first time on the Frontier, the ground forces would have the benefit of substantial close air support. It would prove to have unexpected limitations – for example, in hot weather the aircraft could not take off from Bannu after 0930 because of hot-air turbulence. Low cloud prevented them operating at all over the mountains. But there would come a time very soon when large-scale ground operations would be regarded as impracticable without close air support. Apart from the section of 4.5 inch howitzers, the column contained no British troops, for the first time in a major Frontier expedition.[5]

As a preliminary to the start of operations, the RAF dropped leaflets on the Wazirs and Mahsuds on 4 and 10 November, warning them that if the British terms were not accepted, bombing would start immediately.[6] On a largely illiterate population the leaflets had no discernible effect. The bombing was a more effective operation. Against Kaniguram on 15 November, ten bombers from Mianwali dropped a total of 134 bombs weighing five tons and the Director of Aeronautics at Simla wrote enthusiastically, if somewhat disingenuously, that the results were 'splendid' – a great deal of damage and many estimated casualties.[7] After the initial experience, casualties were probably low because the tribesmen were easily able to find shelter in the hills where there were numerous caves. But it served notice to the tribesmen that they were not safe from attack even in the heart of their country.

The subsequent ground operations proved something of an anticlimax. The Tochi Column was concentrated at Miranshah by 8 November and the terms of submission duly presented to a Wazir jirga next day. The three echelons then advanced without opposition to Datta Khel, where the whole force was concentrated, with ten days' supplies, by 17 November. Climo met virtually the full Tochi Wazir jirga on the 17th; the only absentees were the Madda Khel, inhabiting the area south-east of Datta Khel, and two small sub-sections in the Kaitu Valley, between Datta Khel and Afghan Khost. The British terms, backed up by the threat of aerial bombardment, were accepted there and then.

The threat of bombardment was no idle one; the Madda Khel villages were bombed next day (18 November) and their maliks came in the same evening to accept the terms. The Kaitu Valley sub-sections were bombed some weeks later and similarly capitulated. Like the Madda Khel, they had clearly calculated that their territory was too isolated and difficult of access to be worth an expedition. It was now clear that no area was beyond the striking power of the RAF.

It had been intended to carry out a march through the Kaitu Valley to reinforce the lesson and to provide the troops with operational experience. The political officers, however, advised against this – partly in order to avoid friction and thus delay the carrying-out of the terms agreed at the jirga, and partly in order not to delay operations against the Mahsuds. The column retired therefore on Dardoni where it was broken up on 27 November. Re-named the Derajat Column, it began its march southwards the same day.[8]

The successful and militarily uneventful operations of the Tochi Column had at the back of them a massive administrative operation. There was no broad-gauge (5 ft 6 in) railway into Waziristan. Supplies had to be transhipped at Mari Indus on the east bank of the Indus, ferried across the river to Kalabagh, on the west bank, whence a narrow-gauge (2 ft 6 in) railway ran eighty-five miles to Bannu, with another branch running down to Tank. Bannu was connected to Datta Khel by an unmetalled road, suitable for wheeled transport.[9] From Bannu to Idak transport was by camel, mule and bullock carts; from Idak to Dardoni by Ford van; and from Dardoni to Datta Khel by Ford vans and by camel and mule. Forward of Datta Khel, the Tochi Column relied on its own camel and mule transport.

Rations for twenty-five days were accumulated at Bannu for the whole force; a further fifteen days' supplies were laid in at Dardoni for all troops beyond there. The carrying capacity of the broad-gauge railway was approximately 650 tons a day but from Kalabagh the daily capacity to Bannu was approximately 250 tons and 200 personnel. When the system was in full working order an average of 200 tons of supplies a day was delivered at Datta Khel. To achieve this, very considerable transport resources had to be deployed. To sustain a fighting force of some 8,500, the ration strength of- Waziristan Force eventually reached some 42,000 combatants and' 38,000 non-combatants, reflecting the enormous growth in the administrative and logistical 'tail'.[10]

The ease with which the Tochi Wazirs had been brought to heel could not, however, disguise the serious weaknesses among the Indian infantry. Writing to Montagu, Chelmsford put the matter bluntly:

We have roughly two experienced officers per battalion in the Indian Army. The rest are men of practically no military experience and certainly no frontier war experience. Moreover, the troops on the whole have very short service. The result is that *vis-à-vis* the Wazir and Mahsud our men are inferior, and the officers, through their inexperience, are unable to make up for the deficiencies in the rank and file. It was because of this inexperience of our officers and men that during the recent operations we had to mass such large forces on our frontier.[11]

This frank appreciation makes it even more surprising that stronger efforts were not made to provide some British infantry.

Notes

1   Grant to Chelmsford, No. 2820.R, 9 October 1019 – MSS Eur D 660/25.
2   Monro, *Des patch on operations in Waziristan*, para. 12; *Operations*, 99–100.
3   Detailed composition – *Operations*, Appendix F.
4   The DH9A was a single-engined, two-seater day bomber/reconnaissance aircraft, with a maximum speed of 118 mph, a ceiling of 16,000 feet and an endurance of nearly six hours. It was armed with two machine guns and could carry up to 600 lbs of bombs. The DH10 was a larger, twin-engined machine, with a maximum speed of 112 mph, a ceiling of 16,509 feet and a similar endurance to the DH9A; but it carried three machine guns and a bomb load of 1,380 pounds. The Bristol Fighter had replaced the obsolescent BE2Cs in the summer of 1919. It was a two-seater fighter/reconnaissance machine, with a maximum speed of just over 100 mph, a ceiling of 17,000 feet and an endurance of three hours. It carried two or three machine guns and up to 300 lbs of bombs. In the difficult, hot-weather conditions of the Frontier these performances were reduced but the aircraft was still a significant improvement on the BE2C. For full details see Thetford, *Aircraft of the Royal Air Force since 1918* (London, 5th edition, 1971). 'Operations in Waziristan' – PRO Air 5/1321.
5   The Territorial Army battalions which had largely garrisoned India during the First World War were being repatriated and the regular battalions to replace them were only slowly arriving. But a regular battalion could have been provided at a pinch and the decision was a deliberate one.
6   Text of leaflets and programme of RAF operations from 4 to 11 November 1919 in L/P&S/10/870, No. 145.
7   Director of Aeronautics to War Section, No. 1024–264, 15 November 1919 – ibid, No. 194.
8   From Dardoni the troops marched back to Bannu and then south along the Dera Ismail Khan (DIK) road (not metalled) to Pezu and thence along a heavy, sandy track to Tank, a total distance of some 140 miles. Wheeled transport could not use the Pezu–Tank track and had to go via DHC, adding another eighty miles.
9   Later in 1919 a camel road was constructed, roughly parallel to the main road, from a point four miles west of Bannu to Dardoni and, in due course, to Datta Khel.
10 Detailed composition of Waziristan Force in *Operations*, Appendix C; logistics statistics, Appendix K, 174–81.
11 Chelmsford to Montagu, 8 October 1919 – MSS Eur 523/9.

XVII

Operations against the Mahsuds: Opening Moves

(Maps 10 and 11)

Never in all the long history of the frontier have the dice been so heavily loaded in favour of the tribesmen as they were in November 1919.
                                                          Major General Elliott[1]

The organisational and personnel disadvantages under which the Indian Army was suffering in 1919 have already been enumerated – the absence of regular battalions overseas, the internal security situation inside India, the large numbers of war-time units full of inexperienced and under-trained recruits, the shortage of experienced officers. Despite these problems, which were real enough, that army had nevertheless fought, and won, quickly and decisively, a war on multiple fronts against Afghanistan. Moreover, in at least three respects, the army was better equipped than ever before – the advent of air power, which threatened to revolutionise Frontier warfare, the widespread availability of the light machine gun and, not least, the availability of mechanical transport to increase mobility. If there were officers, such as Skeen and Smyth, who were worried about the quality of the Indian infantry available, there were other, regimental officers, like Ross and Rees, who appeared, in their diaries at least, to have no particular qualms.[2]

There was one other feature which distinguished the forthcoming campaign against the Mahsuds from those which had preceded it – the absence of British infantry. The basic reasons for their absence are clear enough – the Territorial battalions which had garrisoned India during the First World War were being repatriated as fast as possible for demobilisation, while the regular battalions which were replacing them were still arriving or were preoccupied with demobilising time-expired men and absorbing drafts.[3] In this respect they were no better off than the Indian battalions – in terms of acclimatisation, perhaps slightly inferior. But there were still available some of the eight regular battalions left in India in 1914, some of which had just taken part in the recent Anglo-Afghan war.

The first part of the Waziristan campaign – the operations of the Tochi Column – had appeared to pass off well. There had been no serious fighting and certainly no reverses. The Wazirs and Daurs had accepted the fairly stiff terms presented to them promptly, apart from some small sub sections, and had given every sign of not wishing to suffer a major punitive campaign. In the Tochi, the Indian regiments, unsupported by a British contingent, had acquitted themselves with some distinction and had offered no cause for alarm. Those same regiments were now en route to the Derajat to confront the Mahsuds.

There had, however, already been a number of disturbing reverses against the Mahsuds in September and October. It could be argued that the troops involved were largely second-line troops – Imperial Service regiments and regular regiments with no active service experience.[4] The Mahsuds in their own territory could be expected to be a rather tougher nut to crack than the Tochi Wazirs and it may be that the relatively easy successes of the Third Afghan War, backed up by the uneventful operations of the Tochi Column, had bred some complacency.

Both civil and military authorities were agreed that there had to be a greater degree of control than hitherto, linked hopefully with economic development to reduce the dependence of the tribes on crime as a source of income. Skeen's operations must therefore be seen as having a short- and a long-term purpose. The short-term objective was to punish the Mahsuds for their depredations since May 1919; the long-term objective was to lay the foundations for greater control. These objectives were clearly reflected in the terms set out at Khirgi, and it is reasonable to assume that their rejection by the Mahsuds showed that they perceived the underlying message. It followed, however, that if the country was to be put under more direct control, then widespread devastation was to be avoided if possible. The aim must be either to induce submission by a serious show of force and determination or, if that failed, as it was likely to, to hit the Mahsuds' fighting capacity hard, and thus bring them to a more amenable frame of mind.

The internal political and economic situation in India, the problems elsewhere on the Frontier, and the need to relieve the overstretch which the Army in India had been suffering from since 1918 all argued for speed. Delay could only increase the already high Mahsud morale, foster unrest elsewhere, and delay the reorganisation of the Indian Army. The Mahsuds needed to be hit quickly and hard, and to be made to realise that resistance to the British was ultimately pointless. The precise penalties which the Mahsuds would have to pay depended obviously upon the degree of resistance. Many soldiers undoubtedly welcomed the possibility of a stiff resistance as it offered the opportunity of inflicting heavy casualties. If all else failed, then recourse would have to be had to the destruction of crops and houses, but this was not an initial objective.

To bring the Mahsuds to battle it would be necessary to invade their country and, if unavoidable, to advance to Makin and Kaniguram, the

Mahsud heartland. It was the most fertile part of the country and the destruction of the crops would be a severe blow. It could be assumed that the Mahsuds would resist fiercely. The choice of the line of advance was therefore of critical importance.

There were in theory four possible lines of approach:

(i) from Dosalli, in the Tochi Valley, via Razani and Razmak;
(ii) from Khirgi, via Jandola and the Tank Zam;
(iii) a simultaneous advance along both lines;
(iv) an approach via Jandola, the Shahur Zam, and Kundiwam.

The last approach involved forcing the very dangerous defile of the Shahur Tangi and risked an attack from the Afghan troops still occupying Wana. On the face of it, a two-pronged invasion (option iii) offered significant advantages. It would force the tribesmen to divide their forces, keep them off balance, and avoid the risk of a single line of supply. It was an approach which had been successfully used by Kennedy and Gordon in 1881. But the coordination of two columns, even with the use of aircraft and radio, would present difficulties while the logistics, especially transport, would be more expensive in men and effort. Above all, it would require much larger forces. In face of modern, high-velocity, magazine rifles, small columns, such as had been used with success in 1902, ran the risk of disaster; since the Mahsuds would be operating on interior lines and possessed great mobility, each column would need to comprise at least a brigade group, capable of meeting whatever combination the tribesmen were able to throw against it. The harsh fact was that, given the size of the 'tail' that modern forces needed to drag behind them, and the needs of the rest of the Frontier, there was simply not enough transport available to sustain a dual advance. The fact that a single line of advance reduced the opportunity for strategic surprise or deception, and gave the tribesmen the opportunity to concentrate all their strength against it, was seen in some quarters as a positive advantage because it gave an opportunity to inflict severe losses.[5]

With the decision in favour of a single axis of advance, it became a matter of choice between (i) and (ii). Logistically the Tochi route was marginally the easier. Datta Khel is only some twenty-six miles, as the crow rifles, from Kaniguram, and with the Tochi Wazirs temporarily cowed,[6] there would be a relatively safe and easy supply route back to Bannu and Kalabagh. The route involved crossing the Razmak Narai (pass), fifteen miles south of Datta Khel, at a height of 7,000 feet in winter conditions of snow. It would require the construction of a camel road over difficult country and it was thought that camping grounds and water for a two-brigade force would be difficult to find.

The alternative line of advance, from Jandola, also presented significant disadvantages. It was logistically more difficult. Whereas the seventy miles from Bannu to Datta Khel offered a fairly easy road with no great natural obstacles and the only real difficulties lay in the twenty-six miles from Datta Khel to Kaniguram, the route from Tank via Jandola and Makin, to Kaniguram, was militarily more formidable and, in particular, involved forcing two extremely dangerous and difficult defiles – the Ahnai Tangi, ten miles beyond Jandola, and the Barari Tangi, five miles farther on. The route along the Tank Zam would require close protection for supply convoys along its whole length. Finally, an advance from Tank meant moving Skeen's striking force from the Tochi Valley to Tank, a laborious and time-consuming process. All in all, the balance of advantage and disadvantage between the Bannu and Tank lines of advance would seem to have been a narrow one. A factor which swayed some thinking was the fact that an advance from Jandola would almost certainly involve more severe fighting, thus offering the prospect of inflicting heavier casualties on the Mahsuds. Climo's decision ultimately came down in favour of the Jandola route, primarily, it would appear, because of the severe climatic conditions and the hardship involved in the Tochi route.[7]

The only significant change to Skeen's force was the substitution of a British mountain battery (No. 6 Battery RCA, armed with the new 3.7 inch gun) and 27 (Indian) Mountain Battery (armed with 2.75 inch guns) for Nos 33 and 35 Mountain Batteries.[8] Somewhat curiously, there was no heavy (Vickers) machine gun unit although the guns had proved their considerable value elsewhere on the Frontier during the Third Afghan War.

Behind the striking force lay a huge support effort which absorbed several times the manpower directly involved in operations, and absorbed two complete brigades (62 and 68 Brigades) in its protection. There was no direct rail link from India to Dera Ismail Khan; all rail traffic came via the broad-gauge railway to Mari Indus on the east bank of the Indus river and was transhipped to the narrow-gauge railhead at Kalabagh whence a spur of that railway ran down to Tank and then on to Kaur Bridge six miles south of Manzai (in due course an extension was laid from Kaur Bridge to Manzai). This narrow-gauge railway was capable of delivering a daily average of 250 tons of supplies to Kaur Bridge, with a maximum of 300 tons. Although there was no rail link to Dera Ismail Khan, supplies could be unloaded at Darya Khan, opposite DIK on the east bank of the Indus and ferried across and then taken by draft transport to DIK. At the start of the campaign, a Decauville line[9] was laid from DIX to Tank which was able to carry up to 160 tons of supplies, 1,600 sheep and 100 personnel a day; in purely cargo-carrying terms it was the equivalent of 1,000 camels. From Tank, a metalled road for mechanical transport ran via Kaur Bridge to Khirgi; a camel road ran from Tank direct to Khirgi. From Khirgi, a double camel track ran up the Tank Zam. When fully operational, this line of communication was capable of delivering 100 tons of supplies daily to Skeen's force as it advanced.[10]

The protection of the eastern half of this line (No. 1 Section) fell to 62 Brigade,[11] under Brigadier General Worgan (with HQ at DIK and later Tank), who was responsible for the area from Darya Khan to a point half way between Khirgi and Jandola. From there to the Ahnai Tangi, protection of No. 2 Section of the L of C fell to 68 Brigade,[12] under Brigadier General Cordon. Along the L of C were deployed an immense number of ancillary units – Supply Sections, Bakery and Butchery Sections, Signals units, Railway Companies, Transport units of all kinds, Military Labour Corps, hospitals, sanitary units, Post Offices, Veterinary Sections, Remount Depots, Rest Camps, Canteens, Dairies, Transit Messes and all the paraphernalia without which armies could no longer operate. For a striking force of something under 9,000 men the ration strength west of the Indus reached some 90,000.[13]

The terms offered to the Mahsuds at the jirga held at Khirgi on 3 November were virtually identical to those offered to, and accepted by, the Wazirs and Dauds at Datta Khel on 17 November (see Chapter XV). The Mathsuds were given until 11 November to accept; if they did not accept by the given date air operations would follow immediately. Mahsud morale was high. They had inflicted heavy losses on the troops in September and October and had taken their measure; they were therefore confident of their ability to defend their country, especially against a force confined to a single line of approach. Above all, they would appear still to have nourished the expectation that the war with Afghanistan would recommence shortly. Their fighting strength was estimated at approximately 16,000, but a more realistic measure was the number of modern, smokeless powder rifles available. Taking into account the number stolen or acquired since May 1919, and those in the hands of Militia deserters, it was assumed that 3,500 were in Mahsud hands. The Wana Wazirs were estimated to have a fighting strength of 7,000, and taking into account the rifles captured when Wana was evacuated in May 1919, it seems possible that they may have had up to 3,000 modern rifles. Ammunition was in plentiful supply as it was estimated that some 1,000,000 rounds had fallen into tribal hands since May.[14]

The loose bonds of discipline among the tribesmen – and particularly: among the highly independent and individualistic Mahsuds and Wazirs – meant that the assembly, and even more, the maintenance in the field, of large bodies of fighting men was an unpredictable affair. No shame fell on tribesman if he suddenly decided to take himself home and lashkars could disappear as quickly as they had assembled. The tribesman's sense of honour did not require him to continue if he decided that the game was no longer worth the candle. At all times his personal advantage took precedence over any wider consideration. In November 1919 the fact that it was winter, when agriculture was at a standstill, meant that it was easier to assemble lashkars for daylight operations, but equally the men were more reluctant to stay out on the cold hillsides at night. The tribesman travelled light, with only a rifle, a handful of ammunition, a knife and a bag of food, but this meant that he could stay out only a matter of days before returning home to replenish his supplies. Taking all these factors into account, official calculations assumed that the largest Mahsud force likely to be encountered was 3,500.[15]

The Mahsuds failed to reply by 11 November and bombing commenced the next day against Kanigurm, Makin and Maroba. The Mahsuds soon learned to shelter their families in the hills and caves and the bombing then concentrated on targets of opportunity among the tribesmen and their flocks. By 25 November an average of 10,000 lbs of bombs was being dropped daily.[16]

The line of advance that Skeen had chosen – straight up the Tank Zam to Makin and then south to Kaniguram – was the same line followed by Chamberlain in 1860. Like Chamberlain, Skeen would have the two major defiles of the Ahnai and Barari Tangis to force, defended this time by tribesmen armed with long-range, breechloading, magazine rifles and perhaps the odd captured Lewis gun, for which ample stocks of ammunition were available.

The Tank Zam itself is broad for most of the way from Khirgi to the Barari Tangi; much of it is dry in the winter but seamed with numerous deep rivulets which made marching arduous. Although the interior of Waziristan is essentially mountainous and deeply intersected by wadis and nullahs, there are plateaux on either bank of the Tank Zam, which could take a large camp, and even the river bed is wide enough in places for a temporary camp. These camping grounds were invariably dominated by surrounding heights from which the Mahsuds could snipe anything that moved. Establishing the necessary picquets on these heights was expensive in manpower and always susceptible to ambush unless very carefully executed.

The plan for Skeen's advance had been worked on throughout the summer. Its timing depended upon the speed with which the Tochi Wazirs could be brought to submission, and upon the desirability of settling with the Wana Wazirs before the hot weather set in. Taking all these factors into account, Skeen had come up with the following timetable:

14 December	move of troops from Tochi to be completed;
23 December	force to be concentrated at Jandola and Gurlalukach;
11–17 January 1920	force to operate in Tao Dachina and Paskas Valleys;
18–19 January	two days' rest;
21–30 January	advance to Kaniguram;
31 January	return march begins;

| 7 February | force united at Jandola; |
| 14 February | advance on Wana begins.[17] |

On this, sanguine, timetable, the Wana Wazirs could be dealt with before the 1920 hot weather set in. In the event of the Mahsuds submitting quickly, the intention was to switch operations to the Wana Wazirs.[18] The Tochi Wazirs having settled unexpectedly quickly, Skeen was in a position to start five weeks early.

The final plan envisaged an advance in three bounds to Dwa Toi, eight miles from Kaniguram and some four miles from Makin. Ten days' supplies would be collected at Dwa Toi and the column would then advance to Kaniguram; at that point, if there was still no sign of submission, the destruction of crops and supplies would begin. The column would then move on to Makin for seven days to do the same there. It would then retire to Jandola. The destruction of crops and houses is not only distasteful but, in the long run, self-defeating; beyond a certain point it creates more opposition than it overcomes and it complicates the military and logistical problems of the force itself. Moreover, it had never had any lasting effect on the Mahsuds. The authorities hoped that by the time Kaniguram had been reached a sufficiently stern military lesson would have been taught the Mahsuds so as to bring them to terms without any need for this destruction. The official history expressed it in even more optimistic terms:

> it was hoped that the concentration of our striking force in the vicinity of Jandola following on very intensive air operations would cause the Mahsuds to accept our terms and so make an advance into the heart of their country unnecessary and admit of the operations against the Wana Wazirs beginning forthwith.[19]

If the threat of military force did not persuade the tribesmen to submit, then it would be highly desirable to bring the Mahsuds to a major battle as soon as possible, in the hope of inflicting sufficient casualties to obviate the need for a further advance.

The choice of commander was a critical one. Climo, an immensely experienced Frontier soldier and a hard fighting general, might have seemed the obvious choice for an expedition which was clearly going to be difficult and even hazardous. But he was now in command of Waziristan District and Skeen was appointed to command the striking force, although Climo remained in overall charge of operations, reporting direct to Army HQ in Simla. Skeen was an officer of equal Frontier experience and he and Climo were close friends. Of the former, an admirer wrote:

> Of all the generals I have met I would put Skeen in the highest class. He lacked only one thing, important in a general, and that was robust

health... [Climo] and Skeen were two of the best leaders of troops the Indian Army has ever produced.[20]

Skeen's initial concentration point for his striking force was Khirgi, on the Tank Zam, sixteen miles north-west of Tank. Ross's battalion, the 103rd LI, was one of the earliest to arrive from the Tochi; it made the fifty-mile march from Bannu to Khirgi in six days, which was probably about par for the course. His battalion arrived at Khirgi on 8 December.[21]

As the troops of his striking force began to arrive at Khirgi, Skeen fed them forward to Jandola, eight miles ahead. From Jandola, two battalions, with two guns, moved forward on 11 December to establish permanent picquets at Spinkai Raghza, one and a half miles ahead, to cover the first step of the main advance. The Mahsuds reacted fiercely and the fighting lasted three days, the force suffering forty-six casualties. Skeen, with 67 Brigade and other elements, reached Jandola on 17 December. The normal composition of the Striking Force settled down at two mountain batteries, a company of Sappers and Miners, a signal company, six infantry battalions and a pioneer battalion, with two field ambulances and a bearer unit, totalling altogether about 8,500 combatants, plus some 2,800 camels and 1,100 mules, carrying four days' supplies and stores which included substantial quantities of barbed wire, fence picquets and explosives. Each battalion had sixteen Lewis guns, distributed among the platoons, as well as sixteen discharger cups for rifle grenades. It was, by the standards of the times, a well-equipped force and to support it Skeen could call on the squadron of Bristol Fighters at Tank and Bannu and DH9A and DH10 bombers from Mianwali. As will be seen, the two brigades seldom moved together, one normally staying at the previous camp until the next camp had been established.

The problem of protecting the route and the camps of the force could be solved in either of two ways – by temporary or permanent picquets. Temporary picquets, where the picquet was sent up from the column as it advanced, and then withdrawn as it passed, or put out round a camp each day, had hitherto been the more usual course. But it was very expensive in manpower, exhausting for the troops and very open to ambush, particularly in the withdrawal; to extricate a picquet in difficulties could delay a column for some hours.

The alternative was permanent picquets, inhabiting a strong defensive work, covered by barbed wire and equipped with grenades and Lewis guns. It was not necessarily cheaper in manpower but, once firmly established, the picquets were almost immune from attack and the only real danger lay in the garrison relaxing and growing careless in its routine. The establishment of permanent picquets, however, was an obvious prelude to an advance and the tribesmen invariably sought to prevent or obstruct their construction. Much of the fiercest fighting of the campaign was fought round the establishment of these picquets and it frequently required the involvement of a full brigade, extending over two days, to complete the establishment of a single picquet.

Given the fact that Skeen's expedition was no quick in-and-out affair but a sustained advance likely to last up to three months, with the consequent need for daily supply convoys, the decision was taken to use permanent picquets to protect the line of advance of the force. Given the fighting quality of the infantry initially available, it proved a wise decision – temporary picqueting was a skilled operation, which required very close adherence to complex procedures, and even experienced troops could easily get into difficulties. With the level of experience and training existing initially among Skeen's troops, disasters would have been almost inevitable.[22]

Apart from the fighting round Spinkai Raghza, Mahsud reaction had been largely restricted to constant sniping. But on 17 December, while Mahsud maliks were in the camp at Jandola, ostensibly seeking peace talks with Skeen, a fierce attack was made on the troops constructing picquets to guard the camp. The troops were forced back and one picquet overrun. The attackers were eventually driven back in the face of rifle, Lewis gun and artillery fire with some twenty casualties but the troops had lost thirty-four. It was a taste of the fierce fighting to come and of the boldness of the Mahsud tactics.

On 18 December Skeen moved forward some three and a half miles to a new camping ground at Palosina. Gordon was despatched to Dotak, on the west bank of the Tank Zam, at its confluence with the Shahur Zam, to protect the left and rear of Skeen's advance over the Sarkai Ridge due north of Jandola, which dominated the Palosina plain from the south. His advance went smoothly, partly due to low-flying aerial support. By 1630 the force, including transport, was concentrated on the Palosina camping ground, where it was to spend an eventful ten days. From Palosina, Skeen could either advance northwards up the Tank Zam (as planned) or westwards along the Shahur Zam. Unsure at this stage of his real intentions, the Mahsuds had assembled a lashkar of some 2,000 farther up the Tank Zam; a smaller Wana Wazir lashkar was reported to be heading down the Shahur Zam, towards Dotak. Skeen had thus succeeded for the moment in dividing and wrong-footing the opposition.

At Palosina, the camp occupied a large plateau on the east bank of the Tank Zam, exactly where Chamberlain had camped sixty years earlier, and the scene of the great night attack on 19 April 1860. To the north the site was protected by the Spinkai Ridge and to the south by the Sarkai Ridge, both going up to 3,000 feet. Skeen was taking no chances and the whole camp was surrounded by a breast-high stone wall, beyond which was a barbed wire entanglement.[23] A picquet (Water Picquet) was established on the edge of the west bank to cover parties drawing water from the Tank Zam.

On the west bank, the dominant feature was Mandanna Hill, almost opposite Palosina, where the Tank Zam curved westwards. Below Mandanna Hill the river bank dropped some 200 feet into the bed of the river which at this point was 600 feet wide. Mandanna Hill was the key to a further advance up the Tank Zam and it was essential for Skeen to have it in his hands before making another move. The attack on Mandanna Hill on 19 December was entrusted to the 55th Rifles and the 103rd LI, under the overall command of Lieutenant Colonel Herdon (55th Rifles), sup ported by the artillery in Palosina Camp.[24] Serious opposition was not expected and the attacking force numbered only 950. The 55th (Coke's Rifles) was a Frontier regiment of long standing, with a good reputation, while the 103rd (a Mahratta regiment) had performed well in the Tochi Valley. There had, however, been no effective aerial reconnaissance and reconnaissance on the ground had necessarily been difficult. Knowledge of the ground over which the troops would have to operate was thus sketchy.

Immediately opposite Palosina, the west bank of the Tank Zam rises steeply to a narrow plateau, which runs roughly NNW towards Mandanna Hill. The western side of the plateau is dominated by two small features – 'Black and White Hill' to the south, and 'Red Rocks' roughly half way up towards Mandanna Hill. Farther west still, running almost parallel to the plateau but divided from it by a steep ravine, was a series of tangled features. These features, reading from south to north, were 'Black Breasts', 'White Breasts', 'Sandbag Hill', 'Comb Rocks', and 'Broken Hill', some 700 yards south of Mandanna.[25]

There are three versions extant of what happened on 19 December – the version in the official history,[26] Ross's account[27] and that of Rees.[28]

Skeen was present at the scene of operations and the official account must lean heavily on his version. According to this account, the 103rd seized 'Red Rocks' and 'Sandbag Hill', while one company of the 55th seized the lower slopes of 'Sandbag Hill' and 'Broken Boulders', on the right of the 103rd; the remainder of the 55th was in position on the left of the 103rd. For an hour the 103rd struggled in face of fierce Mahsud opposition to seize 'Comb Rocks'. Having lost heavily, the battalion was then fiercely attacked by a body of Mahsuds issuing from the depression between 'Sandbag Hill' and 'Comb Rocks'. The battalion was forced back and without supports the retirement became a rout, sweeping the 55th along with it, all the way back to Palosina. This is by no means a clear account; in particular it has the bulk of the 55th on the left of the 103rd.

Ross, who was an interested spectator in Palosina, has a somewhat different account. According to him, Herdon had planned to occupy 'Black and White Hill' to protect his flank and to make his main advance along the river bed under cover of the picquet established by his regiment the day before, and then to assault Mandanna on the shortest possible line from there. Such a plan clearly depended for its success upon there being no serious enemy intervention from the area west of the plateau. Ross claims that this plan was overruled by Skeen, who ordered Herdon to seize the features progressively from the south, starting with 'Red Rocks' and extending northwards through 'Sandbag Hill', 'Broken Boulders', 'Comb Rocks' and 'Broken Hill', finally assaulting Mandanna Hill itself. According to this account, the 103rd, supported by the artillery firing across the Tank Zam, managed to get on to the lower slopes of Broken Boulders' where it came under intense fire to its left and rear from 'Black and White Hill'. When the battalion, with the 55th on its left, attempted to move forward to seize 'Comb Rocks' and 'Broken Hill', preparatory to the final assault on Mandanna Hill, it came under intense fire from 'Comb Rocks'. For an hour the battalion tried unsuccessfully to seize 'Comb Rocks', losing its acting CO and two other British officers killed, two officers wounded as well as five Indian officers. A counter attack by the Mahsuds finally threw the troops off 'Sandbag Hill' and they then began to retire. The retirement soon became a rout and both battalions retired in complete disorder across the Tank Zam, arriving back in camp 'very shaken'.

Rees's account is different again. According to him, the 55th were on the right and their covering parties almost reached the lower slopes of Mandanna Hill. The 103rd, apparently on the left, sent a party to occupy 'Black and White Hill'. Just after 1030 Rees saw through his field glasses a part of the 103rd retreating from 'Black and White Hill'. At the same time the forward troops of the 55th were attacked by a small party of Mahsuds and promptly bolted. Their panic infected the rest of the battalion which promptly fled also, leaving the unfortunate Herdon by himself.[29]

Clearly these three accounts cannot be reconciled. The official account makes no mention of Herdon's original plan being countermanded and, whereas Ross has the 55th on the left of the 103rd, Rees has it the other way about. There are other inconsistencies which it is impractical and perhaps pointless to attempt to elucidate. Ross naturally was concerned for the honour of his regiment, but he also had the advantage of hearing the accounts of the survivors from his regiment. If Ross is to be believed, then Skeen also had a direct personal interest in the eventual official account. Rees is perhaps the least reliable of the witnesses; he clearly did not know what the actual plan of operations was and his sketch plan, made from memory in 1925, is highly inaccurate.[30] What may be significant in this context is that Skeen subsequently chose to retain the 55th in the force, while sending back the 103rd. But equally that may simply have been due to the fact that Skeen knew the 55th as a famous Frontier regiment, whereas the 103rd was a Bombay regiment, and not well known to him previously.

At this distance in time, the precise sequence of events is impossible to determine. What is clear is that two regular battalions of the Indian

Army had been forced to flee in panic, losing ninety-five killed and 140 wounded, with 131 rifles and ten Lewis guns, in the process. The Mahsuds admitted to thirteen killed and forty wounded.[31] Lucas himself was apparently caught up in the panic and just made it back to the Tank Zam.[32]

The verdict in the official history is suitably ambiguous:

> The reverse was due to several causes, the chief of which was the neglect to observe the principle of distribution in depth. There was no reserve of troops and the small local supports were insufficient to restore the situation when the retirement became general.[33]

It was presumably intended to be a criticism of Herdon, who was in direct command. But given the presence of Skeen and Lucas, the difficulties of the terrain and the unexpected strength of Mahsud opposition, it can equally be read as a criticism of the higher command. The troops were criticised for not being masters of their weapons and for helplessness when their officers were disabled or killed.

Whatever the precise sequence of events, it is now possible to see with the benefit of hindsight the basic causes of the debacle – first, the lack of adequate reconnaissance; secondly, the use of too small a force, and third, the inadequate training and discipline of the troops engaged. The inability of commanders adequately to reconnoitre the ground in hostile, hilly country is always a problem, but the deficiency can be rectified by aerial reconnaissance. Why this was not available in this case is something of a mystery but may have been due to ground commanders' unfamiliarity with the use of aircraft. Two passes by a single aircraft constituted the sum total of air support that day[34] – more sustained air support, as subsequently became a *sine qua non*, might well have turned the tide or at least enabled the troops to retire in some sort of order.

Given the ignorance of the topography, it was tempting fate to entrust this important operation to two battalions only; when the operation was repeated the following day, even a full brigade proved inadequate. The reasons for the lack of training and experience among the troops have already been discussed. The 55th were lucky enough to be given a second chance and ultimately proved one of Skeen's most reliable battalions. The 103rd paid the price and were relegated to L of C duties and then sent back to India.

The troops passed an uneasy night. The whole force was much shaken by the scale and nature of the defeat, and fears of a night attack, such as that on the brigade camp at Wana in November 1894,[35] were present in many minds. Given the state of the force's morale, such an attack might well have produced a disaster on a scale never seen on the Frontier.

Notes

1 Major General J C Elliott, *The Frontier* 1849–1947 (London, 1968), 249.

2 Diaries of Colonel Harry Ross (NAM 8004–60) and Second Lieutenant Douglas Rees (NAM 6706–21).

3 Between 9 May and 9 September 1919 the 2nd North Staffordshires, for example, received drafts totalling three officers and 321 other ranks. Battalion strength on 18 May 1919 was twenty officers and 472 ORs; it reached a peak of twenty officers and 535 ORs on 29 June but when it arrived back at Jamrud on 9 September 1919 it was down to sixteen officers and 379 ORs – Adjutant's diary, 2nd Battalion the North Staffordshire Regiment (copy in possession of SCR Burton Esq.).

4 Cf the disasters round Manjhi in October 1919 involving the Bhopal Lancers, an Indian States Forces unit which had arrived on the Frontier only in June 1919, having seen no active service, and the 1/150th Infantry, a war-time battalion raised only in 1918, and which had also arrived on the Frontier only in June without previous active service experience.

5 It is thus argued in *Operations*, 93: 'a single line of advance by encouraging a vast display of tribal force and inducing a sense of security from other points enables our forces to bring the tribesmen to battle and to inflict casualties which in every action of importance were, considerably heavier than our own.' Apart from the slight but significant confusion of tense, this sits rather uncomfortably with the recorded uneasiness of senior officers about the fighting quality of the troops. It is clearly a case of 'post hoc…'.

6 Nevertheless, the Tochi Wazirs took the opportunity to suspend payment of their fines in money and rifles pending the outcome of the campaign against the Mahsuds – Viceroy to SofS, No. 325-S, 20 March 1920 – L/MIL/7/15939, 496.

7 Climo to CGS, 20 October 1919 – L/P&S/10/870, No. 90. The chosen route was that followed by Chamberlain in 1860 – see *Operations*, 14–17 and *Frontier and Overseas Expeditions*, Vol. I.

8 The detailed composition of the Derajat column initially was two squadrons 31st Lancers, two troops 21st Cavalry, No. 6 Mountain Battery RGA, 27 Mountain Battery, 55 Field Company Bengal Sappers and Miners, 74 Company Bombay Sappers and Miners, (43 Brigade) 4/39 Garwhal Rifles, 57 Rifles, 82 and 2/152 Punjabis (67 Brigade) 55 Rifles, 1/103 LI, 104 Rifles, 2/112 Infantry, together with 3/34 and 2/61 Pioneers. No. 35 Mountain Battery from the Tochi eventually joined the L of C when Skeen advanced.

9 The 60cm Decauville light railway had been used extensively in France. It was easy to lay (and take up) and its light petrol or diesel engines could haul surprising tonnages.

10 For ration strengths and logistic organisation, see *Operations*, Appendix K, 174–85.

11 16 Cavalry, 21st Cavalry (less one squadron) and 27th Light Cavalry, one section 35 Mountain Battery, Nos 6 and 7 Armoured Motor Batteries, 2/90 Punjabis, 2/94 Infantry, 2/102 Grenadiers, 2/113 Infantry, 2/127 Baluch, 2/150 Infantry. Note: as the campaign developed these allocations changed as battalions moved up to join the striking force and were replaced by battalions from the striking force.

12　One troop 21st Cavalry, two sections 35 Mountain Battery, 75 Field Company Bombay Sappers and Miners, 3 Guides, 2/19 and 2/76 Punjabis, 109 Infantry.

13　See *Operations*, Appendix K, 174.

14　The tribesmen possessed large quantities of older weapons – Sniders, Martini-Henrys, jezails, etc. – indeed every fighting man probably owned a gun of some sort, but these did not fire smokeless powder. It was the use of smokeless powder, which rendered the firer almost invisible, that constituted the major tactical shock of the campaign. 'In the fighting against the Mahsuds in 1919 and 1920, I was at my command post during twenty three actions in which at least a brigade was employed, with anything from three hundred to five thousand men up against us... during the whole of that time I saw only two puffs from black powder.' Skeen, *Passing It On: Short talks on tribal fighting on the North-West Frontier of India* (Aldershot, 1932), 12.

15　Tribal strengths in *Operations*, 96–7.

16　Monro, *Despatch*, para 16.

17　Skeen to War Section, No. G-109, 22 November 1919 – L/P&S/10/870. No. 268.

18　L/MIL/17/4119, Appendix 106.

19　*Operations*, 92.

20　Sir John Smyth, *Milestones* (London, 1979), 62.

21　Ross's diary, 185.

22　For a detailed description of the complex procedure for temporary picqueting, see Skeen, op cit.

23　*Memoirs of Second Lieutenant Douglas Rees, 3/34th Pioneers* – NAM 6706–21, 179.

24　Although Ross was the senior, the Brigade Commander (Lucas) had asked him not to go out in order to allow Herdon to command, presumably because he believed Herdon to be the more experienced Frontier officer – Ross, 187.

25　See Map 11 and detailed topographical plan and panoramic photograph in *Operations*, opposite 100.

26　*Operations*, 101–2.

27　Ross, 188–9.

28　Rees, 179–82.

29　'Hughie' Herdon was left alone in tears but was allowed to retire unharmed by the Mahsuds who apparently included some ex-soldiers of the 55th – Rees, 182.

30　Rees, opp. 180.

31　Losses in *Operations*, 102.

32　'General Lucas was leading by a couple of lengths as they swept past the newly established Water Picquet but was fouled by his Brigade Major who used his elbows just as they were entering the ravine.' – Rees, 182.

33　*Operations*, 102.

34　De Watteville, 105.

35　For a detailed description of the attack on the camp at Wana on the night of 2/3 November 1894, see Nevill, 151–3.

XVIII

Crisis and Reorganisation

(Map 11)

The fighting on the 19th had made clear to the Mahsuds the axis of Skeen's advance; with morale high, they could now concentrate along the line of the Tank Zam.

For Skeen, it was clearly essential to restore morale among the troops as quickly as possible and to limit the damaging effect on the tribes. In the circumstances, he had little option but to repeat the operation against Mandanna Hill the following day (20 December), using a larger force. Climo had already ordered up 68 Brigade and suggested that Skeen should wait until this reinforcement was available:

> 68 Brigade moving to join Skeen. Have pointed out to Skeen that it could possibly be advantageous to await arrival of this fresh brigade before attacking but am leaving this to his judgement.[1]

The force to be employed comprised a full brigade and two sections of 55 Company 1st (Bengal) Sappers and Miners.[2] The plan was essentially the same as that adopted on the preceding day, but this time it included occupying 'Black and White Hill', a tacit admission that a mistake had been made the previous day. This time also there was continuous support from the RAF, which bombed and machine gunned the reverse slopes of 'Comb Rocks' and targets of opportunity.[3] With heavy air and artillery support, Mandanna Hill was occupied for a cost of only three killed and fifteen wounded; Mahsud casualties were believed to have been heavier than on the previous day. Work immediately started on constructing a permanent picquet post. Numbers of tribesmen had been observed in the Tank Zam to the north of Mandanna Hill but by 1530 the picquet post, although incomplete, was considered strong enough to leave a garrison for the night. By 1630 the covering troops were back in camp at Palosina, leaving behind a garrison of 100 men of 2/19th Punjabis, under Captain Cuthbert.[4] The post was exposed to fire from 'Comb Rocks' and 'Broken Hill' at ranges of 300 – 600 yards[5] but well within covering range of the artillery some 1,200 yards away.

195

At 1645 Cuthbert reported by field telephone that tribesmen were collecting north and west of his position; from Palosina a party could be seen in the Tank Zam at the foot of Mandanna Hill. Ross recorded what he next saw from the camp:

> My tent was not far from the Artillery camp and I saw the gunners suddenly open fire in a westerly direction. On enquiring why they were doing this, I was told to look at Mandanna Hill, and there I beheld the whole of the picquet rushing pell mell down the side of the hill into the river bed while the hill top was in possession of the Mahsuds.[6]

In their panic the men allowed their rifles and equipment to be snatched from them by the Mahsuds as they fled. The casualties amounted to eighteen killed and sixty wounded; Cuthbert and eleven Sikhs were killed defending the post.

It appears that the garrison, having dumped rifles and equipment inside the half-finished post, were outside the post, carrying up blankets, water and reserve ammunition, when they were suddenly fired upon from 'Comb Rocks' and 'Broken Hill'. Under this covering fire, two parties of Mahsud swordsmen climbed up the hill from north and west, and attacked the post. Cuthbert was killed leading a counter-attack and most of the men then panicked and fled. Subsequent intelligence suggested that the Mahsuds had not planned an attack but simply seized upon a fleeting mistake. It emphasised both their tactical acumen and the lack of experience among the troops. The Mahsuds acquired nearly 100 rifles, 10,000 rounds of ammunition and several boxes of hand grenades. Skeen's original doubts about the quality of the troops allotted to him were now being justified.[7]

Skeen was in an unenviable position. He had suffered two successive defeats; losing in the process over 300 men killed and wounded. Three battalions had been severely mauled,[8] and there was now a grave doubt about the fighting capacity of the rest of his infantry. He could no longer be sure that they were capable of coping with the Mahsuds.

The future of the campaign now hung in the balance. It was a critical test of Skeen's leadership. Postponing the problem of Mandanna Hill, he decided to launch an attack next day (21 June) to establish a permanent picquet on 'Black Hill' (Tarakai), some 1,300 yards due north of the camp. The operation had no great tactical importance – although it overlooked the camp, the hill was too far away to offer any real threat – but Skeen urgently needed a success to restore the confidence of his shaken troops. The attack was entrusted to three fresh battalions (82 Punjabis, 109 and 2/112 Infantry), with 55 Company 1st (Bengal) Sappers and Miners and two companies 3/34 Pioneers to construct the picquet post.

'Black Hill' (3,264 feet) is at the southern end of a steep ridge running roughly north and south; at the northern end is Sagarzai Peak (3,584 feet), some 1,200 yards away. The ground around 'Black Hill' is rough and difficult, and offered good cover and good fire positions; it was nevertheless well within gun range from Palosina.

The attack initially went well and 'Black Hill' was seized without opposition by 1030 and construction of the defences put in hand immediately. Considerable numbers of tribesmen had been seen crossing the Tank Zam towards 'Black Hill' and when the defences were only half finished a party was seen assembling half way between Sagarzai and 'Black Hill'. Just after 1330 heavy rifle fire was brought down on the position and a large body of Mahsud swordsmen swept over the hill. The covering troops protecting the right front of the picquet panicked and fled, exposing the other troops who also retired precipitately. The two companies of the 3rd/34th Pioneers working on the half-finished post were left isolated. The walls had reached a height of only two feet and the only protection was a single strand of barbed wire. Nevertheless the Sikhs under their four British officers repulsed four attacks.

Meanwhile, the remainder of the troops was rallied on a ridge half way back to camp. Their counter-attack reached the foot of 'Black Hill' but could get no farther. The Pioneers finally ran short of ammunition and grenades, and were forced to withdraw when a fifth attack developed. The Mahsuds, some 800 strong, occupied 'Black Hill' where they were engaged by the guns from the camp who now had a clear field of fire. At 1600 the troops were ordered back to camp. Casualties amounted to sixty-six killed or missing and 256 wounded; Mahsud casualties, largely caused by artillery fire, were later reported as 250 killed and 300 seriously wounded. Despite their casualties, victory clearly remained with the tribesmen.[9]

The Mahsud attack was described as: one of the best examples of fire and shock action. The organisation of their fire power was perfect. At ranges up to 1,500 yards, and from positions on which our artillery fire could be brought to bear, their riflemen developed a volume of aimed fire under which their swordsmen scaled the hill unseen and unscathed.[10]

The attack on 'Black Hill' may have been a more critical affair than was appreciated at the time. Enquiries made subsequently by the Political officer, Major Quinan, indicated that the poor performance of the troops on19 and 20 December had encouraged the Mahsuds to plan an all-out attack on the camp from all sides. It was planned for mid-day because the Mahsuds had noticed that the aircraft normally returned to base at this me to replenish and let the pilots have lunch. The signal for the assault was to be the victorious Mahsuds descending the southern slopes of 'Black Hill'. The gallant defence of the 3/34th had prevented this and without the agreed signal the rest of the attackers had dispersed.[11] Given the state of morale in the force, a major attack might have produced a disaster of unparalleled proportions. Skeen recognised the vital significance of the Pioneers' defence when, in an Order of the Day, 'Black Hill' was re-named 'Pioneer Picquet'. For the first time, a unit of the force had stood and fought the tribesmen to a standstill.

Some air support had been available but it had clearly been less effective than on the 20th. For the second day in succession a post had had to be left uncompleted late in the day, which would seem to suggest that the establishment of permanent picquets required more careful planning and organisation if further disasters of this kind were to be avoided. The inability of a substantial body of troops, with air and artillery support, to fend off the Mahsud attacks and to counter-attack successfully, now raised in even more acute form the question of the infantry's fighting capacity. Subsequent examination of the ground showed that the temporary sangars constructed by the covering parties were poorly designed and situated.

What had been a grave situation in the force was now a critical one. The Brigade Major of 43 Brigade, 'Jackie' Smyth, summed it up later:

> In two days we had only advanced three miles and had suffered three resounding defeats; three battalions had been so severely mauled that they were in need of a rest, and perhaps worst of all, the confidence of the troops had been badly shaken. We had realised that our troops were untrained in mountain warfare and that they would have to buy their experience but we had hoped that the price would not be so high. Only a few people, myself included, realised how close we had come to a debacle.[12]

Skeen could now no longer trust the fighting capacity of his infantry. He was faced with the gravest situation in Frontier warfare since the critical days of the Ambeyla campaign fifty-six years earlier. In this crisis, he requested the use of poison gas. The seriousness of the situation was emphasised by Climo to AHQ:

> Report by Skeen that loss of picquet was due to hurried retreat of, firstly, 109th, and, secondly, 82nd, which left picquet isolated. Counter attack failed as troops refused to face them in spite of gun and aeroplane support. His attack today will be undertaken by fresh troops and picquet will be held by selected company of 100 rifles of 76th. Should these fresh troops show same weakness Skeen considers that serious situation will arise. A feature of the fighting is our bad rifle practice, many of the men had no really steady training since recruits course. Against tribesmen this is fatal to success. He considers only set off to our present unsatisfactory situation is use of gas and serious results may arise from hesitation to use it. Sight of five

battalions all in retreat in front of tribesmen has undoubtedly shaken morale of troops. Indian gunners not free from this feeling... I wish strongly to endorse advisability of using gas for if today's operation fails we cannot afford to reject any method by which superiority over tribesmen may be restored.[13]

The request was a measure of the desperate nature of the situation in which Skeen found himself. His troops were not trained in, or equipped for, gas warfare and the necessary equipment and supplies were not available in India.

The possibility and desirability of using gas against the tribesmen on the Frontier had, for nearly a year, been under active discussion, as part of a wider discussion in England about the retention of gas as a weapon by the British Army.[14] The General Staff in London and Churchill, the Secretary of State for War, were keen to avoid any international ban on the use of poison gas because they saw it as an effective and economical weapon which could shorten operations and hence save lives, particularly in colonial, or so-called 'savage' warfare, in India, Iraq, Egypt and elsewhere in Africa. They were aware that poison gas as a weapon had aroused strong public repulsion and that its use would produce political problems both at home and abroad. They argued, however, that gas had actually proved less lethal on the Western Front than artillery fire, that against savages who mutilated casualties it was absurd to have scruples about the use of gas, and that it would greatly assist in dealing with the numerous military problems which faced Britain in the immediate post war period.

In India, Chelmsford and Monro were initially opposed to its use on the Frontier. Nevertheless, Army HQ considered that the Army in India must be in a position to retaliate if gas was to be used against it, and requested that Brigadier General Charles Ffoulkes, the leading gas expert, should be sent out to investigate and advise. Ffoulkes sailed on 11 June 1919, while the Third Afghan War was still in progress. He found many military commanders, including Barrett, Climo, Skeen and Wapshare, in favour of its use, in different degrees of enthusiasm.[15] Even Hamilton Grant and the Agent to the Governor-General in Baluchistan, were prepared to accept its use.[16] Grant was positively enthusiastic:

Tribal warfare is so difficult that we cannot afford to throw away any weapon which can help us in the prompt settlement of frontier difficulties.[17]

Dobbs, the Foreign Secretary, once he had consulted Ffoulkes, was also in favour. Leslie, Skeen's Chief of Staff, told Ffoulkes that officers were generally in favour 'as the best means of reducing the casualty list'.[18] In face of this pressure, Chelmsford and Monro agreed reluctantly to gas being adopted as a weapon for frontier warfare; they were not prepared to have it used without warning or against civilian disturbances such as had culminated in the massacre at Amritsar.[19]

Skeen's and Climo's request was therefore made in a receptive atmosphere. The problem was that the necessary equipment and expertise did not exist in India. Some gas shells and protective clothing were shipped out to India for trials and experiment in July 1919 and further items were sent out in January 1920. A requisition for 16,000 shells and 10,000 gas masks, however, was blocked by Lord Sinha, the Under Secretary of State for India.[20] Montagu was entirely opposed to the use of gas against the tribesmen and the Afghans except in retaliation.[21] He believed that its use would have serious political and moral consequences and insisted that it should not be used without reference to him. However, even if the necessary requisitions had been passed, there would have been insufficient time to manufacture and ship these stores out to India so as to have any significant effect on the Waziristan campaign. The Cabinet as a whole was divided on the issue and, although it agreed with some reluctance to the War Office continuing to experiment and carry out trials, the matter went no further than that; by 1939 the British Army was trained in defensive measures against gas but had no offensive capability. In India a temporary Travelling Gas School was set up in September 1920, [22] thereafter the matter lapsed.

In the meantime, Skeen and Climo had met the Chief of the General Staff (Lieutenant General Sir George Kirkpatrick) at Khirgi on 21 December to ask for reinforcements and particularly for Gurkha battalions whose fighting capacity and background as hillmen was deemed to make them better suited to mountain warfare. Accordingly, the 2/19th and 82nd Punjabis, and the 103rd and 2/112th infantry[23] were withdrawn to the L of C and replaced in the Striking Force by 4/39 Garwhalis and 2/76th and 2/152nd Punjabis from 43 Brigade, pending the arrival of Gurkha battalions. It was agreed at the same meeting that in future no operations would be undertaken at less than brigade strength and that all picquets would be fully consolidated before they were occupied.

Despite his anxieties, Skeen was determined not to surrender the initiative to the tribesmen and on 22 December he re-occupied 'Black Hill' without significant opposition and successfully established a permanent picquet there; the RAF flew thirteen sorties with Bristol Fighters in support. The true scale of the Mahsud losses then became apparent – bodies were found on or around the hill even though it was normally a matter of honour for the tribesmen to carry away their dead.[24] Equally significantly, many rifles were found abandoned. Spies reported many burials at Kotkai, four miles away, up the Tank Zam, and there were reports of many dead and wounded being carried off to their villages.[25]

The operations on the 22nd can be seen as the beginning of the renaissance of Skeen's force. Two good, fresh battalions – the 57th (Wilde's)

Rifles and the 4/39th Gharwalis – reached Skeen on 22 December. But the 22nd also marked the highly significant moment when air power came of age on the Frontier. Reporting to Army HQ, on 24 December, Skeen noted that:

Aeroplanes were prohibited from operating in the hills by heavy clouds and in consequence I am not pushing operations until the weather has sufficiently cleared to admit of adequate cooperation from the air.[26]

It was recognition that major ground operation could or should no longer be carried out in daylight without air support. It followed from this that further advances would be dependent upon suitable flying weather. It was a major turning point in Frontier warfare. A few days later, Skeen proposed to Army HQ that the DH9s of 99 Squadron and the DH10s of 7 squadron operating in his support should be replaced by Bristol Fighters which he believed were more useful for tactical purposes.[27]

Skeen's troops, in any case, needed a period of rest and recuperation after the stresses of the previous few days. This enforced halt coincided with information that the Mahsud maliks were anxious to discuss a settlement and were asking for active operations to be suspended pending talks; Skeen was doubtful of their sincerity. In agreeing to meet them at Jandola, he proposed to increase the number of tribal rifles to be surrendered and to insist on advancing to Makin to receive all of the money and rifles to be surrendered, a clear sign perhaps of renewed confidence.[28] In the meantime, despite, or perhaps because of, these overtures, he resumed operations on 25 December against Mandanna; This time, all went smoothly. Large numbers of tribesmen were observed north of Mandanna but they were continuously harassed from the air and did not interfere. Operations continued next day in order to complete the picquet defences which had been demolished by the tribesmen. Thereafter the picquet was not disturbed. On 27 December a picquet was established on 'Chalk Hill', a quarter of a mile north of Mandanna Hill, on the east bank of the Tank Zam.

The operations of 25–27 December can now be seen to have marked a turning point in the campaign. After the failures of 19–21 December the campaign had hung in the balance. If, as had begun to seem possible, the troops in the Striking Force were unable to cope with the Mahsuds fighting on their own ground, then the viability, not only of the campaign but of the whole policy in regard to Waziristan, would have had to be rethought, as in the last analysis that policy depended upon the successful application of military force.

There still remained after 27 December the likelihood of severe fighting before Kaniguram could be reached; the dangerous defiles of the Ahnai and Barari Tangis still lay ahead. But in an indefinable and imperceptible way the crisis point had been passed and the balance had begun to tilt away from the Mahsuds. That shift may not have been readily perceptible to those in the Striking Force and indeed the situation from a military point of view was not yet fully under control. Much remained to be done in re-organising the force and in integrating new units into the force. But the tactical decisions made at the meeting with the CGS on 21 December would prove decisive.

The Mahsud maliks reached Jandola on 28 December, despite having been told that operations would not be suspended *pro tem*, and on the following day Climo held a jirga; the only absentees were the Abdullai subdivision occupying the country round Makin. In view of the opposition so far encountered, the original terms were stiffened by the permanent confiscation of another 100 modern tribal rifles. The maliks were told that the advance would continue pending payment of the fine and the surrender of rifles. These terms were accepted and signed and sealed by the Mahsud representatives present.[29]

The occupation of 'Chalk Hill' on 27 December had removed any remaining uncertainty about the direction of Skeen's advance and on 29 December he, with 43 Brigade and two battalions from 67 Brigade (2/76th Punjabis and 109th Infantry), moved some four and a half miles up the Tank Zam to Kotkai. HQ 67 Brigade and 55 Rifles joined them there on 6 January 1920, leaving only the 103rd LI at Palosina. This ended, effectively, the first phase of the operations.

From its starting point at Jandola the force had advanced less than nine miles in ten days and Kaniguram still lay thirty-five miles ahead. In those ten days the terms of the initial military equation had shifted significantly. The quantity of ammunition in Mahsud hands and the presence of many hundreds of trained ex-Militia men in their ranks had enabled the Mahsuds to develop fire and movement tactics of a sophistication and effectiveness not seen before in Frontier warfare, and the troops had, initially at least, been unable to cope with them. The military balance had been significantly adjusted by the increasing use and effectiveness of aircraft and by the success of the new 3.7 inch gun whose high angle of elevation enabled it to perform virtually as a howitzer, reaching areas of hidden ground which the 2.75 inch mountain gun could not.[30] It was unfortunate that more were not available in India. But much heavy fighting clearly lay ahead and both commanders and troops had much to learn.

The learning curve was bound to be a steep one. As Climo put it:

> Those operations have shown the vital necessity of regaining some standard of musketry efficiency. Marksmanship and fire discipline are two of the first essentials in frontier fighting, and the present Indian Army as a general rule has never learnt these two arts. The result is

the men have no faith in their rifles, they have little self- confidence and look to auxiliaries such as Artillery, aeroplanes and Lewis guns for their protection and to win the battle... practically none of the junior British officers have had experience of hill warfare and experience of warfare against a civilised and organised enemy is not necessarily good training for hill warfare against a savage enemy.[31]

These arts could be acquired only with blood and experience.

Notes

1. Climo to War Section, AHQ, No. 115-G-12, 20 December 1919 – L/MIL/17/4, Appendix 160.
2. 2/19 Punjabis, 1/55 Rifles, 1/109 Infantry, 2/112 Infantry, two companies 3/34 Pioneers.
3. Four Bristol Fighters and nine DH9As and DH10s made twenty-seven flights up until 1700 hours; a further six aircraft engaged targets up and down the Tank Zam. For a resumé of the RAF's operations, see Army HQ War Diary for December, Appendix 126 – L/MIL/17/5/4119.
4. Leonard Arthur Cuthbert, commissioned 1917.
5. The Short Magazine Lee-Enfield was sighted out to more than 2,000 yards.
6. Ross, 189.
7. According to Rees, Skeen thought that there was too great a preponderance of Muslim troops but that he had been told to get on with it or be replaced – Rees, 189. Rees was a very junior officer and he was probably reporting camp gossip rather than direct knowledge. But he may not be far from the truth. In February 1929 Skeen wrote to HQ Wazirforce expressing doubts about the willingness of Muslim troops to fight other Muslims, and suggesting that the proportion of Muslim troops in garrisons in Waziristan needed to be watched carefully – Skeen to DAAQ Wazirforce, No. 28-47-C.A., 22 February 1920 – L/MIL/7/18853.
8. 55th Rifles, 103rd LI and 2/19th Punjabis.
9. Casualties in *Operations*, 106.
10. Ibid, 106. The four British officers with the Pioneers had served in France and were trained Lewis gunners; all four were wounded but brought back safely to camp in a splendid display of skill and leadership by the Indian officers and NCOs.
11. Douglas Rees, *Pioneer Picquet* (1954).
12. Sir John Smyth, *Milestones* (London, 1979), 70.
13. Climo to War Section, Army Headquarters, No. 115-G-10, 22 December 1919 – L/MIL/17/4119, Appendix 180.
14. See L/MIL/7/19238; also E M Spiers, 'Gas and the North-West Frontier', *Journal of Strategic Studies*, Vol. 6, No. 4, 94–112.
15. Director of Staff Duties, War Office, to CGS India, No. 121/1/622 (S.D.2), 11 June 1919 – L/M 19238.
16. Spiers, 102–3.
17. Grant to Dobbs, 12 December 1919 – papers of 'Major General Ffoulkes, J.63 – Liddell Hart Centre for Military Archives, London.

18 Leslie to Ffoulkes, 10 January 1920, Ffoulkes J.63.

19 Viceroy in Council to Secretary of State, Despatch No. 12 of 1919,12 February 1920 – L/MIL/7/19238.

20 Army Department India to War Office, 14 February 1920, PRO WO 32/5185; Sinha to Cubitt (War Office), 5 March 1920, ibid.

21 Secretary of State to Viceroy, Military No. 47, 17 July 1919.

22 *Army Instruction (India)* No. 733 of 1920, 21 September.

23 Ross believed that the 82nd and 2/112th were relegated partly because they were originally Bombay Army regiments, which had been under a slur since the defeat at Maiwand in July 1880 – Ross, 190. In fact the 82nd was a former Madras Army regiment – see John Gaylor, *Sons of John Company: the Indian and Pakistan Armies 1903–1991* (Tunbridge Wells, 1992). But undoubtedly there was still a prejudice in favour of regiments from Northern India, the so-called. 'martial races', which Roberts had nurtured – see Brian Robson, *Roberts in India* (London, 1993).

24 Skeen to War Section, AHQ, No. G-237, 23 December 1919 – L/P&S/10/870, No. 431.

25 On 26 December 1919 the Political Agent in the Tochi reported that up to that time the Mahsuds were reported to have lost 380 killed and 560 wounded – Army HQ War Diary for December 1919, Appendix 215. It may be assumed that the majority of these were incurred on 21 December.

26 Skeen to War Section, No. 249, 24 December 1919 – War Diary, December 1919, Appendix 197 – L/M Ibid, Appendix 219.

27 Ibid, Appendix 219.

28 Ibid, Appendix 204 – Skeen to War Section, No. G-C-31, 25 December 1919.

29 Ibid, Appendix 230 – Skeen to War Section, No. G-C-40, 29 December 1919.

30 The maximum elevation of the 2.75 inch mountain gun was roughly 23°; for the 3.7 inch it was 44° – Graham, *History of the Indian Mountain Artillery*, Appendix V, 446.

31 Waziristan Force Weekly Appreciation for week ending 30 December 1919 – PRO WO 106/56.

XIX

The Second Phase

(Maps 10 and 12)

Ahead of the Striking Force now lay the Ahnai Tangi, the first of the major topographical obstacles in the way of the advance. Skeen therefore halted for nine days at Kotkai to lay in supplies and to establish a series of permanent picquets along the route back to Jandola to give protection to his supply convoys and road communications. At the same time he established four picquets north of Kotkai as a preliminary to forcing the Tangi.

Despite the signature of peace terms at Jandola on 29 December, the establishment of these picquets encountered fierce opposition. On 1 January a picquet under construction between Palosina and Kotkai was attacked; the attackers were driven off with rifles and grenades at a cost of eighty-four killed and wounded, including three British officers.[1] A more serious reverse occurred on 2 January 1920 in the course of constructing a permanent picquet on 'Scrub Hill' (Kotkai North), 2,500 yards north of Kotkai, on the west bank of the Tank Zam.[2] The covering troops (4/39 Garwhalis) reached their position on the Spin Ghara ridge north of the picquet without serious difficulty but then came under continuous sniping, culminating in three determined attacks which got to stone throwing distance.

The attacks were driven off but difficulties with casualties[3] delayed withdrawal of the covering battalion until 1515. By then a strong force of Mahsuds had established themselves immediately below the crest of the ridge held by the Garwhalis. Attempts with grenades and stones to dislodge them were frustrated by intense fire from surrounding peaks. When the rear party of the battalion came to withdraw – always the most dangerous moment in this type of warfare – these tribesmen rushed forward on the heels of the retiring troops. Lieutenant Kenny, with ten men, turned back in an attempt to delay the tribal rush. He and his party were annihilated but managed to delay the Mahsud rush until the rest of the troops had got safely away.[4] The Mahsuds were then caught by shell fire and were estimated to have lost seventy-seven dead and wounded. The Garwhalis, a 'new' battalion, raised only in October 1918, lost thirty-five killed and forty-three wounded in this affair,[5] but they showed that the

Indian troops were beginning to recover their fighting spirit. Nevertheless, through a blunder which more experienced troops (and commanders) would not have committed, the picquet on 'Scrub Hill', as well as that on 'Whitechapel', 1,500 yards farther north, was left unfinished and unoccupied. They were re-occupied on 5 January but in the fighting the troops lost eight killed and forty wounded. The heavy British casualties in these two affairs were a sharp reminder of the perils which under-trained and inexperienced troops faced when opposed to a tactically astute and experienced enemy, fighting on familiar ground.

Some four miles north of Kotkai the Ahnai Tangi barred the route up the Tank Zam. Lightly armed troops could by-pass it, over the surrounding hills, but its seizure was essential for a large force, moving with artillery and baggage, and for the subsequent supply convoys. The actual defile was only thirty yards wide and about eighty yards long, overhung by precipitous sides, rising 150 feet above the floor of the river. The approach to the Tangi from south and south-west was guarded by the Spin Gara range of hills, rising to 700 feet; between the range and the river there was a plateau intersected by numerous ravines across which the troops could move only in single file. The south-eastern approaches to the Tangi were commanded by the Konr range, rising to 1,200 feet.

The position was immensely strong and the Mahsuds could be expected to defend it stubbornly. A fresh lashkar of 2,500–3,000 was believed to be assembling and there were rumours of a large force of Wana Wazirs moving to assist.

On 7 January 43 Brigade moved out from Kotkai and occupied the heights along the eastern bank of the Tank Zam for a distance of three miles, protecting the right flank of 67 Brigade which was to move across the plateau below Spin Gara and seize the western approach to the Ahnai Tangi.

By 1100 hours 67 Brigade was ready to attack the western approach to the Tangi, but the Mahsuds had now massed on the slopes of the Konr massif to the east whence they could direct fire on to the Tangi and its approaches. Until they could be shifted, an attack on the Tangi was impracticable. It was equally clear that they could not be shifted in the time remaining and the two brigades withdrew to camp at Kotkai. Losses amounted to ten killed and thirty-four wounded, mainly in the operations on the east bank.

It was obvious now that no serious operation could be mounted against the Tangi unless the east bank and the slopes of the Konr massif could be controlled. But the ground on that side was considered too difficult to attack the Tangi from and Skeen decided to mount his attack, as before, on the west bank across the plateau below the Spin Gara but to neutralise opposition from the east bank by establishing a strong permanent picquet south-east of Zeriwam, about two and a half miles north of Kotkai. At the same time 67 Brigade would establish a camp some two miles nearer to the Tangi to provide an easier jumping-off point for the eventual attack on the Tangi.

On 9 January 67 Brigade moved up the Tank Zam and established camp at Gana Kach while 43 Brigade began the construction of the picquet south-east of Zeriwam. By 1100 the picquet was half-finished and the garrison was moving up to occupy it. At this point the Mahsuds opened an intense fire on the covering troops who were driven back with serious losses. Aid was sent up from 67 Brigade, but by 1500 the picquet was still not finished and 43 Brigade was withdrawn; losses amounted to eighteen killed and forty-two wounded. An attempt to repeat the operation next day (10 January) met the same fate; the covering troops were overwhelmed by intense rifle fire and losses amounted to twenty-four killed and eighty-four wounded. Tribal casualties were put at forty-seven killed and wounded.

The two days' fighting had cost Skeen nearly 170 casualties and he was no nearer seizing the Tangi. His failure was in part due to a lack of air support caused by indifferent weather and a shortage of machines. He decided that further delay in seizing the Ahnai Tangi could only increase tribal opposition and make the task even more difficult. He decided to mount the most hazardous of all mountain warfare operations – a night march. Even over relatively easy ground, with experienced troops, this is a difficult operation to execute successfully; in the dark, troops easily lose direction and cohesion, commanders lose control, fire support is virtually impossible to provide and, against an alert enemy, surprise is easily lost. On the other hand, if it can be carried out successfully, it can be extremely effective.[6] In January 1920 circumstances slightly favoured Skeen – the weather meant that the Mahsuds were unlikely to be sleeping out on hills, the moon was past its full, and the darkness meant that the absence of air support would not be so important. Nevertheless, given the state of training and experience of his troops, Skeen was taking a significant gamble – disaster was at least as likely as success, or so it would seem at this distance.

His plan was for 43 Brigade[7] to move out at 0500 on 11 January so as to be in position at dawn (around 0715) to attack two features on the Konr Massif. Lucas, with 67 Brigade[8] would move out at 0300 to occupy the Spin Ghara range and from there, simultaneously with 67 Brigade's attack, to attack the west side of the Ahnai Tangi. None knew better than Skeen the nature of the gamble he was taking:

The General told me himself afterwards that he lay in his camp bed with his hands over his ears waiting to hear the crackle of Mahsud rifles.[9]

The operation took the Mahsuds by surprise; by 1000 67 Brigade had seized the western side of the Tangi and by 111543 Brigade had seized the opposite side and the Tangi was in Skeen's hands at the modest cost of five killed and twenty-eight wounded.[10] Much of the success was due to the effective cooperation of the RAF's DH9As and Bristol Fighters which made some twenty flights over the Tangi as soon as it was light, keeping the tribesmen's heads down. Picquets were quickly established to hold the Tangi itself and 43 Brigade then withdrew to the camp at Kotkai; 67 Brigade formed a new camp a mile south of the Tangi, on the west side, close to the village of Gana Kach.

The effect of this success on the Mahsuds was considerable. They had not expected the troops to be able to move at night and this now created a further uncertainty in their minds. The Mahsuds themselves had apparently concentrated on defending the east bank because their assumed that Skeen intended to occupy and devastate the Shuza Valley on that side; the defence of the west side of the Tangi had been left to the Wana and Tochi Wazirs. The result was not therefore designed to improve relations between the tribes and the lashkar which had been occupying the Tangi now split up, some going northwards to Shimanzai Kach, two and a half miles along the Tank Zam, others retiring eastwards into the Shuza Valley.

The 12th January was spent in constructing roads for the transport along the bed of the Tank Zam. The picquets on the Tangi were relieved so that 67 Brigade was at full strength for the next advance. Skeen, with Column HQ and attached troops, joined 67 Brigade at the Ahnai Camp on the 13th. The same afternoon an advanced picquet was attacked, leaving three killed and three wounded, and demonstrating that the Mahsuds were still full of fight.

On 14 January the whole Striking Force passed through the Ahnai Tangi in four echelons.[11] The Advanced Guard consisted of the 55th Rifles, two companies 2/5th Gurkhas[12] and two guns of 27 Mountain Battery, under Lieutenant Colonel Herdon. 55th Rifles had orders to move straight up the bed of the Tank Zam, while a flank guard, consisting of the remainder of 2/5th Gurkhas, under Lieutenant Colonel Crowdy, of the Gurkhas, moved along the east bank. The main body[13] followed the Advanced Guard up the river bed, while some distance behind, Lucas, with 2/9 Gurkhas, 57th Rifles, 109 Infantry, a section each of Nos 6 and 27 Mountain Batteries, escorted the huge baggage train of some 4,000 animals. Surplus transport and the sick and wounded returned to Kotkai, escorted by two companies 61 Pioneers.

Beyond the Ahnai Tangi the country presented an exceptionally difficult tactical problem. A mile beyond the exit a steep ravine, Zaghbir Pal, joins the Tank Zam from the north. It is separated from the Tank Zam by a long, narrow ridge, which ends in a flat-topped hill, named 'Flathead Left', which dominated the Tank Zam Valley from a height of 900 feet above the river bed. Some 1,200 yards north of 'Flathead Left' a tangle of high cliffs on the east bank of the Tank Zam commanded the whole of the river bed, preventing any further advance. Finally, 1,200 yards to the NNE of 'Flathead Left' was a higher peak called 'Flathead Right', separated from 'Flathead Left' by a very steep ravine, known as 'Marble Arch'. Progress up the Tank Zam depended upon occupying 'Flathead Left' in the first instance; further progress depended upon occupying 'Marble Arch'. But both were dominated by 'Flathead Right' at ranges of 900–1,200 yards. This fact was not apparently obvious in advance.

Skeen's plan was for Crowdy's flank guard to seize 'Flathead Left' while Herdon's Advanced Guard moved up the river bed and seized 'Marble Arch'. At Asa Khan, a mile beyond the Ahnai Tangi, Herdon's Advanced Guard came under heavy and accurate rifle fire from both 'Marble Arch' and 'Flathead Right'; at the same time it was fiercely attacked by a party of some forty tribesmen emerging from a nullah on the east bank. The Advanced Guard was thrown into some confusion but order was eventually restored. Meanwhile Crowdy had occupied 'Flathead Left' but was now under fierce attack from 'Flathead Right'; with their ammunition running out, the Gurkhas were forced to carry out a series of bayonet charges in which Crowdy was killed. Eventually the Gurkhas were reinforced by 2/76th Punjabis from the Main Body and by a company of 2/9th Gurkhas which Lucas sent up from the Rear Guard.

By midday 'Flathead Left' was securely held but attempts by 2/76th Punjabis to seize 'Flathead Right' could make no progress and 'Marble Arch' was still in Mahsud hands. By 1330 Skeen's advance was stalled and as he now had the rearguard and the transport on his hands it was too late to retreat through the Tangi. He was forced to camp where he was, in the bed of the Tank Zam. It was a dangerous position, dominated by the surrounding hills, only one of which was in his hands. The tribesmen with their acute tactical sense had correctly perceived that the loss of 'Flathead Left' would put Skeen's whole force in a critical situation. Four determined assaults under heavy covering fire were made on the troops occupying 'Flathead Left', the last of which was beaten off with bayonets, stones and grenades. Air support had played a major part in the retention of 'Flathead Left', the RAF maintaining a constant patrol over the hill; when their ammunition ran out the pilots had remained overhead, keeping the Mahsuds' heads down and forestalling attacks. Three machines were forced down but the crews succeeded in escaping. The situation was finally stabilised in the late afternoon with the arrival of two further companies of 2/9th Gurkhas.

On the west side of the Tank Zam, Mahsuds were reported in the late afternoon to be assembling for an attack on the camp and two companies of 109 Infantry were sent to seize a feature known as 'Dazzle Hill', overlooking the ravine where the tribesmen were reported to be assembling.

The companies were unable to seize the hill but managed to hold on to their ground and prevented the camp being attacked from that direction.

This ended the severest day's fighting of the campaign. The tribesmen were estimated to have totalled 4,000, including a large contingent of Wana Wazirs. They had correctly appreciated that Skeen was bound to attempt to occupy 'Flathead Left' and had made their preparations accordingly – hence the bitter fighting there. They had fought with the utmost determination, using their firepower in a classic display of fire and movement, but they were estimated later to have lost some 400 killed and wounded, as well as many rifles.[14] Skeen had lost 382 men killed and wounded, including nine British officers killed and six wounded, one of the heaviest day's losses in the history of Frontier warfare. But Skeen could replace his losses – the Mahsuds and Wazirs could not. Taken in conjunction with the losses sustained on 'Black Hill', the Mahsuds in particular had now lost at least a thousand men.

Although Skeen had not achieved his immediate objectives, he could draw distinct comfort from the clearly improved performance of his infantry. The arrival of additional Gurkha battalions had obviously strengthened his force, but on 14 January the 2/76th Punjabis and 109th Infantry had also fought well. His troops had begun, man for man, to match their opponents. The fighting on the 14th can be seen to mark a turning point in the campaign. Henceforth Skeen could proceed with greater speed and confidence.

It may reasonably be asked at this point what had happened to the peace terms signed by the Mahsud maliks at Jandola on 29 December. The answer lies in the Mahsud character and in the peculiar nature of Mahsud society. The dominant characteristic of the Mahsud was his fierce independence – in a sense, every man was his own malik. Each Mahsud therefore made up his own mind about the desirability of giving in to the Government, weighing carefully the prospects of resistance, the likely terms which might be squeezed out and, not least, his own profit and loss. To a degree uncommon elsewhere on the Frontier, the maliks carried little weight or responsibility, and their agreements did not automatically bind other Mahsuds.[15] Mahsud morale at the end of 1919 was still high. They had just inflicted a series of stunning defeats on the troops and it would not have been surprising if many of them thought that further determined resistance might lead to the terms agreed at Jandola being watered down or even proved incapable of enforcement. Constancy and adherence to his bond were not dominant Mahsud characteristics.

Notes

1   Ross, 197.

2   Beyond Kotkai, the Tank Zam is often called the Takki Zam.

3   It was an inviolable rule in Frontier warfare that the wounded were never left behind, whatever the difficulties involved.

4   Kenny was deservedly awarded a posthumous VC, the second of two VCs awarded in the campaign (see Appendix 4).

5   Casualties in *Operations*, 110. De Watteville, 118, gives the casualties as 'not far short of 120' but gives no source.

6   Roberts' night attack at the Peiwar Kotal on 1/2 December 1878 is the only comparable operation which springs readily to mind – see Robson, *The Road to Kabul*, 84–5.

7   4/39th Garwhalis, 109th Infantry, 2/152nd Punjabis and two companies 2/150th Infantry. Only the Garwhalis and 2/152nd Punjabis had been in the Brigade since the start of the campaign.

8   55th Rifles, 57th Rifles, 2/76th Punjabis, 2/5th Gurkhas. Only the 55th and 57th Rifles had been present since December.

9   Smyth, 72.

10 *Operations*, 114.

11 Derajat Column Order No. 59, issued at 1600 on 1 January.

12 The 2/5th, the first of the Gurkha battalions requested by Skeen, joined the force on 9 January, followed over the next week by 2/9th, 4/3rd and 3/11th Gurkhas. They replaced 2/19th and 82nd Punjabis, 103rd and 2/212th Infantry, relegated to L of C duties.

13 One troop 21st Cavalry, two guns No. 6 Mountain Battery, two guns 27 Mountain Battery, 2/76th Punjabis, 3/34th Pioneers, 109th Infantry and 55 Company Sappers and Miners. *Operations*, Appendix H states that two sections No. 6 MB accompanied the main body, but Skeen's operational order (Note 11 above) is clear that only one section was to accompany the main body.

14 *Operations*, 117.

15 It was the main reason why the so-called 'Sandeman system' of working through the tribal representatives, which had proved so successful in Baluchistan, had failed when applied in Waziristan – see Chapter XIV.

XX

The Barari Tangi

(Map 13)

The end of the fighting on 14 January marked the end of a distir stage in the operations.

In defending the Ahnai Tangi, the Mahsuds had assembled one of the largest forces ever seen on the Frontier; even more significantly, it had included at least 700 Wana Wazirs, who fully understood that their ultimate fate depended upon what happened to the Mahsuds. In the upshot, the tribesmen had been fought to a standstill and had suffered exceptionally heavy casualties. Skeen had also lost heavily but his losses could readily be replaced;[1] much more significantly, the performance of his troops on 13/14 January indicated that his force was recovering from the low level of morale and fighting capacity which it had reached a month earlier after the failures round Mandarina and 'Black Hill'. While his force clearly needed careful handling to avoid any further reverses, Skeen could begin to be cautiously confident that his infantry were now capable of defeating the Mahsuds on their own ground.

Of this phase of the operations, both the official history and de Watteville (echoing the official history) take the view that it had broken the enemy's resistance.[2] That view tends to overlook the fighting which followed and Skeen could certainly not plan on that assumption.

He remained in camp at Asa Khan until 17 January, putting out picquets to protect his very awkwardly placed camp there, and preparing for his next advance. His troops needed rest after the severe fighting, there were wounded to be evacuated, and the changeover of battalions required time for integration and reorganisation.[3] A permanent picquet was established on 'Marble Arch', which was found to be unoccupied, on 15 January, the Mahsuds and Wazirs having dispersed, carrying away their dead and wounded. There was continued sniping and minor activity, and daily losses on the British side averaged four killed and ten wounded.[4] The Wazirs were reported to have declared that they had no intention of returning to carry on the fighting and the Mahsuds now made tentative overtures to the Political Officer at Jandola for peace. In the light of the peace terms agreed to on 29 December, these were treated with scepticism as merely a tactic for delaying a further British advance. There was certainly no evidence that the anti-British faction led by Fazl Din and Musa Khan had lost its influence. Climo himself was under pressure from AHQ India to limit the further advance of the Striking Force, in order to deal with the Wana Wazirs before the hot weather. He insisted that he should not be required to halt before 28 January and then only if the Mahsuds had made full and unconditional submission.

On 18 January Skeen and 67 Brigade moved forward four miles to the Sorarogha plateau, on the west bank of the Tank Zam, about one and three quarter miles short of the next formidable obstacle, the Barari Tangi, leaving 43 Brigade at Kotkai. Skeen had advanced fourteen miles in just over six weeks. Not the least of his trials was the fact that his troops were now operating in severe winter conditions.[5] The actual advance to Sorarogha was not contested, but the establishment of two camp picquets in the afternoon was fiercely opposed and one could not be established until next day; casualties amounted to eight killed and fourteen wounded.

The Sorarogha plateau, on the west bank of the Tank Zam, some 300 feet above the river, offered an extensive flat area, amply sufficient for the whole of the Striking Force and its transport, and even more important, providing space for a landing ground. It was free from any immediate threat – the nearest high ground was the Sarkai Ghar range (5,200 feet), nearly two miles to the north-west. That would need to be held before the Barari Tangi could be seized but in the meantime it could be ignored. Hitherto, air cover had been patchy even though it was now recognised as vital. Conditions were largely outside RAF control – bad weather, obsolescent aircraft and the need to operate at the limits of their range, from Bannu or Tank or, in the case of the bombers, from the far side of the Indus. Certainly, nothing could be laid at the door of the pilots who had behaved with great devotion and gallantry, frequently diving in mock attacks when ammunition was exhausted. But even when aircraft were available, their effective use was hampered by ineffective ground-to-air communications. Most of these problems would be eased by the availability of aircraft on the spot at Sorarogha.[6]

The Force halted at Sorarogha for nine days. The troops had fought more than twenty actions of at least brigade strength in the thirty days between 19 December and 20 January, and they clearly needed a period of rest. Skeen needed time to plan the next phase of his operations and he needed in particular to amass the ten days' supplies which it had been agreed were necessary for the next stage of the advance. The lines of communication had not so far been seriously threatened – a curious piece of neglect by the Mahsuds – but the next stage of the advance would bring the Force close to the centre of Mahsud territory where their resistance could reasonably be expected to stiffen.

Despite repeated appeals and even threats, the Afghan commander at Wana, Shah Daula, had hitherto refused to lend his two ancient 6-pounder mountain guns to the Mahsuds although he provided small quantities of rifle ammunition. Emissaries sent to Khost to seek assistance from the Afghan tribes there had come back empty-handed. The steady British advance and the severe losses suffered by the Mahsuds and Wazirs in the fighting in January now led some of the more prominent anti-British elements in Khost to fear that the Mahsuds might be weakening in their opposition to the British invasion. Quantities of ammunition and promises of men and guns began to reach the Mahsuds from Khost in the second half of January. Even Shah Daula began to exert himself by collecting a fresh lashkar of Wana Wazirs which he promised to accompany with his two guns. This aid (or the promises of it) threatened to make Skeen's next task – the forcing of the Barari Tangi – a particularly formidable one.

If the Ahnai Tangi had been a difficult nut to crack, the Barari Tangi appeared even more difficult. Just over two miles north of Sorarogha,[7] the Tank Zam cuts through the Sarkai Ghar range which runs roughly south-west to north-east. The valley then bends sharply to the west at a point where the Barari Algad (stream) comes in from the north; the Tangi itself lies just beyond this confluence. The defile is some 300 yards long and sixty yards wide and is dominated by steep hills in all four directions. In particular a force attempting to penetrate it is open to attack from an enemy coming down on its rear from the Barari Algad. Before Skeen could penetrate the Tangi, he would first have to seize the Sarkai Ghar ridge on both sides of the river. He would then have to seize the high bluffs ('Barari Centre') which divide the Barari Algad from the Tank Zam. Once through the defile his advance would be threatened from the end of a steep ridge to the south (the aptly named 'Gibraltar'),[8] and by a similar but even more formidable position on the opposite bank aptly called 'The Barrier'. If these positions were held by the tribesmen in force, it promised to be an interesting tactical exercise.

Operations began on 23 January when Lucas made a night march, with 65th Rifles, 2/5th and 2/9th Gurkhas, to seize the shoulder of the Sarkai Ghar south-west of the Tank Zam. By 1345 he had completed a permanent picquet there ('Bluff'), under heavy fire from Mahsuds in the village of Ahmadwam, across the river. His retirement was closely followed up, but he succeeded in reaching camp under cover of artillery support and air cover from Bristol Fighters operating from Sorarogha. Bad weather, which stopped the RAF flying, prevented operations on 24 January. Next day, despite some opposition, the Sarkai Ghar shoulder to the north-west of the lank Zam was seized by 57th Rifles and a permanent picquet ('Barari Left') established there.

With both sides of the entrance to the Barari Tangi in his hands, Skeen could now mount his attack on the Tangi itself. On 26 January 43 Brigade moved up to Sorarogha from Kotkai and the whole force was now available. Overtures for a cessation of hostilities came to nothing; it seemed clear that the Mahsuds had no intention of abiding by the terms agreed at Jandola, probably because they still hoped for Afghan aid. Climo now sanctioned the destruction of Mahsud property as the force advanced, a measure hitherto avoided.

Under the mullah Fazl Din and the malik Musa Than, a lashkar of some 1,200 had been assembled in the neighbourhood of the Barari Tangi. If they elected to stand and defend the Tangi, as was to be assumed, then it might be possible to pin them down long enough to inflict sufficient casualties to bring resistance to an end. Either way, Skeen had to seize 'Barari Centre', which dominated the passage through the defile, and then the even more serious obstacle of 'The Barrier' which blocked any advance beyond. The crest of 'The Barrier' was only a few yards wide; it fell away gently to the north-east, offering an easy line of retreat for its defenders. Conversely, the south-west, or front, face, up which the troops would have to attack, was steep and precipitous. To reduce casualties, Skeen decided to attempt another night march and early morning attack to seize both obstacles before the tribesmen were in position.

Accordingly, at 0530[9] on 28 January Lucas left camp with 67 Brigade, consisting of 55th Rifles, 2/5th Gurkhas, 109th Infantry and two companies of 3rd Guides. By daybreak (0700), he was in possession of 'Barari Centre' and ready to cover the attack on 'The Barrier'. That attack was to be carried out by 43 Brigade (Gwyn-Thomas), consisting of an advance guard of 57th Rifles and 2/150th Infantry, followed by a special assault force of 4/39th Garwhalis and two companies of 2/9th Gurkhas, which was to seize 'The Barrier'. The advance guard pushed up the Tank Zam and through the Tangi, encountering only light opposition from the Mahsud picquets. Surprised or disheartened, the Mahsuds failed to defend 'The Barrier' which was in the troops' hands by 1000. Meanwhile the advance guard had continued its advance up the Tank Zam, detaching a picquet to occupy 'Gibraltar'. It came under accurate fire and it was only after two companies of 2/9th Gurkhas had been sent up that the position. was consolidated after dark, under heavy sniping. Skeen and 43 Brigade camped at Ahmadwam, on the edge of the Tank Zam, just beyond the Tangi. There was no space for 67 Brigade and the transport, which went back to Sorarogha.

British losses were seven killed and sixty-two wounded, a remarkably small bill for such a potentially difficult operation. Tribal losses were put at sixteen killed and twenty wounded, which reflected the fact that the Mahsuds had been taken by surprise and were present only in small numbers.

The seizure of the Barari Tangi was a model of how such operations should be carried out and reflected credit on both commanders and troops. It is difficult to envisage it being carried out by the Force six weeks earlier. If there was a moment, therefore, when the Striking Force came of age and the success of the whole campaign seemed assured, it was the successful conclusion of the operations on 28 January.

Notes

1 The losses in British officers presented a particular problem. The establishment in Indian battalions was only twelve as compared with thirty-six or so in a British battalion. Calls had gone out for officers on leave or overseas to return but these were not immediately available. The loss of fifteen officers in one day was therefore serious.

2 *Operations*, 120; De Watteville, 132.

3 The composition of brigades was now as follows:
43 Brigade
4/39th Garwhalis, 57th Rifles, 3rd Guides (from 68 Brigade), 2/152nd Punjab Infantry;
67 Brigade
55th Rifles, 2/9th Gurkhas, 4/3rd Gurkhas, 2/5th Gurkhas.
In addition Skeen had as Column troops 3/34th Pioneers and 3/11th Gurkhas. The composition of his infantry is revealing.

4 *Operations*, 119.

5 'It was bitterly cold weather now, hard frosts and cold winds. . . The night of 23/24th January was a very stormy one. The wind was terrific and the rain came down in torrents. In the morning the hills all round were covered in snow.' – Ross, 193.

6 The downside was the need for a supply of petrol in cans, which put a further strain on the supply chain.

7 *Operations* gives the distance as one and a quarter miles, but this is contradicted by its own maps.

8 Reconnaissance had not, apparently, disclosed the existence of 'Gibraltar' – *Operations*, 123.

9 *Operations*, 125; De Watteville says 0500.

XXI

The Advance to Makin

(Map 10)

The 29th January was spent by the troops in finishing construction of the various picquet defences. Heavy rain in the evening turned the camp at Ahmadwam into a morass and any further advance was postponed until 1 February. That night there was a mild panic in the camp, set off by a jumpy sentry in one of the camp picquets; the 2/150th distinguished itself by firing off some 4,000 rounds.[1]

Although he had successfully forced the two major choke points in his way, Skeen was still less than half way to Kaniguram and it was beginning to seem improbable that the campaign against the Wana Wazirs could be undertaken before the hot weather began. In an effort to speed up matters, fresh peace terms were sent to the Mahsuds:

(a) the original terms of 3 November, as modified at Jandola on 29 December 1919,[2] were withdrawn;

(b) fresh negotiations would not be opened until the stipulated number of rifles had been handed in and the fines paid in full;

(c) a further 200 Government rifles must be handed in to avoid the devastation of Kaniguram, and the same number to save Makin;

d)unless these terms were accepted, punitive measures i.e. devastation, would start when the Force reached Janjal (near Dwa Toi).

Despite their losses and the growing fighting power of the Striking Force, Mahsud morale remained high. By 29 January a Mahsud lashkar of some 1,200 had been joined by Shah Daula with a large Wana Wazir lashkar and the famous mountain guns. A preliminary outing for those guns on 29 January during some skirmishing round Ahmadwam was a fiasco. Their range did not exceed 2,000 yards and most of the shells were duds. Nevertheless, Shah Daula's arrival with his guns and a Wana Wazir lashkar rekindled Mahsud enthusiasm. By 30 January a force of some 4,000 tribesmen, armed with modem rifles, supported by half as many armed with older weapons, had collected ahead of Skeen's force. This was probably as large a force as had been assembled hitherto. The main body was reported to be round Shin Konr, some three and a half to four miles from Ahmadwam; the remainder were scattered in small groups between.

Skeen's objective was Piazha Raghza,[3] some seven miles beyond his present camp at Ahmadwam and a similar distance from Makin. The country beyond the Barari Tangi was different but equally difficult, with deep, narrow ravines feeding into the Tank Zam, the hills on either side covered with bushes and scrub which gave excellent cover for snipers and effective camouflage against air reconnaissance.

Faced with the prospect of having to fight his way through the heavy opposition reported ahead of him, Skeen decided to try another night advance. It was a significant illustration of the faith he could now place in his troops. On 1 February Gwyn-Thomas moved out at 0315 with a force of three battalions, with Pioneers and Sappers and Miners.[4] By daylight he had gained control of the heights along the east side of the river for a distance of some two miles. An hour after Gwyn-Thomas, a second force of one and a half battalions, with a section of 27 Mountain Battery, advanced to gain control of the west side as far as Aka Khel, some two and a half miles from the starting point. There was little opposition and Shah Daula's guns, firing from Shin Konr, were quickly silenced by a couple of rounds from the section of 27 Mountain Battery on the Aka Khel plateau.[5]

When daylight came, the RAF was able to support the advance with reconnaissance and by harassing parties of tribesmen. Casualties had amounted to ten killed and sixteen wounded; the tribesmen were estimated to have lost about seventy killed and wounded, mainly from air attack. At trifling cost, Skeen had achieved complete surprise and taken a significant step forwards towards Piazha Raghza and Makin. Significantly, the Mahsuds made no attempt to retake any of the heights lost along the Tank Zam. They were reported to have been disheartened by the failure of Shah Daula's vaunted artillery and by a realisation that the Amir's representative, Hajji Abdur Raziq, was not, after all, in a position to effect a favourable settlement on their behalf with the British.

Although many Mahsuds now dispersed to their homes, sufficient remained to constitute a significant threat to Skeen's further advance. Yet again he resorted to the by-now familiar tactic of a night advance. The operation on the night of 2/3 February had to be halted because of sleet, snow and a biting wind which caused great hardship to the troops.[6] The bad weather prevented a resumption until 5 February when the advanced troops moved out of camp at 0100, followed by the main body at 0530. There was 25° degrees of frost and a piercing wind. Troops crossing the bed of the Tank Zam found their boots and puttees encased in ice Construction of sangars meant digging out icy stones from the frozen ground. It was, altogether, tactically and climatically, a severe test of the troops' endurance. Their performance obviously surprised the tribesmen who were accustomed to sheltering in the villages in such weather.

By 1700 hours that day the column was concentrated at Janjal, an advance of some four miles, at a cost of a single casualty. Next day (6 February) the columnn reached its objective of the plateau on the edge of the Piazha Algad known as Piazha Raghza, where it rested and consolidated for a week. Convoys of supplies could now run right through from Sorarogha and were soon delivering up to 100 tons of supplies a day. Sorarogha was occupied by 67 Brigade and a battalion of 43 Brigade.

The next week or so was spent in constructing permanent picquets along the route to Makin, as far as Dwa Toi,[7] where the Tank Zam divides into the Baddar Toi, which eventually leads down to Kaniguram, and the Dara Toi which leads on to Makin. The weather remained atrocious, with now and rain, and the troops were issued with leather jerkins. The weather hampered the supply convoys and the desired reserve of ten days' of supplies was accumulated only with difficulty.

The stay at Piazha Raghza gave time to communicate new terms to the tribesmen. All previous agreements were cancelled and the tribesmen were told that no further discussions would take place until all fines had been paid and all the rifles previously stipulated had been handed in.[8] Furthermore they were told that Makin and Kaniguram would be destroyed unless 200 more rifles were surrendered for each site. Thus, they faced a potential loss of 700 rifles for an indeterminate period. It remained to be seen whether the Mahsuds would or could accept these terms.

The surrender of rifles presented peculiarly difficult problems for the tribesmen – not merely because of the financial penalty involved but because the rifle was an essential part of the tribesman's being. It protected him against his enemies and without it he considered himself naked. There were practical problems too. Some rifles were owned in common by several tribesmen. A tribesman might own more than one and lend them out to others in which case he stood to pay a disproportionate penalty. Similarly, as the Government specified modem rifles, those with more ancient weapons would escape penalty. There was also the problem of 'face' for the tribe as a whole. All in all, the penalty now imposed was a very severe one and one which might simply stiffen resistance. To increase the pressure on the Mahsuds, the troops now began a deliberate process of destroying villages in the vicinity.[9]

At Piazha Raghza, Skeen was only seven miles from the area known as Makin and about eleven miles from Kaniguram, the Mahsud 'capital'. The climax of the campaign, which had taken far longer to reach than had been expected, was now at hand. Skeen planned to leave 43 Brigade at Piazha Raghza to become No. 3 Lines of Communications Section and to take forward with him a strengthened 67 Brigade, totalling about 3,000 men.[10] The column began its advance on 15 February and endured constant sniping until it reached camp at Marobi, about three and a half miles on from Piazha Raghza, and the home of Fazl Din. Next day it moved on to form a large camp on the west side of the Taud China stream which ran due north from its junction with the Dara Toi. Here the Force was only some two miles from the principal village of Makin.[11]

Opposition so far had been confined to persistent sniping, but on 17 February a detachment of 4/3rd Gurkhas gathering firewood from a demolished village near the camp was fiercely attacked by a party of fifty Mahsuds. They were driven off but a dozen or so holed up in a village. The whole battalion was soon engaged, but the opposition could not be overcome without the prospect of heavy casualties. Even then, the withdrawal with the wounded could not be effected until dusk. In that action alone, casualties amounted to ten killed and thirty-seven wounded; since the 15th the column had lost fourteen killed and sixty-nine wounded.

Makin is the generic name given to the area on either side of the Dara Toi and Dashkai Algad Valley which runs for some two and a half miles north-westwards from Marobi.[12] It is extensively wooded and, by Waziristan standards, very fertile and therefore extensively cultivated. But the area is surrounded by hills and seamed with ravines and wooded spurs. There were three or four large villages, numerous small ones and a large number of defensive, mud-brick towers.

To safeguard the camp at Taud China it was essential to occupy the heights known as 'Tree Hill' and 'Split Hill',[13] respectively half a mile north-west and three quarters of a mile west of the extensive camp area. 'Split Hill' was occupied without difficulty on the morning of 19 February, but by a very rare mistake 4/3rd Gurkhas initially occupied the hill adjoining 'Tree Hill'. The remainder of the force moved out at about 0600 to begin the work of destruction. It proved a less than satisfactory day. The ground below 'Tree Hill' was difficult. It was dominated by three villages on high ground, as well as by a number of towers. In advancing, the troops were hampered by numerous walls surrounding the cultivated fields. To add to the problems, 3/11th Gurkhas came under fire from the Force's own guns, firing from the camp, and were compelled to fall back. The ground surrendered was immediately occupied by the Mahsuds who then succeeded in forcing back 2/9th Gurkhas on the right flank. The extrication of the numerous casualties again took time, and by the time the troops were back in camp, they had lost thirty-four killed and twenty-eight wounded. All that there was to show for these heavy casualties was the destruction of a handful of towers and houses. The Mahsuds admitted to the loss of sixteen killed and twenty-eight wounded, but they had been encouraged in their opposition.

Next day (20 February) the troops moved out to construct a permanent picquet post on 'Split Hill' and to commence the destruction of the villages in the area. It was now a new form of warfare. The forested nature of the country and the presence of so many walls and buildings gave good cover to snipers, even at close range, and the troops engaged in demolition were especially vulnerable. In these conditions, speed and accuracy of timing, particularly in the demolition of towers and houses, was vital and the scope for errors was large. In the course of the day, seventeen towers, 160 houses and numerous retaining walls in the fields were demolished but casualties were again heavy – twenty-seven killed and sixty-three wounded. Mahsud losses, by their account, were slight. In two days Skeen had now lost over 150 men.

For the next nine days the work of destruction continued. The 3.7 inch guns, firing as howitzers, prove an easy and effective method of destroying towers without incurring casualties. Marobi, the home of Fazl Din and his equally notorious father, the Mullah Powindah, was among the villages destroyed, only the mosque being left standing. At Makin, Musa Khan's tower was blown up, utilising an unexploded RAF 100lb bomb.

The first fruits of the policy of destruction appeared on 21 February when the Umar Khel sub-section of Mahsuds offered to surrender immediately twelve captured Government rifles provided that their villages on the south side of the Dara Toi were spared, and this offer was accepted. Eight days later, on 29 February, a deputation of maliks arrived in camp to bargain for the safety of Kaniguram. They produced 103 Government rifles, 103 tribal rifles as well as 2,400 rupees, in exchange for a promise not to destroy Kaniguram. But many of the Government rifles were without their bolts and magazines. It was a typical piece of Mahsud duplicity and the maliks were told to take the rifles away and that the advance on Kaniguram would begin. Trickery or not, the fact that the rifles were left and the maliks promised to try to bring in the remainder suggested that at long last Mahsud submission was in sight.

It was clearly time for the Force to move on even though the farther recesses of Makin had not been visited – in particular, the villages stretching along the deep gorge of the Dashkai Algad, to the north-west. Its wooded crags and its narrowness offered every prospect of heavy casualties and it was decided that the potential casualties were not worth likely gains. The force had now been operating in the heart of the Mahsud country for a fortnight, inflicting serious devastation and, although casualties had been heavy, there had been no serious reverse. That situation could not be guaranteed to continue if the Force remained there indefinitely; the law of diminishing returns was bound to set in at some point. The moment had come to try to bring the campaign to a close by occupying the Mahsud 'capital' of Kaniguram.

Withdrawal from the hornets' nest of Makin required careful planning because it was to be expected that the Mahsuds, angry at the devastation, would lose no chance to harry the retiring troops and to inflict heavy casualties if they could. The main withdrawal began in the early hours of 1 March with the evacuation of the picquet posts on 'Tree Hill' and 'Split Hill'. The main body left camp at 0615, leaving behind a number of booby traps. The tribesmen appear to have been taken by surprise and the troops were scarcely harassed. The whole force was back at Dwa Toi by the afternoon of 1 March, with trifling casualties. 43 Brigade had assisted by establishing picquets up the valley of the Baddar Toi, preventing attack from that direction, as well as preparing for the advance on Kaniguram. The only blemish on the withdrawal was an attack at close range on one of the picquets on the south bank of the Dara Toi. The garrison of Punjabi Muslims lost two killed and, unusually, six prisoners. These were later released and subsequently court-martialled for cowardice; the death sentences were later commuted to three years imprisonment.[14] It was the only occasion during the campaign when disciplinary action of this kind was taken; given the events on Mandanna Hill and 'Black Hill', this action can be seen paradoxically as evidence of the great improvement in morale which had taken place.

Notes

1   According to Rees, who remarked that 'as a Guy Fawkes Day display the show might easily have been considered a huge success' – Rees, 259.
2   At Khirgi in November 1919 the Mahsuds had been required to hand back all rifles stolen or seized from Government sources; in addition, 200 rifles were to be handed in as a surety for good faith. At Jandola on 29 December the fine had been increased by another 100 rifles.
3   'Raghza' comes from the same root as 'Rogha', meaning a plateau on the edge of a river.
4   Skeen was 'leapfrogging' his brigades forward. In this case, 43 Brigade undertook the advance to Piazha Raghza while 67 Brigade remained at Sorarogha.
5   'Suddenly there was a loud explosion from the far bank about a half-mile forward and I saw a small black cloud at the bottom of a cliff face . . . With quite a thrill we realised that this must be Shah Daula himself in action. After he had fired three rounds – one of which I saw bursting as shrapnel about ninety feet up in the air above nothing in particular – there was another bang from that direction but this time it was from one of our shells. From then onwards we heard no further sound from the Mahsud artillery.' – Rees, 243. They were 6 pounders, slightly smaller than the British 2.75 inch guns.
     According to Rees, the first round fired by 27 Mountain Battery caused rock fall which blocked the entrance to the cave in which Shah Daula, Musa Khan, Fazl Din and the guns were sheltering, and they were only able to dig themselves out later that night – Rees, 243. An agreeable story if true.
6   'Over my shoes and stockings – in fact up to the knees – there was a case of ice perhaps nearly half an inch thick. The few unfortunate Sappers who had sat down in the river were by then wearing outer garments that were as stiff as a board and must have been about as comfortable as a suit of armour.' ibid, 251.
7   In Pashto, Dwa Toi means 'two streams'.
8   See Note 2.
9   It was discovered that 15 pounds of gun cotton was enough to demolish a tower, provided that the hatch at the top was closed in order to keep in the power

of the explosion. The mud houses were destroyed by bringing down the roof supports with a slab of gun cotton and then setting light to them – Rees, op cit, 230–1; 261. Huts were systematically looted before being burned.

10 2/5th, 2/9th and 4/3rd Gurkhas, 55th Rifles, 3/34th Pioneers, No. 6 Mountain Battery RGA, No. 27 Mountain Battery, 55 Field Company 3rd Sappers and Miners, with medical, supply and transport elements; 3/11th Gurkhas joined on 16 February direct from India.

11 *Operations*, 133, refers to it as a small town; it is perhaps more accurate to describe it as the main village of the area.

12 See the excellent topographical map (No. 5) in *Operations*.

13 See L/MIL/7/ 18854 – extracts from Column Commander's report.

14 *Operations*, 139.

XXII

The Climax of the Campaign
(Map 10)

The campaign was now close to its climax. The route to Kaniguram lay south-westwards from Dwa Toi, along the bed of the Baddar Toi. The country was close and well wooded, offering, as at Makin, innumerable opportunities for sniping and ambush at close range. It was therefore essential to picquet the route closely. The first picquets along the route were established by 43 Brigade, from its base at Piazha Raghza, the rifle grenade proving a useful weapon in flushing out snipers from the wooded slopes.

The promises made by the maliks on 29 February to try to assemble the full number of rifles in order to spare Kaniguram had not been fulfilled. Information from spies indicated that the maliks had given up all hope of collecting the additional rifles and had gone home. No great hopes had been entertained of their success and their failure was a disappointment rather than a blow.

At 0530 on 3 March Skeen's advance guard from 67 Brigade, consisting of two battalions, a section of 27 Mountain Battery and half of 55 Company with Sappers and Miners, moved out from Piazha Raghza towards Kaniguram. The early part of the route lay between steep, bush covered bluffs which commanded the track at short-range. The official history scribed it as the most difficult of all the defiles traversed by the troops since leaving Jandola.[1] In attempting it, Skeen was showing great confidence in the skill and morale of his troops – a significant illustration of the change which had developed in the column over the last three months.

The immediate task of the advance guard was to establish a chain of five permanent picquets[2] to protect the route as far as Ladha, some six and a half miles ahead. Almost as soon as it entered the Baddar Toi, the column came under intense sniping from tribesmen concealed on the wooded sides of the valley. Effective artillery fire enabled it to secure its first objective, an important wooded spur on the west side of the valley, known 'The Dam'.[3] By late afternoon the whole striking force was concentrated at Ladha, some five miles from Kaniguram, at a cost of one killed and nine wounded. These casualties suggested that the Mahsuds were beginning to abandon organised opposition.

Permanent picquets were now established round Ladha to control the exit from the Baddar Toi into more open country, to provide a strong point on which the column could fall back in the event of a major attack. A short stretch of camel track was built to by-pass another difficult defile a mile ahead, at Piaozar. The advance on Kaniguram was resumed on 6 March and the force camped that afternoon on a terraced plateau on the east side of the valley, some 700 yards south of Kaniguram itself. Apart from some sniping, which caused thirteen casualties, there had been no opposition. Skeen had thus reached his final objective after twelve weeks at a cost of some 600 killed and missing and nearly 1,700 wounded, very nearly the equivalent of a brigade's worth of troops.[4]

Kaniguram was the nearest approximation to a town that existed in Waziristan, with over 1,000 houses, five towers, a large covered bazaar and a number of rifle and knife factories, all huddled together along the slopes of a ridge, in five or six terraces, so close together that the flat roof of one terrace acted as a pathway for the next terrace.[5] The permanent inhabitants were mainly Urmars, a small non-Pathan tribe, who lived there on sufferance from the Mahsuds and who in turn shouldered the burden of accommodating and feeding those attending the major Mahsud assemblies held there.[6]

With the arrival of Skeen's striking force at the Mahsud 'capital', having successfully fought his way through every opposition, military and physical, and inflicted exceptionally heavy losses,[7] it might have been expected that the Mahsuds, recognising the apparent hopelessness of further armed resistance and anxious to avoid further destruction, would have been ready to sue for peace. Of that, there was no sign; the maliks had apparently abandoned any attempts to assemble the required fines in rifles and money, and had simply gone home.

In this impasse, the British options were limited. Continuing destruction was an option of diminishing returns; beyond a certain point it could only produce a tribal backlash of opposition. Isolated in the heart of Mahsud territory, with only the brigade at Piazha Raghza and air cover available as support, Skeen would be facing disaster in the case of a full scale tribal resurgence. Simply to camp at Kaniguram indefinitely was not a practical option for the same reason. Further devastation ran the risk of being counter-productive as the resources of the countryside would be required to sustain any large force. The permanent occupation of the heart of Waziristan was not in any case a policy which the Indian Government was yet prepared to face. Withdrawal without having brought the Mahsuds to accept the terms laid down would negate the whole purpose and cost of the campaign and destroy any hopes of peace indefinitely:

it was impossible to force this tribe of unruly and obdurate individuals, recognising no responsible leaders and no form of organised government, to make any engagements or to keep such promises if made, once the troops had left the country.[8]

The British explanation of this blank wall of Mahsud obduracy was that the Mahsuds had been misled by former leniency and were unable to grasp that this time the Government was determined to enforce its terms, having finally reached a turning point in its attitude to the Mahsuds. On this reasoning, the only course immediately open to the British authorities was to keep Skeen's force where it was in order to give the Mahsuds further time to come to their senses.[9] Time was not unfortunately on the British side. The weather was atrocious, with heavy snow and rain, and it as increasingly difficult for the supply convoys to get through on a regular basis. Isolated in the heart of the Mahsud country the risk to Skeen's force could only grow. Moreover, there was still the Wana Wazirs to deal with. It is unlikely that the Mahsuds had not already followed the same reasoning and, having accepted the futility of further direct opposition, had decided to play a waiting game.

In face of this impasse, it was important to keep the column active as inactivity could only embolden the tribesmen to resume guerilla attacks. There was useful work to be done in surveying the country round Kaniguram and in punishing the recalcitrant inhabitants of the upper Baddar Toi. Their country had not been visited by troops for many years and they appeared to assume they were beyond Skeen's reach.

A strong force of all arms, comprising six guns and 2,600 infantry, encumbered with 2,000 transport animals, moved out on the morning of 6 April, heading south and then north-west up the Baddar Toi. It reached Sine Tzha, some six miles from Kaniguram, that afternoon, where it destroyed villages and towers. Next day it moved on another four miles to Giga Khel, where more towers were blown up. The withdrawal that afternoon was closely followed up by some 300 tribesmen from the Shakai valley, who succeeded in wiping out a small party of 4/3rd Gurkhas who became trapped in a narrow ravine.[10] The retirement next day to Kaniguram was again closely followed up by the tribesmen but a single aircraft gave valuable support and the column was back at Kaniguram by 1600 hours. Total casualties were fifteen killed and forty-five wounded; the enemy, mainly Wana Wazirs, were estimated to have lost about the same. The troops had not succeeded in demolishing all the towers they had planned to, and the tribesmen had certainly shown no signs of being overawed. Honours were at best even.[11] It gave much food for thought.

If Skeen was in an awkward position, the Mahsuds, faced with a large force of troops camped outside their 'capital', faced a dilemma of their own. No doubt to Skeen's relief, most of the tribal sections of the Mahsuds now began to make efforts to assemble the necessary rifles and monetary fine. The troops concentrated throughout the rest of April on building a road suitable for mechanical transport back to Ladha. There was clearly little prospect of the Mahsuds producing all the rifles and fines which had originally been insisted upon, and in a dramatic change of policy the Government decided to create a permanent base in the heart of Mahsud territory, at Ladha. The troops at Kaniguram moved back there at beginning of May to begin the work of creating this permanent base.

The Derajat Column was formally broken up on 7 May 1920 but the forces in Waziristan remained. The new base at Ladha was garrisoned by 67 Brigade, together with a mountain artillery battery, a battalion of pioneers and a field company of sappers and miners. 43 Brigade remained at Piazha Raghza, while 68 Brigade remained at Sororogha and 62 Brigade at Tank. The equivalent of a division thus remained deployed in Southern Waziristan while in Northern Waziristan two brigades remained in the Tochi valley.

Thus ended, in the words of the official history,

a Frontier campaign of unparalleled hard fighting and severity. The enemy fought with a determination and courage which has rarely, if ever, been encountered by our troops in similar operations. The character of the terrain, combined with trying and arduous climate conditions, alone presented difficulties before which the more seasoned troops might well have hesitated.[12]

The military and political results of that campaign will be considered in the succeeding chapters.

Notes

1 *Operations*, 141.
2 'Dam', 'Pekin West', 'Red Hill', 'Dirty Tower' and 'Upper Chakoti'
3 *Operations*, Map 5.
4 For detailed figures, see Chapter XXIII.
5 Rees, 279.
6 For the Urmars, see Caroe, op cit, 23.
7 See Note 4 above.
8 *Operations*, 142–3.
9 Ibid, 144.
10 The official account says that the opposition round Giga Khel was mainly Wazirs from the Shakai Valley to the SW, although Giga Khel was a Mahsud (Abdur Rahman Khel) village – *Operations*, 144.
11 Rees, who accompanied the expedition, commented wryly:
'We had set out to persuade the Abdur Rahman Khel to hand over thirty captured rifles and, if possible, a fine by the implied threat of the destruction of their villages. We had blown up a total of four towers and damaged a handful of the houses but otherwise Giga Khel remained intact. During the operations they had captured a further fifteen of our rifles. On reflection, the coercion does not seem to have been an unqualified success.' – Rees, 295.
12 *Operations*, 144-5.

XXIII

The New Policy in Operation: Waziristan 1920–47

(Map 14)

Battle casualties in the Derajat Column totalled 366 killed, 237 missing and 1,683 wounded. Deaths from sickness and wounds among troops and followers in Waziristan Force as a whole between 26 October 1919 and 1 May 1920 totalled 1,329, out of total hospital admissions of 33,439, from an average strength of just over 83,000 troops and civilians. I have not found separate figures for Skeen's force but, on a pro-rata basis, deaths from sickness and wounds would have totalled about twenty, which is almost certainly too low, given the severity of the conditions. Overall, Skeen's casualties in killed, missing, and died of wounds or sickness thus totalled at least 2,500, equivalent to roughly half his original striking force of four battalions.[1]

Detailed casualties among Wazirs and Mahsuds are unknown. Estimated battle casualties exceeded 1,000 killed and there is likely to have been a significant number of deaths among the wounded because of their more primitive medical facilities. It seems likely that battle casualties in killed and died of wounds exceeded 1,400, about two and a half times those of the troops.[2] Deaths from sickness may well have been smaller because of greater hardiness and better acclimatisation. Civilian casualties, from bombing, privation and disease are not calculable. Tribal casualties were sustained against a much smaller military potential[3] and were therefore proportionately more serious.

The financial cost to the Government of India over and above normal peace-time expenditure was estimated at 13 crores of rupees (roughly £350,000 at the then exchange rate of 10 rupees to £1).[4]

By any standards it had been a costly and bloody campaign. The results could not be considered satisfactory for either side. The tribesmen had lost very heavily in men and property. They had been forced to surrender several hundred modern rifles (although not ammunition), and they had been unable to prevent the Army penetrating to their heartland. They were faced with a permanent garrison of regular troops at Ladha,[5] close to their 'capital'; more ominously, they were being forced to accept the construction of a permanent road network which would open up their country and significantly limit their previous independence. It remained to be seen whether, and by how much, these losses might be offset by greater prosperity and employment. Either way, they faced a future which would never be quite the same.

If the Mahsuds and Wazirs were overall losers, the Army and the Indian Government could not be said to be winners. Despite heavy casualties and even heavier expenditure, the Army had not gained its objectives. It had succeeded in penetrating to the Mahsud heartland and it had inflicted severe losses. But it had not succeeded in forcing the Mahsuds to surrender the rifles and pay the fines which had been part of the original terms at the jirga at Khirgi in November 1919. In the early stages of the campaign, the troops had sustained defeats of a kind never before seen in Frontier warfare and which would have lasting effects on the organisation and training of the Indian Army. Above all, the Mahsuds had not permanently been brought to heel. Within months there would be further attacks and in due course further large-scale operations. The Mahsuds, if temporarily cowed, were not defeated nor was their aggressive independence of spirit curbed.

The formal disbandment of the Derajat Column in May 1920 left much unfinished business. That the Mahsuds were not cowed was immediately obvious. Sniping between Ladha and Piazha Raghza became so troublesome that early in July 1920 a force of three battalions and the mountain battery from Ladha undertook a punitive expedition into Makin. The withdrawal was fiercely followed up, with hand-to-hand fighting which cost the 4/39th Garwhal Rifles sixty casualties. In September and October there was a series of raids in the area south of Tank, while in the remainder of the year attacks on convoys were endemic along the whole line from Jandola to Ladha, and casualties continued to mount. The focus of this activity was regarded as Makin. Air bombing had ceased to be effective, because the tribesmen had become adept at seeking shelter in caves and dug-outs. The two 6 inch howitzers laboriously dragged up to Ladha in the autumn of 1920 were used instead, to carry out constant and intermittent shelling of the Makin villages.[6] Women and children had been warned in advance to leave the area and shelling was carried out on a daily basis whenever movement was spotted.[7]

There remained the problem of Wana. The Afghans had been in possession of the fort since 1919. Their presence and the activities of their agents in the surrounding district kept alive the belief that the Ami would eventually take a hand in the affairs of Waziristan and thus strengthened the intransigence of the Wana Wazirs. Although there were elements of the Wana Wazirs who wished to come to terms with the Government, their influence was nullified by the Afghan influence which had been strengthened by the arrival of a virulently anti-British Afghan gent, Hajji Abdur Raziq (or Razak), in the early part of 1920.

To the British authorities it was clear that there could be no peace in that corner of Waziristan until the Afghans were expelled from Wana and the Wazirs suitably punished. If this was not done, then the situation at Wana would continue to be a source of unrest throughout Waziristan. In the autumn of 1920 the point was driven home when the Wazirs raided a regular army post between Manzai and Tank, making off with rifles.

The original plan had been to complete operations against the Mahsuds by the third week in February or, at latest, the end of March, in time to undertake a punitive expedition against the Wana Wazirs and to re-occupy Wana in April and May 1920, before the hot weather. The length of time taken to deal with the Mahsuds had destroyed that timetable. It was now too late to complete a campaign against the Wazirs before the hot weather set in. The operations had therefore to be postponed until the cold weather in the autumn of 1920.

The delay was not entirely unwelcome. There were serious lessons to be learned from the fighting against the Mahsuds. Despite the improved performance of the Indian infantry in the later stages of the Mahsud campaign, the unhappy experiences in the early weeks had left problems of training and morale which needed addressing urgently. The return to more normal conditions in India as well as in the Indian Army, after the immediate post-war chaos and instability, offered an opportunity to start to rectify some of the defects.

In the autumn of 1920 a force under Major General W S Leslie[8] began to assemble at Jandola for action against the Wana Wazirs. It comprised two infantry brigades (Nos 23 and 24), two 4-gun mountain batteries (No. 6 British), armed with 3.7 inch guns, and No. 15 (Indian), armed with the improved but still obsolescent, 2.75 inch mountain gun),[9] two pioneer battalions, a machine gun company, 14 Field Company, 2nd (Madras) Sappers and Miners, assisted by a dedicated RAF squadron. Of the infantry who had served in Skeen's column, only the 4/3rd Gurkhas were now included. Significantly, the force included a unit of heavy machine guns and a British battalion in each brigade, a clear indication that no chances were to be taken this time and a tacit recognition of deficiencies in Skeen's force in 1919–1920.

While the force was assembling, the Wana Wazirs were summoned to a jirga at Murtaza on 10 October 1920 where the Government's terms were presented to them. These were:

(a) a fine of 40,000 rupees;
(b) the surrender of 250 modern, tribal rifles;
(c) the surrender of all Government arms and equipment taken since 1 May 919.

As a pledge of good intent, 20,000 rupees, 300 Government and 200 modern tribal rifles were required to be produced at a further jirga to be held at Murtaza by 10 November 1920. If there was inadequate compliance, the force at Jandola would advance immediately to Wana and destroy crops and houses until the terms had been met.[10]

The Wazirs failed to turn up at Murtaza and there was no sign of compliance. They were known to be divided upon the issue of submission, with the opposition being under the influence of Hajji Abdul Raziq, the Afghan agent. Accordingly, a sustained aerial bombardment began on 11 November, concentrated upon areas known to be frequented by Abdul Raziq.

The Wazirs appealed for aid to the Mahsuds but were rebuffed. The Mahsuds apparently took the view that, but for Wazir incitement, they (the Mahsuds) might have given in earlier and saved themselves heavy losses. There was clearly little honour among thieves. The Mahsud attitude simplified the choice of route open to Leslie. The traditional route from Tank to Wana via the Gomal Valley had the advantage that it lay for the most part outside tribal territory and offered no particular natural obstacle. The alternative route via the Shahur Zam was shorter but ran through Mahsud territory and included the very dangerous defile of the Shahur Tangi – perhaps even more fearsome than the Barari Tangi.

Relying on the promise of Mahsud non-intervention, the choice was made in favour of the Shahur route although the intention had in effect been telegraphed already by the choice of Jandola as the assembly point. Leslie's force began its advance on 12 November. It proved to be something of a promenade. The Shahur Tangi was traversed without a shot being fired and when the force reached Sarwekai, half way to Wana, on 18 November, it found the old Militia fort there occupied by a force friendly Mahsuds, who had apparently already warned off a force Wana Wazirs headed by Abdul Raziq. Leslie halted there for a month to give the more pacific elements among the Wana Wazirs an opportunity to persuade the rest of the tribe to make peace as quickly as possible. By 15 December 24,000 rupees, fifty-one Government and eighty-seven tribe rifles had been handed over. This still fell far short of the original terms and the advance on Wana was resumed on 16 December. Two days later the force encountered its only serious opposition near Karab Kot, some six miles short of Wana. A night march by 4/3rd Gurkhas, supported by mountain guns and a section of machine guns, surprised the tribesmen and forced them to retreat, at a cost of only four British casualties. Wana was reached on 22 December.

The Government now faced exactly the same frustrating impasse as Kaniguram eight months earlier. The Wazirs' 'capital' had been occupied and the surrounding inhabitants had paid their share of the fines and were anxious for peace. The more recalcitrant sections showed no signs accepting the terms offered and there was no obvious way of forcing them to do so. Most of them were semi-nomadic, moving freely to and fro across the border with Afghanistan. They owned neither houses, nor land nor crops so there was nothing to destroy and the tribesmen could take refuge across the border if matters got too hot. As at Kaniguram, the only option appeared to be to remain in Wana indefinitely, in the hope that time would weaken the tribes' obstinacy. The force therefore remained at Wana until the spring of 1921 by which time the major part of the rifles and money demanded had been surrendered. The British battalions were withdrawn because of the approach of the hot weather and a garrison consisting of four infantry battalions, two mountain batteries, a field company of Sappers and Miners and some Militia, remained at Wana for two years; for much of the time, there was also a cavalry squadron.[11]

The retention of a regular garrison at Wana entailed a long line of supply from Jandola, divided into two sections for the purpose of protection – Section 1 from Jandola to Dargai Oba, roughly eighteen miles from Wana, and including the Shahur Tangi, and Section 2, from Dargai Oba to Wana. Although there were no major disasters, sniping and attacks on convoys became endemic and the Indian Army had another running sore on its hands. The strain on the troops was severe; as the CinC wrote in his despatch of 23 October 1921:

> The occupation of such a country as Waziristan is a severe strain on the troops who have to face arduous and dangerous duties daily. The scorching heat of summer, followed by a bitter winter, demands a very high standard of endurance from all troops employed upon protective duties, whether on permanent picquets or on road protection.[12]

With the completion in 1923 of the great central road from Tank, via Jandola and Razmak, to Bannu, it was decided in 1923 to withdraw the regular garrison from Wana and to leave it to be occupied by khassadars[13] and the occasional Militia patrol.[14]

The Waziristan campaign had shown up serious defects in the recruitment, training and organisation of the Indian infantry. Training in the use of personal weapons and light machine guns needed to be intensified, and mountain warfare tactics, at NCO, junior officer and unit level, needed to taught more thoroughly. Commanders and troops required practice in operating with aircraft, which would clearly be a major factor in all subsequent Frontier campaigns. Many of these defects had arisen from the difficult and dangerous internal situation in India in 1919, and from the almost inevitable confusion which followed the conclusion of the First World War. But at the root of these problems lay the archaic organisation the corps of infantry.

In 1919 the great bulk of the infantry was still organised in single-battalion regiments.[15] Since 1886 the regiments had been loosely associated in small groups sharing a common centre. Recruits were liable to serve in any of the associated regiments in an emergency. But each regiment retained its own separate responsibilities for recruiting, training and personnel administration. When a regiment went on active service, it left behind a small depot. Apart from some minor administrative efficiencies, the only real benefit was that in an emergency, cross-posting, and hence reinforcement of regiments on active service, became slightly easier. But the system was cumbrous. By 1919 there were over fifty centres and 115 regimental depots, each depot competing for recruits and training facilities.

While the defects of the single-battalion regimental organisation had been clear for many years – they had been glaringly exposed in the First World War – the Waziristan campaign made it clear that reorganisation was now essential if the defects in training and reinforcement which had been exposed were to be overcome speedily. The reorganisation of the Indian Army which followed in 1921–2 was based upon amalgamation into larger units. In the first phase in 1921 the infantry and pioneer regiments were brought together in groups of four to five, one of which acted as the training battalion, located at the group centre. This battalion was responsible for recruiting as well as training and reinforcement. This system was taken to its logical conclusion in 1922 when the groups were amalgamated into single regiments. The 280 battalions existing at the beginning of 1919 had, through disbandment and amalgamation, been brought down to 127 single-battalion regiments and were now reduced to twenty-two large regiments.[16] This immensely eased the problem of reinforcements, notably of officers; under the old system, the supply of officers to replace casualties was often extremely difficult and often meant the supply of replacement officers who were not familiar with the men they had to command. Battalions which had suffered significant battle casualties could now, under the new system, be rapidly supplied with trained men and officers from the regimental centre.

Before 1914, in line with the theory of 'the martial races',[17] only certain regiments had been considered suitable for service on the Frontier. The regiments which had formerly constituted the old Punjab Frontier Force were the most obvious examples, but in addition Sikh, Gurkha, Garwhali and Punjabi regiments were also considered suitable. Regiments from the south and east – the Madras regiments, the old Bengal regiments and most of the Bombay regiments – were not normally employed on the Frontier. The experiences of 1919–20 persuaded the Indian authorities that in future all regiments must be available and able to serve there, and must be trained accordingly and, as far as possible, rotated through the Frontier.

It is arguable that, without these organisational changes and increased military flexibility that they permitted, the greatly increased military commitment in Waziristan which the new 'modified forward' policy entailed could not have been sustained. That policy, which had been foreshadowed to some extent at the jirga with the Mahsuds at Khirgi on 3 November 1919 (see Chapter XV) with the announcement of a proposed programme of road building, took formal shape in May 1920 when the Secretary of State gave guarded approval to Chelmsford's proposals for the future control of Waziristan.[18] Chelmsford proposed the permanent occupation of a position in Central Waziristan in the neighbourhood of Makin, a chain of Militia posts along the Gomal to Wana, and a series of strategic roads, including a central road for motor vehicles connecting the Tochi with Khirgi via the new base in Makin.[19] In due course the central position was fixed as Razmak in place of Ladha; the central road was completed in 1923.

The military burden of this policy was very significant. In May 1919 there were no regular troops stationed inside the Administrative Boundary; the military presence inside the Tribal Area was maintained by a handful of posts manned by the North and South Waziristan Militias. The nearest regular troops were a strong brigade group located at Bannu and Dardoni, and a weak brigade group in the Derajat, based on Dera Ismail Khan, with the most forward detachment at Jandola.[20]

In May 1920 on the Ladha–Jandola line alone there were four complete brigades.[21] By the end of 1920 this had been reduced to strong brigade groups at Ladha and Wana, as well as two full brigades in the Tochi valley (at Dardoni and Bannu) and a further brigade in the Derajat, at Tank. Waziristan was now absorbing rather more than the equivalent of a division. If the long supply and administrative 'tail', which armies now required, is added in, together with the reserves held outside Waziristan, then the country was absorbing something approaching a fifth of the Army in India.[22]

The new policy had naturally taken account of the military's views. It as perhaps unfortunate that three of the viceroy's senior military advisers in this matter – the CinC (Rawlinson), the Deputy Chief of the General Staff (Montgomery) and the Commander Waziristan District (Matheson) were British Service officers with virtually no direct experience of the Frontier and its peculiar problems.

By contrast, the opposition to the new policy had its focus in two political officers of immense Frontier experience – Sir George Roos-Keppel, who had retired as Chief Commissioner of the North-West Frontier Province at the end of the Third Afghan War, and Sir John Maffey his successor – and Barrett's Chief Political Adviser in the Waziristan campaign. They embodied in an extreme form the opposing 'Forrward' and 'Close Border' policies which dominated thinking on the Frontier question for the whole of the British occupation. Roos-Keppel's views were simple and drastic. He condemned what he saw as a policy 'burn and scuttle' (or 'butcher and bolt' as others described it):

the Government of India should lay down and follow a definite policy of civilising the Frontier tribes up to the Durand line, first by crushing their fighting power and disarming them and then, by making roads through their countries and establishing and maintaining order, which would be welcomed by a large percentage who are tired of the anarchy which prevails in tribal territory.[23]

He was opposed to the partial occupation of Waziristan and would not hold anything forward of Miranshah and Jandola. In his view, the tribesmen could not be relied upon wherever the subject of Islam was involved and they should not be enlisted in the Indian Army or any of civil forces, i.e Militia and Police.

Roos-Keppel had served on the Frontier, as soldier and political officer for more than thirty years. No one knew it and its people better than he did. But by 1919 his views and attitude were increasingly considered out of date, and discounted accordingly.

Nevertheless, his successor, Grant, took much the same view:

there is no doubt that the only final solution to the problem is to occupy the country, but for this to be effective more must be done than merely the occupying of commanding positions by large bodies of troops. Mobile columns must traverse the whole country, disarmament of the people must be carried out, the introduction of civil administration on rough line must be effected, revenue at nominated rates must be assessed, and in addition to main mechanised communications, posts and roads should be constructed fit for pack transport... [24]

If this was not practicable, then he recommended that Sarwekai and the Shahur Tangi should be held, and there should be a main road from the Tochi to Razmak, which should be held permanently. If this was done then it would not be necessary to link Jandola to Razmak or hold the Barari Tangi, Makin and Kaniguram. He clearly believed that by holding Razmak to the north and Sarwekai and the Shahur Tangi to the south the Mahsuds could be squeezed if necessary between two halves of a nut cracker, thus obviating the need for a central road.

In retrospect, there was never a moment post-war when the Government of India possessed the resources to occupy and administer Waziristan, let alone the whole tribal territory up to the Afghan frontier; no conquerer in history, even Alexander, had ever attempted it. Like Grant's, Roos-Keppel's proposals did not directly attack the econonomic question. He had done much to provide educational facilities for the tribes but failed to see the corollary, that better education would create a demand for better economic opportunities and for political representation such as was already being introduced in India as a result of the Montague–Chelmsford reforms.

He was in reality the last great representative of the 'paternalistic' school of Frontier administration which had domated the 19th century.[25]

Maffey's arguments, presented in a paper produced in August 1922,[26] were diametrically opposed to those of his predecessor. He pointed out forcefully that the Government of India had been toying with the Frontier problem since 1847 but it still had no fixed policy or principles on which base a policy:

> This great blood-sucking Frontier which has drained us of men and money for nearly a hundred years is still the playground of chance decisions, personal predilictions and professional ambitions.[27]

In his view, there was a major and a minor problem. The major problem was Afghanistan; the minor problem was the tribes. In practice, the attention of the Government and the Army was almost exclusively fixed on the latter.[28] He believed that the presence of the army in tribal territory was a constant provocation and temptation to the tribesmen. His solution was to withdraw completely from tribal territory and to protect the settled areas by defending the Administrative Border; the only exceptions to this would be the Khyber, the Malakand, the Kurram and the Tochi as far as Miranshah, whose retention Maffey justified on strategic grounds vis à vis Afghanistan.[29] Any incursions or outrages across that border would be invariably and immediately punished. Otherwise the tribes would be left to their own devices. The revolutionary character of his proposals lay in the suggestion that the army would be forbidden to enter tribal territory, and that the job of enforcing this policy of 'zero tolerance' would be given to the RAF. It followed from this that he was wholly opposed to the stationing of any troops in tribal territory and to the road proposals in Waziristan which he believed would bring little permanent economic benefit to the tribes and would simply encourage the army to interfere in tribal territory. Instead, he believed that the important thing was to build a system of lateral roads along the Administrative Border to enable military forces to move quickly against any tribal incursions.

Maffey was an officer pf immense ability and the outstanding Frontier officer of his generation. Before taking over as Chief Commissioner, he had been Private Secretary to the Viceroy (Lord Chelmsford), a post of great influence and normally held only by the ablest men in the Indian Civil Service. Something of that self-confidence is reflected in his paper which is written forcefully and with notable frankness of expression. It is perhaps fair to say that it reflects also a faint trace of the traditional distrust between the political officer and the soldier.

Far more intriguing is the connection between the views expressed in his paper and those being expressed at exactly the same moment in a report submitted to the Viceroy by Air Vice-Marshal Sir John Salmond, who had been invited to India to report on the state of the RAF there.[30] Significantly, his formal terms of reference laid stress upon the economies which might be realised by the wider use of the RAF.

Salmond had spent time with Maffey, touring portions of the Frontier, and his Report included a detailed proposal for the RAF to assume responsibility for controlling the Waziristan tribes. It did not go as far as Maffey's paper in excluding the Army completely. There were probably two reasons for this; firstly, the RAF's success in air control, in Iraq, Somaliland and the Sudan, had been in close cooperation with ground forces, and, secondly, in 1922 the RAF was fighting for its continued independence and Salmond and the Air Staff were cautious about treading on too many toes. Any expansion of the role of the RAF in India was likely to lead to economies in the size of the Indian Army and thus likely to be opposed by the military authorities on grounds of self-interest.[31] Maffey was not hampered by such considerations and it would not be unreasonable to suppose that his (bolder) proposals for the use of airpower represented the covert ambitions of the Air Staff.[32]

Although the views of Roos-Keppel and Maffey represented the extreme poles of Frontier thinking, they had in common a deep opposition to the 'modified forward' policy about to be implemented in Waziristan Both men disappeared quickly from the scene – Roos-Keppel died in 1921 while Maffey resigned in 1924 in protest at the Waziristan policy. He went on to be Governor of various places and to receive a peerage in 1947. But with him went the last real chance of a radical solution to a problem which continued to bedevil the British administration down to 1947.

It is fair to recognise that Maffey did not address squarely the economic problems of the tribesmen. He assumed that with the cessation of 'butcher and bolt' the tribal economic life would develop of its own accord:

> The Pathans of the borderland are virile and active-minded. When they find that mischief does not pay, they soon turn their hands to something that does.[33]

The new 'modified forward' policy, once it had begun to be implemented could not easily be reversed. The Government of India and the Army had invested too much prestige and expense in it and it had therefore to be given a full trial. The policy was in large part devised to prevent further Afghan incursions such as had occurred in 1919 when the Afghans occupied Wana. Afghan intrigues among the British tribes could never be prevented, but the assumption was that the new policy, together with the treaty of friendship signed in 1921, would make this more difficult.

The new policy received an early test. The approaching completion of the central motor road up the Tank Zam in the spring of 1922 prompted the military authorities to withdraw from Ladha and to construct a new base instead at Razmak, just outside Mahsud territory. Rumours circulated among the Mahsuds that the troops were to be withdrawn completely from Central Waziristan. The resulting unrest led to a series of attacks and outrages. In consequence, work on the central road was temporarily suspended beyond Dara Twoi in December, which increased the unrest, stimulating afresh the old rumours that the British were about to pull out of Waziristan and hand it over to Afghanistan. Work on the road, however, was resumed under the direct protection of the Ladha Brigade, while the RAF began bombing the insurgents. The situation did not improve and in January 1923 it was decided to undertake yet another punitive expedition. The 9th Brigade at Ladha was to rendezvous with the 5th and 7th Brigades, which were covering the construction of Razmak, in Makin. The three brigades met at Taud China on 4 February, having encountered little serious fighting and having few casualties. They then proceeded to devastate Makin until the hostile tribal sections submitted on 22 February. Jirgas representing the whole Mahsud tribe met later in March and accepted the terms offered. The three brigades then dispersed back to their original stations, having suffered 137 casualties.[34]

Several factors may be adduced to explain the speed and low cost of this operation – the Indian Army had begun to recover from the low point reached in 1919 and troops were better trained and more experienced, the use of two dedicated squadrons of aircraft, operating from Dardoni, in the Tochi valley, enabled the tribesmen to be continually harassed and prevented from concentrating in any numbers, and the central road, whose construction had been hurried on, had fulfilled its aim of enabling troops and supplies to be moved quickly and efficiently. These factors would become permanent features of future operations. From a military stand point, the new policy could be said to have passed its first test satisfactorily. But it could also be argued that the most significant feature of the campaign was that it should have been necessary at all, barely two years after the 1919–20 campaign. From the political point of view, the effectiveess of the new policy remained unproven.

In 1924 it was decided to set up Waziristan District, with HQ at Dera Ismail Khan. Political control of the territory beyond the Administrative border, which had been effectively in the hands of the Army since 1920, was handed back to the Resident. At this stage, the forces in Waziristan totalled four brigades (one at Razmak, two on the lines of communication back to, and including, Bannu, and one covering the L of C from Tank to Jandola, the most forward regular garrison in the south). Forward patrolling was undertaken by the two reconstituted militias (now called the Tochi Scouts and South Waziristan Scouts) totalling 4,000 men.

In March 1925 Bristol Fighters and DH 9A light bombers were employed on their own in an experiment to punish a small body of Mahsuds living just north of the Shahur Tangi. It proved entirely successful, at a cost of one aircraft and its crew, going some way to validating both Salmond's and Maffey's proposals.

In the eleven years which followed, the combination of regular troops; Scouts and the RAF succeeded in reducing substantially the number of tribal outrages. The brigades at Razmak and Bannu carried out frequent 'promenades', making use of the new road system, which was substantially complete by 1936. But it proved impossible in practice to conceal preparations for these operations from the tribesmen and there was a steady drain of casualties from sniping. In effect, the troops in Waziristan remained permanently on active service, although the permanent facilities at Wana and Razmak were gradually improved to provide at least a semblance of peace-time conditions. True to form, there was a drag hunt at Wana.

The relative quiescence after 1925 came to an abrupt end in 1936. It is not necessary here to go into the tortuous course of the Islam Bibi affair which led to a major uprising.[35] What is significant is that it brought to prominence a Tori Khel Wazir, Mirza Ali Khan, better known to history a the Fakir of Ipi. Previously known only for his reputation as a religious man, he became virulently anti-British as a consequence of this affair. His appeal lay partly in his claim that the British were interfering in religious matters (always a strong rallying cry among the fanatical tribesmen); partly in the fact that he was appealing to a new generation who had no direct knowledge of the heavy losses suffered in 1919–20, and partly also in the fact that the constitutional changes in India – and particularly the installation of Congress governments in the major provinces – had led tribal onlookers to conclude that British rule in India was coming to an end.

The Tori Khel[36] somewhat disingenuously professed their inability to arrest the Fakir unless supported by troops. It was recognised by the. Indian authorities that sending an expedition into the Khaisora Valley ran the risk of stirring up a general rising, but on balance this was considered preferable to inaction. Accordingly, early in November 1936, in what was expected to be a relatively peaceful 'showing the flag' demonstration, the brigade at Razmak (RAZCOL)[37] moved eastwards down the Khaisora Valley to rendezvous at Bichhe Kashkai[38] with a force of two battalions (TOCOL) moving southwards from Mir Ali in the Tochi Valley.

RAZCOL, after a march of twelve miles, during which it encountered significant opposition, reached the rendezvous late on the evening of 20 November 1936. The commander of TOCOL had been warned of strong oposition led by the Fakir of Ipi in person but, despite the relative weakness of his force, decided to press on. By early afternoon on the 25th he was facing strong opposition and had already suffered heavy casualties, particularly among the transport. Efforts to move on proved fruitless and he was forced to make camp late that night, several miles tort of Bichhe Kashkai. Next morning (26 November) RAZCOL sent two battalions and a mountain battery to help and by mid-day the two columns had joined up at Bichhe Kashkai. They were now short of ammunition, there were many casualties to be evacuated and they were rationed only until the evening of the 27th. In these circumstances the District Commander decided to withdraw both columns northwards to Mir Ali. Despite fierce attacks on the rear guard, the two columns reached Mir Ali on the evening of the 27th, having lost in total just over a hundred men. What had started out as a demonstration of force had turned into something of a fighting retreat.

The military authorities had been warned of likely opposition, but the scale of it had been underestimated and the plan to rendezvous at Bichhe Kashkai in one day was optimistic. The absence of serious fighting since 1925 had perhaps encouraged a certain degree of false security. The result was a spectacular boost to the Fakir of Ipi's prestige and a rapid growth in tribal hostility.

The logic of Frontier policy led inevitably to a major campaign which lasted until December 1937, directed essentially at one man. In the course the operations, the Fakir flitted across Waziristan, recruiting Wazirs, Mahsuds, Daurs, Bhitannis and trans-border Afghans to oppose the British. On the British side, operations reached a level of effort exceeding that of 1919–20. They were under the direct control of the GOC Northern Command, General Sir John Coleridge, and in due course the whole of the Infantry Division was brought in to back up the permanent Waziristan garrison. Four squadrons of aircraft were deployed in direct support (exactly as Salmond had proposed in 1922) and light tanks appeared on the Frontier for the first time in operations.

By the end of 1937, after heavy fighting, the influence of the Fakir was declining as the tribes counted up their losses. The Fakir himself was never captured and the campaign fizzled out, rather than coming to a definite conclusion, in December 1937. The troops involved, as well as the Scouts, received the India General Service Medal 1936, with the bar North-West Frontier 1936–37.[39]

Perhaps the most significant aspect of the 1936–7 campaign was the fact the Mahsuds as a tribe stayed clear of it, although small parties of them took part on an opportunistic basis. The abstention of the tribe as a whole was probably due mainly to the fact that the Fakir was a Wazir. But it may also be that there was an element of schadenfreude as the Tochi Wazirs had escaped lightly in 1919 by giving in early. Clearly, if Mahsuds had supported the Tochi Wazirs, the campaign would have been a very much more serious and prolonged affair. Tribal individualism and their inability to stand together had, yet again, played into British hands. But those who had assumed that after 1919 the Wazirs could be discounted as a serious threat had been sharply disabused.

That the Mahsuds had lost none of their aggression or tactical skill was demonstrated in spectacular fashion in April 1937, when a convoy of lorries escorted by four armoured cars was ambushed in the Shahur Tangi.

In the chaos which followed, fifty-two officers and men were killed and fifty-three wounded. It was a chilling illustration of the ever prevalent risk of disaster on the Frontier, and of the effect that concerted Mahsud hostility might have had on the fighting farther north. It was an illustration also that the mechanisation of transport and its consequent restriction to a fixed road system presented problems of its own.

The problem of protecting mechanised convoys was never fully solved. Constant patrolling by the Scouts, the use of permanent picquets and better intelligence were the keys, but in the type of terrain which was Waziristan, ambushes by dissident groups of tribesmen could never excluded. But the network of strategic roads originally conceived in 1911 was complete by 1939 and undoubtedly the increased mobility that this conferred on the Government forces reduced the opportunities and increased the hazards for the tribesmen.

It has been claimed that the 1936–7 campaign had the important effect of keeping the tribes quiescent throughout the Second World War.[40] That may, however, somewhat exaggerate the position. Certainly, there was no major trouble, requiring a full-scale punitive expedition on the scale 1919–20 or 1936–7. The Fakir of Ipi, however, continued to foment trouble and found a new role in spreading Axis propaganda supplied to him by the German and Italian embassies in Kabul, and both Wazirs and Mahsuds remained ready to seize any aggressive opportunities which presented themselves. In August 1940, for example, the Tochi Scouts suffered a significant disaster at Tappi, in the Tochi Valley, and in June 1942 there was another serious affair near Datta Khel.[41] In May 1942 the Fakir of Ipi besieged the fort at Datta Khel for three months before it could be relieved. The period 1940–5 could only be described as a difficult and uneasy one, rendered the more dangerous by the drain of experienced British officers and troops to other theatres.[42]

Pakistan took over responsibility for Waziristan in August 1947 and two months later, all regular forces were withdrawn. The South Waziristan Scouts continued to garrison Wana but the advanced posts of Lac Sorarogha and Kotkai were abandoned. In Northern Waziristan, the Fakir of Ipi still exercised considerable influence among the Wazirs and were minor incidents, but Razmak was evacuated without trouble. The Pakistan Government and Army naturally benefited from being co-religionists with the tribesmen, as well as from the fact that under the ethnic cleansing' which took place in August 1947, Hindu communities and traders largely disappeared from the Frontier. Raiding fellow Muslims and defying a Muslim government became increasingly difficult to justify. But it is also right to recognise the wisdom of the Pakistan Government's policy in introducing schools and colleges, and even a Frontier university at Peshawar. The Mahsuds, in particular, with their keen intelligence and force of character, benefited from the educational and economic opportunities which opened up after 1947, exactly as Maffey had predicted more than twenty years before.

This progress made after 1947 raises in acute form the issue of British policy in Waziristan after 1921. The policy of opening up the country by roads and of stationing large bodies of regular troops inside tribal territory received its acid test in 1936–7. On the face of it, the need to bring a complete infantry division, in addition to a regular garrison of three brigades and 4,000 militia, and the apparent lack of a clear conclusion to the operations, suggests ultimately the failure of that policy. It had undoubtedly been an expensive one in men, money and resources.

On the credit side the policy had brought some direct economic benefits to the tribesmen in terms of employment on the roads, in transport contracts, and in the employment of tribal khassadars. For the Army it was claimed that it provided the best training in the world. That was probably a fair comment in terms of basic skills such as weapons handling, mobility, assessing ground, and speed of reaction. But it bore little relationship to armoured warfare which would be encountered in the Western Desert and North-West Europe in 1940. For the RAF, it taught basic airmanship and perhaps survival skills, but otherwise the machines and tactics bore little or no resemblance to the air war of 1939–45. Overall, the correctness of the 'modified forward' policy pursued in Waziristan between 1920 and 1945 remains unproven.

The alternatives also remain unproven because they were not tried by the British. Roos-Keppel's extreme 'forward' policy, which would have entailed the complete occupation of Waziristan, was almost certainly impracticable – the military resources required were simply not available in peacetime even if there had been the political will in India and London. Roos-Keppel, however, understood the importance of providing education for the tribesmen, and in theory at least permanent occupation could have provided the foundation for that expansion of economic opportunity which was the only permanent solution to the tribal problem.

Maffey's extreme 'close border' proposal tackled the economic problem from a different angle. His thesis was that deprived of the opportunity to raid and loot, their natural intelligence and aggressiveness would have driven the tribesmen to find other economic outlets for their energies. On the face of it, Maffey's solution was an attractive one. There can be little doubt that the presence of the army in Waziristan was a provocation and a source of aggression for Mahsuds and Wazirs alike. Maffey and others believed that, far from being daunted, the tribesmen welcomed the excitement of fighting the troops. The experience of the RAF in Iraq, Somaliland, the Sudan and Arabia gave substantial ground for believing that a policy of air control in Waziristan stood a substantial chance of being effective, although the details needed to be worked out.[43] There was attraction, too, in the other aspect of Maffey's scheme – the importance of encouraging the inhabitants along the border of the settled area to undertake their own defence. The policy was not without risk. If the British withdrew from Waziristan, what would be the attitude of Afghanistan and what would be the attitude of the tribes towards Afghanistan? If the policy proved unsuccessful, what would be involved in attempting to reverse it and move back into Waziristan? What would be the precise cost of maintaining a hermetically sealed border and a zero tolerance policy? History seemed to show that a civilised static society could never live permanently at peace with savage neighbours – the Romans, the Russians and the British all seemed to have found that out.

In 1944, at the height of the war against the Japanese, the CinC India, General Sir Claude Auchinleck, himself an experienced Frontier officer., appointed a committee under Lieutenant General Sir Francis Tuker, a highly intelligent and experienced Frontier officer, to examine post-war Frontier policy. That committee came up in effect with Maffey's old proposals – the withdrawal of regular troops from the tribal areas, leaving those areas to the militias, coupled with ever-present air support.[44] But the sun had almost set on the British occupation of India and the proposals never got beyond the drawing board.

When Pakistan took over in August 1947, its first step was to withdraw all regular army units from the tribal areas, leaving it to the militias. That the Pakistan Government has had substantially less trouble from the Mahsuds and Wazirs than the British did is, of course, a function among other things of co-religion; the tribesmen did not have the same incentive to trouble an independent Muslim government as they had done an alien British Government. But the Pakistan Government has also poured money into the country on education and development projects and the tribesmen have fulfilled Maffey's prophesy and seized the new economic opportunities open to them.

The Pakistan experience, although not without its blips vis à vis the tribesmen, points to the real failure of British policy in Waziristan, to treat it as basically a military problem rather than an economic one, to deal with it in terms of repression rather than opportunity, both political and economic. The world has moved on since 1919, for the tribes as well as governments. The tribesman is no longer content to live the spartan, poverty-stricken if independent life that he once did. Since 1945 political developments elsewhere have encouraged him to demand a degree of political independence and responsibility. Such a thing would have been incomprehensible to Roos-Keppel and probably even to Maffey.

Autres temps autres moeurs. What was possible in 1947 was not necessarily possible in 1922 and hindsight is not an infallible tool for historians. Nevertheless, in surveying the events of 1919–20, one has a feeling of an opportunity lost.

Notes

1　Casualties from *Operations*, Appendices I and 1 172–3 and passim.

2　Author's estimates.

3　Official estimates gave the fighting strength of the Mahsuds in November 1919 as 11,200 and that of the Wana Wazirs as 11,900 – *Operations*, Appendix L, 186–7.

4　Salmond Report, Appendix III, paragraph 9.

5　The permanent brigade camp was moved from Ladha to Razmak in 1922.

6　The howitzers had a range of 9,500 yards and fired a shell weighing 86 pounds.

7　*Despatch by His Excellency General Lord Rawlinson of Trent on the operations of the Waziristan Force for the period 1st April to 31st December 1921* (Simla, 24 May 1922).

8　Leslie had been Skeen's Chief of Staff during the Mahsud operations – see Biographical Notes.

9　The mountain batteries were officially designated 'pack' batteries in October 1920 but reverted to being 'mountain' batteries in 1927 – see Graham, op cit, 190. I have used the term 'mountain' throughout to avoid confusion.

10　*Despatch by His Excellency General Lord Rawlinson of Trent on the operations of the Waziristan Force for the period 8th May 1920 to 31st March 1921* (Delhi,1921) – copy in L/MIL/17/13/121.

11　Rawlinson, Despatch. De Watteville, 176, gives the garrison as six battalions, one and a half mountain batteries, a half company of the Machine Gun Corps and a field company of Sappers and Miners. His figures, however, clearly relate to the garrison immediately after the re-occupation.

12　*Despatch*, para 34.

13　Khassadars were tribal police, employed to patrol the roads and prevent minor transgressions. They were not uniformed and provided their own rifles. They were used extensively on the Frontier and did useful work, provided their tribal loyalties were not tried too far.

14　Wana was re-occupied by the regular army in 1929 and thereafter retained until 1947.

15　The 39th Garwhal Rifles and the ten Gurkha regiments had two battalions each.

16　Thirty-two, if one includes the ten two-battalion Gurkha regiments. As an example of how the system worked, the 14th, 15th, 35th, 36th and 45th Sikhs became the 1st–4th and 10th Battalions of the new 11th Sikh Regiment. The cavalry regiments were amalgamated to form twenty-one who were then linked to share seven depots, with one regiment becoming the training regiment there. For details of this and subsequent reorganisations, see John Gaylor, *Sons of John Company* (Tunbridge Wells, 1992) and *The Army in India and its Evolution* (Government Press, Calcutta, 1924).

17　For the 'martial race' theory, propagated powerfully by Lord Roberts, see Brian Robson, *Roberts in India: the military papers of Field Marshal Lord Roberts 1876–1893* (London, 1993), xvii, 257–8 and passim; also Sir George McMunn, *The Martial Races of India* (London, 1932).

18　SofS to Viceroy, No. 1714, 12 May 1920 – L/MIL/7/15939, 466.

19　Viceroy to SofS, No. 332-S, 23 March 1920 – ibid, 490–5.

20　The brigade at Bannu comprised a cavalry regiment, a mountain battery, two armoured motor batteries (armoured cars) and four battalions of infantry. The Derajat brigade comprised a cavalry regiment, a mountain battery, one armoured motor battery and three battalions of infantry. *Operations* Appendix D.

21 At Ladha, Piazha Raghza, Kotkai and Tank, a total of two squadrons of cavalry, nineteen battalions of infantry, three mountain batteries and three field companies of Sappers and Miners – Rawlinson, *Despatch on Waziristan 8th May 1920 to 31st March 1921*, Appendix I.

22 Small wonder that Maffey referred bitingly to the Army holding a long communications trench called the Ladha Line – long, expensive to maintain, littered with the skeletons of animals and motor vehicles – quoted in Elliott, 263.

23 Roos-Keppel to Viceroy 10 August 1919, 2 – Barrett papers. This was effectively his swan-song – he retired very shortly afterwards and died in 1921.

24 Grant to Foreign Secretary, No. 194, 26 February 1920 – L/P&S/10/870, No. 31.

25 For Roos-Keppel's personality and attitude, see Caroe, 422–5.

26 *Unsolicited views on an unsolved Problem*, dated 2 August 1922 – RAF Museun Hendon, reference B2609 (Salmond papers), hereafter cited as Maffey.

27 Ibid, 2.

28 Not exclusively; as late as 1934, the Army was drawing up plans for a war with Afghanistan – see L/MIL/17/14/21.

29 Maffey does not actually spell this out but it is clear from his text – Maffey, 6

30 *Report by Air Vice-Marshal Sir John Salmond KCB, CMG, CVO, DSO on the Royal Air Force in India*, dated August 1922 – RAF Museum, Salmond papers reference B2690.

31 'I feel that any opposition by the Army in India to my proposals is based less on conviction as to their impractability, than on the natural fear that they may lead to a further reduction in an Army already reduced to a point considerably below pre-war strength.' – *Salmond Report*, paragraph 38.

32 For a more detailed analysis of the Salmond Report, see this author's article in the *Journal of the RAF Historical Society*. For a more detailed discussion of the RAF's attitude on air control, see David Omissi, *Air Power and Colonial Control* (Manchester, 1991).

33 Maffey, 19.

34 *Despatch by His Excellency General Lord Rawlinson of Trent on the Operations of. the Waziristan Force for the period 1st January 1922 to 20th April 1923* (Simla 1923); *Official History of Operations on the N.W. Frontier of India 1920–35* (Delhi 1945). For the post-1919 budgetary difficulties, see Anirudh Deshpande 'Military Reform in the Aftermath of the Great War: Intentions and Compulsions of British Military Policy 1919–1925' in Gupta and Deshpande, *The British Raj and its Indian Armed Forces 1857–1939*.

35 In essence, the case concerned the elopement of an under-age Hindu girl with a young Muslim student. Claims that she had been abducted against her will and forcibly converted to Islam followed and both sides claimed custody. The case followed a tortuous course through the civil courts, with conflicting judgements being reached at each stage.

36 The Tori Khel inhabited the country between the Tochi and the upper reaches of the Khaisora and Shaktu rivers.

37 One British and three Indian battalions, with three mountain batteries.

38 In the Khaisora Valley, due south of Idak.

39 For a detailed study of this campaign, see *Official History of he Operations on the*

North-West Frontier of India 1936–37 (Delhi,1943).

40 See, for example, Elliott, op cit, 280–1.
41 For these affairs, see Chenevix Trench, 226–37.
42 For a portrait of this period, see Chenevix Trench, 241–60.
43 For a more detailed discussion of the use of air power in this way, see David Omissi, op cit.
44 *Report of the Frontier Committee 1945* (Simla,1945).

XXIV

Reflections

The campaign in Waziristan in the winter of 1919–20 marked a major change in the terms of Frontier warfare. At the heart of that change lay the advent of the modem, small-bore, magazine rifle, firing smokeless powder cartridges. It was not a new phenomenon. By 1910 large numbers of such rifles were arriving on the Frontier via the Persian Gulf and the Mekran coast of Baluchistan,[1] and causing concern. In 1910 the first detailed analysis of tribal strengths and weapons suggested that the trans-border tribes possessed already some 63,000 breechloaders as against some 40,000 muzzle loaders, although not all of the breechloaders were modern, magazine rifles.[2] A year later, Fraser Lovat wrote prophetically that:

> The tribesmen on the North-West Frontier are now armed as they were never armed before, and we shall discover the results of our carelessness in the tale of the dead and wounded if we ever have to send a big expedition into the hills between the Khyber and the Gomal.[3]

By the beginning of 1919 the situation was even worse. Estimates of modem rifles had risen to some 140,000, while the number of black powder weapons had remained roughly the same.[4] Large numbers of Lee Enfield rifles were captured from the Militias and troops in the early part of 1919, together with very large stocks of ammunition. At the same time desertions from the Militias and the existence of time-expired regulars meant that there were significant numbers of trained soldiers in the tribal ranks.[5]

The significance of the small-bore, magazine rifle lay in its longer range,[6] the rapidity of fire, using a magazine,[7] and its comparative invisibility, using smokeless powder. The greater range meant that protective picquets needed to be sited much farther away from the camp troops they were protecting, and this in itself increased the risk of ambush and the difficulty of giving covering fire; in Waziristan it meant that the establishment of a permanent picquet post became a brigade operation. The volume of fire which could now be produced by a comparatively small body of men and the presence of trained men among the tribesmen enabled them to carry out sophisticated fire plans under cover of which their swordsmen could rush the troops. The outstanding example was the attack on 'Black Hill' on 21 December 1919. Nothing approaching it had been seen on the Frontier before and it came as a very disagreeable shock to British commanders. Finally, the combination of long-range and smokeless powder, aided by the dust-coloured clothing which most tribesmen wore, enabled them to indulge in daylight sniping with comparative impunity. Even from the air they were extremely difficult to spot.

Between 1910 and 1919 there was only one significant expedition on the Frontier – that against the Mahsuds in 1917.[8] For different reasons, neither side was anxious for a full-scale war and, although there was some serious fighting, the, expedition was over within a fortnight. The sea change which had come over the Frontier with the advent of large numbers of modern rifles had not, in consequence, fully manifested itself.

The Army in India attempted to meet the new situation on the Front in 1919 in two main ways. The most obvious way was the deployment the modem technology developed on the Western Front. Chief among the relevant technologies was the development of the machine gun and in particular the light machine (Lewis) gun. The heavy machine gun – the Vickers gun – had developed into a powerful adjunct to the artillery, capable of laying down a dense barrage of fire at ranges of up to 2,500 yards. Its importance and application had been recognised by the formation of a special corps, the Machine Gun Corps, operating in a number of specialised mobile roles – on motorcycles, on lorries and in armoured cars.[9] It was also capable of being carried by animal transport and, if necessary, it was man-portable. Armoured car (Armoured Motor Batteries) were used on both the Tochi and Derajat Lines of Communication, but were unable to accompany Skeen's column because the terrain was too difficult. A number of heavy machine guns were deployed in defence of posts on the L of C, but in what seems a surprising omission no heavy machine gun unit accompanied Skeen's column. Such a unit might materially have assisted his troops on a number of occasions. In theory, the Vickers gun was man-portable and had frequently been used in that way on the Western Front. In practice, the climate and topographical conditions on the Frontier made this difficult and brought into greater prominence the use of the Lewis gun. Its lightness made it easily portable, it fired rifle ammunition which eased the problem of supply, and its rate of fire added greatly to the firepower of the infantry. It was particularly valuable in the defence of picquet posts whose garrisons could be reduced as a result. The Lewis gun, however lost much of its effectiveness in the hands of untrained troops and after the disasters of December 1919 the guns were withdrawn from rifle companies and concentrated at battalion level as a temporary measure.

Apart from the machine gun, the grenade, both in the form of the small, easily thrown Mills bomb and the rifle grenade, discharged from a cup fitted to the rifle, had become perhaps the infantry's most useful weapon; it was used extensively in Waziristan by both sides, as the tribesmen succeeded in the early stages in capturing significant stocks. The hand grenade, however, had a downside since excessive reliance on it tended to diminish reliance on, and familiarity with, the rifle, a serious error on the Frontier and one which was responsible for the defeats of the early part of the campaign. Unfortunately, the recovery of skill and confidence in the rifle required time and training which was not readily available. Of the other technologies in existence at infantry level, a surprising omission in Waziristan was the use of the trench (Stokes) mortar, although a small number of the larger, 3 inch variety were deployed along the L of C.[10] With its high trajectory and its ability to search dead ground, it would seem to have been well suited to tactical requirements on the Frontier. It was, however, still relatively crude and the rifle grenade, albeit with much shorter range, appears to have met the need.

On the Western Front, artillery had proved the biggest killer and the weapons themselves had developed accordingly. They were, however, generally too heavy and lacking in mobility for the Frontier. But a new 3.7 inch mountain howitzer was available in India and was used extensively in Waziristan where its ability to drop shells over the crest of hills and ridges was of great value, a value diminished by the absence of a shrapnel shell. In time it would become the standard mountain artillery weapon, but in 1919 it needed to be supplemented by the obsolescent 2.75 inch mountain gun.[11]

Poison gas in the form of shells and bombs containing mustard gas was available in India and its use had been raised by the Secretary of State at the beginning of the Third Afghan War, probably as a result of the War Office having raised it via military channels.[12] At that stage Chelmsford did not think its use either necessary or politic.[13] But the early debacles in Waziristan raised the question of its use more urgently. The military as a whole, from Skeen upwards, were generally in favour, but whereas Skeen was primarily in favour in order to meet an immediate tactical dilemma, Climo sought to justify its use by a more sophisticated argument:

I am strongly of the opinion that the use of gas should be introduced. I am more strongly than ever of this opinion; not because I am doubtful of the power of the troops to carry things with these and other operations, but because I consider that when an enemy confronts us who has all the advantages of the savage backed by rifles as good as our own, we should turn to science to compensate in every possible way for the disadvantages which our more civilised conditions and manner of war places on our troops.[14]

Its use was wisely vetoed by London; apart from the domestic and international political fall-out, the practical problems of delivery were matched by the danger of its use with under-trained troops.[15]

The most important development in military technology in the first two decades of the 20th century was the internal combustion engine. By 1919 it was becoming a major factor in Frontier warfare, first, in the form of motor transport, notably the ubiquitous Ford van, secondly in the form of the armoured car, and finally in the shape of the aeroplane.

Wherever the road system allowed it to be used, motorised transport immensely increased the mobility of troops – the reinforcement of Landi Kotal on 5 and 7 May 1919 was a classic example; Dyer's use of lorries to tow his guns up to Thal was another. But its major importance lay in speeding up and easing the problem of supply; for planning purposes, it was assumed that one 3-ton lorry could carry the equivalent of between fifteen and thirty camels (depending on the tyres) and had twice the radius of action.[16] This was of particular importance because of the enormous increase in the quantity and variety of stores, ammunition and petrol which the post-war army required.

Its use naturally depended on the existence of motorable roads, few of which existed in Waziristan in 1919. Thus Skeen in 1919–20 had no option but to rely upon pack transport beyond Jandola, and to drag along with him thousands of pack animals whose protection and feeding greatly complicated his operations. This factor was a major determinant in the decision in 1919 to open up Waziristan with a network of motorable roads

Armoured cars, operated in the first instance by the short-lived Machine Gun Corps, proved useful in patrolling the Lines of Communication and in escorting convoys, but they were severely limited in where they could go, and on the whole did not play a significant role in 1919–20. One other use of the internal combustion engine may be noticed at this point – the narrow-gauge Decauville railway laid between Dera Ismail Khan, Tank and, ultimately, Khirgi, which used small, petrol-driven locomotives[17] and proved of great value in shifting men and supplies.

The major technological development affecting the Frontier and the Waziristan campaign in particular was the aeroplane. It had first appeared on the Frontier in the 1916 Mohmand campaign, and again in Waziristan in 1917. It had played a comparatively small part in the recent Afghan war, its most noteworthy exploit being the lone bombing raid on Kabul on May 1919, which was credited by the Commander in Chief (Monro) with playing a major part in the decision of the Amir to sue for peace.[18] That its value was already perceived is evidenced by the fact that the occupation of Dakka on 13 May 1919 was immediately followed by the construction of a landing ground. The aircraft available then – principally the BE2C – were, however, primitive, with very limited performance and high unreliability.[19] Thus it would be true to say that by the end of the Third Afghan

War the aeroplane was seen by the military authorities as a useful, but not vital, adjunct to ground operations on the Frontier. It was the campaign in Waziristan in 1919–20 which saw it emerge as an essential element of all future operations.

By the end of 1919, better aircraft were available – notably the versatile two-seat Bristol Fighter, which equipped No. 20 Squadron at Tank and Bannu.[20] Like other aircraft of this period, it had been developed in the conditions of the Western Front where range had been less important than payload, and serviceability remained low. In its first role – reconnaissance – the aeroplane had mixed success on the Frontier. Visual reconnaissance proved less effective than expected. The tribesman in his dust-coloured clothing was never easy to spot on his native hills; he was accustomed to remaining still for long periods and adept at finding cover; spotting him was a matter of experience. But by enabling commanders to 'see over the hill', visual reconnaissance had proved valuable in the difficult, tangled terrain of Waziristan.[21] Photographic reconnaissance was perhaps even more valuable because it enabled commanders at all levels to study in advance the actual ground over which they would have to operate. From photographs accurate maps could be produced and disseminated. As yet there was no speedy way of getting the results of aerial photography up to the front line although Skeen had both a survey and a photographic section with him.

For the actual troops on the ground, reconnaissance came second in value to battlefield support. Experience in Waziristan quickly showed that air cover was vital in keeping the tribesmen's heads down and preventing their movement in daylight. Against aircraft the tribesman had no direct defence except his rifle, and although aircraft were vulnerable to a lucky pot shot and were brought down from time to time, it took exceptional boldness to remain on an open hillside when aircraft were overhead, machine gunning and bombing. The effect of aircraft was such that on occasion pilots who had run out of ammunition and bombs were able to keep the tribesmen in check simply by circling and making mock attacks.[22]

The bombing of villages proved a relative failure. The bombs available were not particularly effective against mud brick and a high proportion were duds. The tribesmen and their families quickly became adept at finding shelter in the numerous caves and under rocky crags, and mud houses were easily rebuilt. As bombing was always preceded by formal notice it was in some senses a charade. Nevertheless, there were occasions when intransigent tribal sections whose villages were considered too remote to make an expedition worthwhile were reduced to submission by a short, sharp bombing campaign.[23]

The turning point in the use of air power on the Frontier can be pin-pointed to the conference on 21 December 1919 when Skeen and Climo accepted that in future no major daylight operation should be undertaken unless air cover was available. Thereafter ground operations were cancelled when weather conditions prevented flying. When the force moved to Sorarogha an essential adjunct to the main camp was a landing ground for the Bristol Fighters.[24] In the 1923 campaign, the use of close air support was taken a logical stage further with the introduction of a system of 'on call' aircraft, the forerunner of the 'cab rank' system employed in North-West Europe in 1944.

Apart from a shortage of spare parts and engines, leading to low serviceability, the RAF suffered from a major problem of communication with the ground. The aircraft then in service on the Frontier were not fitted with radio, although the Army had a very small number of mobile sets in Waziristan. Ground-to-air communication depended upon visual signals laid out on the ground, first, the Popham panel, and then linen strips.[25] These could convey only basic information such as the position of own troops, and the estimated strength, direction and distance of the enemy. It was not always possible to lay out the panels or strips, and they were not readily capable of keeping track of a fast-moving battle or of signalling commanders' intentions. Pilots could drop messages by hand, but these were liable to go astray and it was in any case impossible to signal back a reply. This lack of effective two-way communication was a particular handicap to the artillery as it greatly hampered accurate spotting. It was a particular handicap in the case of the new 3.7 inch gun, with its high trajectory and ability to search 'dead ground'.

A second handicap for pilots was a lack of experience of flying over tribal territory and thus gaining experience of the peculiar conditions of the Frontier. This was strictly controlled by the political officers, who were anxious not to stir up the tribesmen. In peace-time, therefore, the pilots were short of experience, both of the topography and the actual air conditions over the mountains. In putting forward his proposal for the RAF to take over the role of punishing the tribesmen in Waziristan Salmond laid stress upon the need for pilots to have greater liberty to fly over tribal territory in peace-time.[26] These problems hampered the development of a clear, codified doctrine on the use of air power over the Frontier.

The problems of the RAF were compounded by the inferior military status of the RAF in India vis à vis the Army. Omissi has pointed out that in 1920 the Air Officer Commanding in India ranked in order of precedence with the Vice Chairman of the Imperial Council of Agricultural Research.[27] In a bureaucracy and a society where precedence was extremely important and rigidly regulated, it was a significant handicap and among Salmond's recommendations was the upgrading of the AC post from Air Commodore to Air Vice-Marshal and his appointment as an extra Member of the Viceroy's Council. From a bureaucratic point of view, it was probably a greater handicap that the RAF did not even have its own sub-head in the

Indian budget but merely appeared as part of the Army's budget. It is easy to see that when money was tight, as it almost always was, the RAF was not first in the queue.[28] Indeed, Salmond suggested that much of the Army's reluctance to accept the potentialities of air power was due to the fear that, if accepted, the result would be a reduction in the size of the army.[29]

While technology was a part of the answer to the changed conditions of Frontier warfare, it could not be the full answer. The individual infantry soldier remained the most important weapon and it was clear that the new conditions placed a heavy emphasis upon individual initiative and leadership, and hence upon individual and unit training, as well as upon new tactical thinking.

Recognition of the problem had led in 1916 to the opening of a Mountain Warfare School in May 1916 for Territorial Army officers and NCOs; it held four week-long courses, training a total of twenty-seven officers and 108 NCOs, before closing down.[30] Some unfortunate experiences in Waziristan in 1917 led to the School being re-opened at Abbottabad in March 1917. The School had an infantry company, a cavalry squadron, a heavy machine gun detachment and a battery of mountain guns attached to it for demonstration purposes. Run by an expert in mountain warfare, Lieutenant Colonel W Villiers-Stuart, the course appears to have been well-regarded by those who attended. When it closed down again towards the end of 1917, 524 officers of all grades, WOs and NCOs had passed through it. The experiences of the 1917 Waziristan campaign led to it being opened again in April 1918. Some 360 senior and junior officers were trained before the School closed yet again in October 1918.

In all, the School trained nearly a thousand officers and just over 200 WOs and NCOs in the period of its existence.[31] Impressive as the numbers may seem, many of the officers and other ranks came from the British battalions in India and the output to the Indian Army was comparatively small. It was, in numerical terms, only a fraction of the requirement and it seems, in retrospect, to have been a singularly short-sighted decision not have retained it permanently instead of closing it down at the beginning of each cold weather unit training season. Allowing for the other demands on men and resources in India between 1914 and 1919, it seems clear that the importance of training to meet the new conditions of warfare on the Frontier had not been fully grasped.

Little could be done in the very short term to improve the training of the battalions who would be involved in Waziristan; even basic training among many of the war-time Indian battalions was inadequate. As Smyth put it brutally, experience and training would have to be bought in blood. It was not only the inexperience and inadequate training of the troop which caused concern. There were a small number of incidents in which Muslim troops had not performed satisfactorily, leading in one case to courts-martial. Writing to the Deputy Adjutant and Assistant Quartermaster at Army HQ, Skeen called attention to the uneasiness felt about Muslim troops on the Frontier, and suggesting that care would be needed in the composition of future garrisons there.[32]

Apart from the use of new or newish technology, tactical innovations on the ground were few. The range of modern rifles meant that picquets had to be pushed out much farther – typically a thousand yards or so. In turn that meant the use of more troops to cover their construction, and increased the risk of ambush or surprise attack. It made logical sense therefore to establish permanent picquets. The use of barbed wire, Lewis guns and grenades made such permanent posts, once established, virtually impregnable.

The use of permanent picquets to protect lines of communication was not new on the Frontier – they had been used extensively along the Khyber line, for example, during the Second Afghan War.[33] Their use during an expedition of limited duration was, however, relatively novel. The marked absence of attacks on convoys and the supply line generally during the campaign attested to their success. But they did tie up manpower and re-supply and the relief of the garrisons required careful planning.

The major tactical innovation on the British side was undoubtedly the use of night marches. Hitherto, they had seldom been used on the Frontier[34] because of the difficulties of command and control in the darkness and because of the ever-present risk of troops losing their way and blundering into ambush.[35] For these reasons, despite the obvious benefit of surprise, night attacks had been seen as hazardous, even with experienced troops. Skeen's use of a night advance to overcome Mahsud opposition on 11 January 1920, using troops whose inexperience and lack of training had hitherto been marked, was therefore an act of considerable courage, especially as it meant dividing his forces on opposite sides of river. Its success had two benefits – it greatly increased the morale of the troops, hitherto in a state of decline because of successive failures, starting with the attack on Mandanna Hill on 19 December 1919, and it led Skeen to use the same tactic with increasing frequency. By the time the campaign ended, there were signs that the tactic was beginning to lose its initial impact and that the Mahsuds were beginning to react positively to it.[36] Nevertheless, night movement as a tactic was now a firm part of mountain warfare and it found its counterpart at unit level in night patrolling and ambushes.[37] The use of booby traps became common and Skeen was at pains to emphasise to his subordinate commanders their value in creating surprise and insecurity among the Mahsuds, instead of vice versa as before.[38]

The campaign in Waziristan in 1919–20 was fought without the employment of British troops other than in No. 6 Mountain Battery RCA. It was by no means the first Frontier expedition fought with Indian troops only – the Black Mountain expedition of 1852, the Jowaki expedition of 1877, and the first Miranzai expedition of 1891 were examples. But no expedition since 1891 had been without British infantry. The decision in 1919 not to include a British battalion was bound up with the problem of post-war demobilisation and reliefs. The Territorial Army battalions which had largely garrisoned India between 1914 and 1918 were on their way home to demobilisation and disbandment. The eight regular battalions which had been left in India after 1914 were in process of being relieved by fresh battalions coming out from England, and they had in any case begun to lose large numbers of time-expired men. The difficulty of finding battalions to serve in Waziristan is therefore understandable. But the question remains as to whether British troops would have prevented the earlier disasters. The answer hinges on experience and training. In terms of simple soldiering experience, the British battalions in India, Regular or Territorial, all of whom had been there for at least three years and embodied for longer, had the edge over most of the Indian battalions, very few of which had been in existence for much over a year. The disadvantage that that produced in discipline, morale and basic skills is clear. They had also benefited disproportionately from the mountain warfare course run in 1917 and 1918. The sum of these factors leads almost inevitably to the conclusion that the inclusion of a British battalion in each brigade would have strengthened the cutting edge of Skeen's force and, in all probability, prevented the early setbacks. By the end of the campaign, the Indian battalions had sensibly improved in experience and training and were well able to cope with the tribesmen. It is noteworthy that in the expedition against the Wana Wazirs at the end of 1920 there was a British battalion in each brigade. The Waziristan expedition in 1919–20 may therefore be considered an unfortunate aberration.

The formidable fire and movement tactics evolved by the Mahsuds were not matched by an equal strategic skill. Tribal differences between Mahsuds and Wazirs, and the ingrained, suspicious individualism of the tribesmen meant that they were never able to deploy their maximum strength.[39] The Tochi Wazirs, living within relatively easy range of the Army at Bannu and Miramshah, were quickly subdued and brought to heel. The Government was then free to operate against the Mahsuds with a fair degree of safety. The Wana Wazirs sent a contingent to assist the Mahsuds in defending the Barari Tangi, taking with them the two famous Afghan mountain guns from Wana. This rare example of tribal cooperation, however, proved unfruitful. The guns were a ludicrous disappointment and the Mahsuds were left with a grievance against the Wazirs who, they believed, had encouraged them to resist, thus suffering heavy losses. The Mahsuds took their revenge by withholding help to the Wana Wazirs during the subsequent reoccupation of Wana, to the extent of giving the British free passage through the Shahur Tangi.[40]

If the Mahsuds can scarcely be criticised for failing to achieve successful strategic combination with the Wazirs, they can be criticised for the strategy they followed. The British decision to follow a single line of advance, along the Tank Zam, had been designed to draw the Mahsuds into a series of pitched battles where serious casualties could be inflicted on them. The Mahsuds allowed themselves to be sucked into this strategy. If Skeen's force suffered exceptionally heavy casualties by Front standards, the Mahsud losses were even more serious because they could not readily be made up. The action on 'Black Hill' on 21 December 1919 was a Pyrrhic victory in this respect, and much the same could be said about the defence of the Ahnai and Barari Tangis.

Most surprising was the singular failure of the Mahsuds to interfere with Skeen's communications and supply line back to Jandola. The days were long gone when troops could live off the supplies they took with them, or could acquire en route, as, for example, Roberts had done in August 1880 when he marched from Kabul to Kandahar. Modern armies required an immensely complicated range of supplies of all kinds including now fuel for aircraft. In consequence, they were less able to withstand any interruption of their supply lines. The Mahsuds made no attempt to interfere with Skeen's convoys or the telegraph and telephone lines which connected him with Jandola and Tank. Such a failure can only partially be explained by the use of permanent picquets. The disaster to the convoy in the Shahur Tangi in April 1937 illustrates what might have been effected. Skeen's force was increasingly vulnerable to attacks along its line of supply the deeper it penetrated into the Mahsud heartland and it would seem in retrospect that important opportunities were missed by the Mahsuds.

In the end, the Derajat Striking Force won through by sheer hard fighting, but at the centre of it was Skeen's qualities as a commander. He had proved tough, resilient, confident and courageous; he amply deserved Smyth's encomium. Behind him, Climo had exercised a wise and discreet supporting role even though he must have itched to be involved in tactical command. The Indian Government was fortunate that the hour had brought forth not one but two men.

Notes

1 A Keppel, *Gun-running and the North-West Indian Frontier* (London, 1911).
2 *Statement of Fighting Strengths and Armaments of Independent Tribes on the North-West Frontier (Cis-Durand Line) 27 June 1910* (Simla, 1910); table in T M Moreman, *The Army in India and the development of Frontier Warfare 1849–1947* (London, 1998), 97.
3 Fraser Lovat, *Arms Traffic* (London, 1911), 43.
4 Moreman, 97.
5 Proportionately fewer perhaps among the Mahsuds because their recruitment into the Indian Army had always been carefully controlled.
6 The Short Magazine Lee-Enfield was sighted out to 2,000 yards; fifteen aimed rounds a minute were perfectly feasible for a trained shot.

7 'The factor which affects everything is the prevalence amongst the tribesmen of low-trajectory rifles with an adequate supply of smokeless ammunition. The tribesmen therefore have the arms and ammunition for covering fire. This they employ, and under its cover they are able to concentrate for attack and carry out much of their approach after concentration. . . Day sniping has increased and is responsible for many casualties. It is most difficult to compete with in broken and hilly country ...' – *Waziristan Force Weekly Appreciation for week ending 6 January 1919* (PRO WO 106/56).

8 I have not overlooked the Mohmand blockade in 1916.

9 There is no published history of the Machine Gun Corps.

10 *Operations,* 166, 167, 168.

11 For both weapons, see Chapter II, Note 14.

12 SofS to Viceroy, No. 1057, 13 May 1919 – CP1O, No. 497.

13 Viceroy to SofS, No. 692-S, 21 May 1919 – ibid, No. 647.

14 Climo to Assistant Adjutant General, No. D.S.-316, 8 January 1919 – L/MIL/7/18853

15 For a wider discussion, see E M Spiers, 'Gas and the North-West Frontier', *Journal of Strategic Studies,* vol. 6, No. 4 (1983), 99–102; also Major General C H Ffoulkes, *'Memorandum on the use of gas in Frontier warfare',* 3 November 1919 – Ffoulkes papers, Liddell Hart Centre for Military Archives, 6/105.

16 *The Army in India and its Evolution* (Calcutta, 1924), Appendix XL, 224. Lorries, however, tended to destroy unmetalled roads.

17 See Chapter XVII above, Note 9.

18 'there is little doubt that this raid was an important factor in producing a desire for peace at the Headquarters of the Afghan Government.' – *Despatch by His Excellency General Sir Charles Carmichael Monro on the Third Afghan War, 1 November 1919* (Simla, 1919).

19 In August 1922 Salmond found seven aircraft serviceable out of a total establishment in India of seventy – Salmond Report, paragraph 64. John Slessor had an engine disintegrate on him in mid-air – J C Slessor, *The Central Blue* (London, 1956).

20 See Chapter XVI above, Note 4.

21 The defeat at Mandanna Hill, on 19 December 1919, was largely due to inadequate knowledge of the topography on the west side of the Tank Zam.

22 For example, over the Ahnai Tangi on 14 January 1920 – see Chapter XX above and *Operations,* 118.

23 For example, the Madda Khel Wazirs were bombed into submission on 18 November 1919 – see Chapter XVI above.

24 See the excellent photograph in *Operations,* 120.

25 Popham panels were made of wood and cloth, with moveable panels. They were clumsy and were soon superseded by linen strips which at least had the advantage of being easier to carry.

26 *Salmond Report,* paragraphs 28 and 29.

27 Omissi, op cit.

28 *Salmond Report,* paragraphs 78, 82–84.5

29 Ibid. paragraph 38.

30 *Report on the principal measures taken in India during the War to maintain training at the standard required in modern war* (Calcutta, 1919).

31 Ibid.

32 Skeen to DAAQ, Wazirforce, No. 28-47-C.A., 22 February 1920 L/MIL/7/18853.

33 Robson, passim.

34 The outstanding example was Roberts' advance on the Peiwar Kotal on the night of 1/2 December 1878 – ibid, 84–5.

35 The risk was not imaginary; during a night advance on 19 February 1919, 4/3 Gurkhas had ended up on the wrong hill.

36 For example, at Makin on 1 March 1920 during the withdrawal of the 'Split Hill' and 'Tree Hill' picquets during the night.

37 *Operations*, 144, 149.

38 L/MIL/7/18853.

39 In October 1919 the fighting strength of the Mahsuds had been put at 17,000 with roughly one modern rifle per man; that of the Tochi and Wana Wazirs at 23,000, with 7,500 modern rifles – Viceroy to Secretary of State, 19 October 1919 (L/P&S/10/8700, No. 80). The official history scales these figures down to roughly 11,000 and 25,000 – *Operations*, Appendix L. They were calculated on the basis of all males over the age of 16. Virtually every man had a firearm of some sort, but the older weapons, firing black powder, were deliberately not used because the smoke gave away the position of the firer. Those without modern weapons could still be used as swordsmen.

40 See Chapter XXIII above.

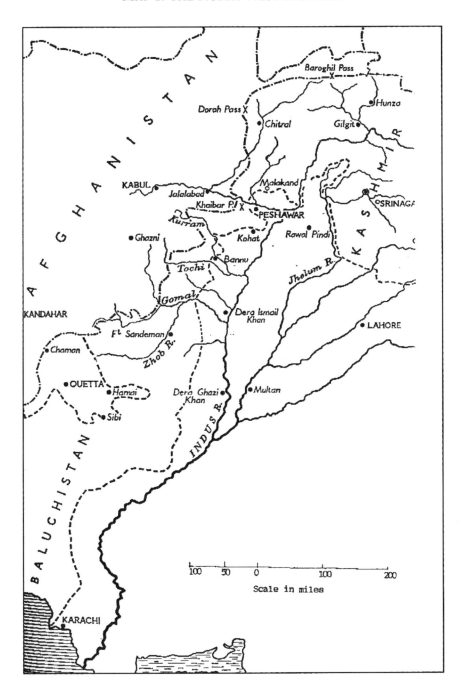

MAP 2: CHITRAL

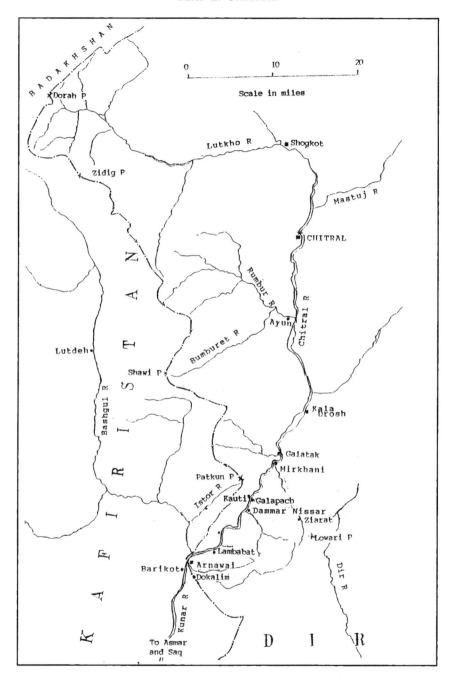

BADAKHSHAN

Dorah P

Lutkho R

Shogkot

Zidig P

Mastuj R

CHITRAL

Rumbur R

Ayun

Chitral R

Bumburet R

Lutdeh

Shawi P

Bashgul R

Kala
Drosh

K A F I R I S T A N

Galatak

Mirkhani

Patkun P

Istor R

Kauti

Galapach

Dammar

Nissar
Ziarat

Lowari P

Lambabat

Dir R

Barikot

Arnawai

Dokalim

Kunar R

To Asmar
and Saq

D   I   R

Scale in miles

0   10   20

MAP 3: THE KHYBER

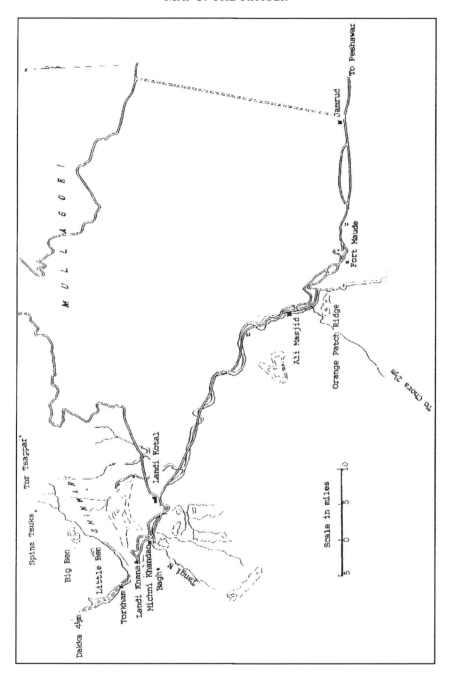

Map 4: Landi Kotal

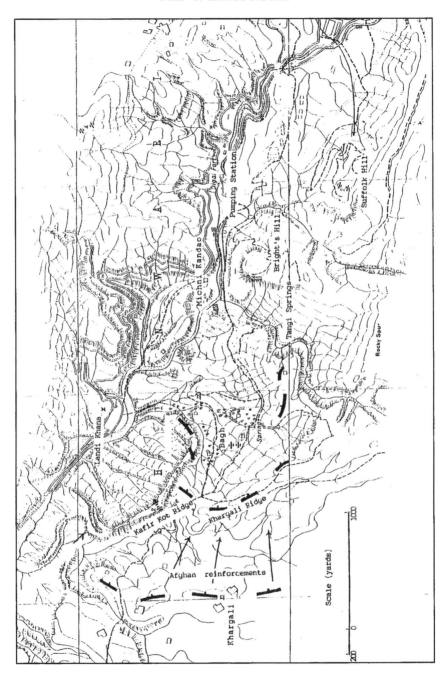

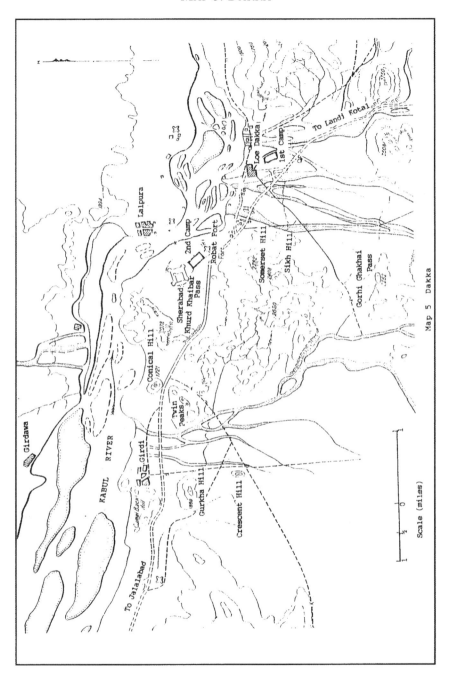

Map 5 Dakka

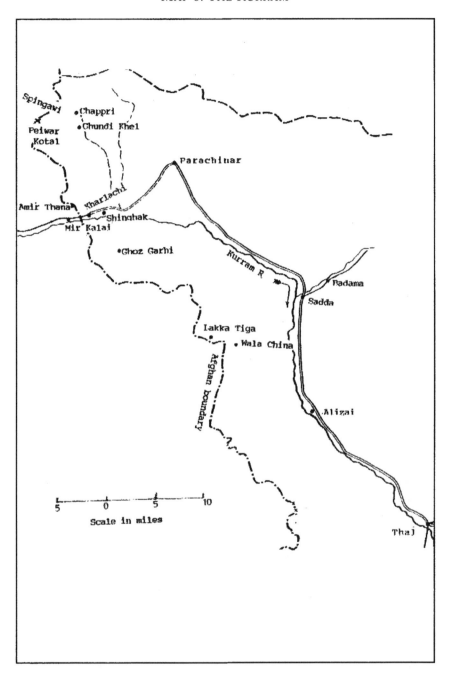

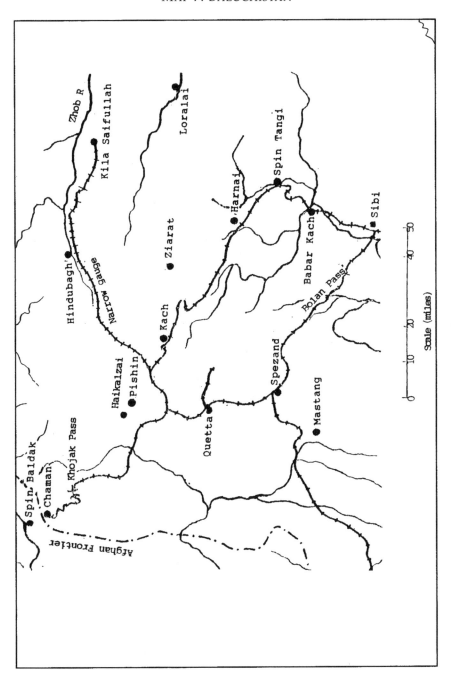

Map 8: Spin Baldak

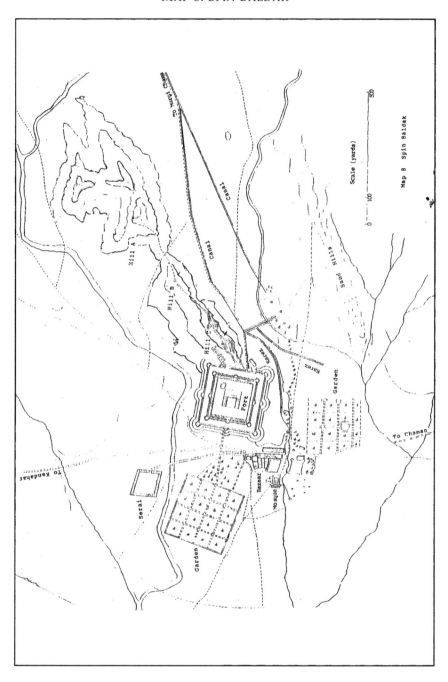

MAP 9: THE ZHOB

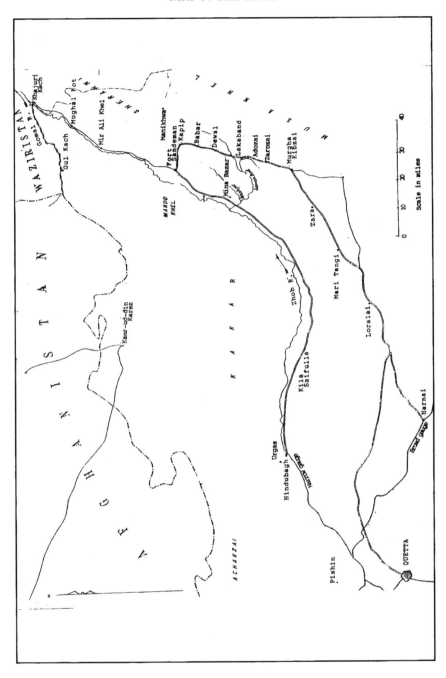

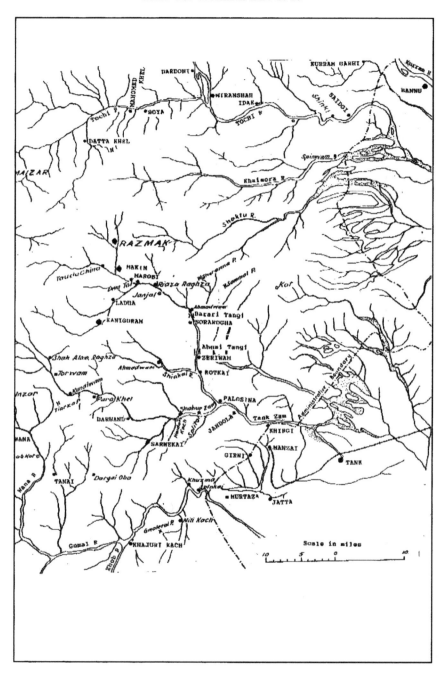

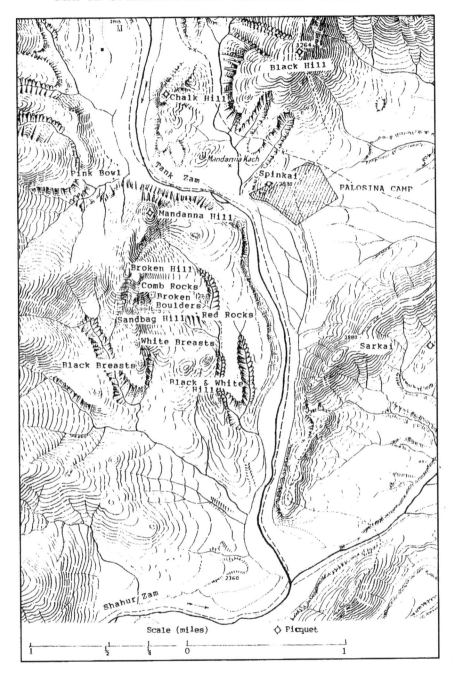

MAP 12: THE AHNAI TANGI

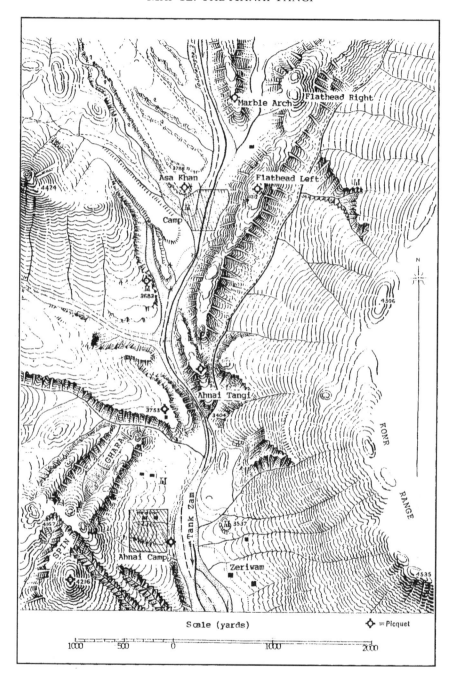

Marble Arch
Flathead Right
Asa Khan
Flathead Left
4474
3788
Camp
4212
3683
4306
N
Ahnai Tangi
3753
3404
KONR
BEGHARA
RANGE
4167
557
SPIN
Ahnai Camp
Tank Zam
Zeriwam
4216
4535

Scale (yards)   ◈ = Picquet
1000   500   0   1000   2000

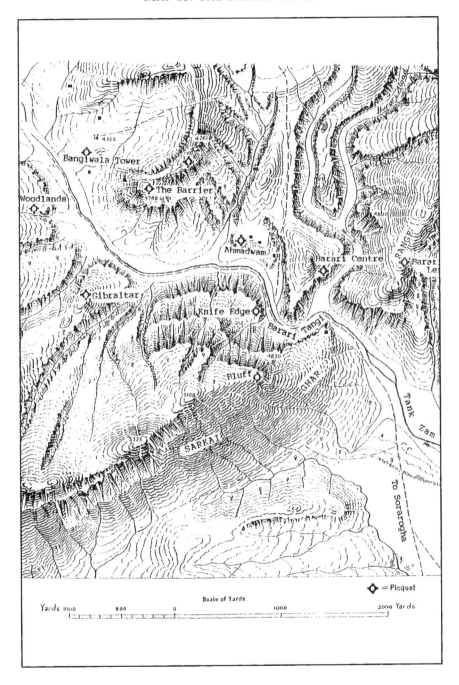

MAP 14: ROAD NETWORK, WAZIRISTAN IN 1936

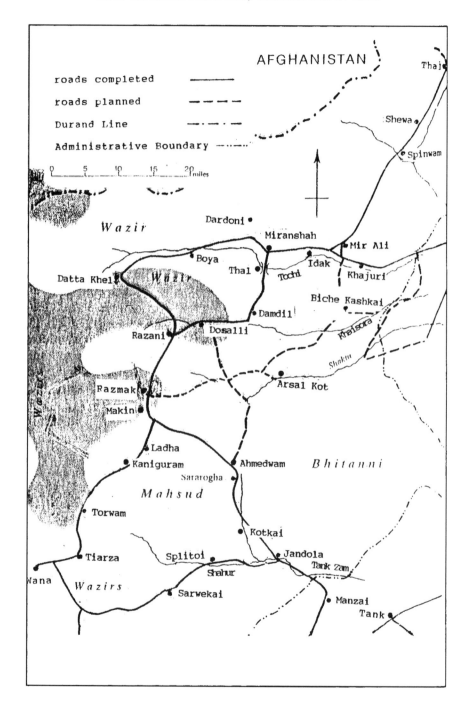

Appendices

Appendix 1: Major Units Involved In The Third Afghan War And Waziristan 1919–20

* = pre-war regular troops; + = Imperial Service (State) troops

British

1st King's Dragoon Guards
M Battery, RHA
38th, 45th, 74th, 77th, 79th, 89th, 90th, 101st, 102nd, l09lst, 1093rd,
1096th, ll04th, 1107th Batteries, Royal Field Artillery
Nos 1, 3, 4, 6, 8, 9 Mountain Batteries, Royal Garrison Artillery
60th Heavy Battery, RGA
Nos 1 2, 3, 4, 5, 6, 7, 8 Armoured Motor Batteries
Nos 15,22,24 Machine Gun Squadrons
Nos 3, 15, 19, 22 Motor Machine Gun Batteries
Nos 260, 263, 270, 281, 285, 286, 288 Machine Gun Companies
2nd Somerset LI
2nd Norfolk Regt
1st Yorkshire Regt
1st Royal Sussex Regt
2/6th Royal Sussex Regt
1st Durham LI
1st South Lancashire Regt
2/4th Border Regt
1/4th Queen's (Royal West Surrey Regt)
2nd Liverpool Regt
1/4th Royal West Kent Regt
1st Duke of Wellington's Regt
1/lst Kent Regt
1/25th London Regt
1/5th Hampshire Regt

Indian

* 1st Lancers
* 3rd Horse
* 4th Cavalry
* 11th Cavalry

* 17th Cavalry
* 23rd Cavalry
* 25th Cavalry
* 27th Cavalry
* 30th Lancers
* 33rd Light Cavalry
* 37th Lancers
  40th Cavalry
  42nd Cavalry
+ Patiala Lancers
+ Alwar Lancers
+ Navanagar Lancers
+ Bhopal Lancers

22nd, 23rd, 24th, 27th, 28th, 30th, 33rd, 35th, 37th, 38th Mountain Batteries
+ Nos 1 and 2 Kashmir Mountain Batteries

Nos 1, 7, 53, 55, 56, 58, 67 Field Coys, 1st (Bengal) Sappers and Miners
Nos 11, 14, 15, 63, 64, 66, 67, 68, 69, 76 Coys, 2nd (Madras) Sappers and Miners
Nos 24, 74, Coys, 3rd (Bombay) Sappers and Miners
+ Sirmoor Sappers
+ Tehri Sappers
+ Malerkotla Sappers
+ Faridkot Sappers

  2/2 Rajput LI
  3rd Guides Infantry
  2/3rd Brahmans
* 1/5th LI
* 1/6th JatLI
  2/10th Jats
* 1/llth Rajputs
* 14th Sikhs
* 1/15th Sikhs
  2/15th Sikhs
* 16th Rajputs
* 1/22nd "
  2/26th "
  2/27th "
* 1/30th "
  2/30th "
* 1/33rd "
  2/33rd "
* 1/35th Sikhs
  2/35th "
* 37th Dogras
* 2/39th Garwhal Rifles
  4/39th " "
* 40th Pathans
  1/41st Dogras
  2/41st Dogras
  2/54th Sikhs
  1/55th Rifles
  2/56th Rifles
  1/57th Rifles

* 1/66th Punjabis
  2/67th   "
* 1/69th   "
  2/69th   "
  2/72nd   "
* 1/76th   "
* 1/82nd   "
  2/89th   "
* 1/90th Infantry
  2/90th   "
* 1/97th   "
  2/98th   "
* 1/102nd Grenadjers
*1/103rd Mahratta LI
* 1/109th Infantry
* 110th Mahratta LI
  2/112th Infantry
  2/113th   "
  2/119th   "
  2/123rd Rifles
* 1/124th Baluchis
  3/124th   "
  2/125th Rifles
* 1/129th Baluchis
  2/129th   "
  1/150th Infantry
  3/150th   "
  1/151st   "
  2/151st   "
  1/152nd   "
  1/153rd   "
  2/153rd   "
  1/154th   "
+ Jind Infantry
+ Gwalior "
+ Patiala   "
+ 1st Kashmir Rifles
+ 2nd Kashmir Rifles
+ 2nd Nepalese Rifles
+ Kapurthala Infantry
+ Nabha Infantry
* 1/12th Pioneers
  2/12th   "
  2/23rd   "
  2/34th   "
  3/34th   "
* 1/61st 2/61st "
* 1/81st 2/81st "
* 2/1st Gurkhas
  3/1st   "
* 2/2nd   "
  3/2nd   "
  4/3rd   "
* 1/4th   "
  3/5th   "

3/6th Gurkhas
* 2/7th   "
3/7th   "
* 2/8th   "
3/8th   "
* 1/9th   "
* 2/9th   "
3/9th   "
* 2/10th "
* 1/11th "
* 2/11th "
3/11th   "
Total: 18 cavalry regiments; 111 infantry regiments.
(For the modern descendants of the Indian units, see John Gaylor, *Sons of John Company*, Tunbridge Wells, 1992)

Appendix 2: Outline Order Of Battle, 6 May 1919

North-West Frontier Force: General Sir Arthur Barrett (HQ Peshawar)

Corps troops

Nos 60 and 68 Heavy Batteries
No. 22 Motor Machine Gun Battery
No.58 Field Company, 1st Sappers and Miners
No. 14 Field Company, 2nd Sappers and Miners
1/55th   (Coke's) Rifles ⎱
2/69th   Punjabis   ⎰ subsequently absorbed into 64 Brigade
2/12th   Pioneers
2/34th   Pioneers
1st Cavalry Brigade: Brigadier General Baldwin (HQ Risalpur)

1st King's Dragoon Guards
1st Lancers
33rd Light Cavalry
M Battery RHA
No. 15 Machine Gun Squadron
No. 1 Field Troop, 1st Sappers and Miners.

10th Cavalry Brigade: Brigadier General Davies (HQ Peshawar)

4th Cavalry
21st Cavalry
20th Lancers
No. 24 Machine Gun Squadron
No. 4 Field Troop, 3rd Sappers and Miners

1st Infantry Division: Major General Fowler (HQ Peshawar)

2st Brigade: Brigadier General Crocker (HQ Peshawar)

2nd Somerset LI
1/15th Sikhs
1/35th Sikhs
1/9th Gurkhas

2nd Brigade: Major General Climo (HQ Nowshera)

2nd North Staffords
2/123rd Rifles
1/11th Gurkhas
2/11th Gurkhas

3rd Brigade: Major General Skeen (HQ Abbotabad)

1st Yorkshires
2/1st Gurkhas
4/3rd Gurkhas
3/11th Gurkhas

Divisional troops

1 sqdn 1st Lancers
Nos 263 and 265 Machine Gun Companies
1/12th Pioneers

4th and 38th Batteries, RHA
77th (Howitzer) Battery, RHA
Nos 6 and 8 Mountain Batteries, RGA
Nos 7 and 56 Field Companies, 1st Sappers and Miners

2nd Infantry Division: Major General Sir C M Dobell (HQ Rawalpindi)

4th Brigade: Brigadier General Peebles (HQ Rawalpirtdi)

1st Durham LI
1/33rd Punjabis
40th Pathans
2/54th Sikhs

5th Brigade: Brigadier General Ridgeway (HQ Gharial)

1st South Lancs
2/35th Sikhs
3/39th Gharwal Rifles
3/5th Gurkhas

6th Brigade: Brigadier General Christian(HQ Chakiala)

1st Royal Sussex
2/33rdPunjabis
2/67th Punjabis
2/8th Gurkhas

Divisional troops

1 squadron 33rd Light Cavalry
1/61st Pioneers
Nos 22 and 286 Machine Gun Companies
89th, 90th, 74th (Howitzer) Batteries, RFA
Nos 3 and 4 Mountain Batteries RGA
Nos 11 and 64 Field Companies, 2nd Sappers and Miners

Peshawar Area

23rd Cavalry
No. 22 (Derajat) Mountain Battery
Nos 1,2, 3 Armoured Motor Batteries
No. 15 Motor Machine Gun Battery
2/4th Border
1/4th Queen's (Royal West Surrey) 37th Dogras
110th Mabratta LI
3/2nd Gurkhas

Malakand posts

2/2 Rajput LI
2/89th Punjabis

Chitral

1 section, 23 (Peshawar) Mountain Battery
1/11th Rajputs
Chitral Section, 2nd Sappers and Miners
Gilgit
Io. 1 Kashmir Mountain Battery ;t, 2nd and 3rd Kashmir Rifles

Kohat Area: Major General Eustace (HQ Kohat)

37th Lancers
23 (Peshawar) and 28 Mountain Batteries
No. 10 Armoured Motor Battery
No. 22 Motor Machine Gun Battery
3rd Guides Infantry
1/57th (Wilde's) Rifles
1/109th Infantry
1/151st Sikhs
3/8th Gurkhas
3/9th Gurkhas
No. 57 Field Company, 1st Sappers and Miners

60 Brigade (HQ Ambala)

2/26th Punjabis
4/39th Garwhal Rifles

Waziristan Force

Bannu Brigade (HQ Bannu)

31st Lancers
33rd (Reserve) Mountain Battery
Nos 5 and 6 Armoured Motor Batteries
No. 55 Field Company, 1st Sappers and Miners
1/41st Dogras
1/103rd Mahratta LI
2/112th Infantry
3/6th Gurkhas

Derajat Area (HQ Dera Ismail Khan)

27th Cavalry
No.27 Mountain Battery
No. 7 Armoured Motor Battery
No. 75 Field Company, 3rd Sappers and Miners
66th Punjabis
1/76thPunjabis
2nd Gurkhas

Baluchistan Force: Lieutenant General Wapshare (HQ Quetta)

Corps troops

Nos 71 and 73 Field Companies. 3rd Sappers and Miners

12th Mounted Brigade (HQ Quetta)
40th, 41st and 42nd Cavalry
No. 22 Machine Gun Squadron
No. 7 Field Troop, 3rd Sappers and Miners

4th Division – (Wapshare) (HQ Quetta)

10th Brigade

2nd Liverpool
1/5th LI
2/56th Rifles

11th Brigade (HQ Quetta)

1st West Yorks
1/22nd Punjabis
1/4th Gurkhas
2/10th Gurkhas

57th Brigade (HQ Quetta)

1/4th Royal West Kent
2/119th Infantry
3/7th Gurkhas
1/129th Baluchis

Divisional troops

25th Cavalry
2/23rd pioneers
Nos 270 and 281 Machine Gun Companies
101st, 102nd, 107th Batteries, RFA
Nos 1 and 9 Mountain Batteries, RGA
Nos 17, 24 and 73 Field Companies, 3rd Sappers and Miners

Baluchistan Area

3rd Horse
Alwar Lancers
Gwalior Lancers
Patiala Lancers
38 Mountain Battery
No. 8 Armoured Motor Battery
No. 19 Motor Machine Gun Battery
2/11th Rajputs
2/15th Sikhs
3/124th Baluchis
3/1st Gurkhas

Appendix 3: Composition Of Forces In Waziristan, November 1919

(Note: as operations progressed, fresh troops were brought in and battalions were shuffled between Skeen's column and the L of C.)

Tochi/Derajat Column (Major General Skeen)

2 sdns 31st Lancers (with Tochi Column only)
1 sdn 21st Cavalry (Derajat Column only)

1 section 4.5 inch howitzers, RFA
No.6 Mountain Battery RGA
27 Indian Mountain Battery (Derajat Column only)
33 Indian Mountain Battery (Tochi Column only)
55 Field Company, 1 Sappers and Miners

No. 16 Pack Wireless Station

3/34 Pioneers
2/61 Pioneers

43 Brigade (Brigadier-General Gwyn-Thomas)
4/39 Garwhal Rifles 1/57Rifles
1/82Punjabis
2/152 Punjabis

67 Brigade (Brigadier-General Lucas)

1/55 Rifles
1/1O3 Mahratta LI
1/109 Infantry (from 17 Dec.)

2/112 Infantry
2/76 Punjabis (from 21 Dec.)
3 Guides Infantry (from 18 Jan. 20)

Tochi L of C

No. 1 Section (Brigadier-General MacLachlan)

31st Lancers, less 2 sdns
33 Indian Mountain Battery
1 section 15 pounders, RFA
1 section 6.3 inch (muzzle-loading) howitzers, RGA
No. 5 Armoured Motor Battery

45 Brigade (MacLachian)

2/4 Rajputs
2/25 Punjabis
1/150 Infantry
2/154 Infantry

1 Wireless Station

No. 2 Section (Brigadier-General Walton)

2 sdns 31st Lancers

No.33 Mountain Battery
1 section 15 pounders, RFA

74 Field Company, 3rd Sappers and Miners

47 Brigade (Walton)
2/21 Punjabis
2/69 Punjabis
3/151 Punjabis
3/152 Punjabis

Derajat L of C

No. 1 Section (Brigadier-General Worgan)

16th Cavalry
21st Cavalry, less 1 sdn
27th Light Cavalry
1 section 35 Indian Mountain Battery
1 section 15 pounders RFA
Nos 6 and 7 Armoured Motor Batteries
62 Brigade (Worgan)
2/90 Punjabis
.2/94 Infantry
2 /102 Grenadiers
2/113 Infantry
2/127 Baluchis
2/150 Infantry

1 Stationary Wireless Plant

No. 2 Section (Brigadier-General Gordon)

1 sdn 21st Cavalry
35 Indian Mountain Battery, less 1 section
2 10 pounders

75 Field Company, 3rd Sappers and Miners

68 Brigade
3 Guides Infantry
2/19 Punjabis
2/76 Punjabis
1/109 Infantry

No. 3 Pack Wireless Station

Appendix 4: Campaign Medals And VCs

The campaign medal awarded was the 1908 India General Service Medal, bearing on the obverse a crowned bust of George V and on the reverse a picture of the fort at Jamrud. The ribbon is green with a wide, dark blue stripe down the centre. Three bars were awarded:

'Aghanistan N.W.F.1919' for service in the Third Afghan War between 6 May and 8 August 1919;

'Mahsud 1919–20' for service on the Takki Zam line between 18 December 1919 and 7 May 1920;

'Waziristan 1919–1921' for service in Waziristan between 6 May 1919 and January 1921.

Two VCs were awarded between the outbreak of the Third Afghan War on 6 May 1919 and the official end of operations in Waziristan on 7 May 1920 (both posthumously):

Andrews, Henry John, tempy Captain, Indian Medical Department 'for most conspicuous bravery and devotion to duty' in attending to the wounded during the attack on a convoy near Khajuri, in Northern Waziristan, on 22 October 1919 (*London Gazette*, 10 September 1920).

Kenny, William David, Lieutenant, 4/39th Garwhal Rifles, 'for most conspicuous bravery and devotion to duty' in counter-attacking a large force of Mahsuds to cover the retreat of a company of his regiment at Kotkai, in Southern Waziristan, on 2 January 1920 (*London Gazette*, 10 September 1920).

Biographical Notes

Baldwin, Guy Melfort (1865–1945). Commissioned North Lancashire Regt 1886. Bengal SC 1888. Service in Hazara Expedition 1888, Relief of Chitral 1895 (DSO), North-West Frontier 1897–8. Lt. Col. 1912, Col. 1915. Commanding 10th Cavalry Brigade 1916–19.

Barrett, (Sir) Arthur Arnold (1875–1926). Commissioned 44th Foot 1875. Bengal Staff Corps 1879. Service in Second Afghan War, Hazara Expedition 1888, Miranzai 1891, Hunza-Nagar Expedition 1891, North West Frontier 1897–8, Mesopotamia 1914–15. Lt. Col. 1901, Maj. Gen. 1906, Lt. Gen. 1911, General 1917, Field Marshal 1921. KCB 1908, KCSI 1915, GCSI 1919. Adjutant General India 1909–12, Poona Division 1912–14, Northern Command India 1916–20.

Beynon, (Sir) William George Lawrence (1866–1955). Commissioned Royal Sussex Regt 1887, Bengal SC 1888. Service in Black Mountain Expedition 1888, Chitral 1895, Frontier and Tirah 1897–8, Somaliland 1901, Tibet 1904, Abor Expedition 1911–12, Waziristan 1917, Swat 1915, Mohmands 1916, Third Afghan War 1919, Waziristan 1919–20. Lt. Col. 1913, Maj. Gen. 1917. KCIE 1917.

Climo, (Sir) Skipton Hill (1868–1937). Commissioned Border Regt 1888, Indian SC 1889. Service in North-West Frontier 1897–8, China 1900–1, Tibet 1904, Mohmand Expedition 1908, Egypt 1914–15, Mesopotamia 1915–16, Third Afghan War 1919, Waziristan 1919–20. Lt. Col. 1912, Maj. Gen. 1918, Lt. Gen. 1921, KCB 1921. Divisional Commander 1920–2. Retired 1923.

Coleridge, (Sir) John Francis Stanhope (1878–1951). Commissioned 1898, Indian Army 1900. Service in Tibet Expedition 1903-4, NE frontier 1911–12, 1st World War 1914–18, NW Frontier 1930–2, NW Frontier 1936–7. Lt. Col. 1917, Maj. Gen. 1926, Lt. Gen. 1932, Gen. 1936. Military Secretary India 1926–30, Kohat District 1930, Peshawar District 1930–3, Northern Command 1936-40. KCB 1933. GCB 1940.

Crocker, George Delamain (1862–1938). Commissioned Royal Munster Fusiliers 1889. Lt. Col. 1912, Col. 1916, Hon. Brig. Gen. and retired 1919.

de Burgh, (Sir) Eric (1881–1973). Commissioned Manchester Regt 1903. Indian Army 1904. Service in South Africa 1902, 1st World War 1914–18, Third Afghan War 1919. Lt. Col. 1919, Maj. Gen. 1934, Lt. Gen. 1938, Gen. 1940. KCB 1941. CGS India 1939–41.

Dobell, (Sir) Charles Macpherson (1869–1953). Commissioned Royal Welsh Fusiliers 1890. Service in Hazara Expedition 1891, Crete 1897–8, South Africa 1899–1900, China 1900, Nigeria 1906, 1st World War (West Africa, Egypt, Palestine). Third Afghan War. Lt. Col. 1912, Maj. Gen. 1915, Lt. Gen. 1920. KCB 1916. GOC Rawalpindi Division 1917–20, GOC Northern Army 1920–3.

Dobbs, (Sir) Henry Robert Conway (1871–1934). ICS 1892, Deputy Foreign Secretary 1906, Political Agent, Baluchistan 1908, Political Officer, Mesopotamia 1915–16, Agent to Governor General, Baluchistan 1917–19, Foreign Secretary 1919, High Commissioner, Iraq 1923–9. Retired 1929.

Eustace, Alexander Henry (1863–1939). Commissioned East Surrey Regt 1885, Bengal SC 1887. Service in Hazara 1888, 1891, East Africa 1903-4. Lt. Col. 1907, Maj. Gen. 1917. Retired 1919.

Fagan, Edward Arthur (1871–1955). Commissioned South Staffordshire Regt 1891, Bengal Staff Corps 1894. Lt. Col. 1916, Col. 1919, Maj. Gen. 1924. Military Adviser to Indian States Forces.

Fowler, Charles Astley (1865–1940). Commissioned Devonshire Regt 1885, Bengal SC 1886. Service in Miranzai Expedition 1891, Mohmand Expedition 1908, 1st World War 1914–16, Third Afghan War 1919. Lt. Col. 1907, Col. 1911, Maj. Gen. 1918.

Gordon, John Lewis Randolph (1867–1953). Commissioned Worcestershire Regt 1888, Bengal SC 1891. Service in Chitral 1895, Tirah 1897–8. South Africa 1900, France 1914–15, Egypt (Senussi) 1915–16. Lt. Col. 1914, Brig. 1919.

Grant, (Sir) Hamilton (1872–1937). Indian Civil Service 1895. Foreign Secretary to Govt of India 1914–19, Chief Commissioner NWFP 1919–21; KCIE 1918, KCSI 1922.

Loch, Stewart Gordon (1873–1952). Commissioned Royal Engineers 1893. Service in China 1900, Waziristan 1914, Mahsud Expedition 1917, Third Afghan War 1919. Col. 1917, Temp. Brig. Gen. 1916, BGGS North-West Frontier Force 1917–20, Brigade Comdr 1921.

Lucas, Frederick George (1866–1922). Commissioned East Lancs. Regt 1886, Bengal SC 1888. Lt. Col. 1911, Brig. Gen. 1916. Service in Hazara Expedition 1891, Tirah 1897–8, Waziristan 1901–2, North-West Frontier 1908, Mesopotamia 1915–16, Waziristan 1919–20.

Maclachlan, Thomas Robertson (1870–1921). Commissioned Border Regt 1889, Bengal SC 1893. Service in Mesopotamia 1917–19, Waziristan 1919–20. Lt. Col. 1915, Brig. Gen. 1919.

Macmullen, (Sir) Cyril Norman (1877–1944). Commissioned 1897, Bengal Staff Corps 1898. Col. 1920, Maj. Gen. 1923, Lt. Gen. 1928, Gen. 1931. Adjutant General India 1930-2, GOC Eastern Command 1932-5. GCB, CMG, CIE, DSO.

Macquoid, Charles Edward Every Francis Kirwan (1869–1945). Commissioned Liverpool Regt 1888, Bengal SC 1888. Service in Tirah 1897–8, South Africa 1900, France, Egypt, Mesopotomia 1914–18. Lt. Col. 1914, Col. 1919, tempy. Brig. Gen. 1919.

Maffey, John Loader, 1st Baron Rugby (1877–1969). Indian Civil Service 1899. Political Agent Khyber 1909–12, Deputy Commissioner Peshawar 1914–15, Private Secretary to Viceroy 1916–20, Chief Commissioner North-West Frontier Province 1921–4. Resigned 1924. Governor General Sudan 1926–33, Permanent Under Secretary Colonial Office 1933–7, UK Representative in Eire 1939–49. KCVO 1921, KCMG 1931, KCB 1934, GCMG 1935, peerage 1947.

Matheson, (Sir) Torquil George (1871–1963). Commissioned Coldstream Guards 1894, Lt. Col. 1915, Brig. 1915, Maj. Gen. 1917. Service in South Africa 1900, France 1914–18. GOC Waziristan 1920–3.

Moberley, Frederick James (1867–1952) Commissioned 1888, Indian Army 1891. Service in Martipur 1891, Burma 1891, Chilas 1893, Relief of Chitral 1895, NW Frontier 1897–8, South Africa 1899–1900, Mohmand Expedition 1908, Lt. Col. 1913, Brig. Gen. 1917. DMO India 1917–20 and acting DCGS 1919–20. Retired 1920.

BIOGRAPHICAL NOTES

Molesworth, George Noble (1890–1977). Commissioned Somerset 1st Light Infantry 1910. Service in 1st World War (Malta, China, India), Third Afghan War. Transferred to Indian Army 1928. Director Military Operations and Intelligence India 1938–41, DCGS India 1941–2, Secretary Military Department India Office 1943–4. Maj. Gen. 1941, Lt. Gen. 1944.

Monro, (Sir) Charles Carmichael (1860–1929). Commissioned 1879. Service in Second Afghan War 1879–80, South Africa 1899–1900, Lt. Col. 1903, Lt. Gen. 1915, Gen. 1917. KCB 1915, GCMG 1916, GCB 1919, GCSI 1919, Baronet 1921. Commanded 2nd Division 1914–15, 1st Corps 1915, 3rd Army 1915, CinC Eastern Mediterranean 1915–16, 1st Army 1916, CinC India 1916–20. Governor of Gibraltar 1923–8.

Montagu, Edwin Samuel (1879–1924). MP 1906–22. Under Secretary of State, India Office 1910–14, Chancellor, Duchy of Lancaster 1915, Financial Secretary to the Treasury 1914–16, Minister of Munitions 1916, Secretary of State for India 1917–22.

Rawlinson, Henry Seymour, 1st Lord Rawlinson of Trent (1864–1925). Commissioned KRRC 1884. Service in Third Burma War 1885, Sudan 1897–8, Second Anglo–Boer War 1899–1902. Lt. Col. 1899, Maj. Gen. 1909, Lt. Gen. 1916, Gen. 1917. Commanded 4th Army 1916, British Military Representative, Versailles 1918, Commanded 5th Army 1918, Archangel 1919, Aldershot Command 1919–20, CinC India 1920–5.

Roos-Keppel, (Sir) George (1866–1921). Commissioned Royal Scots Fusiliers 1886. Service Third Burma War 1886–7. Political service 1890, Political Officer, Kurram 1893–9, Political Agent, Khyber 1899–1908, Chief Commissioner, North-West Frontier Province 1908–19, Council of India 1919–21. KCIE 1908, GCIE 1917.

Russell, Guy Hamilton (1882–1958). Commissioned Indian Army 1902. Maj. 1917, Lt. Col. 1926, Col. 1931. Inspecting Officer of Frontier Militia 1931–5.

Salmond, (Sir) John Maitland (1881–1968). Commissioned British Army 1901. Service in Second Anglo–Boer War 1901–2, West Africa 1903–5, 1st World War 1914–18, 2nd World War 1939–45. Joined Royal Flying Corps 1914, CinC REC and RAF France 1918–19, Air Officer Commanding Inland Area 1920–2, Iraq 1922–4, CinC Air Defence of Great Britain 1925–9, Air Member for Personnel 1929–30, Chief of the Air Staff 1930–3. Maj. Gen 1917, Air Marshal 1923, Air Chief Marshal 1929, Marshal of the Royal Air Force 1931.

Sandeman, (Sir) Robert Groves (1835–92). Commissioned Bengal Infantry 1856. Service in Mutiny. Civil and political employment in Punjab 1859–77, Agent to Governor General in Baluchistan 1877–92. KCIE 1879.

Skeen, (Sir) Andrew (1873–1935). Commissioned 1891, Bengal SC 1893. Service in North-West Frontier 1897–8, China 1900, East Africa 1902–4, World War 1 1914–17, Waziristan 1919–20. Lt. Col. 1917, Maj. Gen. 1918, Lt. Gen. 1923, Gen. 1929. KCIE 1921. KCB 1925. Peshawar District 1922–3, GOC Southern Command India 1923-4, CGS India 1924-8. Retired 1929.

Tanner, Charles Oriel Oliphant (1867–19??). Commissioned North Staffordshire Regt 1886, Bombay SC 1888. Lt. Col. 1912, Col. 1918.

Tarver, Alexander Leigh (1871–1941). Commissioned Royal Welch Fusiliers 1890, Indian SC 1893. Service in Bazar Valley Expedition 1908, Mohmand Expedition 1908. Col. 1918, Brig. Gen. 1921, Maj. Gen. 1923, District Commander 1926.

Thesiger, Frederick John Napier, 1st Viscount Chelmsford (1868–1933). Governor of Queensland 1905–9, Governor of New South Wales 1909–13, Viceroy of India 1916–21, First Lord of the Admiralty 1924. Created Viscount 1921.

Tytler (Sir) Harry Christopher (1867–1939). Commissioned Manchester Regt 1886, Bengal SC 1887. Service in Sikkhim 1888, Lushai Expedition 1890–1, Waziristan 1901–2, East Africa 1916–17, Persia 1918–19, Waziristan 1919–20. Lt. Col. 1911, Maj. Gen. 1920. CinC Burma 1924–8. KCB 1926.

Walton, William Crawford (1864–1937). Commissioned Royal Scots Fusiliers 1884, Bombay SC 1886. Service in Burma 1884–5, Persian Gulf 1911, France and Aden 1915–16, Waziristan 1919–20. Lt. Col. 1908, Brig. Gen. 1918.

Wapshare, (Sir) Richard (1860–1932). Commissioned Royal Marines Light Infantry 1880, Bombay SC 1882. Service in Burma 1886–8, East Africa 1914–15, Mesopotamia 1915. Lt. Col. 1904, Maj. Gen. 1915, Lt. Gen. 1918. Commanding Bangalore Brigade 1912–16, 4th Division 1917–20, Baluchistan District 1919–20. KCIE 1920.

Woodyatt, Nigel Gresley (1861–1936) Commissioned 1883, Bengal SC 1886. Lt. Col. 1907, Col. 1911, Maj. Gen. 1917. GOC Waziristan Force 1919, GOC 4th Division 1919–20.

Worgan, Rivers Berney (1881–?). Commissioned Army Service Corps 1900, Indian Army 1905. Service in France 1915–18, Waziristan 1919–20. Lt. Col. 1918, Col. 1921, Brig. Gen. 1917–20, Maj. Gen. 1925.

Bibliography

I Manuscript sources

(i) British Library Oriental and India Office Collections
MSS Eur B 235/4 diary of Colonel Harry Ross (103rd Light Infantry)
"   "   D 523 papers of Edwin Montagu
"   "   D 613 papers of Sir George Roos-Keppel
"   "   D 660 papers of Sir Hamilton Grant
"   "   D 783 papers of Sir Charles Monro
"   "   E 264 papers of 1st Viscount Chelinsford
Military Department papers (L/MIL series)
Foreign and Political Department Secret papers (L/P&S series).

(ii) Imperial War Museum, London.

(iii) RAF Museum, Hendon
B2580–2662   papers of Sir John Salmond.

(iv) National Army Museum, London
6505-55-2   papers of Sir Eric de Burgh
6509-56   papers of Lt. General G N Molesworth
6705-21   diaries of Douglas Rees, 3/34 Pioneers
8004-60   diary of Colonel Harry Ross (typed copy)
7003-3   War diary of B Squadron 37th Lancers
6605-24   Notes by Colonel George Brown on (i) the military history
                   of Waziristan; (ii) the history of Wana and the Gomal Valley.

(v) Public Record Office
Air 5/1321   *Operations against Afghanistan*
WO 106/56   *Waziristan Force Weekly Appreciations.*

(vi) Regimental HQ Duke of Wellington's Regiment, Halifax
1st Battalion War Diary 1919
Baluchistan Force Intelligence Summaries 1919
Miscellaneous reports of 1st Battalion.

(vii) Duke of Wellington's Regiment Museum
Papers relating to attack on Spin Baldak 27 May 1919.

(viii) Papers in private hands
    Papers of Field Marshal Sir Arthur Barrett
    Papers of Brigadier-General G M Baldwin
    Adjutant's diary of 2nd Battalion North Staffordshire Regiment 11 May–9 September 1919.

II Official publications

(i) Army Headquarters India
    The Third Afghan War: Official Account (Calcutta, 1926)
    Operations in Waziristan 1919–1920 (Calcutta, 1921)
    Report on the Action at Dakka 16–17th May 1919 (Simla, 1919)
    Report by Brigadier-General A E Fagan on events between 27th May and 3rd June 1919 in and around Parachinar (Simla, 1919)
    Despatch by His Excellency Sir Charles Carmichael Monro GCB GCSI GCMG ADC on the Third Afghan War (Simla, 1919)
    Despatch from His Excellency General Sir Charles Carmichael Monro GCB GCSI GCMG, ADC on the operations in Waziristan during the period 3rd November 1919 and 7th May 1920 (Simla, 1 August 1920)
    Despatch by His Excellency General Lord Rawlinson of Trent GCB GCVO KCMG ADC, Commander in Chief in India on the operations Of the Waziristan Force for the period 8th May 1920 to 31st March 1921 (Delhi,1921)
    Report by Lieutenant-Colonel F C S Sambourne-Palmer commanding Chitral Force on operations in the Chitral Area (Simla, 1919).

(ii) India Office
    The India List 1919, 1920.

(iv) War Office
    The Army List 1919 (Part 1).

(v) Government of India
    Overseas and Frontier Expeditions, Vol. II North-West Frontier Tribes between the Kabul and Gumal Rivers (Simla, 1908).

(vi) Parliamentary Command Papers
    East India (Afghanistan) *Papers regarding Hostilities with Afghanistan 1919* Cmnd 324, 1919.

III Secondary Works (all books published in London except where otherwise noted)

Adamec, Ludwig, Afghanistan, 1919–1923: *A Diplomatic History* (Berkeley CA, 1967)
Ali, Mohamed, Afghanistan: *The War of Independence 1919* (Kabul, 1960)
Barooah, N K, *India and the official Germany 1886–1914* (Frankfurt, 1971)
Barrow, General Sir George, *The Life of General Sir Charles Carmichael Monro* (1931)
Barthorp, Michael, *The Frontier Ablaze* (1997)
Bruce, J M, *The Aeroplanes of the Royal Flying Corps* (Military Wing) (1982)
Caroe, Sir Olaf, *The Pathans 550 B.C.–A.D.1957* (1958)
Climo, S H, *Mountain Warfare Notes* (Poona, 1921)
de Watteville, H, *Waziristan 1919* (1925)
Dignan, Don, *The Indian revolutionary problem in British diplomacy 1914–1919* (New Delhi,1983)
Durand, Colonel A, *The Making of a Frontier: Five Years' Experience and Adventures in Gilgit, Hunza, Nagar, Chitral and the Eastern Hindu Kush* (1908)
Edwards, H S. *Russian Projects against India, from Czar Peter to General Skoboleff* (1885)

Elliott, Major General J G, *The Frontier 839–1947* (1968)

Fraser, T G, *The intrigues of the German Government and the Ghadr Party against British rule in India 1 914–1918* (PhD thesis, University of London, 1974)

Fraser-Tytler, W K, *Afghanistan* (revised edition 1967)

Gaylor, John, *Sons of John Company: the Indian and Pakistan Armies 1903–1991* (Tunbridge Wells, 1992)

Ghazi, Shah Vali Khan, *Yaddashta-ye man* (Kabul, 1959)

Graham, Brigadier-General C A L, *The History of the Indian Mountain Artillery* (Aldershot, 1957)

Gregorian, Vartan, *The Emergence of Modern Afghanistan: Politics of Reform and Modernisatjon 1818–1 946* (Stanford, 1969)

Gupta, Partha Sarupta and Deshpande, Anirudh, *The British Raj and its Indian Armed Forces 1857–1939* (New Delhi, 2002)

Halley, J, *The Squadrons of the Royal Air Force* (Tonbridge, 1980)

Heathcote, T A, *The Afghan Wars 1839–1919* (1980, 2007)

Hopkirk, Peter, *The Great Game: On Secret Service in High Asia* (1990)

—— *On Secret Service East of Constantinople* (1995)

Jackson, Donovan, *India's Army* (1940)

Jacobsen, Mark, *Rawlinson in India* (Army Records Society, 2002)

Ker, J C, *Political trouble in India* (reprinted Calcutta, 1973)

Moreman, T R, *The Army in India and the Development of Frontier Warfare 1849–1947* (1998)

Molesworth, G N, *Afghanistan 1919* (1962)

Moyes, P J R, *Bomber squadrons of the Royal Air Force and their aircraft* (1964)

Nevill, H L, *Campaigns on the North-West Frontier* (1912)

Niedermayer, Oskar von, *Im Weltkrieg vor Indiens Toren* (Hamburg, 1936)

Omissi, David, *Air Power and Colonial Control* (Manchester, 1991)

Petre, F L, *The 1st King George's Gurkha Rifles: The Malaun Regiment* (RUSI, 1925)

Popplewell, Richard J, *Intelligence and Imperial. Defence: British Intelligence and the Defence of the Indian Empire 1904–1924* (1995)

Poullada, L B, *Reform and Rebellion in Afghanistan, 1919–1929* (New York 1973)

Robertson, Sir George, *Chitral: The story of a Minor Siege* (1898)

Robson, Brian, *The Road to Kabul: the Second Afghan War 1878–1881* (1986)

Rumbold, Sir Algernon, *Watershed in India 1914–1922* (1979)

Sareen, Tilan Raj, *Indian revolutionary movements abroad (1905–1922)* (New Delhi, 1979)

Sandes, E W C, *The Indian Sappers and Miners* (Chatham, 1948)

Shah, Iqbal Ali, *Modern Afghanistan* (1938)

Slessor, (Sir) John, *The Central Blue: Recollections and Reflections* (1956)

Stockdale, E T, *Walk Warily in Waziristan* (llfracombe, 1982)

Strachan, Hew, *The First World War, Vol. 1* (Oxford, 2001)

Swinson, A, *The North-West Frontier 1839–1947* (1967)

Thetford, Owen, *Aircraft of the Royal Air Force since 1918*, (5th edition, 1971)

Trench, Charles Chenevix, *The Frontier Scouts* (1985)

Warren, Alan, *Waziristan, the Fakir of Ipi and the Indian Army: the North-West Frontier Revolt of 1936–37* (Karachi, 2000)

IV Articles

Aeroplane
   Halley J, 'The Kabul Raid' (August 1979), 437–42

The Bugle and Kukri (Journal of 10th Princess Mary's Own Gurkha Rifles) Harding, D W, 'Lt. Colonel R G T Gatherer 1879–1943' (Vol. 5, No. 6, 1986/7), 60–6
—— 'The Young Soldier's Battle' (Vol. 5, No. 12, 1993), 42–8

The Iron Duke (Journal of the Duke of Wellington's Regiment) E C B, 'Chaman and Spin Baldock, 1919' (Vol. 8, No. 23 (1932)), 204-6

Journal of Imperial and Commonwealth History
    Moreman, T R, 'The Arms Trade and the North-West Frontier Pathan tribes 1890–1914' (Vol. 2, No. 22, 187–216)

RAF Quarterly
    'Report on the Air operations in Afghanistan' (Vol. 1, 1930), 45–68

Journal of the Royal United Services Institute
    Young, J R, 'Royal Air Force, North-West Frontier of India, 1915–39' (Vol. 127, 1982), 59–64.

Journal of Strategic Studies
    Spiers, E M, 'Gas and the North-West Frontier' (Vol. 4, No. 6) 94–112.

Index

Ranks are those held at the time. Up to regimental no. 130, the prefix 1/ indicates a pre-1914 regular battalion. In the case of the Garwhal Rifles, and the first ten Gurkha regiments, the prefix 2/ also indicates a pre-war battalion.